THE
REVOLUTION
IS NOW BEGUN

THE
REVOLUTION
IS NOW BEGUN

*The Radical Committees of
Philadelphia, 1765-1776*

RICHARD ALAN RYERSON

University of Pennsylvania Press
1978

Library of Congress Cataloging in Publication Data

Ryerson, Richard A.   1942–
   The Revolution is now begun.

   Bibliography: p.
   Includes index.
    1.   Philadelphia—History—Colonial period, ca. 1600–
1775.   2.   Philadelphia—History—Revolution, 1775–1783.
3.   Pennsylvania—History—Revolution, 1775–1783.
I.   Title.
F158.4.R87   974.8'11'03   77-81444
ISBN 0-8122-7734-1

Composition by Deputy Crown, Inc.

FOR MY FATHER AND MOTHER

Contents

List of Figures

List of Tables

Abbreviations

APS	American Philosophical Society MSS
Duane, ed., *Passages from Marshall*	William Duane, Jr., ed., *Passages from the Remembrancer of Christopher Marshall* (Philadelphia, 1839)
Evans	Charles Evans, ed., *American Bibliography: A Chronological Dictionary of all Books, Pamphlets, and Periodical Publications Printed in the United States of America . . .* [1639–1820] (Chicago, 1903–34)
Force, ed., *American Archives,* 4th Ser.	Peter Force, ed., *American Archives,* 4th Series (Washington, 1837–46)
HSP	Historical Society of Pennsylvania MSS
JAH	*Journal of American History*
Journals	W. C. Ford et al., eds., *Journals of the Continental Congress* (Washington, 1904–37)
Minutes of the Provincial Council	*Minutes of the Provincial Council of Pennsylvania, Colonial Records,* X (Harrisburg, Pa., 1852)
Minutes	Minutes of the Committee of Safety, in *Minutes of the Provincial Council of Pennsylvania*
NJA	*New Jersey Archives,* (Newark, N.J., 1880–1941) 1st Series
N.-Y. Hist. Soc.	New-York Historical Society MSS

N.-Y. Hist. Soc., *Colls.*	*Collections of the New-York Historical Society,* XI (New York, 1878)
Pa. Archives	*Pennsylvania Archives,* several series used (Harrisburg, Pa., 1874–1935)
Pa. Chronicle	*The Pennsylvania Chronicle*
Pa. Evening Post	*The Pennsylvania Evening Post*
Pa. Gaz.	*The Pennsylvania Gazette*
Pa. Hist.	*Pennsylvania History*
Pa. Jour.	*The Pennsylvania Journal*
Pa. Ledger	*The Pennsylvania Ledger*
PMHB	*The Pennsylvania Magazine of History and Biography*
Pa. Packet	*The Pennsylvania Packet*
Rivington's N.-Y. Gaz.	*Rivington's New-York Gazeteer*
Votes and Proceedings	*Votes and Proceedings of the House of Representatives of the Province of Pennsylvania, 1682–1776, in Pennsylvania Archives,* 8th Series
WMQ	*The William and Mary Quarterly*

Table of Symbols

Religion

A	Anglican
B	Baptist
Dutch P	Dutch Presbyterian
FR	French Reformed
GC	German Calvinist
J	Jewish
L	Lutheran
P	Presbyterian
Q	Quaker
(Q)	Of Quaker background, but not a member of the Society of Friends
RC	Roman Catholic
SL	Swedish Lutheran

Wealth

1775	1775 provincial tax assessment
1775c	1775 constables' tax assessment
per head	taxpayer who owned no assessable property

Political Activity

1765-Hughes	delegation that called on Stamp Agent John Hughes
1765m	1765 merchants' nonimportation committee
1765r	1765 retailers' nonimportation committee
1769	1769 merchants' nonimportation committee
1770	1770 nonimportation committee

1773	1773 committee to oppose the landing of tea
19	committee chosen on May 20, 1774
11	committee chosen on June 9, 1774
43	committee chosen on June 18, 1774
66	committee elected on November 12, 1774
100[1]	committee elected on August 16, 1775
100[2]	committee elected on February 16, 1776
CS	Committee of Safety, June 30, 1775– July 20, 1776
CP	Committee of Privates, 1775–76

Acknowledgments

If any credit is due for my taking up the subject of the following pages, it should go to Jack P. Greene, who has a fine gift for encouraging a young graduate student to head off in any direction toward a goal of the student's choosing, and then waiting patiently to see if the student will find his way, all the while expressing confidence that he will prevail. Thus in September 1969, I intended to begin a psychological study of a handful of American Revolutionary leaders in a major urban community; I chose Philadelphia quite arbitrarily. Within a month I made two discoveries. The first, that I could not even determine which Philadelphia leaders might be the most interesting or representative psychological subjects, given the lack of personal information on all of them, was not surprising. My second discovery, however, did surprise me, and it continues to do so today. I found that no detailed narrative of the coming of the Revolution in America's largest city had ever been written, nor was there a single intensive study of the process of radical committee politics within one community anywhere in the British American colonies. Thus while my first discovery terminated my chosen topic, my second find uncovered one which I liked even better. For some time I had been vaguely uneasy that we knew so much about the international ideology and the intercolonial propaganda of the Revolution, but apparently so little about that event's local leaders and their politics. Philadelphia's radical committees afforded me the perfect opportunity to learn more about the revolutionary process in America at the community level. Such is the genesis of the following study.

Now that I have put together whatever I have learned about the political process in the American Revolution, I see more clearly than ever before how deeply indebted I am to so many teachers, librarians and archivists, colleagues, and good friends. My first intense interest in history was awakened by Eric Gruen, now a professor of Roman history at the University of California, Berkeley, who was my college tutor in classical Greek history over a decade ago. A splendid teacher and

xiii

an inspiring scholar, he gave me my first rigorous training in the historian's craft. My enthusiasm for the American Revolution was first kindled by Jack P. Greene, who has provided invaluable guidance and faith in this study from its inception. And in the history seminar at Johns Hopkins University, my colleagues, professors and graduate students alike, completed my formal historical education through their rigorous and perceptive criticism of my early work.

Any historical researcher incurs many debts that he can never repay; but he may make some small recompense by telling other scholars where there are helpful and efficient institutions, and gracious and dedicated archivists and librarians. Although I selected Philadelphia for study arbitrarily, it has been a happy choice. The staffs of the City Hall Archives Department, the Presbyterian Historical Society, and the American Philosophical Society in Philadelphia, and the Friends Historical Library at Swarthmore, have all been most helpful. And as the notes below attest, this study could not have been written without the rich collection of manuscripts, newspapers, and broadsides in the Philadelphia Library Company and the Historical Society of Pennsylvania. Edwin Wolf and Lilian Tonkin of the Library Company, and Edward Hughes, formerly of that institution and now with the Haverford College Library, made my hours at the Company pleasant as well as productive; and Peter Parker, curator of manuscripts at the Historical Society of Pennsylvania, and his former assistants, Thomas Duncan and Vilma Halcombe, helped me thread my way through many a difficult collection. Two institutions outside the Philadelphia area were also valuable, and their staffs friendly and helpful: the New-York Historical Society and the Manuscript Department of the Library of Congress. Finally, I have had generous support for this work over the years from an NDEA fellowship and a Woodrow Wilson Dissertation Fellowship at Johns Hopkins, a University of Texas Research Institute grant, and most pleasantly, a postdoctoral fellowship at the University of Pennsylvania's Bicentennial College.

The publication of this work has been assisted by a grant from the National Endowment for the Humanities, through the Bicentennial College. Earlier versions of parts of chapters 4 and 8 appeared in the *William and Mary Quarterly,* 3d Series, XXXI (1974): 565–88.

Colleagues who read one's manuscript often get too little in return. My readers have all sacrificed valuable time from their own work to give thorough and perceptive readings to several different drafts of this study. The least that I can do is to absolve them of any faults in the finished product. This is only just, for they know well that any errors which appear below are more often due to the author's dogged adherence to his ideas than to any oversight in their critiques. Howard Miller, a Texas colleague, undertook the greatest burden, and his penetrating criticism greatly improved the shape and argument of the first five chapters. Robert Crunden, also of Texas, has been both an excellent reader and a close friend throughout the revision, equally ready to offer criticism and encouragement. Chapter 1, because it is the one part of this study in which I am heavily dependent upon the research of other scholars, presented particular difficulties. Whatever virtues it now has owe much to my fellow graduates of the Johns Hopkins history seminar, Peter Onuf of Columbia University and Alan Tully of the University of British Columbia, and Edward M. Cook, Jr. of the University of Chicago (who also read several other chapters), and to Stephanie Wolf of the Bicentennial College, as well as to Howard Miller. Each of these scholars brought particular knowledge and talents to his or her reading, and I found that I had need of all of them. My colleagues at the Bicentennial College, Stephanie Wolf and Jerrilyn Marston, also read chapters 7 and 9, and their criticisms were most helpful in tightening up the arguments in those extended narratives. Several scholars read a finished draft of the work and made valuable suggestions for the final revision: Richard Beeman and Richard Dunn of the University of Pennsylvania, Mary Maples Dunn of Bryn Mawr College, Robert Middlekauff at Berkeley, and Gary Nash at the University of California at Los Angeles. Professor Nash was particularly generous in helping to improve the presentation of this study's quantitative data.

In addition, Robert Oaks of the University of Texas at Arlington supplied me with important data on nonimportation in 1769. And Burton Spivak, a former Texas colleague now at Brown University, suggested the use of Thomas Paine's splendid observation in *The Rights of Man* as a headquote for the work.

Finally, I would like to thank some very special people who did not read one page of this work as critics and who never located a source for me. They are my close friends, not already named, who have seen me through the long and sometimes discouraging years of writing and revision: John Bullion, Wendy Crunden, Bill and Martha Dolman, my sister Judy Ryerson, Kate Hutchins, Alexander Vucinich, and most of all, Patricia Eberle.

Austin, Texas   Richard Alan Ryerson
May 1977

The instant formal government is abolished, society begins to act: a general association takes place, and common interest produces common security.

Thomas Paine, *The Rights of Man*

Introduction
The Progressive Challenge

In the last quarter century, renewed interest in the American Revolution has generated several excellent studies of the rhetoric, ideology, and psychology of that event. Taken together, these diverse inquiries now afford one comprehensive answer to the question, "Why was there a Revolution?" Yet to establish the perspective upon which this achievement rests, scholars have had to view the Revolution very broadly. Ignoring considerable variation in detail, they have regarded Revolutionary thought as a coherent entity. The object of much recent scholarship—to understand the Revolution in ideological terms—has demanded of its interpreters an overriding commitment to the study of dominant, articulate voices.

But contemporary scholarship's concomitant rejection of an earlier and quite different interpretation of the Revolution has not been without adverse effects. As historians have discarded the view of the Revolution developed by scholars in the Progressive era, they have all too often abandoned their predecessors' interest in political, economic, and social conflict in the Revolutionary era as well. So thorough has been this shift in focus that many historians, in asking why there was a Revolution with ever greater precision, have largely ceased to inquire exactly how that event progressed from inception to completion.

Strictly within the realm of ideology, to be sure, Revolutionary scholars are tackling questions of process. Moreover, as the ideological school of interpretation has become more sophisticated, it has devoted increasing attention to conflict in Revolutionary America.[1] But in the extensive new literature on the Revolution

---

1. Compare the strong "consensus" implications of Edmund S. and Helen M. Morgan, *The Stamp Act Crisis; Prologue to Revolution* (1953), and Bernard Bailyn, *The Ideological Origins of the American Revolution* (1967); the more extensive recognition of elements of discord among Revolutionary-era Americans in Bailyn, *The Origins of American Politics* (1968); and the heavy emphasis upon internal ideological and socio-economic conflict in Gordon S. Wood, *The Creation of the American Republic, 1776–1787* (1969), esp. chap. 12, "The Worthy against the Licentious."

there is as yet little interest in explaining how principles, beliefs, and fears trans-
lated into Revolutionary action. And while political institutions of the colonial
period have been the subject of intensive study, Revolutionary institutions remain
strangely neglected. Only one comprehensive discussion of the new state governments has appeared in the last half century.[2] To turn to the subject at hand, almost
nothing is known of the several hundred committees of correspondence and safety,
which, as established authority slowly expired or suddenly collapsed between
May 1774 and June 1776, became the primary vehicle for providing necessary
leadership, building community solidarity, and translating abstract new concepts
and beliefs into daily policy and practice.[3]

The present study is an attempt to deepen our understanding of this political
mobilization in one colony, Pennsylvania, through an investigation of the formation and operation of its Revolutionary institutions, and of the recruitment of its
Revolutionary leaders. As the colonists developed their revolutionary principles,
they had to disseminate them.[4] As their alienation from Great Britain reached a
critical level, they had to find the means to channel the energy of this alienation
into deliberate public action. What remains unknown is exactly how this happened.
What processes were involved and what new institutions arose? Which pre-
Revolutionary leaders and factions, or parties, were able to engage in Revolutionary activity successfully, and which were discarded or destroyed in favor of
new men arranged in new parties? What factors were crucial in these respective
political successes and failures?

Because most historians have not asked these questions, they do not yet know
to what extent Revolutionary politics were an extension of or a sharp departure
from the political life of the colonial period. After twenty years of contentiously
debating the claim that American society was already democratic before the Revolution,[5] scholars have yet to subject this hypothesis to its most obvious test—a
comparison of the nomination and election procedures, campaigning styles, and
faction or party organizations that prevailed at the local level in the colonial era

---

2. Major exceptions to this generalization include Staughton Lynd, *Class Conflict, Slavery,
and the United States Constitution* (1967), esp. part I; Alfred F. Young, *The Democratic
Republicans of New York: The Origins, 1763–1789* (1967); Merrill Jensen, *The Founding of
a Nation: A History of the American Revolution 1763–1776* (1968); the first half of Pauline
Maier, *From Resistance to Revolution: Colonial Radicals and the Development of American
Opposition to Britain, 1765–1776* (1972); Eric Foner, *Tom Paine and Revolutionary America*
(1976); and several articles and dissertations by Lynd, Young, Roger Champagne, and Jesse
Lemisch, who together form almost a "New York school" of historical interpretation, working
against the grain of the dominant consensus view of the Revolution. Jackson Turner Main,
The Sovereign States, 1775–1783 (1973), treats the new state governments. The only institutional and political overviews of the several state constitutions are Allan Nevins, *The American
States during and after the Revolution* (1924); and Elisha P. Douglass, *Rebels and Democrats:
The Struggle for Equal Political Rights and Majority Rule during the American Revolution*
(1955). Works on individual states in the Revolutionary era are also generally old and out-
dated, and nowhere is this truer than in the case of Pennsylvania.

3. The only full-length study of the committees in any colony is Richard D. Brown, *Revolutionary Politics in Massachusetts: The Boston Committee of Correspondence and the Towns,
1772–1774* (1970).

4. Throughout this study, the author shall use "Revolution" and "Revolutionary" to refer to
the American Revolution in particular, and "revolution" and "revolutionary" to indicate more
general revolutionary phenomena.

5. This hypothesis, the "Brown thesis," first appeared in Robert E. Brown, *Middle-Class
Democracy and the Revolution in Massachusetts, 1691–1780* (1955).

with their counterparts during and after the Revolution. Nor have students of the Revolution developed the methodology needed to determine the merit of Carl Becker's assertion, made over half a century ago, that America's struggle for "home rule" quickly became a struggle to see "who should rule at home."[6] The few historians who have asked these questions, from Becker's day to our own, have failed to answer them in part because they have not examined Revolutionary factions and institutions in any depth; nor have they, with few exceptions, considered the possibilities of quantitative, group-biographical analysis.[7]

A thorough familiarity with the daily business of politics in America's colonial insurrection and revolution—the art of revolutionary political mobilization—is central both to an understanding of the Revolution's pacing and success, and to an appreciation of its specific effects upon the development of America's distinctive political culture. Yet this aspect of political behavior, to which political scientists are now directing considerable attention, remains, half a century after some promising beginnings, at the periphery of Revolutionary scholarship.[8] To restore vital questions of process to the position that their importance merits is a major goal of this study. The principal and more modest object is to advance an explanatory view of the creation of political institutions, the formation of factions and parties, and the recruitment of leaders in Revolutionary Pennsylvania.

AN UNEXPECTED AND UNINTENDED REVOLUTION

When Philadelphia's radical leaders organized their committees for sustained resistance to British imperial policy in 1774, they neither expected nor intended to begin a revolution.[9] There was no conscious revolutionary tradition, in the modern sense of that term, to which they could appeal, and the several upheavals in early modern European history that now appear revolutionary to scholars could

---

6. *The History of Political Parties in the Province of New York, 1760–1776* (1909), p. 22.

7. Three major exceptions are Charles A. Beard, *An Economic Interpretation of the Constitution of the United States* (1913); Forrest McDonald, *We the People: The Economic Origins of the Constitution* (1958); and Jackson Turner Main, *Political Parties before the Constitution* (1973).

8. For a succinct definition of the concept of political mobilization, see J. P. Nettl, *Political Mobilization: A Sociological Analysis of Methods and Concepts* (1967), pp. 32–33. Extended explorations of this concept appear throughout Nettl's work; in Amitai Etzioni, *The Active Society: A Theory of Societal and Political Processes* (1968); in Ted Robert Gurr, *Why Men Rebel* (1970); and, with particular reference to the American Revolution, in Samuel P. Huntington, *Political Order in Changing Societies* (1968), chap. 2.

9. I am indebted to Robert M. Zemsky, *Merchants, Farmers, and River Gods; An Essay in Eighteenth-Century Politics* (1971), p. ix, for the characterization of the Revolution as unexpected.

Because I will employ the label "radical" very frequently in this study, a brief comment about my use of the term may help to clarify my interpretation of Philadelphia's resistance movement. In general, I label "radical" all Philadelphians who sought a fundamental alteration in the relationship between Great Britain and the American colonies, *and* were willing to take the greatest risks to effect that alteration. By 1776, that commitment led many Philadelphians to favor fundamental alterations in their own local government, and in their political culture as well. The concept of "radical" is, therefore, an expanding concept, and naturally leaves some earlier "radicals" behind as it embraces other, newer leaders. It is this fact which requires several brief working definitions of the term at each major stage of the narrative. I will comment on my use of "radical" in chapters 2, 3, 5, 6, 7, and 9.

not have impressed colonial Americans in the same way or to the same degree.[10] Pennsylvanians were not conscious of being in a revolution until the spring of 1776, and as they became aware of their new condition they were at first unwilling to accept its implications. In tracing the intermittently harmonious and contentious interplay of radical committee and conservative Assembly in Pennsylvania, one is struck by the reluctance of even the most zealous anti-British leaders to make any alterations in Pennsylvania's 1701 constitution, or even to vote more than a handful of obstructionist legislators out of office. It was only in May 1776 that Pennsylvania radicals decided to inaugurate major constitutional reform in order to remove their opponents from power. Even at this late date, such a program enjoyed the support of a bare majority of Pennsylvanians.

As a conscious act, then, the American Revolution began in Pennsylvania only in 1776. Yet if the Revolution was unexpected and unintended, it was not accidental. The event was already well begun in two respects as 1776 opened. First, alterations in the thought and attitudes of the colonists came rapidly after 1765, and the outlook of Americans was fully, if unconsciously, revolutionary—in favor of a decisive break with the political past—by 1774.[11] Second, the committee movement itself quietly worked a revolution in Pennsylvania politics every day from May 1774 to July 1776. In these twenty-six months, over one hundred and eighty Philadelphians served on civilian committees. Probably another hundred sat on the city militia's committee of privates. In rural Pennsylvania, another one thousand persons were committeemen on civilian boards alone in this same period. The new men drawn into public life in 1774–76 greatly outnumbered all officeholders in Pennsylvania in the spring of 1774. Perhaps 90 percent of these individuals had never before held public office. Had colonial office-holding patterns continued indefinitely, the vast majority of them could never have entered public service.

These legions of political novices formed the first wave of a new kind of political leadership in Pennsylvania, one based less upon inherited wealth and status than upon the driving ambition of self-made men. The sudden explosion of political opportunities, and of political contention and passion, set off by these new men was crucial in sealing the fate of Pennsylvania's old regime. An onslaught of more than a thousand aggressive young leaders in two years was not to be resisted by a few conservative sheriffs, county commissioners, and justices, a proprietary governor supported by a handful of aging councilors, or an Assembly of forty middle-aged farmers and merchants. The committees, in short, revolutionized Pennsylvania politics not only by what they planned, said, and did, but also by what they were.

Amid the detailed narrative and the complex socio-economic profile of leadership advanced below to explain the transformation of Revolutionary Pennsylvania, the reader should not lose sight of one central point. Whatever democratic roots

---

10. See the treatment of the late sixteenth-century Dutch Revolt, the English Civil War, French Fronde, and Spanish monarchy revolts, all in the 1640s, and Pugachev's peasant rebellion in Russia in the eary 1770s as revolutionary phenomena in Robert Forster and Jack P. Greene, eds., *Preconditions of Revolution in Early Modern Europe* (1970).

11. On the colonists' ideological and emotional preparation for their sudden conversion to independence and republicanism in 1775–76, see Cecilia Kenyon, "Republicanism and Radicalism in the American Revolution: An Old-Fashioned Interpretation," *WMQ*, 3d Ser., XIX (1962): 153–82; Bailyn, *Ideological Origins*, chaps. 2–5; Wood, *Creation of the American Republic*, chap. 1; and Maier, *From Resistance to Revolution*, chap. 9.

it may have had in late seventeenth-century Quaker Whig traditions or in mid-eighteenth-century Scotch-Irish frontier individualism, and whatever its final triumph may have owed to small bands of ultraradicals who occasionally worked in a conspiratorial fashion to overcome the reluctance of Pennsylvanians to support revolutionary change, the Revolution in Pennsylvania was a revolution.[12] As late as 1774 Pennsylvania was governed by an elected oligarchy. Rich in democratic mechanisms, the province was devoid of democratic convictions. By late 1776 the Commonwealth of Pennsylvania was perhaps the most vital participatory democracy in the world. Whatever may have been political reality in Massachusetts or Virginia before or after Independence, the Revolution had transformed Pennsylvanians from insular, docile freemen bowing to their cultural betters—older, wiser, more pious men—into cosmopolitan, contentious citizens eager for national glory and the main chance, and loyal to aggressive young leaders who would secure these prizes for them.[13] In 1760 Pennsylvanians voted. In 1780 they campaigned. Mobilization brought intense, direct participation in political life to thousands. Pre-Revolutionary Pennsylvania had its democratic dimension: it knew government by consent of the governed. Revolutionary Pennsylvania was, for good or ill, a democracy: it struggled with government by mass participation of the governed.

The distinctive character of the Revolution within the context of Pennsylvania history lay in its suddenly exploding intensity. In 1776, and at no other time in Pennsylvania before or since, institutions were suddenly destroyed, traditions overturned, received authority subverted and then rejected, and established elites sent on the road to extinction to be replaced by others. New ideologies entered upon the shoulders of even newer men. Like any revolution, Pennsylvania's upheaval spawned special political bodies, institutions that do not appear when political practice is either business-as-usual or under considerable stress that established organs of government are nevertheless able, if only barely, to handle. These new institutions, the committees, were short-lived, just as was the transitional period over which they presided. The strife and tension that they unintentionally inaugurated lasted longer; the new political elements of which they were composed survived longer still. Most durable, perhaps, was the ideology of the Revolution. But this faith, assessed so brilliantly in recent years, is not the subject of the pages that follow. Our focus is upon the men and institutions that took up that ideology and carried it one last step, out of the realm of theory and rhetoric into the domain of reality and action.

---

12. Theodore Thayer, *Pennsylvania Politics and the Growth of Democracy, 1740–1776* (1953), stresses the liberal strain in Quaker political thought and behavior; Charles H. Lincoln, *The Revolutionary Movement in Pennsylvania, 1760–1776* (1901), sees the paramount influence of Scotch-Irish activism; and David Hawke, *In the Midst of a Revolution* (1961), argues that a handful of zealots conspired to end the power of the established Assembly in the spring of 1776.

13. The argument that Massachusetts and Virginia were democratic both before and after the Revolution appears in Brown, *Middle-Class Democracy*; and in Robert E. and B. Katherine Brown, *Virginia, 1705–1786: Democracy or Aristocracy?* (1964).

1

Pennsylvania's Old Regime

The gentlemen chosen by ballot on the first of *October,* are the only persons before whom every grievance should come; you are the men; you are chosen to represent us on every occasion; in you we have reposed the most unlimited confidence; no body of men are to supersede you; you are the guardians of our rights; we look to you for protection against every encroachment and now implore you to avert every innovation.[1]

A FREEMAN
July 21, 1774

In the decade preceding the outbreak of massive resistance in North America to the imperial policies of Great Britain, formal political life in Pennsylvania was exceptionally quiet. Through Stamp Act demonstrations, the Townshend Act boycott, and the spirited rejection of the East India Company's tea in Philadelphia, provincial magistrates remained, to a remarkable degree, pacific and unruffled. Alone among major British North American colonial legislatures, Pennsylvania's Assembly did not once engage in sharp controversy with the British ministry between the repeal of the Stamp Act and the passage of the Coercive Acts. Moreover, while the ongoing contests between legislatures and governors became pitched battles in colonies to the north and south, Pennsylvania enjoyed a decade of cooperation between its established political factions and institutions of government.

Official Pennsylvania's inner harmony and sense of imperial security arose out of conditions particular to the province. For some years the colony's ruling elite had enjoyed a growing consensus within its own ranks. Periods of partisan contention became increasingly rare; the years 1755–58 and 1764–65 were the last to interrupt Pennsylvania's deeply provincial peace.[2] The structure of government, with its proprietary executive and its small, unevenly apportioned legislature, played a role in sustaining this harmony by partially shielding the colony from imperial pressures and restricting the government to a relatively narrow popular base. But it was Pennsylvania's unique history that most effectively shaped the elitist character of its political life. As the colony matured, well-entrenched Quaker

---

1. "To the Representatives of the Province of Pennsylvania, Now Met in This City," by "A Freeman" [Joseph Galloway?], Force, ed., *American Archives,* 4th ser., I: 607–8n.
2. See Jack P. Greene, "Changing Interpretations of Early American Politics," in Ray A. Billington, ed., *The Reinterpretation of Early American History* (1966), 176–77; James H. Hutson, *Pennsylvania Politics, 1746–1770: The Movement for Royal Government and Its Consequences* (1972); and Appendix A below.

traditions of harmony and stability—and of oligarchy—became increasingly powerful. The province's settled area, population, and wealth all grew rapidly in the eighteenth century, yet local government and the Assembly expanded very slowly, affording political participation to an ever smaller portion of the electorate. Legislative representation became more uneven and remote, while Philadelphia's rapid expansion quickly outstripped the governing capacity of its archaic corporation government.[3]

Pennsylvania's leaders were admirably suited for this increasingly static polity. Governor's councilors, proprietary officials, and Philadelphia corporation members held their positions for life. The assemblymen, securing their seats in annual elections that were seldom contested, enjoyed tenures of long duration. There had been sporadic attempts to make Pennsylvania's political culture more competitive, but the occasional appearance of party conflict in the Quaker-dominated Assembly arose largely from spontaneous reactions to temporary conditions. Neither the Quakers and their allies nor the proprietary adherents were able or eager to involve an extensive electorate in their quarrels for long, and the proprietary group's inability to capitalize on opportunities to build up its legislative power meant that in the spring of 1774 the Quaker party leadership in the Pennsylvania Assembly had faced no serious challenge in many years.[4]

When the imperial problem became the imperial crisis, and governments in every colony were called upon to take a stand, Pennsylvania's assemblymen had to struggle to meet the challenge that lawmakers in most other colonies had been facing squarely for a decade. In the spring of 1776, they failed, losing control of the established government and retiring in disgrace. Their inability to provide firm leadership in the Revolutionary crisis, at a time when their counterparts in several other legislatures retained a sure grip on their provinces' resistance movements, grew out of the structure and early history of Pennsylvania's government, and the values and behavior of its dominant Quaker elite in the decade of hesitation and doubt that preceded the Boston Port Act.

THE STRUCTURE OF GOVERNMENT AND PARTY

Of the first importance in Pennsylvania's response to the imperial crisis was the fact that it had a proprietary executive that insulated the province in large measure both from imperial pressures and from the kind of executive-legislative battles

---

3. Jack P. Greene, "The Growth of Political Stability: An Interpretation of Political Development in the Anglo-American Colonies, 1660–1760," in John Parker and Carol Urness, eds., *The American Revolution: A Heritage of Change* (1973), pp. 26–52, argues that most major British North American colonies were becoming politically demobilized in the decades before the Stamp Act. The present writer estimates that in 1710 each Pennsylvania assemblyman had, on the average, 1,077 constituents (total population); in 1730, 1,633; in 1750, 3,176; and in 1770, 5,694. These figures are based upon population estimates in James T. Lemon, *The Best Poor Man's Country: A Geographical Study of Early Southeastern Pennsylvania* (1972), p. 23, table 7.

4. See Gary B. Nash, "The Transformation of Urban Politics, 1700–1765," *JAH*, LX (1973–74): 605–9, 612–16, 618–19, 622–32. Nash makes an excellent case for growing political mobilization in Philadelphia and other colonial cities in the mid-eighteenth century, but this mobilization was still sporadic; more important, in Pennsylvania, at least, it remained almost entirely urban.

that were raging throughout much of British North America. Pennsylvania's governor was appointed by the province's proprietor and served at his pleasure. To assist him in formulating policy, the governor had a small Council, which had no legislative powers. The Penn family insisted that their governor's first duty was to protect their financial interests, which centered in the management and sale of their vast land holdings, and they pitted a succession of their deputies against the Assembly over the taxation of undeveloped property, appropriations for defense, and the conduct of diplomacy with the Indians, often through binding or secret instructions that the assemblymen found particularly offensive.[5] Pennsylvania's governors entered this contest with even fewer weapons than their colleagues in the royal colonies, for they lacked any constitutional authority to prorogue or dissolve their legislature. Thus the chief executive of Pennsylvania was a man with many duties to perform, several interests to protect, and no secure base of power.

The provincial Assembly was the most important branch of Pennsylvania's established government in the Revolutionary crisis. Like other colonial legislatures, Pennsylvania's House had acquired great powers in the course of defending its constituents' rights against executive authority since the founding of the colony.[6] Indeed, its freedom of action was almost without parallel in British North America, because, under the Pennsylvania Constitution of 1701, it could neither be checked by a hostile Council nor dismissed by an angry executive. And under Pennsylvania's election laws, this legislature was highly accountable to its constituents. Elections for every seat were annual, voting was by secret ballot, and there were no special qualifications for candidacy. The franchise was quite broad. In rural areas nearly every farmer, whether British or naturalized German, had the vote. The suffrage for Philadelphia's two burgesses, while more restricted, probably allowed from one-third to one-half of the City's adult white males to cast a ballot.[7]

In the second and third decades of the eighteenth century, however, a rapidly coalescing indigenous Quaker elite altered this once open Assembly. By 1730 control of the House had passed to long-settled rural areas thoroughly dominated

5. See William R. Shepherd, *History of Proprietary Government in Pennsylvania* (1896), part 2, chaps. 1–4, 11. These disagreements between proprietor and Assembly, extending throughout Pennsylvania's colonial period, were strongest in the 1750s and early 1760s. See William S. Hanna, *Benjamin Franklin and Pennsylvania Politics* (1964); and Hutson, *Pennsylvania Politics*, chaps. 1–2.

6. See Leonard W. Labaree, *Royal Government in America: A Study of the British Colonial System before 1783* (1930); Jack P. Greene, *The Quest for Power: The Lower Houses of Assembly in the Southern Royal Colonies, 1689–1776* (1963); and Sister Joan de Lourdes Leonard, "The Organization and Procedure of the Pennsylvania Assembly, 1682–1776," *PMHB*, LXXII (1948): 215–39, 376–412.

7. Sister Joan de Lourdes Leonard, "Elections in Colonial Pennsylvania," *WMQ*, 3d ser., XI (1954): 385–401; Albert Edward McKinley, *The Suffrage Franchise in the Thirteen English Colonies in America* (1905), pp. 275, 279, 282; and Chilton Williamson, *American Suffrage from Property to Democracy* (1960), pp. 33–34. The contention of Lincoln, *Revolutionary Movement*, p. 45, that the effective franchise was many times more extensive in rural Pennsylvania than in Philadelphia is demonstrably exaggerated. Benjamin H. Newcomb, "Effects of the Stamp Act on Colonial Pennsylvania Politics," *WMQ*, 3d Ser., XXIII (1966): 257–72, finds that on the basis of voting returns in the Franklin Papers, LXIX: 98, APS, about 2,000 persons voted in the City in 1765, which was about 50 percent of Philadelphia's adult white males. Thayer, *Pennsylvania Politics*, p. 102, gives the same percentage for 1766.

Throughout this study, I use "City" to refer to the corporate City of Philadelphia, and to the electoral district coterminous with it, bounded by Vine and South streets. I use "city" to mean the larger urban area, including Southwark and the Northern Liberties.

by local Quaker leaders, and to their allies, the Quaker mercantile elite of Phila-delphia.[8] The increasing overrepresentation of the original eastern counties in a chamber that avoided major reapportionment helped to secure this control against any challenge from either non-Quaker Philadelphia or the newer western counties.

Only in 1756 did members of the Society of Friends become a minority in the Assembly, and then only because several Quaker lawmakers resigned their seats when service during the Seven Years War would have violated their pacific princi-ples.[9] The mid-century Quaker party, an unusually stable coalition of Anglican, former Quaker, and worldly Quaker lawmakers, never lost control of the House before the Revolution.[10] And while the belief of some contemporaries that the majority of Pennsylvania's assemblymen were still Quakers in early 1776 was clearly mistaken, Friends and former Friends with strong Quaker ties did hold very nearly half of the seats in the House until October 1775.[11]

The only force within the established government that ever attempted to counter-balance the dominant Quaker party was the small proprietary faction whose members clustered around the Penns and filled the Council. But for either the proprietary faction or any third group outside the established government to chal-lenge the Quaker party was no simple matter. That party's dominant position in Pennsylvania politics rested on three foundations even more solid than Assembly malapportionment.

---

8. Gary B. Nash, *Quakers and Politics, 1682–1726* (1968), chap. 7, discusses the formation of this Quaker political elite and its subsequent stabilizing and closing up of Pennsylvania's polity.

9. See Frederick B. Tolles, *Meeting House and Counting House: The Quaker Merchants of Colonial Philadelphia* (1948), pp. 234–43. This abstention from political activity was not, however, a permanent one; by 1760 more members again "affirmed" than "swore" their fidelity to the British Crown (Theodore Thayer, "The Quaker Party of Pennsylvania, 1755–1765," *PMHB*, LXXI [1947]: 21n). Richard Bauman, *For the Reputation of Truth: Politics, Religion, and Conflict among the Pennsylvania Quakers 1750–1800* (1971), p. 27, points out that this new Quaker majority included several lawmakers who behaved as Quakers and who so regarded themselves, as their affirming testifies, but who were not in good standing in the Society of Friends. In a study of the Revolution, however, it is important to emphasize that Friends who were disciplined or disowned before 1775 were usually charged with marrying outside of the Society, or with some other domestic infraction of Quaker order, and not with violating the sect's pacifist doctrine.

10. From this point in this study, I will use the term "Quaker party" for the Quaker fac-tion, both because it has been commonly employed by colonial observers and modern scholars alike, and because this dominant Quaker-Anglican coalition of assemblymen had several attri-butes of a modern party. It had major objectives that were consistent over time; it carefully composed election tickets in Philadelphia and in several rural counties; and everyone knew who its members were. It did not, of course, have the elaborate organizational structure of a modern political party. The proprietary group I label a "faction" because it was not a broadly-based, effective nominating and electing organization. It had little internal discipline, and the identities of its members are often uncertain.

11. Note, for example, Charles Thomson's observations on the Assembly, N.-Y. Hist. Soc., *Colls.*, XI (1878): 281. The present writer estimates that Friends in good standing and legis-lators behaving as Friends and widely regarded as Quakers by non-Quaker contemporaries held seventeen of the forty seats in the 1773–74 Assembly. See Bauman, *For the Reputation of Truth*, pp. 19, 27, 106, 111–12, 146; and table 1 and Appendix B below. For other estimates of Quakers in the Assembly in 1773–74, which count only members of the Society in good standing, see Hermann Wellenreuther, *Glaube und Politik in Pennsylvania 1681–1776: Die Wandlungen der Obrigkeitsdoktrin und des* Peace Testimony *der Quaker* (Cologne, 1972), esp. pp. 432–37, who finds only twelve Quaker lawmakers; and the careful estimate of Wayne L. Bockelman and Owen S. Ireland, "The Internal Revolution in Pennsylvania: An Ethnic-Religious Interpretation," *Pa. Hist.*, XLI (1974): 124–59, who find fifteen Quaker lawmakers.

First, the tradition of seriously contesting elections, which had flourished in the colony's early years when the Quaker community was deeply divided over secular issues, had nearly expired in Pennsylvania in the 1730s, and all efforts by non-Quakers to revive it were unsuccessful. Second, since the 1730s Quaker assemblymen had ridden a strong and steady political wave. Consistently espousing popular rights and interests against the often greedy policies of the proprietors, they had given two generations of Pennsylvanians peace with the Indians, a sound currency, and effective laws. Dissatisfaction with their leadership was minimal in peacetime, and even in Pennsylvania's rare periods of electoral strife, most rural counties, especially the Quaker strongholds, Bucks and Chester, remained largely immune to factional contests.[12] Finally, the depth and extent of Quaker party power prevented the proprietary faction from developing along lines that would make an effective challenge to that power possible. Routinely shut out of the Assembly, the proprietary adherents remained a small cluster of Philadelphia merchants and major landowners who curried favor with the Penns and supported their policies on land development, relations with the Indians, defense, and finance in return for appointive offices and valuable options on western land and in the Indian trade.[13]

It was visionary for such a political clique—itself barely a faction—to think that it could attract many voters away from the Quaker party, and in the fifteen years before Independence, its only strong drive to secure power in the House came in the elections of 1764 and 1765, in response to the Quaker party's ill-timed campaign to royalize Pennsylvania. But the proprietary faction proved incapable of turning even this unpopular Quaker party program to more than a fleeting advantage.[14] After 1765 proprietary supporters had to be content with their control of the executive and the Council, thereby resigning themselves to a protracted truce with their opponents.

If by the late 1760s the Quaker party was as dominant in Pennsylvania as it had ever been, and had proved equal to every challenge, surviving even the ultimate test of a major war, how were the events of the 1770s able to destroy it? One part of the answer lies in the background and careers of the party leaders who responded to those events.

PENNSYLVANIA'S RULERS

At every level Pennsylvania's officials reinforced the province's resistance to change. The governorship, held for many decades by employees of the Penns, returned to members of that family in the 1760s and 1770s. John Penn administered the province from 1763 to 1771, and from 1773 to Independence. His younger brother Richard was interim governor from 1771 to 1773. John Penn began his first term in bitter quarrels with his Assembly, but in his two administrations he became increasingly flexible and, above all, cautious. As he evolved from

---

12. See Thayer, "Quaker Party," pp. 38–42.
13. Hanna, *Franklin and Politics*, pp. 18–21, 154; and Hutson, *Pennsylvania Politics*, pp. 148–50.
14. Hutson, *Pennsylvania Politics*, chap. 3. See also Hanna, *Franklin and Politics*, pp. 148–87; Morgan and Morgan, *Stamp Act Crisis*, pp. 301–24; Thayer, "Quaker Party," pp. 38–42; and Newcomb, "Effects of the Stamp Act," pp. 266–68.

a deputy for absentee proprietors with little independent authority (1763) to the colony's junior proprietor with plenary power (1771), and then to the chief proprietor (1775), his unpopularity with the Assembly steadily diminished. A man at once prudent and indolent, John Penn hoped to secure his quiet life style and vast estate by avoiding all commitments in an uncertain world. He defended Pennsylvania to the British ministry, and the British ministry to Pennsylvania, as far as he dared. As the Revolutionary crisis unfolded, however, he apparently concluded that his only prudent course of action was a desperately optimistic, unshakable passivity.[15]

The Council that advised John Penn in his last administration had ten members. The typical councilor was a wealthy Anglican in his fifties with over a decade of service behind him. Only three men joined the Council between 1764 and Independence. The younger and the more recently appointed councilors were the most regular in attending sessions in the 1770s, but several of their elders were still fairly active. The most important aspect of the councilors' careers was their close identification with the interests of the proprietors. Their number included the provincial secretary, a former governor, the secretary of the provincial land office, the clerk of the supreme court, the attorney general, and the chief justice. The only councilor who kept any distance between himself and the Penn family was William Logan, the Council's lone Quaker.[16]

The councilors' response to the coming Revolution closely resembled that of John Penn. With the exception of the youngest councilor, Andrew Allen, who was at first an active patriot and then a loyalist emigré, and of the venerable Dr. Thomas Cadwalader, who remained an ardent Whig, they simply avoided and ignored the conflict. For these men to lead the populace against the Crown or to identify with popular needs and desires in any way was out of the question. Their whole lives had been directed to different ends, and their only source of power was the Penns. Of the seven native-born councilors who lived beyond 1776, Andrew Allen went over to General Howe and four others became neutrals suspected of loyalist sympathies. Only Dr. Cadwalader remained a zealous patriot to his death.[17]

The Pennsylvania Assembly had forty members in 1774: the three original counties on the Delaware elected twenty-four of them; the eight newer counties selected fourteen delegates; and the City of Philadelphia chose two burgesses. Because the newer counties were not granted additional Assembly seats as their populations grew, the House was heavily malapportioned by mid-century. In 1760 Lancaster County had as many taxable inhabitants as Philadelphia County, but

---

15. See the sketch in Allen Johnson and Dumas Malone, eds., *The Dictionary of American Biography* (1928–44), XIV: 430; Hutson, *Pennsylvania Politics*, pp. 80–83; Leonard, "Organization of the Assembly," pp. 406–7, and n. 116; and Shepherd, *Proprietary Government*, pp. 196–204.

16. Charles P. Keith, *The Provincial Councillors of Pennsylvania, 1733–1776* (1883), *passim; Minutes of the Provincial Council*, X: 179–276; G. B. Warden, "The Proprietary Group in Pennsylvania, 1754–1764," *WMQ*, 3d Ser., XXI (1964): 371–74, 377, 382; and Hutson, *Pennsylvania Politics*, p. 104.

17. On Andrew Allen, see Henry J. Young, "Treason and Its Punishment in Revolutionary Pennsylvania," *PMHB*, XC (1966): 292–93. Dr. Cadwalader was a leader in Philadelphia's resistance to the importation of tea. The four councilors suspected by their fellow citizens of loyalist sympathies were James Tilghman, Edward Shippen, Jr., Benjamin Chew, and James Hamilton. Tilghman, Shippen, and Chew had, with Allen, been the most active councilors in the period 1774–75.

chose only half as many legislators. Berks, Cumberland, and York counties bore a similar underrepresentation. At the other extreme, Bucks County had as many delegates as Philadelphia County, but only about half as many inhabitants.[18] There was little competition for the majority of these seats, and between 1751 and 1775 an average of only 21 percent of the delegates left office annually. In no year between the great Quaker withdrawal of 1756 and Independence did the turnover exceed 31 percent, and several years in which major issues agitated the province, in particular 1765 and 1774, saw only an average turnover.[19]

Pennsylvania's legislators formed a homogeneous group for a province of such diversity. Of the forty assemblymen serving in the 1773–74 session whose ages are known, the greatest number were in their forties or fifties.[20] Third- and fourth-generation colonials of English and Welsh stock dominated the House; immigrant and second-generation Scots, Scotch-Irish, or Germans held relatively few seats. Most of the lawmakers followed the same vocations as did the majority of their constituents. Farmers and millers held rural seats; urban delegates were usually merchants. Few were lawyers; fewer still were gentlemen-officials or, toward the other end of the social scale, craftsmen and shopkeepers.

In real and personal wealth these men were largely of the upper ranks. Few were really wealthy, but the delegates' fortunes varied greatly from one district to another. Philadelphia's two burgesses enjoyed ample incomes, and most of the delegates representing Philadelphia County were either middle-aged, wealthy city tradesmen or leading figures in their respective agricultural communities. Bucks and Chester counties present a different picture. Nearly every representative from these counties was among the most prosperous farmers and millers in his district, but the land holdings of these delegates were seldom exceptionally large. Scores of men in their neighborhoods had farms of similar size. The newer counties selected more heterogeneous delegations. Their members were either lawyers and retail merchants in the county seats or farmers from smaller communities who owned large plots of land.

The characteristic of Pennsylvania's lawmakers that most affected their reaction to major crises, however, and especially crises with a military dimension, was their religious background and outlook. Nearly one-half of the assemblymen were Quakers, and only in October 1775, when several Friends withdrew from the annual Assembly election rather than face the management of a war, did their legislative predominance end. Several Anglicans and Presbyterians also sat in the Assembly, in about equal numbers. The remaining handful of lawmakers included two Baptists, a French Calvinist, and several men of unknown denomination (see table 1).

On the eve of the Revolution, veteran lawmakers thoroughly dominated the

---

18. Lincoln, *Revolutionary Movement*, p. 47, expresses this malapportionment, as of 1760, in a quantitative model.

19. For the exact figures, see Appendix A below.

20. This session, running with recesses from mid-October 1773 to September 1774, has been selected for intensive study because it was the last to be thoroughly dominated by the Quaker party leadership of Joseph Galloway. It thus represents the succession of annual conservative legislatures against which the Dickinson-Thomson patriot faction struggled in the decade before the Boston Port Act. The portrait data on its members, summarized in this and the two following paragraphs and in table 1, are given in Appendix B. The sources for all portrait data are given in the notes to chapter 4.

TABLE 1

The Denominational Status of Pennsylvania Assemblymen, 1773–1774 Session[a]

Presbyterian	4[b]	Affiliations that traditionally inclined their members toward moderate or radical positions on questions of resisting imperial authority
Baptist	2	
Anglican, not formerly Quaker	6[c]	
Other	2[d]	
Unknown or uncertain, not Quaker	8	
Former Quaker	1[e]	Affiliations that traditionally inclined their members toward conservative positions on questions of resisting imperial authority
Quakers by current behavior	7[f]	
Quakers in good standing	10[g]	

a. Bockelman and Ireland, "Internal Revolution," p. 158, find a somewhat different breakdown: 5 Presbyterians, 2 Baptists, 8 Anglicans, 1 French Reformed, 1 Moravian, 1 Presbyterian or Anglican, 7 unknowns, and 15 Quakers.

b. There were certainly a few more among the frontier delegates, here counted as "unknowns," but I have been unable to find firm data on them. See n. a above.

c. Here again there were certainly three or four more, and both Franklin, counted as "other," and Galloway, who had been raised a Quaker, had some affiliation with the Anglican church by the 1760s.

d. Joseph Ferree, French Reformed, and Franklin, whom I find impossible to classify.

e. Joseph Galloway.

f. This number includes several men firmly identified as Quaker by Wellenreuther (see n. 11 in this chapter), or Bockelman and Ireland, or by nonofficial contemporary references, but who are not listed in Quaker meeting records as members of the Society in good standing in 1773–74.

g. Each of these men appears either in Quaker records, collected in William Wade Hinshaw, ed., *Encyclopedia of American Quaker Genealogy*, II (1938), or in a contemporary account of the Society's attempt to discipline its members for political or military involvement in the Revolution.

Pennsylvania Assembly, as they had since the 1730s. Seventeen of the thirty-nine legislators present in the 1773–74 session had completed five or more terms before the October 1773 election, and nine had at least a decade of experience. These men controlled the Assembly's committees, and the speaker was one of their three most senior members.[21]

The great majority of these assemblymen had long enjoyed a secure hold on their offices, and those changes which did occur in House membership were due to a veteran's voluntary retirement as often as to his electoral defeat. Indeed, so strong was the commitment of the voters to incumbents that of the twenty-three announcements by legislators of a desire to end their Assembly service placed in the *Pennsylvania Gazette* between 1771 and 1775, twelve were ignored by the electorate. In 1771, eight assemblymen attempted to leave office, but only one was not returned for another term—the zealous anti-Quaker party leader John Dickinson.[22] In the early 1770s, a Quaker legislator representing Bucks or Chester County evidently found it almost as difficult to leave the House as it had been to enter it. As late as the summer of 1774, the Pennsylvania Assembly was firmly in the con-

21. See Appendix C.
22. *Pa. Gaz.*, Sept. 26, 1771; Sept. 23, 1772; Sept. 22, 1773; and Sept. 27, 1775. See also *Pa. Packet,* Sept. 19, 1774.

trol of seasoned lawmakers whose security in office rested on an apparent widespread satisfaction among their constituents with their work.

A small circle of these veteran legislators controlled the House by securing the selection of one of their number as speaker and, through him, distributing the seats on the chamber's standing committees among themselves. The basic character of any Assembly session was always manifest in the personality and political outlook of the current speaker. He appointed all House committee members and thereby shaped every bill, address, and resolve.[23] From October 1766 to September 1774, Joseph Galloway led the House. Galloway was perhaps Philadelphia's most prominent lawyer, and one of Pennsylvania's largest landowners. Raised a Friend, he left the Meeting as a young man, but had very close Quaker, and Anglican, ties. Galloway had been groomed to head the Quaker party by the fiercely antiproprietary and for many years zealously proroyal Benjamin Franklin. But Galloway never experienced his teacher's bitter disillusionment with the British political nation, and in responding to the imperial crisis he remained an unshakable ultraconservative. It was he who shaped the House that entered the Revolution and who determined, to the extent that any one man could, that the Assembly would be ill prepared for the sudden changes in thought and action that the Revolution would demand of it.[24]

In the spring of 1774, nine Quaker party leaders, first elected between 1756 and 1769, filled just over half of the seats on the Assembly's four standing committees. It was these men—Benjamin Chapman (first elected in 1766), Joseph Galloway (1756), John Foulke (1769), and William Rodman (1763) of Bucks County; Charles Humphreys (1763), John Morton (1756), and Isaac Pearson (1761) of Chester County; and Michael Hillegas (1765) and Samuel Rhoads (1761) of Philadelphia County—who dominated the Assembly when the Coercive Acts reached America. Of the nine, only Hillegas and Morton had not been raised in the Society of Friends. These lawmakers were the heart of Quaker party power in 1774.

To explain the inability of Pennsylvania's assemblymen to sustain their effective leadership and secure their constituents' traditionally warm and loyal support in the Revolutionary crisis, or to step aside gracefully and allow new men to lead the province, must be a central objective of any treatment of the collapse of Pennsylvania's established government. The economic, social, and cultural background of the legislators suggests a few broad motives for their behavior. First, they were middle-aged, successful, substantial men. Many had considerable power and long public careers that they could defend only by continuing to govern, even in a crisis that they could not handle. Second, in their places of residence, occupations, and fortunes, they were fairly representative of their constituents. Their own unwillingness to cope with the Revolution after 1775 may reflect an inability among a large portion of the Pennsylvania electorate to face the imperial crisis squarely. Finally, in a province that was perhaps one-tenth Quaker and no more than one-fifth pacifist, strict Friends comprised over one-third of the House, and a particularly veteran third.[25] Allied with members who had close cultural ties to the Society of Friends, this powerful pacifist block was nearly a majority.

---

23. See Leonard, "Organization of the Assembly," esp. pp. 225–32, 236–38, and 385–88.

24. See Hutson, *Pennsylvania Politics*, pp. 220–30, 235–36, 240.

25. On the size of Pennsylvania's Quaker and pacifist populations, see Lemon, *Best Poor Man's Country*, p. 18 and n. 6.

These were fundamental determinants of the Assembly's conservatism at the onset of the Revolution. But a fuller comprehension of their recurrent obstruction of radical resistance to British policy, and ultimately of their determined opposition to independence in 1776, requires a more detailed view of the assemblymen at work in the two decades before the Revolution. If Pennsylvania's lawmakers had been diarists who revealed just how they related imperial problems to their general conception of their political world, historians would know better why this Assembly resisted the Revolution with such determination. But the legislators were men of action—or inaction; their deeds from the late 1750s to the early 1770s must speak for them.

PENNSYLVANIA'S ASSEMBLY AND THE GROWING IMPERIAL CRISIS

The overriding concerns of every legislature in British North America in the eighteenth century were its dominant political role within its province and the political autonomy of that province within the empire. Any challenge to this autonomy, whether by the local governor or by political leaders and imperial officials in Britain, had to be resisted. But their particular histories taught different assemblies to look for their enemies in different places, and to expect them to appear in different forms. From the 1750s to the 1770s, the increasingly self-conscious, defensive Quaker party leaders who controlled the Pennsylvania Assembly saw two enemies: their province's Scotch-Irish Presbyterians and their proprietor, Thomas Penn.

In 1756 provincial and imperial pressures together drove Pennsylvania into war against the Delaware Indians. Many Quaker assemblymen resigned their seats in this moral crisis, but others did not, and in the early 1760s several Friends returned to the House to dominate their Quaker party once more. Under attack by Presbyterians and proprietary spokesmen for refusing to defend the frontier, and by powerful leaders of their own Society of Friends for continuing in worldly office, yet determined not to surrender their sect's unique position in the province, these Quaker legislators gradually developed a siege mentality. Pontiac's fresh Indian attacks upon the frontier, the retaliatory massacre of several Christian Indians at Conestoga by Scotch-Irish farmers, and the march of these angry "Paxton Boys" on Philadelphia in early 1764 only heightened this feeling.[26] In May 1764, incensed by proprietor Thomas Penn's attempt to control the province's financial affairs and outraged by the close relations that, they were sure, existed between the proprietary faction and the uncontrollable Scotch-Irish frontiersmen, the Quaker party endorsed Benjamin Franklin's plan to secure royal government. For the next four years, party leaders stubbornly pursued this dream of royalization.[27]

Through the early 1760s, the Assembly's struggles with its two opponents conferred many benefits upon Pennsylvania. The provincial government, over the bitter protests of the Scotch-Irish frontiersmen, worked out disputes with Indian

---

26. Tolles, *Meeting House and Counting House,* chaps. 1, 10; Bauman, *For the Reputation of Truth,* chaps. 2–6; and Hutson, *Pennsylvania Politics,* chaps. 1–3. Of these authorities, Hutson most clearly suggests the growth of a "siege mentality," although he does not use the phrase.

27. Hutson, *Pennsylvania Politics,* chaps. 3–4. Throughout this section the author is especially indebted to Mr. Hutson, whose study of Pennsylvania politics in the 1760s and 1770s is both thematically original and consistently penetrating and authoritative.

tribes peacefully and cheaply, and in 1764 the Assembly forced Thomas Penn to pay a share of the community's tax burden.[28] After the Stamp Act crisis, however, the Assembly's perception that Presbyterians and the proprietor remained the greatest dangers to liberty and peace in Pennsylvania became myopic and harmful for two reasons.

First, the Friends' fear of a Presbyterian challenge to many decades of tolerant, pacific Quaker government grew from a concern in the 1730s and 1740s to an obsession in the 1750s and 1760s. Overreacting to the threat of Presbyterian domination, the Quaker party, traditionally a popular, "country" party, gradually became a narrowly partisan faction.[29] Pennsylvania's legislators had always identified the province with its founding sect, but now they confounded Pennsylvania's political interests with the interests of its assemblymen, whose Quaker backers had become a distinct minority in the province. Ignoring changing realities and dismissing suggested new policies, they clung tenaciously to their offices—and to a Pennsylvania that was rapidly becoming vulnerable to interference from the center of the empire.

Second, whenever the legislators looked to London, the proprietor eclipsed both George III and Parliament from their view. Pennsylvania's assemblymen resented controls from England as keenly as any colonial lawmakers, but it was Thomas Penn, not the King's ministers, who had struggled for a decade to curb their power. Thus while they were quick to take offense at Penn's instructions to his deputies, they were slow to react to the more dangerous innovations of the Privy Council and Parliament. So bitter was their hatred of Thomas Penn's attempts to dominate them that in 1764 they supported Franklin's campaign to royalize the province, even when it appeared that thousands of Pennsylvanians, including many Quakers, strongly opposed royalization. This decision and the subsequent legislative policies that it inspired shaped the Assembly's reaction to imperial measures, directly from 1764 to 1768, and indirectly, but still powerfully, until 1774.[30]

The Assembly's timing in requesting royal government, however, could hardly have been more unfortunate. In 1764 Parliament passed the Sugar and Currency acts. The former statute burdened Philadelphia's West Indies trade; the latter, banning all colonial legal-tender acts, hurt all Pennsylvanians and directly offended the lawmakers themselves, who had framed some of British North America's soundest paper-currency legislation. The Stamp Act followed in 1765, and while 1766 brought a respite, 1767 brought the Townshend duties. These policies presented the Assembly with two problems that no other colonial legislature faced. First, it made the public acceptance of any royalization plan more remote than ever. Second, public reaction to British policy was so turbulent and disruptive that the province stood the risk of alienating the British ministry just as Franklin was trying to persuade it to take on the government of Pennsylvania.[31]

---

28. Hutson, *Pennsylvania Politics*, pp. 117, 169, 180–81.

29. See Bauman, *For the Reputation of Truth*, chaps. 8–9; and Hutson, *Pennsylvania Politics*, pp. 192–94, 199–202.

30. Hutson, *Pennsylvania Politics*, chap. 4.

31. Note Hutson's very original argument on this point, *Pennsylvania Politics*, pp. 192–93. A turbulent and even violent Pennsylvania might, of course, have encouraged royalization in the new era of stronger imperial controls. But the assemblymen, remembering the imperial indolence of the previous generation, assumed that Britain would avoid directly governing a difficult colony. Moreover, they sought royal government, not royal discipline, and would have feared deeply any royalization that was brought on by their province's misbehavior.

These difficulties prompted a two-part response by Quaker party leaders. They persistently tried to convince their constituents that the Assembly, in securing royal government, would not agree to the surrender of any of the province's rights and privileges, and that Britain's new imperial policies, while unfortunate, were not disastrous, and could be reversed by respectful petitions to the Crown and Parliament and by the orderly lobbying of Franklin and other colonial agents in London. At the same time, they worked to suppress all disorderly demonstrations in Pennsylvania so that the province would stand out as a model of loyalty to the empire.[32]

Behind this second effort lay an emotion which, although present among the upper classes in every British North American colony, appears to have been of central importance in shaping the behavior of Quaker party leaders in the 1760s and early 1770s—a deep-seated fear of mobs, demagogues, and all extraconstitutional activity. The Society of Friends, a closely disciplined, communitarian people, who had established a stable elite in Pennsylvania in the 1720s, were hostile to any form of popular enthusiasm, especially if it had a potential for violence; and many Pennsylvanians of English stock, both Quaker and non-Quaker, were equally concerned over the aspirations of their increasingly numerous German and Scotch-Irish neighbors.

In times of stress, party leaders revealed how deep these fears ran. As early as 1751, Benjamin Franklin had pointed with alarm to the rising tide of "Palatine Boors" flooding the colony.[33] In 1765, Samuel Wharton, a prominent Quaker party merchant, saw a horde of "low drunken Dutch," mere "tinkers" and "cobblers," brought to the polls by the Presbyterians to vote the Quakers out of office.[34] In October 1773, Abel James, an East India Company tea agent, a Quaker, and a former assemblyman, extended an invitation to Samuel's brother, Thomas Wharton, Sr., who was also a tea agent, to visit James' suburban home in Frankford, where there were "fewer of the Yahoo Race," so that they might quietly discuss their plans to land dutied tea.[35] In July 1774, these fears found their strongest expression in the polemic of an anonymous Quaker party pamphleteer (probably Joseph Galloway), who urged the Assembly to ignore the instructions of the extraconstitutional provincial convention of freemen that had gathered to oppose Britain's Coercive Acts. The author opened with the observation of the philosopher and historian David Hume, who declared that "all numerous Assemblies, however composed, are mere mobs, and swayed in their debates by the least motive."[36]

---

32. Hutson, *Pennsylvania Politics,* pp. 178, 194–98 (and see *Votes and Proceedings,* VII: 5682–83); Hutson, "An Investigation of the Inarticulate: Philadelphia's White Oaks," *WMQ,* 3d Ser., XXVIII (1971): 3–25; and Joseph Galloway's public letters defending British policy: "Americanus," *Pa. Jour.,* Aug. 29, 1765; "A Chester County Farmer," *Pa. Gaz.,* June 24, 1768; and "A. B.," *Pa. Chronicle,* July 25, 1768.

33. "Observations Concerning the Increase of Mankind," in Leonard W. Labaree et al., eds., *The Papers of Benjamin Franklin* (1959–), IV: 234, hereafter *Franklin Papers.* See also Franklin to James Parker, Mar. 20, 1751, *Franklin Papers,* IV: 120–121; and Franklin to Peter Collinson, May 9, 1753, *Franklin Papers,* IV: 483–85.

34. Wharton to William Franklin, Sept. 29, 1765, Franklin Papers, APS, cited in Hutson, *Pennsylvania Politics,* pp. 171, 173.

35. Loose letter dated Oct. 16, 1773, in "1773" folder, "1771–1820" box, Thomas Wharton, Sr. Collection, HSP. It is not certain whether James was referring to Germans, Presbyterians, or Philadelphia's lower classes generally.

36. "To the Representatives of the Province, . . ." by "A Freeman," *Rivington's N.-Y. Gaz.,* July 28, 1774 (also in Force, ed., *American Archives,* 4th Ser., I: 607–8n). On the attribution of this piece to Galloway, see chapter 3 below.

Mobs, especially Presbyterian and German mobs, deeply alarmed Quaker party assemblymen. As masses of Pennsylvanians gathered more frequently and in greater numbers to oppose British imperial policy, Quaker party leaders struggled to stifle all riotous, disrespectful protests, even while trying to convince their constituents that British policies were really harmless. Both tasks fell primarily to Joseph Galloway, who, with Franklin, led the movement for royal government. For several years Galloway was remarkably successful in both endeavors. Working through Philadelphia's merchants' associations and mechanics' clubs, especially the "White Oaks," a society of shipwrights, he kept the province quiet in 1765, while other colonies engaged in riot and destruction.[37] And as the difficulties of securing royal government mounted, Galloway's own power inside the legislature grew. In 1766 the royalizers, now at the height of their power within the Assembly, rejected the moderate leadership of their former speakers, Isaac Norris and Joseph Fox, and placed Galloway in the speaker's chair.[38]

But the Quaker party's initial success in keeping Pennsylvania a quiet, dutiful colony was not without cost. To the extent that successive British ministries cared about Pennsylvania's good behavior at all, they accorded the credit not to Galloway and the Quaker party, who deserved it, but to the proprietor's mild-mannered nephew, Governor John Penn.[39] Yet the Assembly's misguided attempt to win royal favor did make an impact: it rapidly changed the Quaker "country" party into a "court" party. This remarkable transformation in party identity began as soon as the Assembly and Speaker Joseph Galloway adopted the role of imperial apologists to defend virtually unlimited Parliamentary and prerogative powers.[40] And because the proprietary faction was also trying to please the British ministry, although with the opposite goal of thwarting royalization, the Assembly, the governor, and the proprietor soon got on much better and by the early 1770s had few outstanding differences.[41]

The real importance of the royalization movement, despite its failure, lay in its power to shape the Assembly's reaction to the imperial crisis. The naïveté and passivity of the legislators in this campaign, so strikingly at odds with the behavior of other colonial assemblies in the decade before the Boston Port Act, had two effects. First, it eroded the confidence that most Pennsylvanians had in their representatives. Second, it gradually insulated the lawmakers from the grim realities of London's new imperial program. This insulation protected their naïveté and made the voluntary abandonment of their passivity more unlikely. Some sense of

---

37. Hutson, *Pennsylvania Politics,* pp. 192–200; and "White Oaks," pp. 3–25.

38. Hutson, *Pennsylvania Politics,* pp. 156–57, 174, 179–80, 220. Norris, speaker from 1750 to 1764, was gravely ill in 1765 and died in 1766, but he had been personally cool toward his younger rivals Franklin and Galloway since at least 1761 (see Hutson, p. 156), and had strong reservations about royalization. Joseph Fox, speaker in 1765, also opposed royalization as a goal, although he may, like several Quaker party leaders, have thought it a good weapon with which to coerce Thomas Penn to allow his undeveloped lands to be taxed.

39. Hutson, *Pennsylvania Politics,* pp. 199–200, 215–28.

40. Note especially Galloway's charge, in the articles signed "A Chester County Farmer," *Pa. Gaz.,* June 24, 1768, and "A. B.," *Pa. Chronicle,* July 25, 1768, that the nonimportation movement against the Townshend duties was simply a ploy by New England to hurt the trade of other colonies.

41. Hutson, *Pennsylvania Politics,* pp. 200–202, 236–40. These insights into the character transformation of Pennsylvania's factions are perhaps Hutson's most important contribution to our understanding of the background of the Revolution in that province.

this process, and of the way in which it resembled the behavior of Governor Penn and his Council, emerges from a brief narrative of the response of Pennsylvania's leaders both to British policy and to the reactions of other colonies to that policy in this last decade of the colonial era.

At the outset of the imperial crisis, Pennsylvania's lawmakers were keenly aware that imperial authority might be abused. Upon initiating their campaign to remove the proprietors from power, they had directed their London agent Richard Jackson to take particular care that Pennsylvania lose none of its rights and privileges, granted under various charters, in the course of the transition. Soon thereafter, at the suggestion of the Massachusetts House of Representatives, they instructed Jackson to cooperate with other colonial agents in opposing the Sugar Act and the projected Stamp Act (September 1764). Yet the legislators passed no resolves against the claims of Parliament, nor is there any evidence that they communicated with the assembly of any other colony on these matters. Pennsylvania's Assembly would resist all such cooperative, "continental" activity throughout the deepening imperial crisis.[42]

The one great exception to this firmly independent policy came in the fall of 1765 when, aroused by the public clamor over the Stamp Act and again prompted by a letter from the Massachusetts House, the legislators framed several pointed resolves against British claims to taxation powers in the colonies and named four delegates to the Stamp Act Congress (September 1765).[43] But Pennsylvania's assemblymen were still not disillusioned with the British government. On January 21, 1766, just seven days after preparing a memorial against the Currency Act of 1764, the legislators advised their London agents, in response to a query from them, that they should by no means drop their efforts to make Pennsylvania a royal province.[44] And in June, upon learning of the repeal of the Stamp Act, they drafted a memorial to George III, which combined effusive praise of that monarch with compliments to their own restraint in reacting to the law, a restraint that contrasted so favorably, they reminded him, with that of certain other colonies. Finally, still eager to prove themselves worthy of royal government, they passed a statute complying with Parliament's Quartering Act of 1765, which New York was contesting at that very moment.[45]

Governor Penn and his Council, themselves most anxious to retain royal favor, played a much smaller role in the Stamp Act crisis, and only took notice of the whole affair upon receiving letters from the British ministry that expressed concern over resistance to the law and urged that order be maintained. Penn simply replied that Pennsylvania was remaining orderly. In June 1766 the ministry informed Penn of the repeal of the act and directed him to urge the legislature to express its gratitude to Great Britain. Penn immediately complied. Thereafter, he and his

---

42. *Votes and Proceedings,* VII: 5615, 5627–29, 5635, 5643–46, 5675–76. The narrative in this section rests upon the *Minutes of the Provincial Council,* IX: 282–784, and X: 1–276; *Votes and Proceedings,* VII: 5570–6590, and VIII: 6591–7085; and Hutson, *Pennsylvania Politics,* chaps. 2–4.
43. *Votes and Proceedings,* VII: 5765–69, 5778–81.
44. *Votes and Proceedings,* VII: 5818–20, 5824–26, 5837.
45. *Votes and Proceedings,* VII: 5877–82, 5884–85; Hutson, *Pennsylvania Politics,* p. 216.

Council were left in peace until the passage of the Townshend duties, when the Crown bothered them only once.[46]

The Assembly also proceeded upon its business undisturbed until February 1768, when it perfunctorily instructed its London agents, Benjamin Franklin and Richard Jackson, to cooperate with other colonial agents in lobbying against the Townshend duties, if the other agents should happen to initiate such an effort. In May the House received a third appeal from the Massachusetts assembly. This was the famous Circular Letter of February 1768, which Speaker Galloway laid before the chamber. Characteristically, Pennsylvania's lawmakers made no response to this appeal to protest the British ministry's new fiscal and military policies, but quietly adjourned for the summer.[47] It was during this recess that Galloway submitted his anonymous essays defending the Townshend duties to the Philadelphia press.

At the next Assembly session in September, the public outcry over the new revenue duties, which Galloway's arguments could not dispel, and a direct challenge to the autonomy of the House by the British ministry combined to end the lawmakers' silence. On September 13, Governor Penn sent to the legislature a letter directed to him from the new Secretary for the Colonies, Lord Hillsborough, which pointedly expressed the Crown's desire that Pennsylvania's Assembly ignore the Massachusetts Circular Letter. This instruction further directed Penn to prorogue the Assembly (which Penn had no constitutional authority to do) if it became disrespectful toward either the King or Parliament. On the same day, Galloway presented a letter from Virginia's House of Burgesses supporting Massachusetts' appeal.[48]

Insulted by Hillsborough's directive, which was the strongest executive edict they had ever received from any source, the legislators immediately resolved that under Pennsylvania's 1701 charter the Assembly alone had the power to adjourn its own sessions, and that it could communicate with any colonial legislature whenever it wished on any topic. They then approved more respectful memorials to the King and to each House of Parliament protesting against the Townshend duties and forwarded them to Franklin and Jackson for presentation in London. Finally, the House answered Virginia's letter. It is worth noting, however, that although Pennsylvania's lawmakers had finally done what Massachusetts had urged, they wrote no reply to the Circular Letter.[49]

Through September 1768, in fact, the Pennsylvania Assembly, in its vain attempt to secure royal government, was still pursuing what one of that body's most perceptive historians has called "the politics of ingratiation."[50] In late October this policy abruptly collapsed when Joseph Galloway received a letter from Benjamin Franklin, who finally admitted, after nearly four years of lobbying with several ministers, that Pennsylvania had no hope of becoming a royal colony in the fore-

46. *Minutes of the Provincial Council*, IX: 297–300, 308–12, 341–43, 345; Hutson, *Pennsylvania Politics*, p. 199.

47. *Votes and Proceedings*, VII: 6168–69, 6181–84.

48. *Votes and Proceedings*, VII: 6187–92; and *Minutes of the Provincial Council*, IX: 545–47.

49. *Votes and Proceedings*, VII: 6193, 6244–45, 6269–82.

50. Hutson, *Pennsylvania Politics*, pp. 194, 216–27.

seeable future. It was at this point, with the strongest incentives for loyalty to a more centralized British Empire rudely snatched away from above, and with the demand for commercial resistance to the British ministry becoming uncontrollable from below, that the Assembly began to lose the respect of its province.[51]

Yet the erosion of Assembly power and the transformation of Assembly policy were gradual in the years following the Townshend duties. John Dickinson and Charles Thomson, who had broken with the Quaker party in 1764 over the royalization issue, now began to construct a new faction to resist British policies, but Galloway and his colleagues refused either to cooperate with the new movement or to compete with it by opposing British policy on their own. Rather than evolve back into a "country" party, and thereby accept as allies their old enemies Dickinson and Thomson, and the upstart Presbyterians, the Quaker forces sought, and gradually secured, an alliance with Pennsylvania's other "court" faction, the older, more conservative Anglican members of the proprietary clique.[52]

The energies of Quaker party veterans were now directed simply to defending their legislative power for six more years. They remained loyal to the British ministry, although they no longer expected any reward, partly because their local political enemies opposed British policy. Fully as central to their motivation, however, was the fact that their perceptions and behavior in the 1750s and 1760s, particularly as these developed in their four-year campaign to earn royal government, had not prepared them for the new political world which, under the steady blows of the British ministry, was beginning to take shape around them.

Thus while the Townshend Act boycott agitated Philadelphia, the Assembly remained calm. When the province entered the "quiet period" (1771–72), its legislature was well ahead of it. In 1769 and again in 1770, the legislators endorsed their previous instructions to Franklin and Jackson, quite as if nothing had happened, and avoided all resolves against British policy and all communication with other colonies.[53] These same years were even kinder to Governor John Penn and to his brother Richard, governor from 1771 to 1773. Following the issuance of Lord Hillsborough's letter of 1768, the British government left Pennsylvania's governor and Council undisturbed for nearly six years.

It was not until 1773 that the anxieties of several other colonial legislatures over the direction of imperial affairs combined to ruffle the serenity of the Pennsylvania Assembly. Alarmed by the implications of the royal investigation that followed the burning of the *Gaspee* in Rhode Island, the legislatures of Virginia, Massachusetts, Rhode Island, and Connecticut wrote to Pennsylvania's House urging a system of legislative committees of correspondence devoted strictly to intercolonial communication concerning the imperial crisis. The Assembly, having no desire to engage in any such communication, simply empowered its existing standing committee for correspondence to handle this task, which that body had been performing competently—if rarely—for years, rather than set up a new committee, the course shortly taken by every other colony that rebelled against British rule. The Assembly then instructed Speaker Galloway to inform each legislature on the continent of its "action." The major imperial issue of 1773, the East India Com-

51. Hutson, *Pennsylvania Politics*, pp. 227–30, 236; and chapter 2 below.
52. Hutson, *Pennsylvania Politics*, pp. 229, 236–40.
53. *Votes and Proceedings*, VII: 6290, 6451, 6525–26.

pany's attempt to sell tea in America, was never mentioned in the Assembly's journals, and it is quite possible that the subject never arose in the House.[54]

Thus matters stood when Paul Revere rode into Philadelphia on May 18, 1774, with an appeal from the Boston Committee of Correspondence for aid and support in resisting the Boston Port Act. Within a few short months the Pennsylvania Assembly, pressured by powerful forces within the province, moved unwillingly into the thick of the imperial crisis.

In the decade of rising imperial tensions, Quaker party veterans persisted in seeing Pennsylvanians as a people apart; the interests of their province and those of other colonies were distinct, and unconnected. Thus a major tactic in the Assembly's royalization campaign had been to insure that Pennsylvania appear not only to be a well-behaved province in an absolute sense, but that it appear better behaved than its neighbors. In its obsequious message of gratitude to George III for the repeal of the Stamp Act (June 1766), the House drew pointed comparisons between its behavior and that of "certain other colonies" (that is, New York and Massachusetts).[55] After 1766 the Assembly never initiated correspondence with another colonial legislature about imperial affairs, nor did it often reply to letters from other assemblies, especially to those from the zealots of Massachusetts Bay.

The Assembly's stubborn isolation did not go unnoticed in Pennsylvania. Writing in 1768, the anonymous patriot "Pacificus," who may have been John Dickinson, was as caustic about Galloway's sycophancy as he was acute about its cause:

> How beautiful does this prudent, peaceable, dutiful and submissive behavior of this province appear, when put in contrast with such hot-headed proceedings [of other colonies]. What applause do we not deserve, and shall we not receive—From his Majesty's ministers? And what rewards will those worthy men be entitled to, whose loyalty to their sovereign, and duty to Great-Britain, have lulled and composed us into so deep a love of public tranquility? With what ease might all public affairs be carried on, if all the other colonies could be persuaded to pursue the same pacific plan: The ministry and parliament would do their business, and our business too, in peace and quiet.[56]

Throughout the continental colonies, too, official Pennsylvania began to acquire a nasty reputation. In a period when intercolonial cooperation was fast becoming a staple of a new American creed, Pennsylvania's legislature stood noticeably apart.

THE LIMITS OF PENNSYLVANIA'S PROVINCIAL POLITY

Pennsylvania's history as a proprietary colony had given it both positive and negative political capacities on the eve of the Revolution. Its experience clearly

---

54. *Votes and Proceedings,* VIII: 6969–76, 6983–85, 7037, 7044–45, 7074–76.

55. *Votes and Proceedings,* VII: 5884–85.

56. "To the Public" by "Pacificus" [Philadelphia, William Goddard], July 16, 1768; reprinted and discussed in David L. Jacobson, "The Puzzle of 'Pacificus,'" *Pa. Hist.,* XXXI (1964): 406–18; quotation on pp. 414–15. The suggestion that Dickinson may have been the author of this piece is mine.

retarded the development of a healthy fear of imperial authority and the creation of the political rhetoric and machinery needed to oppose the British Crown and Parliament. But when the conflict began in earnest, the province had an unusual advantage: it could, and did, entirely ignore Governor John Penn and his Council and create an extraconstitutional executive and a provincial militia with only minor adjustments to its governmental structure.

Yet even these dramatic measures did not secure the province for the Assembly, and the legislature's opposition to independence in 1775–76 finally destroyed its badly strained credibility and terminated its authority. Why, at the eleventh hour, did Pennsylvania's lawmakers fail? The several particular causes of their political behavior suggested here together yield one broad answer. So totally had traditional Quaker and proprietary elites dominated the political process in Pennsylvania that no leaders, factions, or ideas that arose independently could claim any political legitimacy. In such a narrow, static political environment, Pennsylvania's established leaders felt that either to accommodate or to step aside for other men would be to enter an unknown world in which rank amateurs of dubious backgrounds, suspect intentions, and irresponsible programs would suddenly become the leaders of their community. For both Quaker and proprietary partisans, the prospect of forgetting past differences and allying with one another to preserve the securely elitist society they knew, even at the risk of failing to defend Pennsylvania's autonomy within the British Empire, was far preferable to jumping off into the unknown.

One must ultimately conclude that Pennsylvania's proprietary government and Quaker-dominated political traditions were hostile to the development of a political culture that could face the challenge of any mass armed insurrection for colonial independence. The province had developed unique traditions, its factions were without close parallel in other colonies, and many of its inhabitants were unusually insular both in their attitudes and in their allegiances. The colony's leaders could neither look upon London in the same way as their counterparts in other colonies nor understand what these other colonial spokesmen were thinking or doing. When the British closed the port of Boston in June 1774, Pennsylvania's assemblymen had suddenly to begin two activities that they had long avoided: taking a good look at the world outside their borders and cooperating with their colonial neighbors.

The Birth of
Radical Politics

What the radical cause lacked was . . . an organization divorced from the
control of the merchant class.[1]

ARTHUR M. SCHLESINGER, SR.

Early in the year 1764, when they felt their livelihood threatened by the recently
revitalized Molasses Act of 1733, Philadelphia's merchants named a committee to
request that the Pennsylvania Assembly petition Parliament for a change in the
statute.[2] Neither their action nor the instrument of its implementation was in the
least remarkable. Local ad hoc committees were familiar to every reasonably well-
informed British American. The Quakers and other dissenting sects and several
occupational groups had long employed them to petition governing officials both
in England and in America, or to place their interests and ideas before the public.[3]
Perhaps it is the familiarity of this tradition which has obscured the significance
of other committees formed throughout British North America in the fall of 1765.
These nonsectarian, extraconstitutional local bodies initiated economic boycotts
that vitally affected every inhabitant of the major colonial seaports, but their
activities were ultimately political in nature. In colonies where established leaders
refused to oppose aggressive new British policies with determination, the local
committee quickly became the primary vehicle by which new leaders aroused their
neighbors to radical resistance. In Pennsylvania the history of the committee movement and that of the growth of radical politics are nearly identical.[4] There the

---

1. Arthur M. Schlesinger, *The Colonial Merchants and the American Revolution, 1763–
1776* (1918), p. 255.
2. Ibid., p. 61.
3. See N. C. Hunt, *Two Early Political Associations* (1961); Carl Bridenbaugh, *Mitre and
Sceptre: Transatlantic Faiths, Ideas, Personalities, and Politics, 1689–1776* (1962).
4. In the period 1765–73 in Philadelphia, "radical" resistance leaders were those who opposed
any and all attempts by Great Britain to tax America, internally or externally, who favored
comprehensive nonimportation boycotts to arrest such taxation, and who refused, in May–
September 1770, to moderate the city's boycott in response to Great Britain's decision to repeal
a part of the Townshend revenue duties. In addition, radical leaders consistently placed
ideological commitment ahead of local social and political considerations. They did not hesitate
to reject the leadership of Philadelphia's mercantile elite when that elite abandoned the boycott

development of local committees was indispensable to the success of the Revolution. And it was Philadelphia's committee leaders who initiated this Revolution and, above all others, shaped its progress day by day until Independence.

THE YEARS OF DEFEAT

Contemporaries and historians alike have observed that Pennsylvania's reaction to the Stamp Act was far milder than that of New York or New England.[5] The province's local officials were far from unanimous in opposing the act. During the mass meetings convened to denounce the statute in September and October 1765, most members of the Philadelphia City Corporation were conspicuous by their absence. The Assembly came within one vote of declining to send delegates to the Stamp Act Congress, and Joseph Galloway, the rising young leader of the Quaker party, worked assiduously—and successfully—to prevent public tumults. Even among Philadelphia's mechanics, many were cool toward mob action directed against the tax.[6]

Pennsylvania's restraint in expressing displeasure over the Stamp Act does not indicate a lack of resentment against the statute. Rather, it demonstrates the persistence of factional quarrels over a unique blend of local and imperial issues. Pennsylvania's established leaders treated the act's appearance as just another event in the ongoing Quaker-proprietary contest over royalizing the province, an event to be seized as political ammunition, or ignored as another political annoyance, depending upon one's loyalties. Much of the feeling behind the Assembly's reluctance to send delegates to the Stamp Act Congress, the demonstrations against Stamp Agent John Hughes held on September 16 and October 5, and Galloway's enlistment of pro-Quaker party and pro-Franklin workers to keep the city quiet arose directly out of ongoing factional struggles.[7]

The removal of these partisan elements from the equation highlights more important features of Philadelphia's Stamp Act crisis. First, Philadelphians did force John Hughes to agree, on October 5, not to execute his commission as stamp agent until an agent in some other colony first executed his commission. Second, while the committee that negotiated this agreement with Hughes was highly partisan, it appears to have had the support of most Philadelphians, not because it was pro-proprietary, or anti-Quaker, but because it opposed the Stamp Act.[8] Finally, Philadelphians made a further response to the tax, a response that was nonpartisan.

---

in 1770, in favor of a new leadership drawn in part from other occupational groups. After 1770, the radicals' primary criterion for an effective political leader was no longer his social standing, but his determination to resist British power.

5. On the Stamp Act crisis in Philadelphia, see Hutson, *Pennsylvania Politics,* pp. 190–200, and "White Oaks," pp. 3–25; Newcomb, "Effects of the Stamp Act," pp. 257–72; Morgan and Morgan, *Stamp Act Crisis,* chap. 14; and Schlesinger, *Colonial Merchants,* pp. 73, 79–81.

6. Morgan and Morgan, *Stamp Act Crisis,* pp. 315, 317; Hutson, "White Oaks," pp. 18–21.

7. Hutson, *Pennsylvania Politics,* pp. 194–98, and "White Oaks," pp. 18–19; Deborah Franklin to Benjamin Franklin, Oct. 8–13, 1765, *Franklin Papers,* XII: 301; and Morgan and Morgan, *Stamp Act Crisis,* pp. 315–17.

8. Hughes gives a full account of the delegation's negotiations with him in his letters to the commissioners of the Stamp Office in London (APS).

In early November 1765, a large gathering of importers and retailers formed an association to boycott British goods from January 1 to May 1, 1766, with the provision that if the Stamp Act were not then repealed, they should meet again to consider an extension of the ban.[9] To execute this agreement, which had the most thorough support of any boycott in Philadelphia before 1774, the meeting chose two small committees, one of major importers, the other of shopkeepers. The merchants' committee had a Quaker majority, but only two prominent political leaders sat on this board, one from each provincial faction. The retailers' committee had an Anglican majority and was without prominent political leaders.[10] These committeemen first circulated copies of the association agreement throughout the town and secured several hundred signatures, and then proceeded to examine every ship entering the port, and every shop that might be handling forbidden goods. Although this tradesmen's boycott affected all Philadelphians, the committeemen acted as if they were merely performing an essential service for their occupational group. Yet because every profession and class supported them, they could easily enforce nonimportation. The only prominent Philadelphians known to have disapproved of the association were the two leading proponents of the Quaker party's "politics of ingratiation," John Hughes and Joseph Galloway.[11]

The debut of the local resistance committee in Philadelphia was a fortunate one. Although Philadelphians differed over the proper limits of resistance to what they believed to be an unconstitutional British law, most favored economic pressure as a proper and pacific means to redress their grievances.[12] Charles Thomson's attempt to force Hughes into a full resignation of his commission failed in November, and in February, William Bradford admitted that political divisions continued to keep the city's Sons of Liberty from expressing the opposition to British policy which they felt.[13] The tradesmen's boycott association, however, was never questioned. In 1766 it appeared likely that Philadelphia's merchants would take the lead in any future commercial protest against imperial policy, should the need for protest arise.

Yet in 1768, when British policies next aroused Philadelphia, the same merchants who had responded so vigorously in 1765–66 were surprisingly reluctant to act.[14] Only persistent efforts by local resistance leaders, steady pressure from merchants in other ports, particularly in New York, a declining provincial economy,

---

9. Schlesinger, *Colonial Merchants,* p. 79.

10. See chapter 4, and Appendixes D and E below.

11. See the manuscript agreement of the association in the Historical Society of Pennsylvania; Schlesinger, *Colonial Merchants,* p. 81; and Hutson, *Pennsylvania Politics,* p. 194.

12. Even Philadelphia's Quakers, Schlesinger notes, were among the association's strongest supporters (*Colonial Merchants,* p. 191).

13. Hutson, "White Oaks," pp. 19–20; William Bradford to the Sons of Liberty in New York, Feb. 15, 1766, and the letters of that organization to Bradford, Feb. 13, 21, 1766, in "Manuscripts Relating to Non-Importation Agreements, 1766–1775," APS (hereafter "Non-Importation MSS").

14. This account of the years 1767–70 in Philadelphia is based upon manuscripts in the HSP and APS, the city's newspapers, and Schlesinger, *Colonial Merchants,* pp. 105–239, which after nearly sixty years is still the best general account of nonimportation, both in Philadelphia and in other colonial cities. Also see Arthur L. Jenson, *The Maritime Commerce of Colonial Philadelphia* (1963), pp. 172–95; Hutson, *Pennsylvania Politics,* pp. 219–36, and "White Oaks," pp. 22–24; and Robert F. Oaks, "Philadelphia Merchants and the First Continental Congress," *Pa. Hist.,* XL (1973): 149–66.

and the realization that they could not secure the repeal of the Townshend duties by petitions alone forced the city's major merchants into a new boycott. A major reason for the merchants' hesitancy to associate was the widespread feeling that the Townshend duties were less threatening than the Stamp Act and did not justify the great sacrifices of nonimportation.[15] Even after a year of increasingly frustrating economic conditions, discouraging news from England, and a vigorous local propaganda campaign had shaken this conviction, the hostility toward British policy among Philadelphia's major importers was less intense than it had been in 1765. This very fact, however, led to a development of critical importance in the evolution of Philadelphia's Revolutionary institutions: the work of resistance orators and writers now became an essential part of the political equation in Philadelphia.

The campaign to renew nonimportation in Philadelphia opened in March and April 1768 with appeals to the city's merchants from importers in Boston and New York to join them in an association; and with impassioned pleas by John Dickinson and Charles Thomson that the merchants realize the danger that the new trade duties posed to their liberties and fortunes. Joseph Galloway was convinced that Dickinson's *Farmer's Letters* and Thomson's oratory were simply the product of personal ambition and partisan zeal. Other Philadelphians knew better. Dickinson had stood with the proprietary faction against the Assembly majority since 1764, and Galloway was his bitter personal and political enemy. But Dickinson's opposition to the Quaker party's "politics of ingratiation" owed more to his strong distrust of royal government than to any attachment to the interests of the proprietors, with whom he had no connection. Thomson, a friend of Quaker party leader Benjamin Franklin and a former party supporter, never identified with the proprietary faction; instead, he became Philadelphia's first and foremost patriot orator and tactician.[16]

These two close friends used every means at their command to arouse a complacent mercantile community. From December 1767 to February 1768, Dickinson serially published his *Letters from a Pennsylvania Farmer*. Both men addressed meetings of importers in March and April, and in May, Thomson wrote an essay that exhorted the merchants to take action. In June, Dickinson attacked the merchants' faint spirit, and on July 30, both Dickinson and Thomson spoke to a mass meeting organized by the proprietary Allen family, which then drafted instructions to the Assembly requesting that it petition Parliament for a repeal of the Townshend duties. In September 1768, the two harangued yet another meeting of importers.[17]

---

15. See Thomas Wharton, Sr. to Benjamin Franklin, Mar. 29, 1768, cited in Hutson, *Pennsylvania Politics,* p. 222.

16. Dickinson held no office under the proprietors, and he intensely disliked Benjamin Chew, the proprietary faction's leader in the late 1760s, who returned the sentiment (see Hutson, *Pennsylvania Politics,* p. 162). Thomson corresponded with Franklin frequently and was a fellow clubman with a particular interest in the Philosophical Society and the Library Company. See the Charles Thomson Papers, Manuscript Department, Library of Congress, and Hutson, *Pennsylvania Politics,* p. 235.

17. For the full debate over nonimportation in 1768, see the letter of Boston's merchants to seven Philadelphia importers, Aug. 11, 1768, "Non-Importation MSS," APS; and political items in *Pa. Gaz.,* Mar. 31, May 12, June 24, Aug. 4 and 11, and Sept. 22, 1768; and *Pa. Chronicle,* July 25, and Aug. 1, 8, and 15, 1768.

This heroic effort was ultimately successful. In the fall of 1768, a crippled economy, the growing irritation with the new trade duties, the force of Dickinson's and Thomson's arguments, and perhaps also a sudden erosion of discipline and purpose within Galloway's Quaker party finally brought the merchants to an agreement.[18] Philadelphia's major tradesmen pledged to enter into an association in March if relief was not forthcoming from Parliament. Their last supplication to London, presented by English merchants who were friendly to America, brought no results, and on March 10, 1769, over two hundred and fifty merchants subscribed to a boycott against British goods, to begin on April 1 and run until the repeal of the new trade duties. Any revision of this association was to be by a majority vote of the subscribers. To administer the agreement, the merchants chose a single committee of twenty-one members.[19]

Major importers thoroughly dominated Philadelphia's new committee, while retailers played a much smaller role in directing the boycott than they had in the Stamp Act crisis. In 1769, however, the merchant community balanced the city's three major ethnic-religious factions—English Quakers, English Anglicans, and Scotch-Irish Presbyterians—more carefully than they had in 1765. Yet this new committee was also more politically involved than the 1765 merchants' board, even at the outset. It embraced men of divergent social backgrounds and political views, and although all of the committeemen strongly resented the Townshend duties, their commitment to resisting British policy, and especially to making economic sacrifices for matters of principle, varied widely. The merchants' decision to place Charles Thomson on the board is particularly indicative of the committee's character. His inclusion argues that the new board was not to be a gathering of merchants strictly as merchants, like its predecessor, but of politically concerned merchants of every variety. This development arose naturally out of the gradual politicization, and polarization, of Philadelphia's mercantile community in the late 1760s.[20]

The Townshend Act boycott committee was initially as effective as its Stamp Act predecessor. Its members were able to control all prices satisfactorily until the spring of 1770, and to enforce the boycott without applying pressure against individual merchants until January of that year. By 1770, too, they had curbed imports more effectively than either Boston or New York.[21] Yet by August 1769, the board had already suffered its first major setback. Frightened at the rejection of a forbidden cargo in July by a nearly violent mob, Philadelphia's Quaker Monthly Meeting condemned all involvement in committee activity by its members.[22] The unexpected appearance of this major obstacle foreshadowed the dissension that would soon divide Philadelphia's merchant community and lead to the bitter abandonment of nonimportation.

---

18. Hutson, *Pennsylvania Politics,* pp. 227–32, argues that the Quaker party's disillusionment with England over the failure of its royalization campaign ended its opposition to a boycott.

19. Schlesinger, *Colonial Merchants,* pp. 116–20, 128–30; "Non-Importation MSS," vol. 2, f. 6, APS [broadside and MS signatures]. A list of the subscribers is in the James and Drinker Correspondence, Henry Drinker Papers, HSP; the rules of the association, agreed to on Feb. 6, 1769, are in the Charles Thomson Papers, Library of Congress.

20. For a full discussion of the 1769 committee, see chapter 4 below.

21. Schlesinger, *Colonial Merchants,* pp. 191, 193.

22. Schlesinger, *Colonial Merchants,* pp. 191–92, 211; "Minutes of the Philadelphia Monthly Meeting, 1765–1771" [MS, film], pp. 327, 343, Friends Historical Library, Swarthmore College.

Among the many factors determining the success of America's economic boycotts against England, the current interests of the merchants in each port and the degree of their internal unity were always important. Nowhere was this truer than in Philadelphia in 1770. Even as this troubled year began, it appeared that the committee would be unable to fulfill its promise to control the prices of scarce commodities.[23] And in November 1769, if not earlier, chairman John Reynell and several members had resigned from the committee or ceased attending meetings because of irreconcilable divisions within the mercantile community. The Society of Friends' decision to steer clear of committee activity powerfully affected several Quaker committeemen, most notably John Reynell. Perhaps as serious was the opposition of the interests of the major dry goods importers to those of all other importers, and most mechanics. Importers of English manufactured goods had little business as the boycott continued, but West Indian produce and local manufactures kept most other tradesmen busy.[24]

Two developments in the spring of 1770 exacerbated this division. Baltimore's merchants, who had agreed to a less exacting association than had Philadelphia's tradesmen, began selling coarse woolens, imported for the "Indian trade," in the Pennsylvania interior. Philadelphia's committee tried in vain to stop the purchase of these goods by appealing to the patriotism of Susquehanna Valley farmers.[25] Then, early in May, America learned that Parliament had removed all of the Townshend duties except that on tea. Philadelphia's mercantile community quickly divided into those who thought that the principle of taxation involved in this one duty justified the continuation of a general boycott, and those who did not. Most Quaker and most dry goods merchants, who were often the same men, held the latter view. They were considerably encouraged when Newport abandoned its association in May. Envious now of the opportunities opening up for merchants to the north, several Philadelphia importers began to agitate for a revision of the association rules, demanding that only dutied items be barred from entry. The dissension spread quickly, and several more committeemen stopped attending meetings, leaving only eleven members loyal to the boycott.[26]

23. Schlesinger, *Colonial Merchants,* p. 211.

24. Only fifteen committeemen signed the November 25, 1769, letter to the London merchants in *Pa. Gaz.,* June 10, 1770. Those who did not, and hence had probably withdrawn from the committee by this date, included John Reynell, three other Quakers, and the Anglican proprietary supporter Tench Francis. Quaker member Abel James was then in England. The four Quakers probably withdrew reluctantly for religious reasons; Tench Francis must have had more economic motives. In February 1770, the Quaker committeeman Henry Drinker, writing of his own apparently reluctant withdrawal to his partner Abel James, expressed his sorrow at the associators' diminishing commitment to nonimportation, and implied that his sentiment was shared by Reynell (Henry Drinker's letters, *PMHB,* XIV [1890]: 41–42). For data on these committeemen, see chapter 4 below; on the economic interests of both merchants and mechanics, see Schlesinger, *Colonial Merchants,* pp. 127, 218, 229; Hutson, "White Oaks," pp. 22–23; Thayer, *Pennsylvania Politics,* p. 149; Charles S. Olton, "Philadelphia's Mechanics in the First Decade of Revolution 1765–1775," *JAH,* LIX (1972): 311–25, esp. pp. 314–19; Olton's *Artisans for Independence: Philadelphia Mechanics and the American Revolution* (1975), esp. chaps. 2–4; and Foner, *Tom Paine,* chap. 2.

25. Schlesinger, *Colonial Merchants,* p. 218; Henry Drinker to Abel James, Apr. 29, 1770, Henry Drinker's letters, *PMHB,* XIV: 42; and the committee's letter to Lancaster, June 9, 1770, Gratz Collection, Case 8, Box 18, HSP.

26. Schlesinger, *Colonial Merchants,* pp. 215, 218–27; Henry Drinker's letters, *PMHB,* XIV, 42–45; *Pa. Gaz.,* Sept. 20, 27, 1770; *Pa. Chronicle,* Oct. 1, 1770; and table 3 below. By May, four more committeemen evidently no longer attended committee meetings. None of the four was a Quaker, therefore all probably dropped out for economic reasons.

Late in the spring, the new committee chairman, William Fisher, and the board's secretary, Charles Thomson, led the committee in a vigorous counterattack against its critics. In this struggle they gained some new allies. The importers' attempt to end the boycott united the community's many craftsmen and local manufacturers into one "mechanical interest" for the first time in the city's history. Deeply concerned that a heavy importation of British manufactures would ruin the fragile prosperity they had built up during the boycott, the city's craftsmen eagerly responded to Charles Thomson's appeal for their support.[27] On May 23, Philadelphia's "artisans, manufacturers, tradesmen, mechanics, and others" resolved "to render the non-importation, as it now stands, permanent."[28] Deeply moved by a letter from Philadelphia's artisan-hero, Benjamin Franklin, recommending the continuation of the boycott, which Thomson read to them, a large number of mechanics attended the boycott subscribers' June 5 meeting. Their presence on that occasion was probably decisive in the committee's successful defense of non-importation. In July, strong mechanic support was again crucial as the boycott committee persuaded the city's nonimportation subscribers to issue a public condemnation of New York's defection from the common cause.[29]

In early September, however, several of the committeemen who had withdrawn from the board joined several other importers to demand an end to the boycott. Quaker dry goods merchants dominated this brief and successful campaign.[30] These tradesmen surprised the board by calling a meeting of the associators for September 20, giving only the minimum three days' notice provided in the association. At this gathering, the subscribers present voted by a large majority to allow the importation of all nondutied goods, whereupon Charles Thomson, speaking for the committee, declared that the board considered the association dissolved and, with his colleagues, resigned.[31] Most Philadelphians probably still favored a general boycott, and a public meeting, hastily called by proprietary faction and boycott leaders, immediately condemned the defecting merchants and elected the eleven loyal committee members and nine new men, including two builders and two distillers, to form a board committed to the use of economic coercion against British imperial policy. But Philadelphia's mercantile community was now too

---

27. The phrase "mechanical interest" is Alexander Graydon's (*Memoirs of His Own Times With Reminiscences of the Men and Events,* ed. John S. Littel, [Philadelphia, 1846], p. 122). A full treatment of this class is in Olton, *Artisans for Independence,* esp. chap. 5, pp. 41–47; and in Foner, *Tom Paine,* pp. 28–66. Also see Gary B. Nash, "Urban Wealth and Poverty in Prerevolutionary America," *Journal of Interdisciplinary History,* VI (1976): 545–84; and Nash, "Social Change and the Growth of Prerevolutionary Urban Radicalism," in Alfred F. Young, ed., *The American Revolution: Explorations in the History of American Radicalism* (1976), pp. 3–36.

28. Olton, *Artisans for Independence,* pp. 42–44, and "Philadelphia's Mechanics," p. 321; Schlesinger, *Colonial Merchants,* p. 219; *Pa. Gaz.,* May 14, 24, 1770; and *To the Free and Patriotic Inhabitants of the City of Philadelphia and Province of Pennsylvania* (Philadelphia, May 31, 1770).

29. Schlesinger, *Colonial Merchants,* pp. 219–20, 227; Henry Drinker's letters, *PMHB,* XIV: 43–44; *Pa. Chronicle,* May 14, 1770; Benjamin Franklin to Charles Thomson, Mar. 18, 1770, cited in Hutson, *Pennsylvania Politics,* p. 235; and *Pa. Gaz.,* May 24, 1770.

30. See table 3 below. Of the fifteen merchants who demanded a change in the rules on September 12, 1770, seven were Quaker and five or six were Anglican. None is known to have been Presbyterian. Six had been committeemen.

31. Schlesinger, *Colonial Merchants,* pp. 230–31; *Pa. Gaz.,* Sept. 20, 27; and *Pa. Chronicle,* Oct. 1, 1770.

deeply divided to agree on any boycott. The nonimportation movement was dead by October. Major importers at once sent off large orders to England.[32]

The failure of nonimportation in Philadelphia left the city bitterly divided over the proper means to oppose British policy. The resistance movement had suffered a serious defeat. Philadelphia's traditional elites were in disarray. The merchants, severely split and nursing grudges against one another and against traders in other colonial ports, who heartily returned that sentiment, now lost considerable respect in the community. A similar erosion of unity and reputation began among the Quakers, who had always led the city. The Society of Friends' condemnation of committee activity, beginning in 1769, became increasingly inflexible as imperial relations reached a crisis. And with inflexibility came defection within and contempt from outside the Society. The sect's hold upon its members was immediately put to the test: in 1769–70, only four of the seven practicing Quaker committeemen in the city followed their Society's recommendation that they resign from committee service. William Fisher, an old and respected Friend, joined Charles Thomson to defend the nonimportation movement in its last few months.

Yet 1770 did not register only deterioration and defeat: this critical year saw several developments that would be indispensable to Philadelphia in the coming imperial contest. The first achievement was the emergence of a faction that was openly committed to resisting Britain's centralizing policies. This political nucleus began to crystalize around John Dickinson and Charles Thomson in their campaign for nonimportation; its first success in provincial politics resulted from popular resentment against Pennsylvania's established leaders for ignoring or abandoning that campaign. On October 1, just ten days after the termination of the boycott, Joseph Galloway could not secure reelection to the Assembly from Philadelphia County and had to seek a safe seat in Bucks. Fully as galling to the Speaker was the election of his archrival John Dickinson as burgess for the City. The new politics had scored its first small victory.[33]

A crucial ingredient in this victory was the resistance movement's second creation—a politically united, articulate mechanic class.[34] The sudden coalescence of Philadelphia's artisans in May 1770 proved lasting. When the city's importers terminated the general boycott in September, mechanic spokesmen challenged the merchants' right to take this action. Because nonimportation vitally affected the public welfare, they reasoned, the subscribers' decision to alter the association should have been shared by all "Tradesmen [merchants and artisans], Farmers and

---

32. See *Pa. Gaz.*, Sept. 27; and *Pa. Chronicle*, Oct. 1, 1770. For the membership of this board, see table 3 below. The conservative boycott breakers also chose a new committee, but there is no evidence that either the conservative or the radical committee, both named on September 27, ever did anything.

33. *Votes and Proceedings*, VII: 6582. See Hutson, *Pennsylvania Politics*, p. 236, and chap. 4 generally, for a quite different view of the genesis of the patriot faction than the one presented here.

34. In using the term "mechanic class," I am not trying to suggest that all mechanics—artisans, shopkeepers, and small-scale manufacturers—held identical economic or political views, nor that all were class conscious. But the very objective of those who sought to organize the mechanics in the 1770s was to make them conscious of being of one class, and to the extent that mechanics rallied, protested, and voted in blocks, they did achieve this consciousness. Olton, *Artisans for Independence*, chaps. 2–6, gives an extended treatment of this development. Also see the interesting arguments in Foner, *Tom Paine*, pp. 28–66, and Nash, "Social Change and the Growth of Prerevolutionary Urban Radicalism."

other Freemen."[35] On September 27, "A Brother Chip" advised his friends to cast their votes wisely—for candidates favorable to and even of their humble class. Dickinson was not the only beneficiary of this appeal on election day. A craftsman ran for sheriff for the first time in years, and artisans won four of the ten city offices filled by election, an unusually strong showing. In an even sharper break with Philadelphia's elitist traditions, the mechanics put a tailor into the Assembly.[36]

The year 1770 presented the patriot cause with yet another precious gift: the understanding that to forge a strong defense against Great Britain, Philadelphia's resistance leaders had to remain unified and enlist the support of every important subcommunity within their city, rather than relying on any one class.[37] The radicals' political achievements in 1772 and 1773 would prove them quick students of this hard lesson.

TEA AND POLITICS

At first glance, the events occurring between October and December 1773 in Philadelphia closely resemble those of the Stamp Act crisis.[38] The populace quickly grew alarmed over the ministry's attempt to establish a monopoly in the sale of tea and thereby to collect a duty that had been widely avoided through smuggling. As in 1765, popular resentment found a local target, on this occasion the small group of Quaker merchants who had received the exclusive right to sell the East India Company's tea, and especially the firm of James & Drinker. And again, as in 1765, the community chose a delegation to demand that the agents of imperial policy resign their commissions. Finally, at the mass meeting that chose this committee and on the committee itself, proprietary faction members were again prominent.

Yet crucial differences distinguished the years 1765 and 1773 in Philadelphia. First, the impetus for rejecting the tea came from a well-organized propaganda campaign, which was essential to the resistance effort because, as in 1768–70, the public did not perceive so immediate a threat to their liberties as they had in the Stamp Act. Second, the major merchants, although they resented the monopoly that the Tea Act had awarded to only four firms in the city and worked actively in October to prevent the tea's importation, failed to gain that thorough control of the committee, and hence of the resistance movement, that they had enjoyed in 1765 and 1769. The merchants' loss of power in 1773 owed partly to the fact that

---

35. *To the Tradesmen* . . . (Philadelphia, Sept. 24, 1770), by "A Tradesman," quoted in Olton, *Artisans for Independence*, p. 46. Also see the essay by "A Citizen," *Pa. Gaz.,* Oct. 10, 1770.

36. Olton, *Artisans for Independence*, pp. 49–53; *Pa. Gaz.,* Sept. 27, 1770; *Votes and Proceedings*, VII: 6582 (Joseph Parker was the tailor).

37. This is the thrust of Schlesinger's observations on the views of Boston's radicals in the years 1770–72 (*Colonial Merchants*, pp. 254–255), and it applies equally well to Philadelphia's radicals in the years 1770–74.

38. This account of the tea affair is drawn from APS and HSP manuscripts; the letter from Philadelphia's committee to Boston's committee of correspondence, Dec. 25, 1773, Joseph Reed Papers, N.-Y. Hist. Soc.; *Pa. Gaz.,* Dec. 29, 1773; *Pa. Mercury,* Oct. 1, 1791, in *PMHB*, XV (1891): 386–87; Schlesinger, *Colonial Merchants*, pp. 240, 262, 268–81, 290–91; and Benjamin Woods Labaree, *The Boston Tea Party* (1964), pp. 97–103, 156–60.

no association of importers was required to oppose the tea, which could be rejected effectively only by the determination of the whole community to prevent its landing. Fundamentally, however, Philadelphia's major importers were simply outmaneuvered by radical organizers and overwhelmed by zealous mechanics.

Philadelphia's patriot chieftains seized the direction of events at the outset of the tea affair and never relinquished their power.[39] Greatly facilitating their control was the growing coherence of the mechanics. In August 1772, the artisans had formed their own political organization, the Patriotic Society, to promote candidates who would protect their rights and privileges against assault "on [either] side of the Atlantic," and in October they placed artisans in six of the city's ten elected offices.[40] In the same election, Philadelphia's rapidly coalescing resistance faction offered its earliest known ticket for assemblymen to represent the City and County of Philadelphia. In 1772 the radicals' time had not yet come: the politically moderate Quaker candidates whom they endorsed won, but their own leaders, Dickinson, Thomson, and John Cox, Jr., were defeated.[41] In October 1773, just as opposition to the Tea Act began to appear, however, the mechanics increased their share of elected city officers to seven of ten.[42] Taken together, the growing organization of radical spokesmen and the triumph of artisan magistrates argue that Philadelphia was a far more widely politicized town by 1773 than it had been eight years earlier, and politicized, despite the persistence of Quaker-proprietary factionalism, in a new way. The city's response to the Tea Act is the first full measure of this new politics.

Early in October 1773, the Quaker firm of James & Drinker received definite word that it, in company with Thomas & Isaac Wharton, Jonathan Browne, and Gilbert Barkley, was to receive an exclusive commission to sell the large quantities of East India Company tea then being shipped to Philadelphia under a special act of Parliament passed in May. Unfortunately for Abel James and Henry Drinker, their neighbors acquired the same information a few days later and were soon staging America's first heated protest against the Tea Act.[43] The architects of this sudden display of public concern were Thomas Mifflin, William Bradford, editor of the zealous *Pennsylvania Journal,* and Charles Thomson. Mifflin launched the radicals' attack upon the importation of tea with a broadside essay circulated on October 9. Bradford then invited several persons to meet at his London Coffee House on October 14 to devise a strategy for arousing the city. These leaders, spurred on by their old master Thomson, summoned all Philadelphians to a public assembly to consider the danger posed to American liberties by the tax on tea.[44]

---

39. For views giving the major merchants a greater role, see Schlesinger, *Colonial Merchants,* esp. p. 240; and Charles Thomson to William Henry Drayton, N.-Y. Hist. Soc., *Colls.,* XI (1878): 279. Jenson, *Maritime Commerce,* pp. 200–206, like the present writer, sees the radicals in charge from the outset of the tea affair.

40. Olton, *Artisans for Independence,* pp. 50, 55 (quotation); *Pa. Gaz.,* Aug. 19, 1772. Olton argues that the Patriotic Society was at its founding exclusively a mechanic organization, but this is not certain, and it did not remain exclusively mechanic.

41. This slate is entitled "Fellow Citizens and Countrymen" (Philadelphia, Oct. 1, 1772, Evans No. 12387). The ticket's introductory rhetoric certifies its antiestablishment bias.

42. Olton, *Artisans for Independence,* p. 50.

43. See Pigou & Booth (London) to James & Drinker, Aug. 4, 1773, James and Drinker Correspondence; James & Drinker to Pigou & Booth (New York), Sept. 29 and Oct. 3, 1773, Henry Drinker Letter-Book (domestic), both HSP; and Labaree, *Boston Tea Party,* p. 97.

44. Labaree, *Boston Tea Party,* p. 98; essay by "Scaevola" [Mifflin's broadside], *Pa. Jour.,* Oct. 13, 1773; and *Pa. Mercury,* Oct. 1, 1791, in *PMHB,* XV: 386–87.

The October 16 public meeting proved a good indicator of the strength of Philadelphia's resistance movement at the outset of the tea affair. The small number of citizens assembled, quite modest when compared with the great crowds that would gather from December 1773 to Independence, suggests that at first relatively few Philadelphians were deeply concerned over the Tea Act. Moreover, all of the meeting's organizers were either proprietary faction veterans or the more zealous resistance leaders of 1770.[45] Many merchants participated, but the greatest importers were not prominent in the deliberations. Nor were the most influential Quakers anywhere in evidence. The gathering's principal accomplishment was the appointment of a committee of twelve men, who were directed to call upon the tea agents to resign their commissions. Five of the twelve had been zealous opponents of British policy, but not one was a patriot leader of the first rank. The other members were fairly prominent moderate merchants, and included a few veterans of the 1769 committee. They represented Quaker and proprietary forces about equally.[46]

Prior to mid-October, both the exact terms of the Tea Act and the reaction of Philadelphians to it were matters for speculation, and the Company's consignees hoped to sell the tea without great difficulty. But having observed as early as September that the public mood was not favorable, Abel James and Henry Drinker met on October 2 with Isaac and Thomas Wharton and Jonathan Browne to plan a common strategy. The agents then agreed to say as little as possible about the tea in public and to speak and act in unison.[47]

The October 16 committee destroyed this strategy in short order. When it visited the tea agents on October 18, the delegation demanded that the agents declare themselves against selling any dutied tea. Both James & Drinker and Isaac & Thomas Wharton offered a measure of accommodation to this demand, but the Whartons were apparently more cooperative, because on the evening of the eighteenth, the committee reported that their answer was satisfactory, while that of James & Drinker, which the committeemen had copied down verbatim and read publicly, showed a "want of candor."[48] This report immediately caused a permanent falling out between James & Drinker and the Whartons.[49] Thereafter, the Whartons and Jonathan Browne, who shortly subscribed to their declaration, were bound by an irrevocable pledge not to sell East India tea. The firm of James & Drinker, although free of that pledge, was now isolated from Philadelphia's business community.

45. [Henry Drinker] to Pigou & Booth (New York), Oct. 19, 1773 [draft], James and Drinker Correspondence, HSP; Labaree, *Boston Tea Party*, p. 98; and *Pa. Mercury*, Oct. 1, 1791, in *PMHB*, XV: 386–87.

46. *Pa. Gaz.*, Oct. 20, 1773. For a discussion of this committee, see chapter 4 below.

47. Labaree, *Boston Tea Party*, pp. 92–93, 97, 101; James & Drinker to Pigou & Booth (New York), Sept. 29, Oct. 10, 1773, Henry Drinker Letter-Book (domestic), HSP. And see Abel James to Thomas Wharton, Sr., Oct. 16, 1773, Thomas Wharton, Sr. Papers, HSP, quoted in chapter 1 above.

48. See the "Report of the Committee appointed to Wait on the Tea Commissioners, 17 [18] October, 1773" (hereafter "Report"), in "Non-Importation MSS.," APS; Labaree, *Boston Tea Party*, pp. 99–100; James & Drinker to Pigou & Booth (New York), Oct. 19, 1773 [draft], James & Drinker to Pigou & Booth (London), Oct. 26, 1773 [typescript], and James & Drinker to Thomas & Elisha Hutchinson, &c. (Boston), Dec. 17, 1773 [typescript], all James and Drinker Correspondence, HSP.

49. Labaree, *Boston Tea Party*, pp. 101, 157.

Philadelphia's first tea committee, having achieved its purpose, dissolved itself in triumph. Abel James and Henry Drinker had a far less pleasant autumn. Universally regarded with suspicion, they vainly protested their innocence. Caught between their strong sense of business ethics and sizable surety bonds, both of which obligated them to serve the East India Company, and their community's forceful expression of the common interest it perceived, they gradually understood that they would not avoid defeat.[50]

Philadelphia's patriot penmen, meanwhile, insured that the public would not forget that Company tea was a poisonous brew. Before anyone knew for certain whether the old Townshend tea duty would be paid in England or America under the new Tea Act, or indeed if it would be levied at all, they directed their attack at the threat of monopoly. Upon learning in early November that the impost was to be collected in the colonies, they advanced new arguments stressing the act's unconstitutional duties. In a barrage of essays, Thomas Mifflin, Charles Thomson, and Dr. Benjamin Rush scored the importation of tea from every angle. Their campaign peaked in late November, when John Dickinson finally joined them. Writing as "Rusticus," Dickinson portrayed the East India Company as a miniature eastern despot trampling upon every liberty of mankind for material gain. He closed with the suggestion that tea would be only the first of the Company's gifts to America.[51]

The public's enthusiastic reception of these arguments encouraged patriot leaders to bolder measures. On November 27, the twelve men named to the October delegation to the tea agents met with several veterans of the 1769 nonimportation committee and other zealots to plan the city's rejection of the tea ship. Either on this day or within the following week, these men formed a new committee of twenty-four members, including the twelve chosen in October, to prepare the city for the arrival of the tea ship *Polly*. In the selection of members for this board, those who favored a firm resistance to British policy triumphed completely over Philadelphia's more cautious merchants. At least eight of those chosen in October were zealous resistors, while the dozen men added included James Mease, Thomas Mifflin, and Charles Thomson, all committee leaders of the general boycott movement in 1769 and 1770, and the rising young lawyer Joseph Reed, who would soon be Philadelphia's leading patriot standard-bearer.[52]

The selection of the December 1773 committee marks a critical point in the development of radical politics in Philadelphia. Of the major committees created since 1765, it was nearly the youngest, it embraced the broadest range of religious denominations, and it was probably the least affluent. But most important, with the

---

50. See "Report," in "Non-Importation MSS," APS; and the letters of James & Drinker to Pigou & Booth (New York), Sept. 29, Oct. 3, 10, 14, 18, 19, 20, 26, 29, Nov. 6, 20, Dec. 7, 16, 18, 24, 1773, and Pigou & Booth, or Benjamin Booth (New York) to James & Drinker, July 7, Aug. 4, Sept. 29, Oct. 4, 8, 13, 20, 25, 27, 28, Nov. 3, 5, 10, 12, 19, 22, 24, Dec. 16, 20, 24, 31, 1773, in Henry Drinker Letter-Book (domestic), and loose letters in typescript and manuscript, James and Drinker Correspondence, all HSP.

51. See Labaree, *Boston Tea Party*, pp. 98, 100–101, 156–57; and Schlesinger, *Colonial Merchants*, pp. 268–77. Dickinson's essay is in P. L. Ford, ed., *The Writings of John Dickinson, 1764–1774* (1895), I: 459–63.

52. For the number and names of the committeemen, see James & Drinker to Pigou & Booth (London), Nov. 30, 1773, Henry Drinker Letter-Book (foreign), HSP; *Pa. Gaz.*, Dec. 29, 1773; and the letter of the new board to Boston's committee, Dec. 25, 1773, Joseph Reed Papers, N.-Y. Hist. Soc. For a full discussion of this committee, see chapter 4 below.

inclusion of Thomas Mifflin, Charles Thomson, and Joseph Reed, it became the first committee to incorporate the complete nucleus of Philadelphia's patriot faction. The board's energy and success were fully equal to its members' talent and distinction in patriot circles. Within a week it forced Abel James and Henry Drinker to pledge that they would not insist on landing the tea. Shortly thereafter, it insured that thrifty Philadelphians would not be tempted to purchase Company tea by forcing down the price of smuggled tea.[53] Confident that Pennsylvania enjoyed a passive governor and prudent customs officials, the board now felt prepared for the tea's arrival and expected that its rejection would be a simple matter—a public act that all Philadelphians would approve without reservation.

The first news to reach Philadelphia, however, was not of the arrival of the tea ship *Polly,* but of the destruction of the tea at Boston. Although this act shocked the committee, the majority of its members felt that the Boston Tea Party was probably justified by Governor Thomas Hutchinson's intransigence, and nineteen committeemen signed a letter of cautious approval on Christmas Day.[54] On that same evening, the committee learned that the *Polly* had already come up the Delaware River as far as Chester. The next morning, several committeemen stopped the vessel at Gloucester Point and persuaded Captain Ayres to come into town by land to witness the mood of the people for himself. A good turnout at a public meeting to demand that the *Polly* turn back would settle the issue. On Monday, December 27, several thousand inhabitants responded to the summons. Ayres agreed to return to England.[55]

But certain committeemen were not satisfied with merely rejecting the tea, a measure to which few Philadelphians objected. Against the wishes of several of their committee colleagues, these activists capitalized on the crowd's enthusiasm to secure a public resolve endorsing Boston's action. At least one local conservative, the tea agent Thomas Wharton, Sr., credited this triumph to Charles Thomson's talent for intrigue and his shrewd understanding of crowd psychology. Perhaps most Philadelphians did give as little thought to the implications of their endorsement of Boston's Tea Party as Wharton believed. Yet this one resolve was to play a major role in determining the lines of polarization over imperial policy in Philadelphia five months later.[56]

Philadelphia's tea affair was a central event in the early development of the city's committee-resistance movement. This brief episode altered Philadelphia politics in three ways. First, it brought a dozen important radical activists together into a durable nucleus for the new patriot movement. Second, it greatly advanced the process, begun in 1770 and developed in 1772, of defining leaders and factions

---

53. Labaree, *Boston Tea Party,* p. 102; "Report," in "Non-Importation MSS," APS; James & Drinker to Thomas & Elisha Hutchinson, &c. (Boston), Dec. 17, 1773 [typescript], James & Drinker to Pigou & Booth (New York), Dec. 7, 1773, both in James and Drinker Correspondence, HSP; and Schlesinger, *Colonial Merchants,* p. 290.

54. Philadelphia committee to Boston committee, Dec. 25, 1773, Reed Papers, N.-Y. Hist. Soc.

55. *Pa. Gaz.,* Dec. 29, 1773; Labaree, *Boston Tea Party,* pp. 158–59. Perhaps 8,000 persons attended this meeting.

56. See Schlesinger, *Colonial Merchants,* p. 291; and Wharton to Thomas Walpole, May 2, 1774, Thomas Wharton, Sr. Letter-Book, HSP. Wharton observed that "a number of Men met with a View to determine a Measure, generally esteemed salutary . . . are easily led to assent to [another] resolve after [several have] been unanimously entered into, without Considering the Face and Effect of such a resolve."

in ideological rather than in economic, vocational, or religious terms. This development gradually divorced the resistance movement from mercantile leadership.[57] The city now divided clearly along conservative (cautious, legal) versus radical (bold, extralegal) lines over the proper limits of resistance to British policy. Finally, the tea affair's zealous climax would soon stimulate the expression of a deep, broadly based dissent among those Philadelphians who were becoming alarmed at the city's ever more visible and vocal activists. Thus the Tea Act forced the articulation, for the first time, of both the conservative and the radical approaches to opposing British imperial policy.

---

57. Note Schlesinger's remark in *Colonial Merchants,* p. 255, quoted at the head of this chapter.

Chapter

3

Founding the
Committee System

> The Whigs, not satisfied with the vigour of [the Assembly], . . . found means to collect a Convention from the several Counties . . . to inspire the Assembly into some resolution, and at least to do something in conformity [with] the other Colonies. . . . [The] Convention established the Government of Committees. . . . Thus the Public Machine was at length organized and put in motion.[1]

JOSEPH REED

The great achievement of Philadelphia's radical resistance leaders in 1774 was the conversion of their hesitant, divided community from a resigned acceptance of all British authority to a determined opposition to London's new imperial policies. Building upon promising beginnings in 1770 and 1773, Philadelphia's radicals effected their goal in three ways.[2] In May and June, through newspapers, broadsides, and speeches, they persuaded the whole community to pledge its strongest support to a continental congress. In June and July, they built up a comprehensive committee system to coordinate the resistance effort throughout Pennsylvania. And from May until November, step by step, they brought Philadelphia's many occupational, ethnic, and religious groups into a direct participation in resistance activity. Remarkably, after stout moderate and conservative opposition in May, committee radicals were able to work toward their goal in close cooperation with moderate colleagues in June and July. At the convening of the First Continental Congress, Philadelphia was a united community, politically radicalized under the leadership of a broad new elite, and irrevocably committed to the new committee politics.

---

1. "Joseph Reed's Narrative" [n.d., ca. 1777–78], N.-Y. Hist. Soc., *Colls.*, XI (1878): 272–73.
2. In the period May–July 1774, I label those Philadelphians "radical" who most strongly favored a coordinated intercolonial resistance to Britain's Coercive Acts, and who sought to effect that resistance through a continental congress which, they believed, should and would order a comprehensive boycott of British imports. Even more radical than most of the committeemen to whom I give that label, however, were mechanics' spokesmen who favored a unilateral boycott by Philadelphia. "Moderate" committeemen in this period hoped for a congressional boycott that would not call for too great a sacrifice by Philadelphia's mercantile elite, and they sought to moderate America's demands that Britain alter its current imperial policy. "Conservatives" were antiboycott and even anticongress in sentiment. In addition, "moderates" and "conservatives" favored a leadership by the mercantile elite in principle, while "radicals" continued to develop a leadership based primarily upon the commitment of each leader to a vigorous opposition to British imperial policy.

BOSTON AND PHILADELPHIA

Following the tea affair, Philadelphia was quiet for several months. Resentment against Britain remained, but even among the radicals tensions subsided quickly. Most Philadelphians did not appear anxious to know the ministry's response to the Boston Tea Party.[3] In April, however, the city learned of Solicitor General Alexander Wedderburn's bitter attack upon Benjamin Franklin in a January Privy Council session, an attack provoked by Franklin's role in the publication by Massachusetts radicals of Governor Thomas Hutchinson's confidential correspondence with British officials. Incensed by Wedderburn's contemptuous assault upon the venerable Doctor, who in their eyes had merely exposed America's most notorious ministerial tool, zealous Philadelphians burned both Wedderburn and Hutchinson in effigy—and ignited the blaze with an electric spark.[4]

The public mood was now ripe for more startling news. On May 14, Philadelphians learned of the Boston Port Act; four days later, Paul Revere rode into the city with an appeal for support from Boston's Committee of Correspondence.[5] Thomas Mifflin, Joseph Reed, and Charles Thomson immediately began planning to win this support and to encourage Philadelphians to consider the broader implications of the ministry's latest challenge to America's liberties. They decided that if they could persuade John Dickinson to recommend decisive action to the town's economic and political leaders, Philadelphia would support intercolonial resistance to the Port Act. To impel the city into action was a more difficult matter in May, however, than it had been six months earlier. The Port Act reached America with less warning than the Tea Act, and in 1774 resistance leaders could not point to an immediate threat to Philadelphia. Moreover, conservatives and moderates, whether merchants or professionals, Quakers or Anglicans, were moving swiftly to dampen the city's response to Boston's appeal for aid. They had been thoroughly alarmed by the strength of the radicals in the tea affair and were determined to hold Philadelphia to a more moderate course in the current crisis.[6]

Charles Thomson and his friends were fully aware of this conservative resurgence, and carefully planned their May 20 City Tavern meeting to outflank their opponents and commit Philadelphia's moderate merchants to intercolonial cooperation in aiding Boston and defending America's liberties. Their stratagem was to open the meeting with a demand that Philadelphia immediately begin a unilateral boycott of British goods, which would continue until the ministry rescinded its punitive policy. They would push this point so aggressively that the moderates would become thoroughly alarmed. At this point John Dickinson would rise and recommend a more cautious response to the crisis, which would win over the entire gathering.[7]

---

3. Joseph Reed to the earl of Dartmouth, Apr. 4, 1774, in William B. Reed, *The Life and Correspondence of Joseph Reed* (Philadelphia, 1847), pp. 56–57.

4. Thomas Wharton, Sr. to Samuel Wharton, May 3, 1774, Thomas Wharton, Sr. Letter-Book, HSP.

5. See Brown, *Revolutionary Politics in Massachusetts,* pp. 185–99.

6. Thomas Wharton, Sr. to Samuel Wharton, May 17, 1774, and to Thomas Walpole, May 31, 1774, Thomas Wharton, Sr. Letter-Book, HSP; James & Drinker to Pigou & Booth (New York), May 24, 31, 1774, Henry Drinker Letter-Book (domestic), HSP.

7. Thomson to Drayton, N.-Y. Hist. Soc., *Colls.,* XI: 275–76. This account of May 20, 1774, is based primarily upon "Joseph Reed's Narrative" and Charles Thomson's letter to Drayton, both in the published Charles Thomson Papers, N.-Y. Hist. Soc., *Colls.,* XI: 269–86. See Appendix F below for a discussion of these two sources and the problems they present.

The success of this plan was absolutely dependent upon Dickinson's participation, and his timidity in public affairs had increased markedly in the early 1770s.[8] To win him over, Mifflin, Reed, and Thomson visited Dickinson at his Fairhill estate around mid-day on the twentieth. There, in several hours of urgent conversation, the three convinced their host that he should address the meeting. They also revealed their plan for persuading Philadelphia's great merchants to send an encouraging reply to Boston and unite with the other colonies in resisting an arbitrary ministry. At Dickinson's insistence, and as a tactical necessity, they in turn agreed to endorse his motion that the city petition Governor Penn to summon the Assembly into emergency session to consider the crisis.[9]

The four leaders, not wishing to appear a cabal, then separated. Mifflin and Reed set off to town first, leaving Thomson to escort Dickinson. In the City Tavern, over two hundred substantial merchants and lawyers, including Philadelphia's leading Quaker, proprietary, and "Whig" (proresistance) figures, sat down to what was, in effect, a carefully staged production. Reed arose first, read the letters from Boston, and then spoke on the crisis calmly, but with deep feeling. Mifflin and Thomson followed. Speaking with great vehemence, they demanded that Philadelphia initiate a unilateral nonimportation boycott, as Boston's committee had requested. The zealous oratory ended suddenly when Thomson, overcome by the heat of the room and his lack of sleep since Revere's arrival, and perhaps also by the intensity of his own emotion, fainted.[10]

The cautious merchants, now thoroughly distressed, cried out their disapproval of the radicals' proposal, and the meeting became chaotic. At this moment Dickinson, who alone among Philadelphians enjoyed the trust of moderates and radicals alike, rose, quieted the crowd, and spoke calmly and with great effect in favor of petitioning Governor Penn to convene the Assembly to consider the crisis. He then departed hastily, and immediately great confusion broke out in the densely packed room. Thomson, however, soon recovered from his spell, restored order, and moved that a reply of support in principle be sent to Boston at once. The city's leaders quickly approved both this suggestion and Dickinson's petition plan. To answer Boston's letter, correspond with the southern colonies, and circulate the petition to Governor Penn, they appointed a committee.[11]

The decision of May 20 to support Boston and join the intercolonial resistance to British policy was a victory for Philadelphia's radical leaders. The committee created on that evening was a compromise. When the chair called for nominations, both the radicals and the moderates, who were also well organized in advance of the meeting, produced complete tickets. After a brief debate the crowd agreed to combine the two slates into one board.[12] This committee of nineteen members—

8. Thomson, N.-Y. Hist. Soc., *Colls.,* XI: 275–76, argues that it was Dickinson's relative passivity in 1773, coupled with his patriotic zeal between 1765 and 1770, that gave both sides reason to expect his support and led both to regard that support as essential, and thus to pay the highest regard to his recommendations in the current crisis.

9. N.-Y. Hist. Soc., *Colls.,* XI: 276 (Thomson).

10. N.-Y. Hist. Soc., *Colls.,* XI: 271–72 (Reed), and 276–77 (Thomson).

11. N.-Y. Hist. Soc., *Colls.,* XI: 277 (Thomson); *Pa. Gaz.,* May 25, 1774; and Thomas Wharton, Sr. to Thomas Walpole, May 31, 1774, Thomas Wharton, Sr. Letter-Book, HSP. See also N.-Y. Hist. Soc., *Colls.,* XI: 271–72 (Reed); and Dr. William Smith, "Notes and Papers on the Commencement of the American Revolution" [1869 MS transcription, 30 pages] (hereafter, Dr. Smith, "Notes"), p. 9, Dr. William Smith Manuscripts, HSP.

12. N.-Y. Hist. Soc., *Colls.,* XI: 277 (Thomson); George Clymer to Josiah Quincey, Jr., June 13, 1774, Force, ed., *American Archives,* 4th Ser., I: 406–7.

Dickinson probably appeared on both tickets—was quite different from its immediate predecessor, which had endorsed the Boston Tea Party. Its members were older and richer; Quakers and former Quakers held nearly as many seats as they had on the 1769 committee; and all but three of the nineteen were in trade. It was not properly an importers' body, however, because its members were engaged in nearly every kind of large-scale business activity. Strictly speaking, the Nineteen was not a merchants' committee, although Philadelphia's mechanics so regarded it,[13] but a coalition of the city's two major political groups as defined by the nature and degree of their opposition to British policy—the moderates, whether Quaker or proprietary, and the radical Whigs.

From the radicals' viewpoint, the most significant feature of the Nineteen was its high proportion of moderates, including Thomas Penrose, who had refused to sign the December 25, 1773, letter endorsing Boston's Tea Party; Jeremiah Warder, Jr., who probably had refused to sign the same letter; and the Reverend Dr. William Smith, the proprietary faction polemicist. The moderates also counted on John Dickinson, but he would not favor their cause in the summer of 1774. The most important radical members were George Clymer, John Cox, Jr., and Mifflin, Reed, and Thomson.[14] The Nineteen was certainly more conservative than Thomson and his allies would have wished, as the cool letter of support that it sent to Boston on the following day made clear. But Philadelphia's conservative merchants, men like Henry Drinker and Thomas Wharton, Sr., were mistaken in their belief that they had won a victory on May 20. The Nineteen included few men who shared their cautious approach to resisting imperial authority, and none so conservative as Joseph Galloway. Dr. Smith, author of the committee's letter to Boston, was a moderate, not a reactionary. Fourteen of the committeemen would remain patriots; only two would become loyalists.[15]

The measures agreed upon by the May 20 meeting—supporting Boston, writing to the southern colonies, endorsing the idea of a continental congress, and petitioning Governor Penn to call the Assembly—were, with the exception of involving the Assembly, exactly the measures Philadelphia's more radical leaders desired.[16]

---

13. A gathering of 1200 mechanics so labeled the May 20 committee in their meeting of June 9, 1774 (*Pa. Gaz.*, June 15, 1774). For a full treatment of the Nineteen, see chapter 4 below.

For convenience, I will hereafter label the May 20 committee "the Nineteen," following the example of Arthur Schlesinger, Sr., whose *Colonial Merchants* employs capitalized, written-out numbers to denominate committees in both New York (p. 330 ff.) and Philadelphia (p. 345 ff.). I will label Philadelphia's other resistance committees on the same principle: the June 18, 1774 committee will be "the Forty-Three"; the November 12, 1774 committee, "the Sixty-Six"; the August 16, 1775 committee, "the First One Hundred"; and the February 16, 1776 committee, "the Second One Hundred" (see Schlesinger, *Colonial Merchants*, pp. 347, 458). The reader should understand, however, that these labels were seldom, if ever, used by the committees' contemporaries.

14. Here, and elsewhere in this study, committeemen are placed on a conservative-radical spectrum on the basis of their full careers in Philadelphia politics, 1764–76, as well as on the basis of their current—in this case, May 1774—positions on the major questions concerning the imperial crisis.

15. Compare this high incidence of adherence to the resistance among Philadelphia's elite committeemen with the situation in New York City, where nineteen of the committee of Fifty-One, also chosen in May 1774, ultimately became loyalists (Becker, *History of Political Parties,* p. 116n).

16. Thomson, N.-Y. Hist. Soc., *Colls.,* XI: 275–76, felt that the important point on May 20

The manner in which the Nineteen supported Boston, however, immediately caused the radicals concern and embarrassment. On May 21, the committee chose Dr. Smith to draft Philadelphia's reply to Boston.[17] While Smith's letter expressed qualified approval for Boston's fight for America's liberties, it also suggested that the town might consider paying for the tea destroyed in December. The letter rejected Boston's suggestion that Philadelphia begin a boycott, recommending instead a general congress. The tone of the letter was even more disturbing. Its pledge of support in principle was cool, faintly disapproving, and indecisive, and Smith stressed the Nineteen's inability to speak either for Pennsylvania as a whole or even for the city of Philadelphia.

The radical wing of the resistance movement, determined to generate a stronger showing of public support for Boston, now turned briefly from formal committee activity to the direct mobilization of the whole community. Charles Thomson opened this campaign by calling on all Philadelphians to observe June 1, the day on which the Boston Port Act was to go into effect, with a "solemn pause." On this day they would suspend all regular business and soberly consider the imperial crisis. The radicals persuaded a few prominent members of each major religious denomination to meet at William Bradford's London Coffee House to discuss this proposal. There, on Sunday morning, May 29, every man present, except for one Quaker, agreed to the observance.[18] Many Quakers refused to discontinue their labors for the pause, which they regarded as a fast day, and both Anglican and Quaker congregations declined to hold special services. But on June 1, most Philadelphians closed their shops, several churches opened for sermons and prayer, and the muffled bells of Christ Church rang continually. Solemn behavior and a thoughtful expression on nearly every face marked Philadelphia's first display of mass support for Boston.[19]

The "solemn pause" of June 1 accelerated the development of Philadelphia's resistance movement in several ways. First, the observance was the radicals' initial bid in 1774 for support from the whole city. The moderates' domination of the Nineteen had encouraged a passive attitude toward British authority in Philadelphia that Thomson was determined to destroy. In the "solemn pause" he found the perfect vehicle for awakening the city to the dangers of Britain's new imperial

---

was intercolonial cooperation. He regarded the involvement of the Assembly as less important, merely a necessary gambit to gain moderate support. Because the idea of a congress appears in the Nineteen's May 21 letter to Boston, it must have been discussed, at least informally, on May 20, but there is no record of this. The proposal for a congress, which was never controversial in Pennsylvania, probably originated with New York City's radicals (see Becker, *History of Political Parties,* p. 118).

17. *Pa. Gaz.,* June 8, 1774; Dr. William Smith, "Notes," p. 4, HSP.

18. *Pa. Packet,* May 30, 1774; *Pa. Jour.,* June 1, 1774; [Henry Drinker] to Pigou & Booth (New York), May 31, 1774, Henry Drinker Letter-Book (domestic), HSP; Charles Thomson to Isaac Low and the New York Committee, May 29, and n. d., 1774 [typescripts], and James & Drinker to Pigou & Booth (New York), June 9, 1774 [typescript], James and Drinker Correspondence, HSP; Charles Thomson to Isaac Low and the New York Committee, *Rivington's N.-Y. Gaz.,* June 2; and "Veritas" [Jabez Maud Fisher], *Rivington's N.-Y. Gaz.,* July 12, 1774. Two Quakers were present at the meeting, Benjamin Marshall, who endorsed the June 1 observance for himself, but not for the Society of Friends, and Jeremiah Warder, Jr., who either protested the decision openly or remained silent.

19. *Pa. Packet,* June 6, 1774; Duane, ed., *Passages from Marshall,* pp. 6–7; James & Drinker to Pigou & Booth, June 9, 13, July 7, 9, 1774 [typescripts], James and Drinker Correspondence, HSP; "Veritas," *Rivington's N.-Y. Gaz.,* July 12, 1774.

policies, while salvaging Philadelphia's reputation with patriots to the north.[20] Second, the meeting that organized the observance was the first to use explicitly the concept of denominational representation. The conviction that Philadelphia's several religious congregations were the fundamental subcommunities within the city and had to be consulted before any decision affecting the whole community was made now became a major theme in Philadelphia's political mobilization. Finally, the "solemn pause" powerfully affected the city's most conservative leaders. The radicals' preparations for that day, the observance itself, and Charles Thomson's public defense of the observance to the leaders and populace of New York City alarmed many conservative Philadelphians. The radicals' success persuaded these leaders that their faith in the moderate merchants' ability to control the city's politics, which they had held firmly only two weeks earlier, was naively optimistic.

The Society of Friends reacted immediately. On May 30, the leaders of Philadelphia's Meetings announced their opposition to the "solemn pause," and declared that no one attending the May 29 meeting had been authorized to speak for their Society.[21] Criticism of the "solemn pause" by individual Philadelphians remained clandestine in their own city, but soon appeared in the New York press. It began when Charles Thomson informed Isaac Low, the chairman of New York's resistance committee, of Philadelphia's decision to observe June 1.[22] Thomson, attempting to achieve unity by declaring its existence and to defend his city to outsiders, announced that the observance had the support of all denominations in Philadelphia. New York's ultraconservative Quaker committeeman and former tea agent, Benjamin Booth, who had just received a different account of the May 29 meeting from Abel James and Henry Drinker, immediately wrote to his friends requesting more information so that he might destroy Thomson's credibility. James and Drinker responded at once, sending Booth details not only of the May 29 meeting, but also of the extent of the observance of the "solemn pause."[23] As soon as he felt suitably armed, the pugnacious Booth engaged Thomson in a verbal duel, both in the press and by mail. Thomson, however, was too shrewd to reply to his adversary in Philadelphia's journals, nor could Booth gain entrance to them.[24]

---

20. On the importance to the radicals of the other colonies' good opinion of their city and province, see Charles Thomson to Samuel Adams, June 3, 1774, and Thomas Mifflin to Adams, May 26, 1774, Samuel Adams Papers, New York Public Library.

21. *Pa. Gaz.,* June 1, 1774. See also "Veritas," *Rivington's N.-Y. Gaz.,* July 12, 1774.

22. [Henry Drinker] to Pigou & Booth, May 31, June 21, July 5, 1774, Henry Drinker Letter-Book (domestic), HSP; Pigou & Booth to James & Drinker, June 3, 8, 28; Charles Thomson to Isaac Low, May 29, and n. d. [between June 1 and 6]; Benjamin Booth to Thomson, June 8; Thomson to Low, June 10; James & Drinker to Booth, June 13; Booth to James & Drinker, June 16; Booth to Thomson, June 17; James & Drinker to Booth, July 7; and Abel James to Booth, July 9, 1774 [typescripts]. All of these letters are in the James and Drinker Correspondence, HSP, except for Thomson to Low (New York Committee), June 10, and Benjamin Booth to Thomson, June 8, 17, 1774, which appear in *Rivington's N.-Y. Gaz.,* June 30, 1774.

23. [Henry Drinker] to Pigou & Booth, May 31, June 21; Pigou & Booth to James & Drinker, June 3; Thomson to Low, May 29, 1774.

24. Booth to James & Drinker, June 8, 29; Booth to Thomson, June 8; Thomson to Low, n. d., and June 10; Booth to James & Drinker, June 16; Booth to Thomson, June 17; and Booth to James & Drinker, July 13, 1774. The last of these letters contains three notes from Philadelphia editors rejecting Booth's requests to publish in their newspapers: William & Thomas Bradford to Booth, July 4 (*Pa. Journal*); Dunlap to Booth, July 5 (*Pa. Packet*); and Hall & Sellers to Booth, July 5 (*Pa. Gazette*). Also see *Rivington's N.-Y. Gaz.,* July 7, Booth to Thomson (dated July 6); and July 12, 1774, "Veritas."

The private correspondence generated by the Booth-Thomson controversy highlights the impotence of Philadelphia's ultraconservative opposition to the resistance movement in June 1774. Philadelphia's most active conservatives were then Abel James, Henry Drinker, Jabez Fisher, and Samuel Shoemaker.[25] But these four Quaker merchants had no visible adherents, even among the Society of Friends. Many conservative Quakers continued to support the committee movement for several months and refrained from criticizing the more radical committeemen in the hope of moderating committee policy.[26] Others withdrew from politics completely. Even those Friends who actively opposed the resistance were either afraid of public controversy or were unable to gain regular access to the press. Fearful memories of 1773 probably stilled James and Drinker. Yet bolder spirits, Benjamin Booth and Jabez Fisher, were also muffled when Philadelphia's editors, by declining to print any divisive attacks upon the city's resistance policy, effectively suppressed all conservative criticism of the moderate-radical coalition.[27]

By early June, Philadelphia's radical leaders had begun to alter the city's cautious spirit of mid-May. While still relatively weak and lacking the unqualified allegiance of the community, they had again established a committee to direct the resistance and secured several places for themselves on it. They had mobilized support for Boston and for a continental congress, and had only to determine whether they, or the moderates, would be the dominant force in shaping the growth of that support. In this campaign, they had thoroughly alienated only one small and rather passive group of Philadelphians. This success was the beginning of a pattern in Philadelphia's resistance politics. Enemies made at each stage of the Revolutionary movement were too few and too passive to join with other groups already opposed to the movement, so that no effective opposition formed to check the ever stronger and more legitimized patriot faction.

MODERATES AND RADICALS

While Philadelphia's conservatives were deploring Charles Thomson's latest outrage, the Nineteen was circulating its petition for an emergency Assembly session. On June 7, the committee presented the petition, with over nine hundred signatures, to Governor Penn. The governor had been expecting this request since May 20, and had already promised Lord Dartmouth that he would reject it. He did so at once, without giving it even one day's consideration.[28]

This rebuff was of great benefit to Philadelphia's resistance movement. The city's radical leaders had only accepted the decision to petition the governor out of necessity. They strongly favored a continental congress, but they attached little importance to choosing Pennsylvania's delegates to such a body in a constitutional fashion, and they were decidedly cool toward allowing Galloway's Quaker party to

25. On Samuel Shoemaker, see James & Drinker to Booth, July 7; and Booth to James & Drinker, July 13, 1774. On Jabez Maud Fisher, son of Joshua Fisher, see James & Drinker to Pigou & Booth, Aug. 9, 1774, Henry Drinker Letter-Book (domestic), HSP.

26. See Thomas Wharton, Sr. to Samuel Wharton, July 5, 1774, Thomas Wharton, Sr. Letter-Book, HSP.

27. Editors' replies to Booth, cited in note 24 above; James & Drinker to Pigou & Booth, Aug. 9, 1774, Henry Drinker Letter-Book (domestic), HSP.

28. *Minutes of the Provincial Council,* X: 179–80; Penn to Dartmouth, May 31, 1774, Force, ed., *American Archives,* 4th Ser., I: 367–68.

appoint or instruct the colony's spokesmen. They did, however, appreciate the petition's many uses. It immediately won over both John Dickinson and several moderates who may have believed that Penn would grant their request. It was effective in mobilizing public opinion and gave the resistance movement a proper appearance. Finally, the petition's rejection created the best possible pretext for further autonomous action, and Charles Thomson eagerly anticipated Penn's denial.[29]

Penn's veto of constitutional resistance sparked rapid political changes in Philadelphia. The first response was the Nineteen's decision, made sometime between June 7 and 9, to hold a public assembly. This gathering would elect a larger, more comprehensive committee to carry on the work that the Nineteen had begun and settle on a plan to enable the city and the province to resist British imperial policy regardless of Governor Penn's actions.[30] It has been suggested that the Nineteen reached this decision only under pressure from Philadelphia's mechanics, who in turn were organized and directed by the committee's radical wing. The city's political activity in the second week in June does not confirm this hypothesis.[31] John Penn received and rejected the petition to convene the Assembly on June 7. On June 8, a broadside summoned the city's mechanics to a meeting on the following day, at which time a letter from New York's mechanics would be read and America's situation considered. On June 9, twelve hundred mechanics did gather, apparently with the intention of prodding the "merchants' " committee—the Nineteen—to adopt a more decisive policy. At this meeting, however, it was announced that the Nineteen had decided to hold a large public assembly on June 15. The mechanics then appointed their own committee, but decided not to initiate any further activity until the fifteenth.[32] The Nineteen met on June 10 and 11, prepared for the public meeting they had called, and moved it back to June 18, to allow more time for Philadelphia County's rural inhabitants to hear of the gathering and attend.

This sequence of events suggests that it was Penn's rejection of its petition that caused the Nineteen to expand its membership and seek fresh public advice concerning its work. The logic of the situation strongly favors this conclusion. The city's mechanics had had over two weeks to influence the policy of the Nineteen, yet they had remained quiet because they, like all Philadelphians, were waiting to see what the governor would do. When Penn gave his answer, both the mechanics

---

29. N.-Y. Hist. Soc., *Colls.*, XI: 278.

30. The May 20 meeting had intended that all Philadelphia freemen consider altering the committee at a later date, as is clear from the account of its proceedings published in the *Pennsylvania Gazette* on June 8.

31. Schlesinger, *Colonial Merchants*, p. 345. Neither Schlesinger nor Hutson, in *Pennsylvania Politics*, sees Philadelphia's mechanics as an independent force; for these scholars the mechanics become simply the tools of radical strategists like Charles Thomson. But there is no evidence to connect any of Philadelphia's prominent, nonmechanic radical leaders with any mechanics' meeting in 1774. Thus it is likely that the mechanics organized spontaneously at this time, as Olton argues (*Artisans for Independence*, chap. 5, esp. pp. 60–63).

32. *To the Manufacturers and Mechanics of Philadelphia, the Northern Liberties, and District of Southwark* (Philadelphia, June 8, 1774); accounts of the meeting in *Pa. Packet*, June 13; *Pa. Jour.*, June 15; and *Pa. Gaz.*, June 15, 1774. For a discussion of the eleven members of this committee, see chapter 4 below. Most of the eleven, while new to radical politics, were not poor artisans but well-established craftsmen and manufacturers (see portrait data in Appendix G).

and the Nineteen acted within forty-eight hours. The mechanics' June 8 proceedings suggest not so much a hostility toward the Nineteen as a lack of confidence in the board's determination to act. Philadelphia's mechanics, like the radical merchants, were distressed at the number of moderates on the Nineteen. In 1770 they had learned to distrust the merchants and to act independently of them; in May 1774 New York's mechanics had organized to combat merchant timidity in their city, and their independence encouraged Philadelphia's artisans to unite anew.[33] Fearful that the importers might again forego principle for expediency, as they had seen them do in 1770, the mechanics became an increasingly autonomous political force in the summer and fall of 1774, and gradually entered into an alliance with those merchants who were committed to radical resistance policies. The mechanics' spontaneous mobilization forced the Nineteen to recognize both their concern and their political strength, and the Nineteen carefully included several members of the mechanics' June 9 committee on the ticket they composed on June 11 for a new city committee of correspondence.

The Nineteen's June 10–11 meeting was probably its first plenary session since May 21. The board had done important work, but in the three weeks since its creation, Philadelphia's major political events were initiated by committeemen acting privately, or by noncommitteemen: Thomson's radicals, Governor Penn, and the mechanics. On June 10 and 11, the committee again moved to the center of the political stage. To the Nineteen fell the drafting of resolves on the imperial crisis and the construction of a slate of nominees for a new committee, which the public would then consider. Fully conscious of their responsibility, the committeemen declined to shoulder it alone. Following Thomson's example, they invited six persons from each denomination in the city to take part in their deliberations.[34]

The sixty or more leaders who assembled at Philosophical Society Hall on June 10 first drew up resolves setting out the city's resistance policy for popular consideration.[35] The body began with a condemnation of the Boston Port Act, then called for a general congress, and finally resolved that the most suitable agent for choosing congressional delegates was the Pennsylvania Assembly, convened in formal session. Since Governor Penn would not summon the Assembly, however, the gathering felt the necessity of recommending an alternative plan, and here the leaders split sharply. According to Charles Thomson, who has left the only detailed account of these transactions, John Dickinson opened the debate with a novel proposal: that every county in Pennsylvania elect delegates to a provincial convention in the same way that it elected assemblymen. This convention would choose and instruct Pennsylvania's congressmen. Dickinson's address marks the first appearance of this idea in Pennsylvania. The plan, which Thomson also favored, was the dominant strategy of revolutionary mobilization among Philadelphia's

33. On the role of New York's Committee of Mechanics, see Becker, *History of Political Parties*, pp. 119–20.

34. Thomas Wharton, Sr. to Samuel Wharton, July 5, 1774, Thomas Wharton, Sr. Letter-Book, HSP. The Quakers invited were Isaac Howell, Owen Jones, James Pemberton, George Roberts, Samuel Shoemaker, and Wharton himself. All except Howell and Shoemaker attended. The identities of the other denominational spokesmen invited, or of the other denominations represented, are not known.

35. Wharton to Wharton, July 5, 1774, supplies the attendance figure.

radical leaders in mid-June. Its partial achievement in the following month was the first great radical victory of 1774.[36]

At its first appearance, however, Dickinson's proposal encountered stiff opposition from several quarters. Opponents of the plan all favored requesting Joseph Galloway to convene the Assembly unofficially to name Pennsylvania's delegates, but Thomson sensed several incompatible motives behind the common counter-proposal. He believed that Attorney General Andrew Allen and Dr. William Smith, as proprietary faction leaders, sought to insure that any blame Pennsylvania might incur for participating in a congress would fall on Galloway's Quaker party rather than on Governor John Penn. A second set of critics were the Quakers, whom Thomson divided into two groups. The first were the truly religious Friends, who abhorred all conflict and therefore favored a cautious, passive response to the crisis. A more worldly set of Friends included men like Thomas Wharton, Sr., who had interests in Whitehall that any sharp opposition to ministry policy might jeopardize.[37] The final critic, curiously, was the young radical lawyer Joseph Reed, but Thomson had an explanation for his behavior as well. Reed, he thought, wanted to discredit Galloway's Quaker party by involving the assemblymen in preparations for the congress, during which they would so thoroughly disgrace themselves by their reactionary behavior that Pennsylvania's voters would turn them out of office in October.

Thomson's assessment of his neighbors' motives is a brilliant analysis—penetrating, comprehensive, and concise. It is also flawed. This shrewd, pragmatic leader suffered from the same preoccupation with old factional wars that was prevalent among Philadelphia's conservatives.[38] The Quaker-proprietary struggle was rapidly becoming irrelevant, and no man had done more to make it so than Thomson himself. Yet the old perceptions lingered. The motives that Thomson highlighted were still strong, but at a more fundamental level, Andrew Allen, Dr. Smith, and Thomas Wharton, Sr. all favored cautious, traditional protests because their entire careers had taught them that any criticism of governmental authority must take the most legitimate form possible.[39] Moreover, those moderates who were merchants had reason to fear that a provincial convention might openly favor nonimportation, which they hoped to avoid. Joseph Reed's often puzzling career suggests that he, too, may have been speaking partly out of moderation.

The wide divergence between the moderate and radical plans for selecting congressmen caused such a lengthy debate that the leaders had to adjourn to the following day, but they finally hammered out a compromise. In their fourth resolve,

---

36. "Notes on a meeting of a number of Gentlemen convened on the 10 June 1774," in "Memorandum Book, 1754–1774," pp. 159–62, Charles Thomson Papers, Gratz Collection, HSP. This account was personal and even secret, and it is likely that no one saw it during Thomson's lifetime. Dickinson's plan appeared, in modified form, in a radical essay in the *Pennsylvania Journal* on June 22, 1774, the day on which the Forty-Three voted to put it into execution (see below in this chapter).

37. For an excellent reconstruction of the worldview of both pious and worldly Quakers, see Bauman, *For the Reputation of Truth,* chaps. 4–10 and appendix B.

38. For numerous examples of this preoccupation, peruse the James and Drinker, Henry Drinker, and Thomas Wharton, Sr. Papers, 1773–75, HSP.

39. Wharton, in his July 5, 1774 letter to his brother Samuel, gives a vivid picture of his own reaction to Dickinson's resolves, "some of which were expressed in terms We could not Approve of, and therefore after debates which lasted for 10 or 12 hours We took off all the Accrimoneous [*sic*] parts." (Letter-Book, p. 52, HSP).

they recommended that Galloway be requested to convene the Assembly unofficially; in the fifth and sixth resolves, they adopted a part of Dickinson's plan, recommending that "a large and respectable Committee be appointed for the City and County of Philadelphia, to draw up Instructions for [our assemblymen]" and that every county in Pennsylvania take similar action.[40] Two duties now remained: to set the time and place for the public meeting and to compose a slate of nominees for a new committee. To allow time to distribute broadsides of their transactions throughout the County, they postponed the meeting to Saturday, June 18, and voted to hold it in the spacious State House Yard.

The most difficult task facing the June 11 session, after devising a plan for selecting Pennsylvania's congressmen, was the choice of nominees for the committee that would succeed the Nineteen. The ticket of forty persons that they composed was, like the Nineteen itself, a compromise between moderates and radicals. The June 11 slate was an aggregation of four distinct sets of men. Fourteen members of the Nineteen—conservative, moderate, and radical—headed the ticket; the five remaining committeemen, including the ever-cautious John Dickinson, apparently declined further public service. Six of the eleven spokesmen chosen by the mechanics on June 9 were also selected by the June 11 meeting, which greatly strengthened the radicals. The gathering then added six representatives of the more conservative county, probably as a counterbalance to the mechanics. Eleven merchants, two retailers, and a lawyer from the city completed the slate. The ticket was moderate, but with a larger number of prominent radicals than of conservatives. Its balanced composition argues that radical strength in the city remained high despite the conservative resurgence of May.[41]

Philadelphia's radical merchants were not delighted with the resolves or the nominees of June 11, but they quietly accepted the necessity for compromise. Their mechanic allies, however, at once began their own preparations for June 18, and on June 17, a number of artisans and Germans, assembled at the Bunch of Grapes Inn, launched a sharp attack on the June 11 nominees.[42] They called for the exclusion of Dr. Smith, whom they opposed for penning the cool letter to Boston on May 21, and Thomas Wharton, Sr., a former tea agent. And they demanded not forty, but fifty-one committeemen, an obvious reference to New York City's Fifty-One, elected on May 16. That board was in fact more conservative than any Philadelphia had chosen since the Townshend Act boycott, and was only so large because New York's conservatives had insisted on expanding an earlier board of twenty-five, chosen by radical merchants and mechanics.[43] Possibly the leaders of the June 17 meeting did not know this; but in any event they only wanted a convenient pretext to add radical mechanic spokesmen to the June 11 slate without

---

40. "At a Meeting at the Philosophical Society's Hall, June 10th, . . ." (Philadelphia, June 13?, 1774), Evans No. 13534. A particularly interesting specimen of this broadside, with annotations in Dickinson's hand, is in the R. R. Logan Collection, HSP.

41. Because the printed ticket is not extant, the validity of this paragraph rests upon the soundness of the author's assumption that a list of forty names written on a small slip of paper, probably in Dickinson's hand, and entitled "list of Committee," is in fact an accurate version of the June 11 slate. The list is in the R. R. Logan Collection, HSP, and appears, alphabetized with portrait data, as table 6 in chapter 4 below.

42. The existence of this meeting has apparently been overlooked by students of the period. The only source for it is a two-page copy of the proceedings in the John Dickinson material, R. R. Logan Collection, HSP.

43. Becker, *History of Political Parties*, pp. 112–15.

having to demand the removal of conservative merchants, with the exception of Wharton, whom they could not abide. Declaring that neither mechanics nor Germans had an adequate voice on the slate of forty, they proposed the addition of seven mechanics' representatives and six Germans. The gathering's leaders, Isaac Melchior and John Ross, then delivered its resolves to John Dickinson and Thomas Willing, the cochairmen of the June 18 meeting.[44]

On June 18, several thousand qualified voters from Philadelphia and the surrounding rural townships assembled for the most important mass meeting of 1774. All knew the critical issues and their respective proponents. Farthest to the right stood a few pious Quaker merchants: Abel James, Henry Drinker, and the Joshua Fisher family. These Friends, attending despite a recent recommendation by their Society that its members avoid political activity, opposed any measure beyond asking the Pennsylvania Assembly to petition Great Britain for a redress of colonial grievances.[45] A much larger moderate party favored sending delegates to a continental congress, but expected this congress to petition the Crown and Parliament before taking stronger measures. The crucial issue for this group, however, was securing for the Assembly the exclusive right to name and instruct Pennsylvania's congressmen. Dr. William Smith and Thomas Wharton, Sr. were the spokesmen for this faction, which had narrowly dominated the June 10–11 meeting. Their followers included middle-aged Anglican and Quaker merchants and many farmers from Philadelphia County. On the left, a large block of freemen favored a provincial convention that would both nominate and instruct, if it could not elect, Pennsylvania's congressmen. Dickinson, Thomson, and Reed led these young Anglican and Quaker merchants, Presbyterians and Germans of all ages and callings, and city mechanics.[46]

The spirit of compromise that had dominated Philadelphia since mid-May was evident from the opening of the June 18 meeting. The cochairmen chosen were the moderate Anglican merchant Thomas Willing and the somewhat more radical John Dickinson. Following a reading of the June 10–11 resolves, Dr. Smith delivered an address on the need for unity.[47] The freemen then voted on the eight resolves of June 10–11, one by one. Immediately the moderates suffered a major setback. The third and fourth resolves, endorsing in principle the nomination of congressmen by the Assembly in official session, and advising that because of Governor Penn's intransigence Joseph Galloway be requested to convene the House unofficially, were both defeated. Instead, the crowd expressed its confidence in the ability of the new committee they were about to elect to discover the most appropriate

44. See Appendix H.
45. On June 16, the Friends' Meeting for Sufferings advised all Quakers to avoid any involvement in public meetings (see the "Minutes of the Monthly Meeting of the Northern District of Philadelphia," eighth month, 1774, pp. 107–8, on film at Friends Historical Library, Swarthmore College). On the Quaker reactions to the June 18 meeting, see Bauman, *For the Reputation of Truth*, pp. 142–45.
46. Reed, although he had opposed Dickinson's plan for a provincial convention without an accompanying session of the Assembly on June 10, seems not to have disapproved of the idea of a convention in itself, as his energetic work on the new committee of Forty-Three on behalf of such a convention indicates (see below in this chapter).
47. Full official proceedings of this meeting, including Dr. Smith's speech, appear in the *Pennsylvania Gazette*, June 22, 1774.

manner of choosing Pennsylvania's spokesmen in congress.[48] This decision did not prohibit a strong political role for the legislature, but it did both assert the voters' independence of their representatives and suggest a sharp decline in their traditional deference toward them. For the first time in Pennsylvania's history, Philadelphia's freemen had suggested that there were limitations to the competence of their province's legally constituted Assembly.

In the consideration of the June 11 nominations for committeemen that followed, the radicals made further gains, although this required a major concession on their part. While the moderates insisted that the forty be approved or rejected as a unit, the radicals, especially the mechanics, demanded the right to vote on each individual in order to turn out Wharton and Smith, who refused to withdraw. An alliance of radical merchants and mechanics could have carried this issue within the city, but gentry leaders who spoke for the rural freemen insisted that if the forty were not approved as a block, then they must represent only the city. Cochairman Thomas Willing supported them. Bitter exchanges between city and county forces followed, ending only when John Dickinson, assuring his radical followers that every nominee "wished his Country Good," recommended approving the whole ticket.[49]

Dickinson's address probably signaled the radicals' willingness to compromise, because they shortly did agree to vote on the entire ticket, and they were given something in return. Although unit approval of the June 11 nominees terminated the candidacy of the thirteen men nominated by the mechanics and Germans on June 17, the June 18 meeting did make alterations in the ticket. Five obscure men withdrew or were removed from the slate in favor of five more prominent figures, including three members of the Nineteen. The most important addition was John Dickinson, still an indispensable symbol of unified resistance to Great Britain. While this alteration did not make the ticket much more radical, it did make it stronger and more distinguished. And after this modified slate won approval, the innkeeper and mechanic spokesman Isaac Melchior persuaded chairmen Dickinson and Willing that Philadelphia's Germans were underrepresented, and the crowd agreed to add to the board the four most prominent of the six Germans nominated on the previous evening, giving forty-four committeemen. The immediate withdrawal of the influential Quaker leader James Pemberton, who evidently saw in what direction the resistance movement was headed, gave Philadelphia's new Committee of Correspondence its final shape.[50]

The Forty-Three resembled the moderate Nineteen in several ways. Major merchants and manufacturers in their forties, cautious Anglicans and Quakers, and long-established leaders dominated both committees. Indicative of Philadelphia's stiffening resistance, however, were several changes in committee composition. Men in their thirties, Presbyterians and members of two religious denominations, Lutheran and Baptist, whose communicants had heretofore taken little part in

---

48. Pertinent here, in addition to a comparison of the two sets of resolves, cited in notes 40 and 47 above, are Dickinson's annotations on the June [13?] broadside, made during or shortly after the June 18 meeting.

49. "Papers relating to the shipment of tea . . ." (hereafter, "Tea Papers") [mistitled and misdated, authorship unknown, 4 pages], HSP, pp. 1–3; Dickinson's remark is on pp. 2–3.

50. "Tea Papers," p. 3, HSP. On James Pemberton, see Bauman, *For the Reputation of Truth,* pp. 141–43.

public life, merchants of only modest wealth, and for the first time a few artisans, now held several committee seats. The members of the Forty-Three were one-third less affluent, on average, than the Nineteen, and proportionally fewer were members of prominent families. Most important, several followed occupations of modest economic and social status, occupations whose members had traditionally played only a passive role in Philadelphia politics. This reappearance of artisan spokesmen amid the resistance leadership after the brief hiatus of May signaled the development of mechanic activism to the point where Philadelphia's traditional elites could no longer deny the "lower orders" a role in mobilizing and directing the city's political energies.[51]

The election of the broadly comprehensive Forty-Three marks the first inclusion of representatives of all denominations and of all classes above the level of unskilled labor into Philadelphia's political process. Yet this same Forty-Three was the first committee to include several assemblymen, giving it an eminently respectable character that was essential in attracting moderate support. For both reasons, the June 18 election was a major radical triumph. Philadelphia's patriot leaders, while broadening the base of political activity, had kept the city united. For a full month they had contested with the moderates, slowly driving them to stronger measures. Yet they had retained their opponents' toleration and cooperation, if not their admiration. The only Philadelphians who were deeply alienated from resistance politics in the spring of 1774 were the more pious and conservative Quaker merchants. Their dissatisfaction was unavoidable, but not especially dangerous: these Friends were too weak to retard the resistance movement and too intimidated to attempt open opposition.

By June 18, 1774, the Dickinson-Thomson resistance faction had convinced Philadelphians of the need for intercolonial unity and the development of an immediate resistance policy through local mass meetings and extraconstitutional committees. The purpose of these bodies was to formulate a colonial strategy of long-term resistance to British imperial policy under the direction of a continental congress. The grand issue, in June 1774, was whether the committee movement would be accepted by all Pennsylvanians as the legitimate vehicle of resistance to British authority.

THE TRIUMPH OF THE COMMITTEE MOVEMENT

On June 20, the Forty-Three chose Thomas Willing chairman and Charles Thomson secretary, at once establishing its moderate-radical balance. On June 22, the board resolved to ask Joseph Galloway to summon the Assembly. The radicals probably first attempted to quash this proposal, a revival of the moderates' strategy of June 10–11, but soon decided to compromise to preserve resistance unity.[52] This concession prepared the way for the most important decision of the Forty-Three's brief life. The members voted to draft a letter directed to political leaders in every

---

51. See chapter 4, tables 2–6 below. On the rise of the mechanics, see Olton, *Artisans for Independence,* chaps. 4–5.

52. The basic source for the Forty-Three's activity between June 20 and July 11 is an untitled manuscript transcript of the committee's minutes in volume Yi 965 F, Du Simitière Collection, HSP (hereafter, [Minutes]), 24 pages.

county seat in Pennsylvania, urging that their counties choose committees and send delegates to Philadelphia to participate in a provincial convention. This body would advise the Assembly on its choice of and instructions to Pennsylvania's congressmen. The committee did not work out the details of this plan on June 22, because it had first to see if Galloway would call the Assembly before it could issue an invitation to the convention, but the radicals' victory was secure, and John Dickinson, Charles Thomson, and Thomas Mifflin set off directly on a tour of Pennsylvania's interior counties to promote their committee-convention system.[53]

In the spring and summer of 1774, seven British North American colonies held provincial conventions, and three colonies held legislative sessions to select their congressmen. Only Pennsylvania held both a convention and a legislative session simultaneously, with the two bodies composed almost entirely of different men. The Forty-Three's June 22 decision to call both a convention and the Assembly at first appears redundant, simply the product of the radicals' distrust of the legislature and the moderates' distrust of any other body. But the radicals attached a great significance to the committee-convention system. On June 22, Bradford's *Journal* carried an essay by one "J. R---," who favored a provincial convention without an accompanying session of the Assembly.[54] His argument not only illuminates the radicals' feelings toward the Assembly but, far more important, reveals their reasons for establishing the committee-convention system in Pennsylvania.

"J. R---" conceded that an Assembly meeting in official session was "perhaps" the correct instrument for choosing congressmen. But to summon Pennsylvania's assemblymen unofficially for this work, he explained, would cause their deliberations to be without constitutional force. If the people were not consulted in the present crisis, any leaders who wished to act would "have nothing firm under them."[55] For them to assume their constituents' opinions, "J. R---" declared, would be to slip into the error of virtual representation. Only a full and immediate consultation with every freeman could secure the unity of the colonies. If each colony were to create a committee of correspondence in its capital and one in each county seat, composed of committeemen from every district and township, the colonies would possess perfect channels of communication, both for the desires and opinions arising from the people and for the policy decisions coming down from their leaders.

In 1774 the radicals worked to establish this system throughout the province. On June 27, the Forty-Three, having secured Joseph Galloway's pledge to call the assemblymen into special session, appointed Dr. Smith and the radicals James Mease and Joseph Reed to draft its circular letter inviting political leaders in the several counties to send delegates to a convention.[56] Meanwhile, Dickinson, Mifflin, and Thomson, having left Joseph Reed in charge of their program in committee, were touring the Pennsylvania backcountry in this last week of June.[57] The three

---

53. Thomson to Drayton, N.-Y. Hist. Soc., *Colls.,* XI: 279.

54. The identity of "J. R---" is unknown. The author could have been Joseph Reed, but considering the opposition he had expressed on June 10 to the plan that this essay develops, it seems more probable that "J. R---" is merely the pseudonym of another radical spokesman.

55. *Pa. Jour.,* June 22, 1774, p. 2.

56. [Minutes], p. 6.

57. The committee's minutes clearly mark Reed as the radicals' leader between June 23 and July 3, when his three colleagues were traveling. His key radical assistants in committee were James Mease, George Clymer, and John Cox, Jr.

travelers were especially concerned to secure the allegiance of Pennsylvania's Germans to the cause. All the early signs encouraged their expedition. Local patriots had been organizing in Lancaster, Chester, Northampton, and York counties even before their departure, and further meetings in Chester, Lancaster, and Berks counties occurred even as they were making their journey. The sequel to their travels was most heartening: in early July, voters in the five remaining counties gathered, elected committees, and appointed delegates to the provincial convention.[58]

On the evening of June 27, however, just as the radicals' plans for a convention were taking final shape, Governor Penn issued writs for the Assembly to convene on July 18, to meet the challenge of an Indian war that had erupted on the frontier.[59] Penn's sudden decision had two immediate effects. On June 28, the Assembly's conservative leadership, now free of the demeaning necessity of meeting unofficially at the invitation of the Forty-Three if they were to meet at all, replied to the Massachusetts assembly's proposal of May that a continental congress be held in Philadelphia. Pennsylvania's lawmakers approved of the congress, but declared that only colonial legislatures, legally constituted and officially convened, could properly appoint delegates to it. The letter, signed by Joseph Galloway and three conservative colleagues, all members of the Assembly's own committee of correspondence, was clearly designed more for Pennsylvania than for Massachusetts consumption. It appeared in Philadelphia's newspapers just days before the provincial convention—and the emergency Assembly session—began.[60]

But another public address issued on June 28 had a far greater impact upon Pennsylvania. The Forty-Three's circular letter to leaders in the several county

---

58. On the radicals' hopes for the support of the Germans, see N.-Y. Hist. Soc., *Colls.,* XI: 279. The early meetings of rural counties and towns were: Lancaster borough, June 15 (*Pa. Jour.,* June 22); Chester County, June 18 (*Pa. Packet,* June 20); Northampton and York counties, June 21 (*Pa. Gaz.,* June 29 [Northampton], and *Pa. Packet,* July 4 [York]); Chester County, June 25 (*Pa. Gaz.,* July 6); Lancaster County, July 2 ("Minutes of the Lancaster County Committee of Safety," MS volume, Peter Force Collection, Library of Congress); and Berks County, July 2 (*Pa. Gaz.,* July 6). The meetings following the radicals' return were in York County, July 4 (*Pa. Jour.,* July 13); Bucks County, July 9 (*Pa. Packet,* July 18); Lancaster County, July 9 (*Pa. Packet,* July 18); at Carlisle (Cumberland County), and in Bedford County, July 12 (*Pa. Packet,* July 18 [Cumberland], and *Pa. Jour.,* July 20 [Bedford]); and again at Chester, July 13 (*Pa. Packet,* July 18). No records of proceedings in Northumberland and Westmoreland counties have been found, but both counties must have held meetings in early July, because they sent delegates to the provincial convention on July 15.

59. *Minutes of the Provincial Council,* X: 180. Penn may have used the crisis on the frontier merely as a pretext to give the Assembly the opportunity to appoint and instruct Pennsylvania's congressmen officially, thereby undercutting more radical action by a provincial convention of committeemen, as Thomson believed (N.-Y. Hist. Soc., *Colls.,* XI: 278–79). The spread of committee politics deep into rural Pennsylvania in the twenty days since he had rejected the Nineteen's petition to call the House into session must have alarmed the governor. Yet such different leaders as Joseph Reed and Thomas Wharton, Sr. accepted the Indian threat as Penn's real reason for convening the House (N.-Y. Hist. Soc., *Colls.,* XI: 272; Wharton to Samuel Wharton, July 5, 1774, Thomas Wharton, Sr. Letter-Book, HSP).

60. The timing of this letter suggests that its purpose was to attack Pennsylvania's committee movement, because the legislators must have had at least three weeks to reply to Massachusetts' letter of May 28. Moreover, Galloway did not usually reply to the Massachusetts House at all (see chapter 1 above). Interestingly, Thomas Mifflin, a member of the Assembly's committee of correspondence, did not sign this letter, which appears in *Pa. Packet,* July 11, and *Pa. Gaz.,* July 13, 1774. For Galloway's reluctance even to summon his correspondence committee in response to the imperial crisis, see Galloway to Samuel Rhoads and Thomas Mifflin, May 30, 1774, Society Collection, HSP.

seats requested that each county send delegates to meet in convention in Philadelphia on July 15, where they would "assist in framing instructions, and preparing such matters, as may be proper to recommend to our Representatives." The most revealing part of the letter comes at its close, where the authors confidently remark: ". . . we are persuaded you are fully convinced of the necessity of the closest union among ourselves both in sentiment and action; nor can such union be obtained so well by any other method, as by a meeting of the county Committees of each particular province in one place, preparatory to the general congress . . . . and our liberties [can be] fixed upon a permanent foundation . . . . only . . . by a free communion of sentiments."[61]

To appreciate the new spirit of Philadelphia's resistance movement, one need only contrast the tone of this circular letter with that of the Nineteen's May 21 reply to Boston, in which Dr. Smith announced, "To collect the Sense of this large City is difficult; and when their Sense is obtained, they [the Nineteen] must not consider themselves as authorized to judge or to act for this populous Province."[62] Yet Smith himself was on the subcommittee that drafted the circular letter, and he recorded his entire approval of the work of the July provincial convention.[63] By the end of June, committee moderates were beginning to accept the radicals' view of the seriousness of the imperial crisis and to endorse many of their tactics for mobilizing the populace to respond to that crisis.

Philadelphia's craftsmen and shopkeepers, meanwhile, were again grumbling that Dickinson and other patriot leaders were making too many concessions to preserve their alliance with conservative merchants who would ultimately betray America. These charges filled a long, yet often cryptic letter, which the mechanics delivered to Dickinson in early July.[64] Led by radical spokesmen in early June "to expect Resolves big with uncommon Wisdom and Spirit," the mechanics soon discovered "nothing but Timidity, Treachery, and destructive Delays . . . such that the smallest petty Town in the Continent would have been ashamed of."[65] They found themselves still saddled with their enemies (apparently Dr. Smith and Thomas Wharton, Sr.), and the Forty-Three continued to ignore the only policy—an immediate commitment to nonimportation—that could, they believed, rescue Philadelphia from humiliation and defeat. But the mechanics' remonstrance fell upon deaf ears. However treacherous cooperation with the more moderate established leaders in the resistance appeared to these artisans, Dickinson and his colleagues valued it highly. No strong demand for nonimportation was apparent in Philadelphia outside the artisan class. The press was quiet, and the Forty-Three had few enemies.[66] Secure on their left from all but verbal assaults, and enjoying a rough equality in strength with the city's more moderate forces,

---

61. [Minutes], pp. 6–9; *Pa. Packet,* July 4; and *Pa. Gaz.,* and *Pa. Jour.,* July 6, 1774.

62. *Pa. Gaz.,* June 8, 1774.

63. Dr. Smith, "Notes," pp. 17, 29–30.

64. MS letter, the mechanics to John Dickinson, June 27 (P.S., July 4), 1774, item #156, Dickinson material, R. R. Logan Collection, HSP.

65. The quotation appears on page 1 of the MS.

66. Only a few newspaper articles made reference to trade policy at this time: "Letter IV, To the Inhabitants of the British Colonies in America," [John Dickinson], *Pa. Gaz.,* June 15; items by "Anglus Americanus," *Pa. Jour.,* June 22; "The Reflector," *Pa. Packet,* June 20, 27; "A Plain Dealer," *Pa. Gaz.,* July 13; "Brutus," *Pa. Gaz.,* July 20; "Yet a Free Citizen," *Pa. Jour.,* July 20; and minor notices in *Pa. Gaz.,* June 15, 22, 1774.

Philadelphia's radical leaders continued to shape a vigorous yet restrained committee policy.

The work of the Forty-Three on July 4, the busiest session of the committee's brief life, is of the first importance in understanding the goals and tactics of the resistance movement in this crucial summer. Two letters received from Maryland, describing that colony's provincial convention of June 22–25, appear to have influenced the Forty-Three directly and shaped its creation, Pennsylvania's first provincial convention.[67] Maryland's decision to give each county one vote in its June provincial convention, and to settle all debates therein by a simple majority, along with its subsequent recommendation that the continental congress stop all colonial imports and exports at once, could only strengthen Pennsylvania's radicals, who were strongest in the new, thinly populated western counties. But the Forty-Three was not ready to vote for nonimportation. The committee, and the city, were so divided over the necessity of a boycott that they could make no policy recommendation; instead, they played down the whole question of nonimportation and passed it on to the congress for resolution.[68] This was the only position that could win broad support in Philadelphia in July. Cautious merchants and zealous mechanics were still far apart on the proper strategy of economic resistance to Great Britain.

The Forty-Three named eight of its members on July 4 to frame resolves and instructions for consideration by the provincial convention. Fully aware of this drafting committee's opportunity to chart Pennsylvania's political course in the critical months ahead, the Forty-Three balanced its moderate and radical spokesmen evenly. On a conservative-to-radical continuum, Thomas Wharton, Sr., Dr. Smith, Thomas Willing, and probably John Nixon defended the moderate position, while Dickinson, Mifflin, Reed, and Thomson represented the zealots.[69] These eight men, the active core of the Forty-Three, embraced nearly the full spectrum of articulate political opinion in early July 1774.

Not all Philadelphians were willing to accept the Forty-Three's policies, however. For many, the city's failure to endorse a boycott in principle was craven and humiliating. On July 8, a body of "tradesmen," probably the same artisans and retailers who had reproached John Dickinson for accommodating the moderates, appointed a delegation to request that the Forty-Three call another mass meeting for July 15, the day on which the provincial convention was scheduled to meet. On July 9, these delegates reminded the Forty-Three's chairman, Thomas Willing, that neither the Forty-Three nor the coming convention had the power to instruct Pennsylvania's delegates to the congress. And without instructions in favor of a commercial boycott, the mechanics argued, the conservative Assembly's congressional delegates were likely to oppose immediate nonimportation, which the whole congress would probably favor. Their opposition to nonimportation would delay the work of the congress, disgrace Philadelphia, and throw Pennsylvania's resistance movement into confusion.[70]

---

67. [Minutes], pp. 12–15. The letters were sent by the committees in Annapolis (June 26) and Baltimore (June 27). Also see Schlesinger, *Colonial Merchants,* pp. 360–62.
68. [Minutes], p. 16.
69. [Minutes], p. 16.
70. [Minutes], pp. 20–22. The seven mechanics' spokesmen were generally prosperous artisans and retailers. See Appendix I.

On July 11, in their last regular meeting before the provincial convention, the Forty-Three answered the mechanics' criticism. Five committeemen, including Charles Thomson, long popular with Philadelphia's artisans, drafted the board's reply. The Forty-Three declined to hold a mass meeting, explaining that there was not enough time to reach many voters in the countryside, while any independent action by the city might cause a split with patriots in the county. Ignoring the doubts about Galloway and his friends that many of its own members shared with the mechanics, the Forty-Three argued that another mass meeting was, in any event, unsuitable for resolving this issue. The Assembly could more properly instruct congressional delegates than any other body, and the provincial convention was the proper body for instructing the Assembly. The most important point was that everyone invest faith in the forthcoming congress. Whatever strategy of resistance the congress decided to implement, the committeemen declared, they were confident that Pennsylvanians would support it. The Forty-Three's drafting subcommittee was at that moment shaping resolves and instructions to this end. And Philadelphia's established radical leaders were to show themselves determined, in the fall Assembly elections and in the succeeding House votes, to bring Pennsylvania's legislature behind congressional policy. The committee closed with an expression of confidence in the future of the resistance in Philadelphia: "We are now happily united. We are all animated in the general cause and pursuing the constitutional mode for obtaining redress of our grievances. Let us therefore wait the event of the congress."[71]

The Forty-Three here recognized the fragility of the resistance movement and of the harmony between moderates and radicals. The necessary means of maintaining this harmony was the conscious avoidance of all divisive issues that were not absolutely critical. The committee's reply to its critics also suggests how far the movement had come in six weeks: the moderates had been radicalized to favor decisive resistance to Great Britain; the radicals had been moderated to act in a strictly constitutional manner and to restrain their mechanic allies.

On July 15, over seventy Pennsylvania committeemen entered Carpenter's Hall.[72] Thirty-four of Philadelphia's Forty-Three attended, five members came from Bucks County, and Chester and Lancaster each sent eight, but the seven newer counties together had only twenty delegates. The gathering included eleven legislators, a quarter of the House that it was to instruct. This was the high point in legislator participation in Pennsylvania's Revolutionary conventions.[73] Recognizing Philadelphia's dominant position in the province, and in the committee movement, the delegates named Thomas Willing their chairman and Charles Thomson their secretary, the same positions that the two held in the Forty-Three. Next they agreed to give each county one vote in settling all debates.[74] This decision strongly favored the radicals. Conservative strength was concentrated in Philadelphia and in Bucks, Chester, and Lancaster counties, from which the majority of convention

71. [Minutes], pp. 22–24.
72. The official transactions of the provincial convention appear in *Pa. Gaz.,* July 27, 1774, P.S., pp. 1–2; and in the minutes of that body, *Pa. Archives,* 2d Ser., III: 545–622.
73. The eleven included three Philadelphia lawmakers and all four Lancaster County assemblymen. Three of the eleven, Edward Biddle, Thomas Mifflin, and George Ross, were or soon would be Assembly leaders.
74. *Pa. Archives,* 2d Ser., III: 545–46; *Pa. Gaz.,* July 27, 1774, P.S., p. 1.

delegates came. The newer western counties, with their smaller delegations, were consistently more radical.

The convention easily voted eight resolves expressing broad patriot principles and a ninth that declared that a "Congress of Delegates" was essential to "form a general plan of conduct to be observed by all the Colonies" in establishing their rights "and restoring harmony between *Great-Britain* and her Colonies, on a constitutional foundation." The next three resolves sparked sharp debate between conservative and radical spokesmen, which was settled only by a broad compromise. The convention first stated that a suspension of commerce would be most injurious to the province, but asserted that Pennsylvanians were willing to make that sacrifice. In deference to Great Britain, however, they wished "that the Congress should first try the gentler mode of stating our grievances, and making a firm and decent claim of redress." The eleventh and twelfth resolves were a counterbalance to the caution of the tenth. "By a great majority," the convention pledged that Pennsylvanians would join with the other colonies in both nonimportation and nonexportation if congress found these measures expedient because "an unanimity of councils and measures is indispensibly necessary for the common welfare." Against greater conservative opposition, the zealots carried the twelfth resolve, that Pennsylvanians would execute any measure that the congress felt to be essential if the congress received fresh news of hostile Parliamentary action.[75]

In the July 15 resolves, Philadelphia's radical leaders mapped out the course that they wished the resistance movement to follow, while sustaining their alliance with the moderates. Joseph Reed, playing down the real differences between the convention members, remarked that while the debates had been "warm," the disagreements expressed were not "of Sentiment on Principles, only on Modes and Expressions."[76] The appointment on July 16 of eleven delegates to draw up instructions for the Assembly further strengthened the radicals. Dickinson, Reed, and Dr. Smith of the Forty-Three's drafting subcommittee joined delegates from eight other counties. The eleven were predominantly lawyers in their thirties and forties; Dickinson was at once acknowledged their leader. Dr. Smith, who approved the document that they produced, was probably their most conservative member.[77]

On July 18, the eleven reported a lengthy draft of instructions and an essay defending the colonial position in the imperial crisis. Both were principally the work of John Dickinson, who had been preparing them since the Forty-Three appointed its drafting subcommittee on July 4.[78] In the debate over the instructions, Thomas Wharton, Sr. charged that Dickinson's rhetoric was disrespectful to the British government and worked to moderate its tone, while Joseph Reed believed that the concessions Dickinson and his allies wished the congress to secure were more than England would ever grant. Unable to reduce Dickinson's maximum terms, Reed persuaded the convention to add an alternative set of minimum terms.[79]

75. *Pa. Archives,* 2d Ser., III: 546–49; *Pa. Gaz.,* July 27, 1774, P.S., p. 1; and Thomas Wharton, Sr. to Thomas Walpole, Aug. 2, 1774, Thomas Wharton, Sr. Letter-Book, HSP.

76. Reed to Charles Pettit, July 16, 1774, p. 2, Reed Papers, N.-Y. Hist. Soc.

77. *Pa. Archives,* 2d Ser., III: 549. The most important member from the west was James Wilson of Carlisle. On Dr. Smith's approval, see his "Notes," pp. 29–30, Dr. William Smith Papers, HSP.

78. *Pa. Archives,* 2d Ser., III: 549–51.

79. Wharton to Walpole, Aug. 2, 1774, Thomas Wharton, Sr. Letter-Book, HSP; Reed to the earl of Dartmouth, July 25, 1774, in Reed, *Life of Reed,* p. 71. See chapters 5 and 9 below for Reed's later opposition to Dickinson.

After long and heated debates, the convention accepted the amended Instructions on July 20 and presented them to the Assembly on July 21.[80] Two plans giving the convention's maximum and minimum acceptable terms for a congressionally negotiated settlement between Great Britain and America formed the core of the Instructions. The "maximum," or Dickinson, plan demanded the renunciation of all Parliamentary powers of internal legislation in America, all internal and external taxation, all quartering acts, the recent extensions of admiralty court jurisdiction, the Coercive Acts, and a host of trade regulations. In return the convention pledged Pennsylvania's obedience to all other imperial statutes, including the Navigation Acts, and promised to settle an annual revenue upon the Crown subject to Parliamentary control, which would exceed the share of imperial expenses that Pennsylvanians had heretofore paid. The "minimum," or Reed, plan did not mention existing trade duties; it did insist that Parliament renounce all pretensions to frame internal colonial legislation, all future duties and taxes, the quartering acts, the extension of admiralty court jurisdiction, and the Coercive Acts. The delegates then pledged that Pennsylvanians would support any other set of goals approved by congress if it incorporated their general objectives. Pennsylvania's committee leaders, the Instructions emphasized, considered 1774 an opportune time to discuss the entire political and commercial structure of the empire with Crown and Parliament, and they were certain that a more equitable system could be established.

To secure these ends, the delegates hoped that Pennsylvania's congressmen would urge the congress to send a special delegation to England with a full petition and declaration of rights and grievances. If the congress were to call a boycott, however, they insisted that it be binding on all colonies, and continue until their common objectives were achieved. The memory of 1770, when many Philadelphians had learned to distrust merchants in neighboring ports as well as in their own, still rankled. The Instructions then suggested that if England were to make some concessions short of a satisfactory settlement, the colonies could make the boycott correspondingly less restrictive. Unless a congressional nonimportation association was general and impartial, however, the convention foresaw a failure that would leave the colonists with the choice of "tame submission" or "a more dangerous contention."

The convention's Instructions make clear the view that Pennsylvania's resistance leaders held of their province and of the congress, and explain what they hoped to do in the next several months. The delegates knew that Pennsylvania's congressmen were likely to be among the more cautious in the congress. They also sensed, from studying public opinion in other colonies, that the congress would probably vote an immediate boycott. Yet they felt obligated to express the reservations of their constituents concerning nonimportation because no one in Pennsylvania, conservative, moderate, or radical, wanted another 1770.

The expression of sweeping "maximum" terms for an imperial settlement in 1774, however, quite overshadows the convention's caution on nonimportation. These terms demonstrate the radicals' determination that the confrontation with Great Britain over the Coercive Acts not end in another postponement and defu-

---

80. *Pa. Archives,* 2d Ser., III: 549–50. The Resolves and Instructions were published with Dickinson's essay at the direction of the convention as *An Essay on the Constitutional Power of Great Britain Over the Colonies in America* (Philadelphia, 1774). See also *Pa. Archives,* 2d Ser., III: 551–64; and *Pa. Gaz.,* July 27, 1774, P.S.

sion of the conflict, but in the final resolution of the imperial crisis. Thomson's narrative of Pennsylvania's resistance movement in 1774, written for South Carolina congressman William Henry Drayton, conveys this idea powerfully, but he composed that account after the colonies had become independent.[81] The Instructions, however, suggest that Thomson accurately recalled his own feelings in 1774, and those of his friends and colleagues. On learning of the Boston Port Act, the majority of Philadelphia's radical leaders, frustrated after years of recurrent conflict with England, decided that the time had come to forge a permanent settlement of imperial differences. All Philadelphians hoped for this end, of course, but John Dickinson and Charles Thomson decided to take the grand chance to achieve it. With the convention's endorsement of the Instructions, they had convinced their townsmen and delegates from all parts of the province that the time had come to seek this settlement, and that America had a reasonable chance of securing it.

THE ASSEMBLY RESISTS THE RESISTANCE

Pennsylvania's first provincial convention, proud of its work and full of the highest expectations, marched in a body to the State House on July 21 to present its collective wisdom to the lawmakers. The House, however, had finally begun to come to grips with the imperial crisis in its own way. Two days before, the legislators had turned from Penn's Indian problems to consider the convention's call for the appointment of congressmen, and letters from Virginia, Rhode Island, and Massachusetts, all recommending an intercolonial congress. The lawmakers voted to discuss the recommendation in a committee of the whole House on July 21, with their deliberations open to the view of the convention.[82] Speaker Joseph Galloway and at least a third of his House were not eager to participate in any congress, but the Assembly leadership could not afford to ignore the popular demand that Pennsylvania cooperate with the other colonies in resisting England. If the House refused to appoint congressional delegates, the provincial convention would do so itself, which meant that not only Galloway's archrival Dickinson, but also Thomson and other radicals would speak for Pennsylvania.[83] To prevent this, Galloway led the assemblymen in a policy of pointedly ignoring the convention's work and sending delegates to the congress virtually without instructions in order that they would not be committed to do anything.

On the morning of July 21, the convention delegates marched two by two to the State House, where Thomas Willing formally presented the convention's Resolves and Instructions to the Assembly. The convention delegates then informally proposed that three of their number, John Dickinson, James Wilson, and chairman Willing, be named congressmen along with whomever the House might select.[84] The legislators, wrote one observer, sat "with their hats on, [in] great coarse cloth

---

81. N.-Y. Hist. Soc., *Colls.,* XI: 275–80. For a discussion of Thomson's purpose in writing this account, see Appendix F below.

82. *Votes and Proceedings,* VIII: 7087–91.

83. N.-Y. Hist. Soc., *Colls.,* XI: 280.

84. *Votes and Proceedings,* VIII: 7097; Force, ed., *American Archives,* 4th Ser., I: 607n. Thomson mentions only two convention nominees, Dickinson and Wilson (N.-Y. Hist. Soc., *Colls.,* XI: 280).

coats, leather breeches and woolen stockings in the month of July; there was not a speech made the whole time, whether their silence proceeded from their modesty or from their inability to speak I know not."[85] Sensing that the House would make no immediate response, the convention withdrew. The clerk of the Assembly then read the Resolves and Instructions, but the *Votes and Proceedings* do not indicate that any discussion of their contents followed, either on this or any other day.

That evening a brief essay, "To the Representatives of the Province, . . ." by "A Freeman" circulated among the legislators. The author was probably Joseph Galloway himself; the essay has his characteristically acerbic tone. Opening with Hume's observation that "All numerous Assemblies, however composed, are mere mobs, and swayed in their debates by the least motive," "A Freeman" asserted that the Assembly must determine whether "the people of the Province shall assert their rights and privileges on constitutional grounds; or, deviating from the long known and securely trodden paths of prudence and regularity, wander into the maizy labyrinths of perplexity and disorder." The convention, he declared, had no constitutional authority, but was derived from county committees elected at meetings "where, it is notorious, not one fourth of the freeholders attend." The whole committee movement was the product of ambitious agitators. "We know not where such precedents may terminate; setting up a power to controul you, is setting up anarchy above order—IT IS THE BEGINNING OF REPUBLICANISM." Appealing to the assemblymen's pride in their exclusive powers, the author reminded them that the "gentlemen chosen by ballot on the first of *October,* are the only persons before whom every grievance should come; you are the men; you are chosen to represent us on every occasion; . . . no body of men are to supersede you. . . ." He closed with a thinly veiled attack on John Dickinson, charging, ". . . I already see a new *Cassius* rise, [who] asserts that [the convention delegates] only are the men made privy to the desires and wishes of your constituents; and that they have a right to dictate to you what shall be done."[86]

This was strong medicine, too strong for the Philadelphia press, in which "A Freeman" had little chance of publication.[87] But it achieved its intended effect. Early the next morning the House, reversing its July 19 decision to debate openly, formed into a committee of the whole behind closed doors. The legislators discussed the Virginia, Rhode Island, and Massachusetts letters, but evidently ignored the work of the convention, before deciding that Pennsylvania would participate in the congress. Only then did they admit the convention delegates and announce their decision to appoint congressmen; and they deferred selecting those congressmen to that afternoon, again behind closed doors.[88]

The convention was keenly disappointed: the Assembly had totally ignored both its Instructions and its nominees. The delegates returned quietly to Carpenter's Hall and quickly concluded their business. Chairman Willing publicly thanked

---

85. Quoted in Keith, *Provincial Councillors,* p. 228.

86. Force, ed., *American Archives,* 4th Ser., I: 607–8n.

87. The firm of James & Drinker sent the essay to Benjamin Booth on July 23, 1774 (James and Drinker Correspondence [typescript], HSP). Booth received it on July 25, and submitted it to James Rivington, who promptly printed it (*Rivington's N.-Y. Gaz.,* July 28, 1774), along with a brief account of the Assembly's rejection of Dickinson, Willing, and Wilson (Benjamin Booth to [James & Drinker], July 25, 1774, James and Drinker Correspondence, HSP).

88. *Votes and Proceedings,* VIII: 7097–98; Force, ed., *American Archives,* 4th Ser., I: 607n.

Dickinson for his labors; the convention directed Dickinson, Reed, and Thomson to communicate its transactions to the neighboring colonies; and the delegates empowered the Forty-Three, or any fifteen of them, to be "a Committee of Correspondence for the general Committee of this province."[89] Then they adjourned.

Still more distressing news from the Assembly was not long in coming. That afternoon, the House named Speaker Joseph Galloway and Charles Humphreys, archconservatives, John Morton and Samuel Rhoads, more moderate conservatives, George Ross and Edward Biddle, moderates, and the radical Thomas Mifflin as its congressmen.[90] Eight assemblymen, for the most part conservative or moderate, prepared a draft of instructions that the House approved on July 23. Rejecting all "maximum" and "minimum" plans, the Assembly gave its congressmen nearly a free hand:

> The Trust reposed in you is of such a nature, . . . that it is scarcely possible to give you particular Instructions respecting it. We shall therefore only in general direct, that you are to . . . exert your utmost Endeavors to form and adopt a Plan, which shall afford the best Prospect of obtaining a Redress of American Grievances, ascertaining American Rights, and establishing that Union and Harmony which is most essential to the Welfare and Happiness of both Countries. And in doing this, you are strictly charged to avoid every Thing indecent or disrespectful to the Mother State.[91]

For the moment, Pennsylvania's Quaker party had stemmed the Revolutionary tide. The Assembly's instructions to its congressmen blurred the dimensions of the imperial crisis, and afforded enough latitude for Joseph Galloway to seek his own solution to it. So long as he could control his delegation, he could freely develop his plans for imperial harmony and union in congressional debate. But Galloway's policy was essentially foolhardy for two reasons. First, in order not to appear as an obstructionist in his own province, he had to persuade the whole congress to adopt moderate, yet effective, resistance policies. Had Galloway studied the signs coming from both north and south closely, he would have realized that he had little chance of selling his brand of cautious, meticulously constitutional resistance to Pennsylvania's neighbors. In 1774, Americans were convinced that they had potent commercial weapons to use against Great Britain, and the congress proved determined to wield them.

The Speaker's strategy also had a deeper flaw: it was insulting to several thou-

---

89. *Pa. Archives,* 2d Ser., III: 564; *Pa. Gaz.,* July 27, 1774, P.S., p. 2.

90. *Votes and Proceedings,* VIII: 7098–7100. The House probably selected its congressmen on those traditional principles which regularly determined the filling of small, important Assembly committees, choosing senior members from Philadelphia and each of the older and more populous counties. Galloway, in addition to being Speaker, was Bucks County's senior lawmaker with seventeen years of service; John Morton and Charles Humphreys had represented Chester County for sixteen and eleven years; Samuel Rhoads was only third in seniority among Philadelphia County members, but Edward Biddle and George Ross were the senior spokesmen from Berks and Lancaster counties. The zealous Thomas Mifflin had served in the House for only two years, but he was the only burgess for the City of Philadelphia present, and the House, observing its own traditions, could not easily ignore him. Four of the seven— Galloway, Humphreys, Mifflin, and Rhoads—had been raised in the Society of Friends. All except Mifflin had been Quaker party supporters of some regularity, and Galloway, Humphreys, and Morton had been party leaders for over a decade. See Appendix B for portrait data.

91. *Votes and Proceedings,* VIII: 7100–7101. Only three of the eight drafting committee members—John Brown, John Jacobs, and James Webb—were Friends, but two others— Michael Hillegas and George Ross—had been Quaker party regulars.

sand Pennsylvania freemen. The eagerness with which Pennsylvanians formed strong local committees and gathered in provincial convention signaled the freemen's deep distrust of their legislature's willingness to meet the imperial crisis without strong encouragement. Freeholders throughout Pennsylvania, even in ultraconservative Bucks County, strongly supported the provincial convention, and outside of the Society of Friends there was little criticism of the idea. Had the Speaker and his Quaker party appreciated the extent of the transformation worked in provincial politics in the past two months, a transformation that dwarfed the crises the Assembly had weathered in 1764 and in 1770, perhaps they would have tried to avoid so dangerous a political strategy.

Yet the Assembly's policy of July 1774 left Pennsylvania with many options. An Assembly delegation would go to the congress with instructions that allowed it to pursue almost any policy. At all levels the resistance movement in Pennsylvania remained open to influence from every quarter: from the freemen through daily conversation, large public gatherings, and the press; from public opinion in other colonies; from the congress; and perhaps most important, from the further actions of Great Britain. Whatever the intentions of its leaders, the Assembly's July policy amply permitted the further development of Pennsylvania's Revolutionary policies and politics.

THE COMMITTEE MOVEMENT AND THE BEGINNING OF THE REVOLUTION IN PENNSYLVANIA

The Assembly's rejection of the convention's counsel in July 1774 was no more than a temporary setback for the committee movement in Pennsylvania. Only the drama of the legislators' action obscures the resistance leaders' real accomplishment in two short months. The creation of a committee-convention system in 1774, while only the first step in the revolutionary mobilization of the province, was a crucial step. Philadelphia's radical leadership had forced a reluctant Assembly to cooperate with the other colonies in developing a common policy for resisting the British ministry. Speaker Joseph Galloway had shown no interest in responding to the imperial crisis until the June 18 meeting determined that Philadelphia would bring Pennsylvania into the resistance in one way or another. Well might "A Freeman" fulminate against the rise of the committees as "setting up anarchy above order."

One need not accept "A Freeman's" view that the committee movement was illegitimate and anarchic, however. The vast majority of both leaders and followers in Pennsylvania, including nearly every assemblyman from the eight counties north and west of Philadelphia, Bucks, and Chester counties, evidently believed that in holding a convention to instruct the Assembly they were acting in a proper fashion.[92] The ideological beliefs behind this view were common throughout British North America,[93] but Pennsylvania was the only colony that, after learning that its

---

92. Of the fourteen assemblymen representing these eight counties, at least twelve were active in the local committee movement in June and July, and eight were named delegates to the provincial convention.

93. See Richard Buel, Jr., "Democracy and the American Revolution: A Frame of Reference," *WMQ*, 3d Ser., XXI (1964): 165–90, and the citations in Buel's n. 58.

legislature would be able to meet and appoint delegates to a congress, decided to hold a provincial convention anyway. Pennsylvanians would not have chosen new leaders and directed them to issue fresh instructions to the House in the summer of 1774 had they fully trusted that House.

Whatever notions Joseph Galloway held about the sanctity of Pennsylvania's 1701 constitution and its Assembly, a working legitimacy for the resistance meant for most Pennsylvanians simply the popular will properly expressed. Committees carefully chosen and fully instructed by widely advertised and scrupulously conducted meetings of qualified voters satisfied these requirements perfectly, and even Philadelphia's more conservative merchants had no strong grounds for complaint. Even in their confidential writings they could only deplore the disrespect shown Great Britain in particular sets of resolves and the zealous tone of certain speeches, while admitting that the principles that the committee movement disseminated were unassailable.[94]

One key to this success was the committee movement's careful accommodation to, and control of, a broad spectrum of public opinion. Under John Dickinson's and Charles Thomson's guidance, the resistance afforded every position argued in public debate a respectful treatment. Radical leaders responded to the attacks of even their most hostile opponents in general terms, and they never dignified the two most powerful institutions that opposed them, the Society of Friends and the provincial Assembly, with a recognition of their opposition. Philadelphia's newspapers, whose editors strongly favored the radical goal of achieving an early consensus on resistance strategy, refused to print divisive polemics. Every Quaker and every assemblyman who would join the cause was warmly accepted, and committee leaders eschewed attacks upon either individuals or groups. In July Pennsylvania's resistance leadership followed this policy to its logical conclusion. Not only did the provincial convention leave no record in its minutes of its frustrated plan to send John Dickinson, Thomas Willing, and James Wilson to congress, or of anger and disappointment at the treatment accorded it by the Assembly, but the gathering's participants apparently did not even write of these matters to friends and relatives until years later. Instead, the radicals prepared for a sober fall campaign to place their own spokesmen in the Assembly, and thereby formally secure their political gains and support the policies formulated by the First Continental Congress.

By July 1774 a new force, created by a powerful new political faction unknown before 1765 and still weak in 1770, dominated Pennsylvania politics. Although this committee movement was extraconstitutional, most Pennsylvanians regarded it as legitimate. Openly solicited consent was the basis of popular support for the resistance. Beneath committee procedure and radical argument, however, lay another solid foundation for change: the committee movement's aggressive recruitment of new leaders from a broad range of economic, occupational, ethnic, and religious subcommunities both in Philadelphia and across the province. This evolving resistance leadership is of the first importance in the coming of the Revolution in Philadelphia.

---

94. Thomas Wharton, Sr. to Thomas Walpole, Aug. 2, 1774 (crossed out passage in the draft), Thomas Wharton, Sr. Letter-Book, HSP.

Chapter

4

The Revolution
of the Elite

The officers and committee members of the Sons of Liberty were drawn
almost entirely from the middle and upper ranks of colonial society. . . . As
older groups became metamorphosized into resistance cadres, however, their
social bases were consciously broadened.[1]

PAULINE MAIER

Between the Stamp Act crisis and the First Continental Congress, public life in
Philadelphia changed dramatically. A new party embracing a new ideology challenged its Quaker and proprietary opponents with increasing effectiveness. A new
institution offered direct political participation to scores of new leaders and a
deeper involvement in public affairs to thousands of freemen. Although two seasoned veterans of Pennsylvania's factional wars directed this mobilization, their
lieutenants were new to politics.[2] But were these new men different men? Did the
committees that launched the Revolutionary movement in Pennsylvania call forth
leaders who differed in kind from members of the provincial establishment, or were
they much the same men with different names and faces?

The view that the process of colonial resistance to British policy selected and
promoted a new kind of leader, a belief held widely among historians of the literary
record of the Revolution in Philadelphia, finds both ample confirmation and suggestive extension in a quantitative measurement of the economic and social backgrounds of the city's committeemen.[3] Philadelphia's new leadership formed a
broadly based economic and social elite that developed largely outside of, and
increasingly functioned in opposition to, the provincial establishment. This leadership retained two features common to colonial political elites. First, the city's
committeemen were nominated, not elected, and on most occasions relatively small
gatherings of leading citizens made and confirmed the nominations. Second, the
leaders were, with few exceptions, among the wealthiest members of the com-

---

1. Maier, *From Resistance to Revolution*, pp. 86–87.
2. The veterans, of course, were John Dickinson and Charles Thomson. On their political
careers in the 1760s, see chapters 1–2 above; and Hutson, *Pennsylvania Politics,* chaps. 3–4.
3. See especially Lincoln, *Revolutionary Movement*; J. Paul Selsam, *The Pennsylvania
Constitution of 1776, A Study in Revolutionary Democracy* (1936); Robert L. Brunhouse,
The Counter-Revolution in Pennsylvania, 1776–1790 (1942); and Hawke, *Midst of a Revolution.*

munity. At the same time, Philadelphia's new leadership evolved away from the traditional leadership model, exemplified in so many provincial establishments and nonestablishment elites alike, in three respects: it was younger; it embraced a broader range of occupations; and it was growing increasingly pluralistic in ethnic composition and religious affiliation. The early Revolutionary leadership in Philadelphia was, then, a new elite. The imperial crisis would make it a new establishment.

COMMITTEE NOMINATION AND THE NEW POLITICS

Merchants, predominantly wealthy Quaker importers, had always run colonial Philadelphia.[4] In its attempt to reform the structure of imperial commerce in the late 1760s, the mercantile community formed associations of a few hundred tradesmen that claimed the sole right of nominating committees to observe and regulate boycotts of British goods.[5] These committees, however, were invested with the exercise of powers that vitally affected the entire community. In the regularity and public visibility of their procedures, the behavior of Philadelphia's merchant nominators resembles the new politics that Carl Becker saw emerging in New York in the 1760s; and the adoption of these procedures was the first step toward the more modern political world that took shape in America in the 1780s and 1790s.[6] Yet the selection of committeemen by one broad occupational group, which in the 1760s in Philadelphia was largely of one economic class, the wealthy, and one religious sect, the Quakers, more nearly approximated the closed nomination procedure used by Friends who attended the Philadelphia Yearly Meeting of their Society, held just prior to the Assembly elections. Until the 1750s, these religious delegates had regularly set up unopposed Assembly tickets and thereby maintained their denomination's control of Pennsylvania's legislature.[7]

On September 27, 1770, Philadelphia's committee-nomination procedure suddenly changed. Proboycott merchants, disgusted with their antiboycott colleagues, joined mechanics and other freemen in public assembly to name twenty zealous opponents of British policy to a committee representing the entire community.[8] The new committee came to nothing; the new mode of nomination was more productive. In 1772 Philadelphia's mechanics formed the Patriotic Society, the first formally organized, publicly avowed, nonreligious political pressure group in Pennsylvania's history.[9] In the fall of 1773, two meetings open to all freemen named the committees that successfully repelled the East India Company's tea. The nomination to ad hoc resistance institutions that were in effect public bodies was no longer in the gift of one part of the community.

---

4. See Tolles, *Meeting House and Counting House*; and Nash, *Quakers and Politics*.

5. On the nonimportation boycotts as mercantile reform efforts, see Schlesinger's argument in *Colonial Merchants,* chaps. 2–3; on the exclusive nature of the boycott associations, see ibid., esp. p. 255; and chapter 2 above.

6. Becker, *History of Political Parties,* pp. 17–21; William Nisbet Chambers, *Political Parties in a New Nation: The American Experience, 1776–1809* (1963).

7. On the Quakers' informal nomination system, see Bauman, *For the Reputation of Truth,* pp. 3, 10.

8. *Pa. Gaz.,* Sept. 27, 1770; *Pa. Chronicle,* Oct. 1, 1770.

9. See *Pa. Gaz.,* Aug. 19, 1772; and Olton, *Artisans for Independence,* pp. 55–56.

Or so it seemed. The naming of nineteen committeemen on May 20, 1774, by two hundred notables—now less an occupational or denominational elite than an establishment of wealth and public reputation—was a sharp reversal in the radicals' drive to establish public nomination and an explicit dedication to the interests of the larger community as fundamentals of the committee movement. Several of the Nineteen, however, intended this return to the domination of public affairs by a closed elite to be only temporary. And temporary it was. In a policy session held in late May and at a nomination meeting in early June participation gradually broadened. On June 18, Philadelphians firmly established the principle that only popular approval could validate a resistance committee ticket. Because this approval was still by voice vote in large outdoor assemblies, committee selection was not yet entirely legitimized; that would come with the imprimatur of the First Continental Congress and secret ballot elections in the fall. But the transformation from closed interest to open competitive politics was essentially complete by the summer of 1774. Significantly, the degree of domination by the traditional elite at each stage of this transformation—in 1765 and 1769, in 1770 and 1773, in May 1774, and in June 1774—coincides roughly with fluctuations in the wealth and age, and more closely with changes in the occupational diversity, ethnic background, and religious affiliation of the committeemen selected in these years.

THE CHANGING FACE OF THE
PHILADELPHIA COMMITTEE

Some two hundred Philadelphians served on major resistance committees between the Stamp Act crisis and the Declaration of Independence. Seventy-six of these men secured seats before the First Continental Congress began its deliberations.[10] To determine the extent and the timing of this new elite's evolution into a different kind of establishment from that which comprised Pennsylvania officialdom has required answers to seven major questions. To what extent did the same men serve on one committee after another? What was their economic status within their community? How old were the committeemen at the time of their service? How did they make their living? From what countries or colonies did they, or their immediate ancestors, come? To what religious faiths did they belong? Finally, do the answers to these questions change during the years before the Congress, and if they do, is that change indicative of a significant—or even a purposeful—shift in the pattern of leadership recruitment?[11]

---

10. Not included in these numbers are fifteen men who served only on one or more of four minor committees: the seven-man delegation that visited Stamp Agent John Hughes, and the eleven-man retailers' nonimportation committee, both chosen in the fall of 1765; the eleven-man mechanics' committee of June 9, 1774; and the seven-man mechanics' committee of July 8, 1774.

11. The changing composition of the committees was not the only source of economic and social change among the committeemen; the wealth, occupations, and religious affiliations of individual members could and often did change over time. To reduce the task of portraying so large a group to manageable proportions, however, it has seemed best to this writer to use one primary source, the April 1774 provincial tax assessors' reports (see note 14 below) to determine both the members' relative economic standing and their occupations, supplementing these returns with the provincial tax reports of 1769 and 1772 and the constable's survey of 1775 only to fill in lacunae in the 1774 data. Similarly, the testimony of denominational affiliation—pew lists, Quaker records, and even parish graveyard inscription lists—that lay closest to 1774 has always been preferred.

Persistency and Continuity of Service. The short-term persistency of committee service—the number of men on a given committee who sat on the succeeding committee—and the long-term continuity of that service—the number of men on a given board who had previous committee experience—together form one evident pattern of committee membership between 1765 and 1774.[12] First, both the persistency and the continuity of committee service rose slowly despite occasional fluctuations and a gradual increase in committee size (see table 2). This trend argues that neither the struggles between conservative, moderate, and radical resistance leaders for control of the committees, nor the mobilization of new leaders for new, larger boards prevented Philadelphia's resistance leadership from becoming increasingly experienced. Yet there was one sharp break in this growing continuity. Only 30 percent of the 1770 committee sat on the tea committee of 1773, and only 29 percent of the 1773 committeemen had ever served before. This interruption suggests that the tea committee was somehow different from all other boards formed before the Congress.[13] Quite apart from the slender literary evidence on committee activity, certain facts about the committeemen themselves confirm this view of a growing, yet uneven, continuity in leadership.

Wealth. The relative economic status of Philadelphia's committeemen varied from one board to another, as did every major index of their economic and social background, but the long trend was a dramatic decline.[14] Moreover, on every committee the average member had a more modest fortune than did the average member of the provincial establishment. Perhaps more significant is the recurrent correlation between sudden drops in average committee member wealth and a turn to more radical policies. What is at issue, of course, is the interplay between different levels of one broad economic elite: until the First Continental Congress, committee service was still largely the province of Philadelphians with at least a comfortable income.

Yet the differences between material comfort and great fortune are unmistakable.

---

12. The forward-looking persistency index is included here because of increasing committee size. Had only the backward-looking index of continuity been employed, a doubling of committee size would dictate a relatively low percentage of carry-over, even if all members of the first committee served on the second. Thus the fact that seventeen of the nineteen committeemen of May 1774 also sat on the Forty-Three gives a persistence rate of 89 percent, but a continuity rate of only 39.5 percent.

13. There were actually two tea committees, one chosen in October, and the other in late November or early December 1773. Because the first committee was incorporated into the second, however, and because the two were created so close together in time, I discuss them as one.

In this chapter and in chapter 8, I capitalize "Congress" for the First Continental Congress. In the narrative chapters, I use "congress" before September 1774, and "Congress" thereafter.

14. For the data on wealth and occupation I have relied principally on "A Transcript of the Assessment of the Seventeenth 18d. Provincial Tax for the City and County of Philadelphia, taken in April 1774," Pennsylvania Historical and Museum Commission, Harrisburg, Pa., and on a contemporaneous official summary of that transcript, Department of Archives, Philadelphia City Hall, Philadelphia. Figures from this assessment have been supplemented by the 1772 provincial tax assessment, and the 1775 provincial tax assessment, Department of Archives, Philadelphia City Hall, and with a printed summary of the 1769 proprietary tax and the 1774 tax, *Pa. Archives,* 3rd Ser. (Harrisburg, Pa., 1894–99), XIV, XV.

Tax assessment figures are often misleading and sometimes completely inaccurate indexes of the wealth of particular individuals. The assumption made in the economic analysis of the committeemen presented in this study, however, is that such errors tend to average out, so that alterations in the assessments of whole groups of men (the committees) bear some relationship to the collective wealth of these groups.

TABLE 2

Philadelphia's Early Committeemen, 1765–74

	November 1765	March 1769	September 1770	December 1773	May 1774	June 1774
Number of members	11	21	20	24	19	43
Persistency	27%	52%	30%	38%	89%	42%
Long-term continuity	—	29%	60%	29%	68%	58%
1774 tax assessment[a]						
£200+	4(3)	1(1)	3(1)	3	3	5
100–199	2(3)	12(5)	9(6)	4	7	13
45–99	1(—)	3(3)	4(4)	5	3	10
0–44	2(4)	5(7)	4(5)	11	6	15
Unknown	2(1)	—(5)	—(4)	1	—	—
Average	£191(221)	£116(81)	£117(86)	£81	£155	£113
Median	£160(130)	£134(65)	£132(79)	£72	£100	£92
Age						
20–29	—	4	5	3	—	—
30–39	5	8	7	9	7	17
40–49	2	7	6	5	11	16
50+	2	2	1	2	1	6
Unknown	2	—	1	5	—	4
Average[b]	41.0	38.6	36.1	38.8	41.8	41.9
(Base)	(7)	(17)	(16)	(16)	(16)	(35)
Occupation						
Merchants	11[c]	21	16[c]	15	11	23
Manufacturers	—	—	3	3	4	12[d]
Mechanics	—	—	—	1	1	3
Professionals	—	—	1	2[e]	3	3
Other	—	—	—	—	—	2[f]
Unknown	—	—	—	3	—	—
Religion						
Quakers[g]	6	9	5	4	8	13
Anglicans	1	6	6	9	5	9
Presbyterians	2	6	8	5	5	12
Other	—	—	1	3	1	6
Unknown	2	—	—	3	—	3

a. For 1765, 1769, and 1770, the committeemen are also classed according to the 1769 proprietary tax. These figures are given in parentheses. The averages and medians based on the very incomplete 1769 data are also given in parentheses.

b. Based only on those members whose ages are known exactly; those who ages are known approximately have been placed in their deciles.

c. Includes Peter Chevalier, who was both a merchant and a distiller.

d. Includes one rural mill master.

e. One lawyer and one ship captain.

f. Includes one farmer, and one ferry-owner, George Gray, who was probably also a farmer and merchant.

g. Includes Quakers who were disowned by the Society of Friends before 1775, or who had been inactive Friends: one (Samuel Howell) in 1765, 1769, and 1770, four (John Dickinson, Joseph Fox, Thomas Wharton, Jr., and Howell) in May 1774, and three (Dickinson, Wharton, and Howell) in June 1774.

Government officials were much wealthier than committeemen. The ten governor's councilors were assessed an average of £309 by the provincial tax officials in 1774, at a time when only one city taxpayer in ten owned over £45 in assessed property.[15] Sixteen assemblymen living in the city averaged £211.5. Yet on only two city committees did the members average more than £117 in assessed wealth; the mean for tea committeemen was only £81 (see table 2). The general direction of change, with one major exception, was downward: the Forty-Three, chosen in June 1774, was 27 percent less affluent than its predecessor, the Nineteen, and 41 percent less affluent than the Stamp Act boycott merchants' committee. By June 1774 a clear trend toward the election of a more middle-class revolutionary leader appeared to be in the making. Yet to be decided were its duration and magnitude.

If the full dimensions of the movement away from the leadership of Philadelphia's mercantile aristocracy were still uncertain, the close correlation between the election of committeemen of more modest fortune and the radicalization of committee policy was not. Until 1773 this relationship did not prevail.[16] In December of that year, however, the committee that opposed the landing of the East India Company's tea was dominated by men assessed at under £45, an unprecedented participation in Philadelphia politics by merchants—and others—without great fortune. The decision of this board to endorse the Boston Tea Party publicly sparked a reaction by Philadelphia's more conservative leaders. The next city committee, chosen in May 1774, was decidedly cool toward Boston's appeal for colonial solidarity and toward any sacrifice by Pennsylvanians in the common cause. It was also the wealthiest board since 1765. Its successor, the Forty-Three, supported intercolonial resistance more firmly; its members were probably of more modest wealth than all their predecessors except those of 1773.[17] Radicalism, before and after the Congress, was usually paired in committee politics with modest fortune, as was conservatism with substantial wealth.

Philadelphia's committeemen, then, were less wealthy than provincial officials; and increasingly, men of modest fortune were filling committee ranks. Were these

---

15. I am indebted to Professor Gary B. Nash of the University of California at Los Angeles for supplying to me a decile breakdown for the 1774 tax list, which establishes that only 10 percent of the taxpayers in the City of Philadelphia and Southwark were assessed over £45.

16. For example, the average committeeman of 1769 was less affluent (£116) than his counterpart on the merchants' committee of 1765 (£191), but does not seem to have been demonstrably more radical. Moreover, while nine conservative committeemen who resigned from the Townshend Act boycott committee in late 1769 or in 1770, for whom there are 1774 assessment figures, were slightly wealthier (they averaged at least £120, and possibly £168, depending on a questionable name identification) than the eleven more radical members who remained loyal to the boycott (£113), the nine radical members who joined these eleven were perhaps even wealthier (£136) than the conservatives who abandoned it. This would suggest that Schlesinger's argument (*Colonial Merchants*, pp. 191, 218–19, 229–30) that the major disagreement over nonimportation centered on the conflicting economic interests of different kinds of wealthy men—the "wet goods" (West Indies trade) versus the dry goods (British Isles trade) merchants, and manufacturers and professionals versus merchants generally—was probably still valid for Philadelphia as late as 1770 (see below in this chapter).

17. See chapters 2 and 3 above for the narrative and citations that establish the relative conservatism or radicalism of these several committees. I say that the Forty-Three was *probably* of more modest wealth than all of its predecessors except the tea committee because the 1769 and 1770 committees appear much less affluent when measured by the 1769 tax assessments than by the 1774 assessments. The 1769 assessments have an obvious superiority as a measurement for the 1769 and 1770 committees; unfortunately, the 1769 tax roll is far less complete than the 1774 roll. Figures from both rolls are given for 1765, 1769, and 1770 committeemen on tables 2 and 3, and in Appendixes D and E.

simply the merchant sons, nephews, and younger cousins of Quaker and Anglican merchant princes—similar men, but at an earlier stage in their business careers—or is the changing average age of the committeemen inadequate to explain their declining economic status?

Age. It is harder to determine the age of Philadelphia's resistance leaders than any other simple fact about them.[18] Yet from the ages that are known, some important features of the committeemen are clear. First, committeemen were younger than government officials. In 1774 Pennsylvania's ten governor's councilors averaged 56 years of age, and twenty-two assemblymen whose ages are definitely known averaged 45.5 years. On no city resistance committee at any time before Independence, however, was the average member as old as 42, and on the committees chosen in 1769, 1770, 1773, and November 1774, the average fell below 40 (see tables 2 and 12). Second, the membership of the more radical committees was usually younger than that of the more cautious boards. This is particularly noticeable on the 1770 committee.

Yet the committeemen chosen in June 1774 were not younger, but older, than their predecessors. The Forty-Three, less affluent and more radical than the Nineteen, was the oldest of all committees created before Independence. Youth could coincide with radicalism; in the young committees of 1770 and 1773 it did. But radical strategists, while recruiting new men of modest fortune, seem also by 1774 to have been reaching back to the 1760s for more experienced committee leaders, to whom they added several mature citizens new to politics. The changing wealth of the committeemen must have had other foundations than changing age.

Occupation. Philadelphia's new resistance leaders of the early 1770s were not, at the time of their first election, significantly younger than the merchant committeemen of 1765 and 1769, nor were many of them significantly less affluent; yet they were different men. The shift away from a strictly mercantile leadership of the resistance movement, which Philadelphia's mechanics and Arthur Schlesinger, Sr. alike thought necessary to the movement's success after 1770, was one of the most important developments in committee politics in 1773 and 1774.

One may measure the dimensions of this shift in two quite different ways. If by "a merchant" one means any fairly affluent businessman, then merchants heavily dominated committee politics at least until November 1774. Men of this description, whom one may define as those in commerce or manufacturing who were assessed at £45 or more (the top 10 percent of persons taxed in the city in 1774), or who were labeled "merchants" in the tax records, held nineteen of twenty seats on the proboycott committee of 1770; at least eighteen of twenty-four

---

18. The portrait data on age, nationality and nativity, and religious affiliation come from the *Dictionary of American Biography*; *PMHB* (particularly the pre-1920 issues); John W. Jordan et al., eds., *Colonial and Revolutionary Families of Pennsylvania,* 17 vols. (1911–65); William Wade Hinshaw, ed., *Encyclopedia of American Quaker Genealogy,* II (1938); denominational data on Anglicans and Lutherans in *Pa. Archives,* 2d Ser., VIII, IX; *A Record of the Inscriptions on the Tablets and Grave-Stones in the Burial-Grounds of Christ Church, Philadelphia* (Philadelphia, 1864); William White Bronson, *The Inscriptions in St. Peter's Church Yard, Philadelphia* (Camden, N.J., 1879); Norris Stanley Barratt, *Outline of the History of Old St. Paul's Church, Philadelphia, Pennsylvania* (1917); William Montgomery, "Pew Renters of Christ Church, St. Peter's, and St. James' from 1776 to 1815, Compiled from Existing Records" (1948), American Philosophical Society, Philadelphia; manuscript Quaker meeting records on microfilm, Friends Historical Library, Swarthmore College, Swarthmore, Pa.; and manuscript records of Presbyterian congregations, Presbyterian Historical Society, Philadelphia.

places on the 1773 tea committee; fifteen of nineteen seats in May 1774; and at least thirty-three of forty-three in June 1774. They filled all eleven seats on the 1765 merchants' committee, and all twenty-one places on the 1769 committee. Professionals and mechanics—small-scale craftsmen and retailers—secured the few remaining places (see table 2).[19]

So general a classification, however, presents an obvious problem in the context of pre-Revolutionary Philadelphia. The first two of these six committees ran non-importation boycotts; the third tried to extend a boycott; the fourth attacked a tea-importing monopoly; and the last two had to cope with a growing popular demand for yet another boycott. Nonimportation did not affect all Philadelphia businessmen alike, but brought privation or opportunity in differing proportions to British dry goods importers, West Indies and wine islands importers, exporters of foodstuffs, iron manufacturers, distillers, shipbuilders, tanners, grocers, and other large-scale tradesmen, as well as to shopkeepers, artisans, and professionals.[20] In the early stages of the resistance movement, importers and exporters shut out manufacturers, retailers, craftsmen, and professionals from leadership. As the imperial challenge grew more serious, however, Philadelphia's response became more comprehensive. Committees grew larger and more powerful, and their members more fully represented the city's many occupations.

A closer look at the pre-Congress committeemen suggests the scope of this process. On the 1765 merchants' committee, only Peter Chevalier, a distiller, was not a great man of trade. Other shopkeeper and artisan spokesmen sat on the subordinate retailers' board. In 1769, every committeeman was an importer or exporter of some variety. When the proboycott meeting of September 27, 1770, joined nine new men to the eleven radicals of 1769 to make a new committee, however, five of the newcomers were not primarily merchants: Chevalier and William Masters, distillers; Benjamin Loxley, a builder; James Pearson, a prosperous carpenter; and Andrew Allen, a prominent lawyer and proprietary officeholder. In 1773, the tea committee cast its net even more widely, recruiting Benjamin Marshall, an importer, retailer, and metal worker; William Moulder, a grocer; shipbuilder Thomas Penrose; lawyer Joseph Reed; and Robert Whyte, a ship captain (see tables 2–4).

The conservative counterreaction of May 1774 returned men of the greatest wealth to committee leadership, yet prosperous committeemen who were not primarily merchants continued to increase in numbers. Joining the shipwright Penrose and the versatile Benjamin Marshall were Joseph Moulder, a sailmaker, Edward Penington, a sugar-baker, and Joseph Fox, a builder. The celebrated patriot pen-

19. "Mechanics" in this essay will denote master craftsmen and retailers of modest wealth as opposed, on the one hand, to large-scale manufacturers and retailers who were assessed at £45 or more in 1774 and who were sometimes called mechanics or artisans by contemporaries if they were not engaged in importing or exporting; and on the other, to journeymen, apprentices, and unskilled laborers, none of whom, to this writer's knowledge, ever held committee office. Compare this definition with that of Olton, *Artisans for Independence,* pp. ix–x, chaps. 1–2, who limits the terms "artisans," and by implication "mechanics" as well, strictly to craftsmen, including large-scale manufacturers, while excluding shopkeepers, grocers, and other retail suppliers. Olton's definition restricts the term "mechanics" more narrowly than Philadelphians did in their daily use of it; for them, "artisans" seem to have been only a part of the mechanic class. See Foner, *Tom Paine,* chap. 2, for the best brief treatment of the world of Philadelphia's mechanic classes.

20. These distinctions, and especially that between dry and "wet" goods merchants, are central to Schlesinger's understanding of mercantile behavior. See *Colonial Merchants,* chaps. 3–5.

man John Dickinson and Joseph Reed represented the bar, and in Dr. William Smith committee politics acquired its first teacher and cleric. The committee of Forty-Three chosen in June completed this first process—the occupational diversification of a leadership drawn from the economic elite—and began a second—the inclusion of small-scale craftsmen and retailers. Major nonmerchant businessmen included Jacob Barge, sugar-baker and innkeeper; George Gray, a prosperous ferry-owner; brewers Reuben Haines and Anthony Morris, Jr.; baker Christopher Ludwig; blacksmith William Rush; tanner George Schlosser; and Robert Smith, a master builder. More modest tradesmen, who were properly of the mechanic class, included Joseph Moulder, William Moulder, and Isaac Howell, a brewer (see tables 2 and 6).

Ethnic Origins and Birthplaces.   Just as those who were of only modest fortune and those who worked or had once worked with their hands were at last beginning to have their day in Philadelphia politics, so the city's Germans, together with other Philadelphians of several nationalities born outside Pennsylvania, were discovering by 1774 that the Revolution opened up dramatic new political opportunities. Between 1765 and May 1774, fifty-six Englishmen, Scots, Welshmen, or Scotch-Irishmen, and three thoroughly assimilated Frenchmen served on city committees. Yet not one German secured a committee seat in this period. Thus when Philadelphians placed five Germans on the city committee elected in June 1774, they brought that nationality, which comprised at least one-sixth and perhaps as much as one-fourth of the community, into participatory politics for the first time. Thereafter, some 10 to 15 percent of the seats on Philadelphia's committees were held by German-Americans, and in 1776, when the province became an independent commonwealth, Germans began entering the legislature in appreciable numbers for the first time in Pennsylvania's history.[21]

Fully as significant is the number of men born outside the province who became prominent resistance leaders, usually of a radical stamp, even before the extensive repudiation of the established leadership that occurred between late 1774 and 1776. Joseph Reed had moved to the city recently from New Jersey. The principal foreign-born leaders included Robert Morris from England and Charles Thomson from Ulster, and several more obscure committeemen were immigrants from Ulster or Germany. To some extent, the political prominence of immigrants was to be expected in Pennsylvania, because a large proportion of the province's population in the 1770s was not Pennsylvania-born.[22] But Scotch-Irish and German immi-

---

21. See *Pa. Gaz.,* Nov. 16, 1774, Aug. 23, 1775, Feb. 21, 1776, for lists of committeemen. *Votes and Proceedings,* VIII: 7023–24, and *Journals of the House of Representatives of the Commonwealth of Pennsylvania* (Philadelphia, 1782), give the number of Germans in the Assembly. Sam Bass Warner, Jr., estimates that about one-sixth of the city was German in the 1770s (*The Private City: Philadelphia in Three Periods of Its Growth* [1968], pp. 14–15), but the burial and baptismal figures given in "historical Notes and Memoranda respecting Philadelphia, etc.," (Box 2, Item 161, 25, Proud Collection, HSP), in *An Account of the Births and Burials in the United Churches of Christ-Church and St. Peter's . . . From December 25, 1774 to December 25, 1775* (Philadelphia, 1775), and in *An Account of the Baptisms and Burials in all the Churches and Meetings in Philadelphia, From Dec. 25, 1774 to Dec. 25, 1775* (Philadelphia, 1775), suggest that between one-fifth and one-fourth of the city was German in the 1770s.

22. Even the establishment—the governor's Council, Assembly, and Philadelphia Corporation Council—included many persons born outside the province. They usually came from Maryland—most notably, provincial councilor James Tilghman and Assembly Speaker Joseph Galloway—or, less frequently, from New Jersey, New York, or even New England; few were foreign-born (see chapter 1 above, and Appendix B).

grants became far more prominent in the Revolution than they had ever been in either the economic or the political life of pre-Revolutionary Pennsylvania. This is yet another indication that as Pennsylvanians approached the Revolutionary crisis, they increasingly rejected their established, largely native-born leaders.

Religion. Even before the First Continental Congress, apparent correlations were emerging between a strong commitment to the Revolutionary movement in Philadelphia and modest fortune, relative youthfulness, and even a manual occupation or immigrant status. Were most Revolutionaries also members of certain religious denominations? The literary evidence strongly suggests this, indicating that the leading Revolutionaries were Presbyterians; that Quakers became neutrals or even tories; and that Anglicans split, with the younger communicants tending toward radicalism. A quantitative survey of the committeemen, while confirming the general features of this pattern, particularly for the years 1774–76, reveals that at no time before Independence was the relationship between radical activity and religion so simple.

Religious divisions had long been intense in Pennsylvania, despite a traditional public display of harmony and good will among the province's many faiths, and by the mid-eighteenth century these divisions were intimately connected with factional politics in both city and province. They were a determinative factor in Pennsylvania's political life in the 1750s and early 1760s, and recent scholarship suggests that they may have been even more fundamental to political contention in the late 1770s and the 1780s.[23]

In the coming of the Revolution, however, religion played a different role. Several of the greatest radical organizers and propagandists in Philadelphia were indeed Presbyterians: before the Congress, Joseph Reed and Charles Thomson were at the center of the resistance movement, while in 1776, Thomas McKean and Thomas Paine's close friend Dr. Benjamin Rush led the drive for independence. After 1769, moreover, Quakers were advised by the leaders of their sect to eschew committee service, and after 1775 they could not engage in Revolutionary politics without risking disownment by the Society of Friends. Yet Thomas Mifflin was both a Quaker and a hero of the resistance from 1770 until his disownment in 1775 for serving in the Continental Army. Other Philadelphians raised as Quakers, of whom a few were still Friends in good standing until 1775–76, were active committeemen. The most notable, before the Congress, included John Dickinson, William Fisher, who chaired the 1770 boycott committee, Samuel Howell, Benjamin Marshall, and Thomas Wharton, Jr., all moderate to radical in their politics, and Edward Penington, John Reynell, Jeremiah Warder, Jr., and Thomas Wharton, Sr. on the conservative side of the resistance movement. The role of Philadelphia's Anglicans was fully as important. Without the zealous dedication to the resistance of John Cadwalader, James Cannon, George Clymer, Robert Morris, John Nixon,

---

23. The best recent treatments of the religious-political linkage in the 1760s are Hutson, *Pennsylvania Politics,* pp. 200–243; Benjamin H. Newcomb, *Franklin and Galloway, A Political Partnership* (1972), chaps. 8–9; and Bockelman and Ireland, "Internal Revolution," pp. 127–44. For a fresh and stimulating look at this relationship after Independence, see Owen S. Ireland, "The Ethnic-Religious Dimension of Pennsylvania Politics, 1778–1779," *WMQ,* 3d Ser., XXX (1973): 423–48. Bockelman and Ireland emphasize not only religious differences, but also the conflict between Pennsylvanians of English stock, who were predominantly Quaker or Anglican, and the overwhelmingly Scotch-Irish Presbyterians.

and scores of less prominent communicants, the Revolution might well have failed in Philadelphia.

A quantitative assessment of the correlation between religious affiliation and committee activity confirms this overview (table 2; and figure 3, chapter 8). The most heavily Quaker committees, chosen in 1765, 1769, and May 1774, tended to be the most conservative; yet the most radical committees, if the least Quaker, were not the most Presbyterian, as the conventional wisdom on Revolutionary politics would lead one to expect. In fact, Anglicans were usually the most numerous group on the more radical boards. These committees were also more evenly balanced in religious composition than the more conservative boards that preceded them. Throughout the Revolution, linkages between religious affiliation and political activity were evident in relation to the imperial question, just as they had been in provincial matters. To Scotch-Irish Presbyterians, anti-London sentiment came easily, while the prospect of violent resistance would deter the Quakers, who were both a pacifist sect and a minority experiencing a continuing political and economic decline in Pennsylvania. What is important here is the extent to which the committee movement overcame this traditional pattern of political perception and behavior.

The most meaningful and potentially explosive divisions within Philadelphia may well have been those between the leading religious faiths, and the several nationalities that these denominations often incorporated, rather than between economic and occupational groups. To heal those divisions, the city's resistance leaders determined, early on, to secure religiously and ethnically balanced, inclusive committees.[24] The result of their policy was no mere show. Philadelphia's Anglicans, for example, were mobilized: they wrote, rallied, and eventually fought for colonial autonomy. Zealous young Quakers, too, were seduced away from the control of their conservative elders in large numbers. What is most striking in all this is the warm cooperation between radicals of different religious faiths.

Taken together, the committees' growing ethnic diversity and denominational balance gradually set the resistance leadership apart from the more traditional colonial elite, which, in Pennsylvania and elsewhere, tended to embrace a narrow range of nationalities and religious faiths. Philadelphia politics appeared to be moving toward the more pluralistic leadership which was to become so important in America in the nineteenth and twentieth centuries, as heavy immigration created an electorate as easily divided by ethnic and religious antagonisms as by regional, economic, and occupational distinctions.[25] What can alone make this and other alterations in committee composition significant are the degree of their coherence and the likelihood that they were purposeful.

Change and Development. The variations in the wealth, age, occupation, nationality, and religion of Philadelphia's early committeemen form two patterns, just beginning to coalesce by 1774, yet evident enough to suggest the resolution

---

24. See chapter 3 above on Charles Thomson's balanced denominational recruiting in May and June 1774.

25. Representative of the literature emphasizing the ethnic and religious basis of voter preferences in America are Lee Benson, *The Concept of Jacksonian Democracy: New York as a Test Case* (1961); and Seymour Martin Lipset, "Religion and Politics in the American Past and Present," in Robert Lee and Martin Marty, eds., *Religion and Social Conflict* (1964), pp. 69–126.

they would show by Independence. First, those committees that were particularly large (June 1774) or that had an unusually high proportion of men new to committee activity (1773), those whose members were less affluent (1773) and younger (1770 and 1773), and those in which Quakers did not outnumber either Anglicans or Presbyterians (1770 and 1773) adopted a more radical stance than the older, wealthier, more veteran, more mercantile, and more Quaker boards (1765, 1769, and May 1774). Second, no matter how radical the committees became, they continued to draw their members from each of the more influential ethnic and religious groups within the city, and to keep the number of committeemen belonging to each of these groups roughly in balance.

Several factors probably contributed to these leadership patterns. First, the tendency for Philadelphia's younger and less affluent men to act a more radical part than their older and wealthier neighbors, a tendency which was at first not pronounced and became an important trend only gradually, and which embraced numerous glaring individual exceptions, most probably relates to the younger men's relatively small investment in the present compared with their much grander hopes for the future. Wealthy merchants over forty found it harder to take an adventurous attitude toward the Revolution, although several did.[26] For middle-aged Quakers who were past their political and even their economic zenith, passive neutrality or even bitter reaction were natural responses to the imperial crisis. All of this is speculation, however, and lies within the shadowy realm of the motivation of individuals long deceased. More central to our inquiry are the social and collective motives and methods whereby several younger merchants and professionals of modest fortune, a few mechanics, and many heretofore inactive Anglicans, Presbyterians, and Germans came forward as many of the old elite faded, or were forced, into the background.

In part, these new men may have consciously seized on the imperial crisis as their opportunity to play a more important role in politics than even the veteran radicals who sought their support expected or desired. Between 1770 and 1774, the mechanics, in particular, readied themselves to take a leading part in public life.[27] Yet well-to-do and well-educated Philadelphians dominated city politics right up to Independence. In large measure, the changing composition of Philadelphia's political leadership was the product of a conscious, well-planned program, dimly visible as early as 1770 and fully operational by June 1774. Philadelphia's committees were balanced and inclusive because those who com-

---

26. It is important to remember here, however, that the number of affluent, middle-aged radicals was always significant. The age and economic standing of committeemen never showed such steady and readily explicable patterns as those formed by the members' occupational, ethnic, and religious backgrounds, and, one suspects, for good reason. Men were recruited for committee service, in many cases, precisely because they followed a certain trade, or attended a certain church, while their age and wealth were more incidental factors, which, from the little evidence that has survived, were apparently of less interest to most radical organizers.

27. One may trace the gradual organization of the mechanics as a conscious, distinct political force in "A Brother Chip," *Pa. Gaz.,* Sept. 27, 1770; broadside by ten candidates, *Fellow Citizens and Countrymen* (Philadelphia, Oct. 1, 1772); "At a Meeting of Respectable Inhabitants," June 17, 1774, and letter from the mechanics to Dickinson, June 27, 1774, item #156, Dickinson material, R. R. Logan Collection; and letter from a mechanic assembly to the city committee, July 8, 1774, Du Simitière Collection, HSP. The best modern treatments of this process are Schlesinger, *Colonial Merchants,* chaps. 5–8; Hutson, *Pennsylvania Politics,* chap. 4; Newcomb, *Franklin and Galloway,* pp. 212–13; and especially Olton, *Artisans for Independence,* pp. 42–63.

posed the election tickets and led the new boards willed it so. It remains to consider how and why they did this.

EARLY COMMITTEE CONSTRUCTION: THE FIRST
RADICAL DESIGN OF POLITICAL MOBZILIZATION

When Philadelphia's earliest resistance leaders first aroused their neighbors to oppose British policy, their primary technique was oratory, and their principal goal was public awareness.[28] Leaders, all assumed, were at hand: elected government officials, city councilmen, and merchant spokesmen. The small merchants' committee selected in 1765 and the larger board chosen in 1769 initially reinforced this belief. Their largely Quaker, predominantly wealthy, and almost exclusively mercantile membership—the embodiment of the city's trading establishment—energetically administered successful protest boycotts. In 1770, however, the nonimportation movement collapsed amid rancorous disagreements over the proper purpose and extent of commercial resistance to British policy that were rich in economic, cultural, and ideological overtones.

The defeat of nonimportation in Philadelphia (September 20) led directly (September 27) to the popular election of the first city resistance committee to be completely dominated by Pennsylvania's coalescing patriot faction.[29] This new board vainly exhorted the merchants to continue their boycott of British imports. In recruiting members for this committee, resistance leaders found themselves already involved, quite unwillingly, in one established pattern of selection. Ten committeemen chosen in 1769, of whom nine were Quaker or Anglican, had resigned by May 1770; seven of these ten then led the successful drive to end the boycott in September (see table 3). In 1769 the Society of Friends had publicly disapproved of committee politics, and by September 1770 many dry goods merchants, angered by the behavior of importers in Newport and Baltimore, were implacably hostile to continuing the boycott.

It was probably necessity, then, that drove resistance leaders, including a few Quaker and Anglican dry goods importers who had been chosen committeemen in 1769 and had continued to support the boycott, to select nine quite different men to join the eleven committee members who remained loyal to nonimportation. The average newcomer was only thirty-two, eight years younger than the average 1769 committeeman at his election. Five of the nine were artisans, manufacturers, or professionals rather than importers. Five were Anglicans, but only one was a Quaker. The nine were generally prominent and highly successful young businessmen, but several were not of the old Quaker-Anglican mercantile establishment (see table 3).

---

28. It is the author's design, in this section, to summarize the events of 1765–74, and as much of his analysis of them given in chapters 2–3 above as bears directly on leadership recruitment, combining these elements with the prosopographical data presented in the current chapter. The general view offered here is necessarily conjectural, but it is the author's contention that the following picture of the challenge facing the radical leaders, and of their motives and reasoning in framing their response, is the most plausible that is consistent with the fragmentary evidence extant on this topic.

29. See chapter 2, for a discussion of the patriot faction; for a very different view of its formation, see Hutson, *Pennsylvania Politics,* chap. 4.

TABLE 3

Political Leaders in the Nonimportation Controversy, September 1770
Listed in order of wealth within each religious group

(See Table of Symbols, p. xi)

Committeemen chosen in 1769 who opposed the boycott in 1770 (all merchants)[a]

	Age in 1770	Religion	1774 Tax Assessment[b]
James, Abel[c]	ca. 50	Q	£240(330)
Reynell, John	62	Q	140
Drinker, Henry	35	Q	134
Fisher, Thomas[d]	29	Q	12(none)
Warder, Jeremiah [Jr.][e]	26	Q	10(none)
Francis, Tench	40	A	196(127)
West, William	46	A?	143(67)
Swift, Joseph	39	A	88(67)

Committeemen chosen in 1769 who supported the boycott in 1770 (all merchants)

	Age in 1770	Religion	1774 Tax Assessment[b]
Fisher, William	57	Q	£160(117)
Howell, Samuel	40–50?	Q[disowned]	150(197)
Roberts, George	33	Q	148(8)
Mifflin, Thomas	26	Q	83(2)
Benezet, Daniel	47	A	196(167)
Gibson, John	41	A	163(62)
Huston, Alexander	35	P	145
Cox, John, Jr.	30–35?	P	120(112)
Mease, James	25–30?	P	52
Thomson, Charles	41	P	12(5)
Nesbit, John Maxwell	42	P	11

a. Robert Morris (age 36, Anglican, assessed £116), and John Rhea (age 40, no other information), who resigned from the 1769 committee in 1770, but who do not appear to have led the drive against the boycott, are omitted.

b. The 1769 assessments, whenever known, are given in parentheses, next to the 1774 assessments.

c. Abel James was in England in September 1770, but his partner, Henry Drinker, committed the firm to oppose the boycott.

d. This Fisher was an heir to the large mercantile fortune of Joshua Fisher and a partner in Joshua Fisher & Sons.

e. The data here are for Jeremiah Warder, Jr., but his father, age 50, worth £440, may have been the committeeman.

It is unlikely that Dickinson, Thomson, and their allies intended to alter the socio-economic dimension of Philadelphia politics in 1770; they sought to change policies, not political structures. Their efforts to radicalize the establishment in Assembly elections of the early 1770s, and especially in 1772, when they had the support of the mechanics' newly organized Patriotic Society, were not highly suc-

TABLE 3 (*continued*)

Committeemen chosen in 1770 to support the boycott

	Age	Primary Occupation	Religion	Tax Assessment[b]
Pearson, James[f]	25	builder?	Q	£75(48)
Clymer, George	31	merchant	A	230(102)
Cadwalader, John	28	merchant	A?	143(none)
Masters, William	35	distiller	A	107(113)
Shee, John[g]	?	merchant	A	12
Allen, Andrew	30	lawyer	P	290(72)
Roberdeau, Daniel	43	merchant	P?	59(86)
Chevalier, Peter	39	distiller	P	10(23)
Loxley, Benjamin, Jr.	24	builder	B?	300(257)

f. The identification is uncertain due to name duplication; tax assessment figure is from 1772.

g. The tax assessment figure is uncertain (either £12 or £5), due to name duplication.

cessful. Within the city, however, dramatic changes were creating conditions in which the resistance could make greater headway. Radicalized mechanics were winning local offices regularly after 1770, and the Tea Act of 1773 antagonized nearly all Philadelphians by threatening to introduce monopolistic trade practices into their highly competitive market.[30] The mercantile establishment, however, remained divided and largely aloof in 1773, nursing the wounds it had received in 1770. Again radical organizers had to seek committeemen where they could most readily find them: among the younger merchants and manufacturers, the Anglicans, Presbyterians, and Baptists. The 1773 tea committee was probably the least affluent and certainly the least mercantile body chosen in Philadelphia before the First Continental Congress. It was also the most radical (see table 4).

The conservative counterreaction of May 1774 immediately threatened the ability of Philadelphia's radical leaders to recruit the city's committeemen primarily from younger, non-Quaker tradesmen of modest fortune; yet this challenge from the right was probably not entirely unwelcome to radical strategists. The comprehensive mobilization of the city toward which Charles Thomson and his colleagues directed their efforts in 1774 would be far easier to achieve if spokesmen for the older Quaker and Anglican elite involved themselves in resistance activity. This advantage could more than compensate for any moderation of radical resistance policies that the older elite's participation in the cause might effect.

Certain it is that radical strategists immediately accepted the principle of moderate-radical cooperation by agreeing to a fusion committee on May 20. The moderate and radical forces present each proposed ten committee nominees, and the meeting quickly agreed to elect all nineteen (John Dickinson was probably on both tickets). The Nineteen might well appear a throwback to 1769, a largely Quaker board of merchant princes. In fact it was a union of two informally com-

30. See chapter 2 above; Olton, *Artisans for Independence,* pp. 49–58; Schlesinger, *Colonial Merchants,* pp. 264–73n; and Labaree, *Boston Tea Party,* pp. 97–98.

TABLE 4

Members of the Tea Committee, 1773
Listed in order of assessed wealth

(See Table of Symbols, p. xi)

Member	Age in 1773	Primary Occupation	Religion	1774 Tax Assessment
Appointed on October 16				
Loxley, Benjamin	27	carpenter, builder	B?	£300
Blockley, Abraham	ca. 35+	?	B	232
Clymer, George	34	merchant	A	230
Penrose, Thomas[a,b]	39	shipwright	A	196
West, William[a]	49	merchant	A?	143
Knight, Peter[a]	50	merchant	A?	95
Barclay, Thomas	45	merchant	P	74
Wilcocks, John	ca. 59 or 30	merchant	A	72
Warder, Jeremiah, Jr.[a]	29	merchant	Q	10
Moulder, William	49	grocer	B	4
Cadwalader, Lambert	30	merchant	Q?	2
Allen, John[c]	34	merchant	P	per head
Added in November or December				
Marshall, Benjamin	36	merchant, manufacturer	Q	178
Nixon, John	40	merchant	A	108
Mifflin, Thomas	29	merchant	Q	83
Mease, James	30–35?	merchant	P	52
Heysham, William	53	merchant	A	34
Shee, John	?	merchant	A	12
Thomson, Charles	44	merchant	P	12
Reed, Joseph	32	lawyer	P	10
Donaldson, Arthur[d]	?	?	?	8
Whyte, Robert	ca. 35	ship captain	A	8
Carsan, Samuel	?	merchant	?	6
[Unknown Member][a]	?	?	?	?

a. Thomas Penrose and, probably, Peter Knight, Jeremiah Warder, Jr., William West, and one other member of unknown identity declined to sign this committee's letter to Boston endorsing the Tea Party (dated December 25, 1773), and can thereby be regarded as composing this board's conservative wing.

b. Penrose was an Anglican but attended Quaker services after 1770 because of a personal dispute with the rector of his church.

c. Living at home with his father, Chief Justice William Allen.

d. The tax assessment figure for Donaldson is from the 1772 tax assessment.

posed tickets. Neither slate, in all probability, showed the ethnic and religious balance or the occupational diversity that were to become such prominent features of Philadelphia's committees over the next two years. A hypothetical reconstruction of the moderate and radical slates, based on the careers of each committeeman in resistance politics from 1769 to 1776, suggests that moderate nominees were exclusively Quaker and Anglican merchants and manufacturers of the greatest wealth. Radical nominees, a somewhat less wealthy, yet well-established, set of merchants, belonged to several denominations, but Presbyterians dominated their ranks (see table 5).[31]

TABLE 5

Hypothetical Slates of Nominees for the May 20, 1774 Committee
Listed in order of assessed wealth

(See Table of Symbols, p. xi)

		Age in 1774	*Primary Occupation*	*Religion*	*1774 Tax Assesment*
	Radical				
REASONABLY CERTAIN	Dickinson, John	42	lawyer	Q[lapsed]	£710
	Clymer, George	35	merchant	A	230
	Cox, John, Jr.	ca. 35–40	merchant	P	120
	Mifflin, Thomas	30	merchant	Q	83
	Thomson, Charles	45	merchant	P	12
	Reed, Joseph	33	lawyer	P	10
PROBABLE	Marshall, Benjamin	37	merchant, manufacturer	Q	178
	Barclay, Thomas	46	merchant	P	74
	Moulder, Joseph	ca. 40–50?	sailmaker	B?	40
	Nesbit, John Maxwell	46	merchant	P	11
	Moderate				
REASONABLY CERTAIN	Dickinson, John	42	lawyer	Q[lapsed]	710
	Fox, Joseph	64	merchant, builder	Q[disowned]	609
	Penrose, Thomas	40	shipbuilder	A	196
	Penington, Edward	48	sugar-baker	Q	100
	Smith, Dr. William	47	teacher, minister	A	47
	Warder, Jeremiah, Jr.	30	merchant	Q	10
PROBABLE	Gibson, John	45	merchant	A	163
	Howell, Samuel	ca. 40–50	merchant	Q[disowned]	150
	Nixon, John	41	merchant	A	108
	Wharton, Thomas, Jr.	39	merchant	Q[disowned]	86

31. It must be emphasized that these tickets are hypothetical. All we know is (1) that two tickets, of ten nominees each, were proposed; (2) that both were accepted; and (3) that the resulting committee had nineteen men whose names appear in the *Pa. Gaz.*, June 8, 1774.

By the late spring of 1774, Philadelphia's radical leadership had assembled a handful of spokesmen from each of three major ethnic-religious groups in the city. From this foundation, the radicals staged their extensive mobilization of Philadelphians to the cause. The most prominent early Anglican leader was the wealthy young merchant George Clymer, who entered committee politics in 1770. There was no shortage of Presbyterians: William Bradford, John Cox, and Charles Thomson had fought British policy since 1765; James Mease joined them in 1769; and the tea affair brought in Thomas Barclay and Joseph Reed. John Dickinson and Thomas Mifflin had symbolized spirited Quaker resistance since the Townshend Act boycott, and in 1773 Benjamin Marshall became a committeeman. These leaders, especially Cox, Mease, Mifflin, and Reed, gathered around Dickinson and Thomson in May 1774 to form a kind of day-to-day radical planning and task force.

In the last week in May, Charles Thomson became distressed at the complacency of so many of his neighbors toward the Boston Port Act. Perhaps, too, he realized that something more than the rather haphazard enlistment of leaders and casual construction of new committees that had prevailed since 1770 was needed to convert his city to political activism. Whatever his reasoning, he suddenly proposed that on May 29, prominent members of each major religious faith in Philadelphia meet to plan a "solemn pause" for June 1, in thoughtful observance of the Boston Port Act. This invitation was the beginning of a conscious program of balanced denominational representation in Philadelphia's resistance politics.[32] It signaled a basic shift in radical recruitment, away from a free, undisciplined inclusiveness toward a carefully planned solicitation of spokesmen from each of the city's more influential subcommunities.

The second element in the radicals' campaign to involve their entire community in resistance activity was the inclusion of spokesmen for certain occupational groups which, while long vital to the city's economy, had only recently shown a keen interest in public life. But the active involvement in committee politics of petty manufacturers, artisans, and retailers—collectively, and loosely, labeled mechanics by their contemporaries—was not so suddenly effected by radical strategists as the participation of Philadelphia's several religious faiths. The rise of the mechanics was a more gradual process, in which radical merchant organizers and aggressive mechanic leaders alike shared the initiative and sustained the effort. The catalyzing event was perhaps Charles Thomson's appeal to the mechanics, on May 25, 1770, to support nonimportation, but Philadelphia's artisans quickly organized and gained control over their own activities, directing their efforts especially toward the October elections for city offices and seats in the Assembly.[33] From August 1772, the Patriotic Society provided a permanent vehicle for the expression of their political ambitions. Only on June 9, 1774, however, did mechanic consciousness reach a much higher level than it had in 1770. On that day, probably without any prodding from Thomson and his lieutenants, several hundred

---

32. The rough equivalence of Anglicans, Presbyterians, and Quakers on the committees chosen in 1769, 1770, and 1773 suggests that the meetings that nominated these bodies also accepted the idea of denominational balance, but there is no evidence that Philadelphia's resistance leaders were planning committee composition and recruiting in advance of any meetings before May 29, 1774.

33. See Olton, *Artisans for Independence,* pp. 43–50.

mechanics resolved to pressure the "merchants' committee," as they called the Nineteen, to mobilize the province over the head of the governor and Assembly. They selected eleven men, prosperous, but generally not wealthy, manufacturers, to argue their case.[34]

This meeting gave radical strategists their cue for incorporating occupational diversity into the committee movement. On June 11, the moderates, led by Dr. William Smith, Thomas Willing, and Thomas Wharton, Sr., and the radicals directed by Dickinson, Mifflin, Reed, and Thomson, cooperatively composed a ticket of forty nominees for a new committee. The construction of this slate provides the first direct view of the recruiting process at work in Philadelphia. The Nineteen and another forty prominent community leaders, again chosen as spokesmen for the city's several faiths, together devised this ticket. They first nominated fourteen incumbent committeemen who were willing to serve again. To these veterans they added thirteen city merchants, manufacturers, and retailers, and one lawyer, including several of their own number not already in committee service, then six of the eleven mechanics' spokesmen of June 9, and finally six men from the rural areas of Philadelphia County (see table 6).[35]

But the mechanics, unhappy with their modest delegation on the committee slate, quickly discovered another underrepresented ally—the city's Germans. Joint mechanic-German pressure on June 17, warmly welcomed by radical merchants, forced moderate merchant leaders to add four Germans at the June 18 public ratifying meeting. The resulting committee of Forty-Three (after James Pemberton hastily withdrew) showed how far coalition politics had come since 1770, and indeed since May 20, 1774.[36] The committee comprised at least four different, yet

---

34. See chapter 3 above, and Appendix F.

35. For Charles Thomson's view of what happened on June 11, see his "Memorandum Book, 1754–1774" pp. 159–62, Charles Thomson Papers, Gratz Collection, HSP. The ticket discussed here has survived in only one copy, in John Dickinson's handwriting, Dickinson material, R. R. Logan Collection, HSP (see chapter 3 above). This slate probably contained a large proportion of the sixty men present at the meeting that composed it, as the mechanics charged in their June 27 letter to Dickinson, item #156, Dickinson material, pp. 2–3, R. R. Logan Collection, HSP.

36. See chapter 3 above on the June 18 meeting. Those who withdrew or were deleted from the committee were Thomas Barlow, Edward Duffield, John Smith, Lewis Weiss, and John Wharton. Those replacing them were:

	Age	Primary Occupation	Religion	Tax Assessment
Allen, John	35	merchant	P	per head
Dickinson, John	42	lawyer	Q [lapsed]	£710
Nesbit, John Maxwell	46	merchant	P	11
Penrose, Thomas	40	shipbuilder	A	196
Smith, John Bayard	32	merchant	P	12

Four other men were added to the committee to represent the Germans:

	Age	Primary Occupation	Religion	Tax Assessment
Hillegas, Michael	45	merchant	A	£140
Hubley, Adam	30	merchant	A	6
Ludwig, Christopher	54	baker	L	99
Schlosser, George	60	tanner	L?	65

(See Table of Symbols, p. xi.)

TABLE 6

Committee Nominated on June 11, 1774

(See Table of Symbols, p. xi)

	Age in 1774	Primary Occupation	Religion	1774 Tax Assessment
Veterans of the Nineteen (14)				
Barclay, Thomas	46	merchant	P	£74
Clymer, George	35	merchant	A	230
Cox, John, Jr.	ca. 35–40?	merchant	P	120
Howell, Samuel	ca. 40–50?	merchant	Q[disowned]	150
Marshall, Benjamin	37	merchant, manufacturer	Q	178
Mifflin, Thomas	30	merchant	Q	83
Moulder, Joseph	?	sailmaker	B?	40
Nixon, John	41	merchant	A	108
Penington, Edward	48	sugar-baker	Q	100
Reed, Joseph	33	lawyer	P	10
Smith, Dr. William	47	teacher, minister	A	47
Thomson, Charles	45	merchant	P	12
Warder, Jeremiah, Jr.	30	merchant	Q	10
Wharton, Thomas, Jr.	39	merchant	Q[disowned]	86
New city merchants, manufacturers, retailers, and professionals (14)				
Bayard, John	36	merchant	P	11
Chevalier, Peter	43	merchant	P	10
Engle, Paul	?	shopkeeper	?	36
Fitzsimons, Thomas	33	merchant	RC	8

interrelated, coalitions. The first was that between the moderates, who favored a continental congress but opposed a sharp confrontation with England, and the radicals, who sought confrontation, particularly in the form of a nonimportation boycott, and urged the construction of an elaborate political organization to further the resistance. Spokesmen for the two factions were roughly equal in number, but the attitude of many committeemen was still undecided. The second coalition was that of denominations; a rough balance of the major British faiths, Quaker, Anglican, and Presbyterian, and the inclusion of a few Baptists and Lutherans. The third coalition, closely interrelated with the second, was between those of English stock, primarily Quaker and Anglican; the Scotch-Irish, who were overwhelmingly Presbyterian; and the Germans. The final coalition was that between the dominant merchants, who still held a majority of committee seats, a dozen large-scale manufacturers and retailers, and a handful of artisans, shopkeepers, and professionals. This was the first committee in Philadelphia to begin to reflect the complexity of the community it represented.

Table 6 (*continued*)

	Age in 1774	Primary Occupation	Religion	1774 Tax Assessment
Haines, Reuben	47	brewer	Q	238
Mease, James	30–35?	merchant	P	52
Morris, Robert	40	merchant	A	116
Moulder, William	50	grocer	B	4
Pemberton, James[a]	51	merchant	Q	358
Roberts, George	37	merchant	Q	148
Weiss, Lewis[b]	57	lawyer	L or GC	14
Wharton, John[b]	37	shipbuilder, merchant	Q	150
Wharton, Thomas, Sr.	43	merchant	Q	166
Willing, Thomas	43	merchant	A	533

Men named to the mechanics' committee on June 9, 1774 (6)

	Age in 1774	Primary Occupation	Religion	1774 Tax Assessment
Barge, Jacob	53	innkeeper, sugar-baker	?	94
Duffield, Edward[b]	54	clockmaker	A	192
Howell, Isaac	ca. 35–40?	brewer	Q	25
Morris, Anthony, Jr.	36	merchant, brewer	Q	55
Rush, William	56	blacksmith	P	92
Smith, Robert	?	builder	P?	110

County Members (6)

	Age in 1774	Primary Occupation	Religion	1774 Tax Assessment
Barlow, Thomas[b]	?	?	?	?
Erwin, Samuel	?	farmer?	?	28
Gray, George	48	ferry-owner	A	389
Miles, Samuel	34	merchant?	B	105
Roberts, John	53	miller	Q	143
Smith, John[b]	?	?	?	?

a. Pemberton resigned from the committee on or soon after June 18.

b. Weiss, Wharton, Duffield, Barlow, and Smith were not elected to the committee on June 18. See note 36 in this chapter for those who replaced them.

Toward the end of June 1774, after many windings, turnings, and false starts, a coherent policy had emerged for enlisting men to lead Philadelphia in its opposition to imperial centralization. The essential principle of this strategy was the selection of leaders who were thought capable of exercising a powerful influence within each religious, ethnic, and occupational group that could affect Philadelphia's economic and political future. While a broad spectrum of early committee leaders favored this strategy to some degree, and were therefore coalitionists, it seems likely that only those of a more radical inclination—those who wished to initiate bold new resistance programs—fully endorsed this policy. Certainly they alone welcomed the mechanics into committee politics, for it was the radicals who had to acquire new political muscle. Yet they could not afford to alienate too many established leaders and social groups. Their policy goals were more ambitious than those of their conservative opponents; their political mobilization had to be more comprehensive, careful, and thorough.

The necessary conditions and the will and insight to implement this strategy developed slowly. In 1770 and in 1773, radical committee politics appeared headed for sharp confrontation with older and wealthier leaders and with most Quakers, but the resurgence of conservative and moderate strength within the resistance movement in May 1774 forced Thomson and his lieutenants to embrace ideological coalition and broaden the ethnic, religious, and occupational bases of committee power. The innovative maneuvers of May 29, June 11, and June 18, 1774, were thus a response to the challenge of Philadelphia's more conservative forces. And while Charles Thomson's policies of May–June 1774 formed an impressive new strategy for bringing the whole city together behind the resistance, one must ask whether the recruitment pattern and the zealous rhetoric that Thomson and his friends used in the fall of 1773 might have been heading in the opposite direction—toward crippling polarization.

Our general portrait of committee transformation from 1770 to 1774 also suggests another way of expressing the development of the radicals' broad recruiting objectives. The old, established elite of the 1760s was, however unwillingly, the teacher of the new elite of the early 1770s. And whether these elders taught by example, cooperation, or opposition, their lessons were most effective. Viewing the transformation of Philadelphia politics from this perspective at once raises a larger consideration, the nature of the new political elite that was forming between 1770 and 1774.

THE FIRST REVOLUTION OF THE PHILADELPHIA ELITE

In the early 1770s, several dozen Philadelphians entered public life, the largest concentrated influx of new leaders since the city's founding. In June and July 1774, this process spread to every county in Pennsylvania, and in the next two years, the several dozen new leaders would become several hundred. In the strictest sense, then, Philadelphia's resistance leaders were the first wave of a new elite. But again one must ask how these men differed from the merchant princes who had preceded them. Was this a different elite, or just a fresh copy of the older establishment?

The changing age and wealth structure of the committees is not in itself a conclusive index of a changing leadership. Committee age averages fluctuated, and declines in both age and wealth often reflected the succession of sons and nephews—Thomas Fisher, Thomas Mifflin, Jeremiah Warder, Jr., or the younger or junior partners—George Clymer, Robert Morris, to seats held by their elders or by men like their elders. The activity of these participants argues no erosion of mercantile power.

The growing movement away from a largely Quaker, importer leadership, however, tells another story. By June 1774, leaders of several heretofore politically passive subcommittees in Philadelphia—manufacturers, retailers, and craftsmen, Baptists, and Germans—had won a secure place in the councils of their city. Perhaps as important, several men without distinguished family backgrounds, like James Mease and Joseph and William Moulder, and other men with no families in Philadelphia, notably Joseph Reed and Charles Thomson, moved into positions of power. The prominence of these men in the committee movement argues that the early leadership of the resistance was rapidly becoming a new kind of elite.

A comparison of committee leadership with the established government highlights this transformation. First, there was little overlap between the two groups. Only one provincial councilor, Andrew Allen, ever held a committee seat, and of the six committees chosen before the First Continental Congress, two contained no assemblymen and three others had one each. The June 1774 committee included four legislators, but only Thomas Mifflin was active in the board's deliberations.[37] Several early committeemen were members of Philadelphia's Common Council, and a few were aldermen, county justices, and even mayors. These officials rarely comprised more than a fifth of each committee, however, and usually no more than one councilman in ten served on a committee. Of those who did, only a handful were important resistance leaders in this period: William Fisher in 1770; George Clymer in 1773 and 1774; Edward Penington in 1774; and Thomas Willing in 1765 and 1774. Most committee leaders, and most members, held no public office.[38]

Perhaps more significant are the aggregate differences between Pennsylvania officialdom and the early resistance leadership. Pennsylvania's assemblymen ranged from three to seven years older than the average member of the city's several committees. Legislators living in or near Philadelphia were a third wealthier than the prosperous May 1774 committee, and over three-quarters again as rich as both the merchants' 1769 board and the Forty-Three, chosen in June 1774. Their fortunes exceeded those of the average tea committeeman by 161 percent.[39] Assemblymen, too, were overwhelmingly of just two denominations, as were Philadelphia's city councilmen. Until 1772, at least three-quarters of the legislators whose faith is known were Quaker or Anglican, and only in May 1776 did their proportion of the House fall below 60 percent. The committees, while also predominantly Quaker and Anglican, were not so heavily dominated by the establishment faiths in the early 1770s, and the erosion of Quaker and Anglican control had, by June 1774, reduced members of those denominations to a bare majority of committee seats.[40] Finally, where Philadelphia's old mercantile establishment was just that, the new resistance elite had come to embrace shipwrights, brewers, bakers, sugar refiners, builders, lawyers, an innkeeper, a blacksmith, a grocer, a sailmaker, and even a minister. The unquestioned control of local politics by the great import-export merchants was at an end.

The early resistance committees of Philadelphia did not signal the triumph of the common man in politics, whether in reality or in appearance. If the committee-

37. The four assemblymen named to the June 1774 committee were Mifflin, a City burgess, and George Gray, Michael Hillegas, and Samuel Miles, all legislators from Philadelphia County.

38. For a full list of members of Philadelphia's Common Council, see the Appendix to Judith M. Diamondstone's "The Philadelphia Corporation, 1701–1776" (Ph.D. diss., University of Pennsylvania, 1969).

39. The exact figures are as follows: Sixteen assemblymen living in the city, assessed in 1774 (average assessment £211.5), were 82 percent wealthier than the average 1769 committeeman (£116); 36 percent wealthier than the average May 1774 committeemen (£155); and 87 percent wealthier than the average June 1774 committeeman (£113).

40. Bockelman and Ireland, "Internal Revolution," pp. 125–59, esp. p. 158, find that of all assemblymen whose religion was known, the percentage who were Quaker or Anglican ranged from 70 to 88 percent for the sessions sitting between October 1765 and September 1774. For Philadelphia's committees, the percentages for these denominations, again for those whose religion was known, were as follows: 1765, 78 percent; 1769, 71 percent; 1770 (proboycott), 60 percent; 1773, 62 percent; May 1774, 68 percent; and June 1774, 56 percent.

men were rather younger and less affluent, and of a somewhat more varied social background than the official establishment, they were far wealthier than their constituents and came overwhelmingly from a fairly narrow social class. Even in June 1774, most committeemen were merchants; most Philadelphians were not merchants. At a time when only one Philadelphian in ten was assessed over £45, the average committeeman on the poorest committee, that of 1773, was assessed £81. The average assessments on all other boards ran well over £100, arguing that the average committeeman was quite well to do. And while only one Philadelphian in three was a Quaker or an Anglican, from 50 to 71 percent of all members of the several committees were of these denominations.[41] The dynamic properties of the committeemen—their decreasing age and wealth and their increasing pluralism—can easily obscure how traditional an elite the resistance leadership was as late as June 1774. The wealthy, the well connected, the famous, or the supremely talented, those of prestigious occupations, nationalities, and denominations—these were still the men who ran Philadelphia.

The changes that did occur in the leadership of the community, however, are too dramatic, even prior to the First Continental Congress, to be dismissed as insignificant. They instead appear to point up two broad, interdependent processes at work in Philadelphia in the third quarter of the eighteenth century. First, the city itself had been changing gradually over several decades, becoming less Quaker and more German and Scotch-Irish. Manufacturing and small-scale crafts were both becoming more important as the American economy became more complex and as the colonists came to desire more self-sufficiency. These developments suggest that the political elite in Philadelphia, and throughout Pennsylvania, would have changed naturally, without the Revolution.

Yet the pace at which elites evolve and the causes of their transformation often have powerful effects of their own. In Philadelphia, gradual, natural, unconscious alterations suddenly became rapid, and after the First Continental Congress, almost explosive. They were effected by conscious and, from June 1774, carefully planned programs of action. It is not difficult to understand why this change occurred. To challenge the might of Great Britain, either to effect imperial reform or to secure independence, required the strongest possible leadership. In so ambitious an endeavor, the vigorous direction of affairs depended upon the establishment of the strongest bonds between leaders and all members of the community who might choose to contribute, or withhold, their support for the cause. This need, and the load of heavy new tasks facing community spokesmen, dictated a broader recruitment of leaders, in greater numbers, from more varied backgrounds. The first sharp transformation of the Philadelphia elite, then, was the natural product of a changing society suddenly thrust into difficult times: a new elite for a new society, chosen (and self-chosen) to perform unprecedented public services. And this was only Philadelphia's first revolution.

---

41. On the basis of contemporary burial figures for the years 1765–74, this writer estimates the proportions of Philadelphia's several denominations to be as follows: Quakers, 12 percent; Anglicans, 16 percent; Presbyterians, 11 percent; Baptists, 2 percent; Swedish Lutherans, 2 percent; German Lutherans, 15 percent; German Calvinists, 6 percent; Roman Catholics, 4 percent; white "strangers," 24 percent; and blacks, 9 percent (from "Historical Notes and Memoranda respecting Philad.ᵃ &c," Item #161, Box 2, Robert Proud Collection, HSP). In saying that from 50 to 71 percent of committeemen were Quakers or Anglicans, I here include all committeemen; the figures in note 40 above, which range from 56 to 78 percent, include only those for whom a religious faith is known.

The Legitimization
of Radical Politics

Indeed I know of no Power in this Country that can protect an opposer of the
publick Voice and Conduct.[1]

JOSEPH REED
September 26, 1774

In the summer of 1774, Pennsylvanians had thrashed out fundamental questions of
principle and settled upon the general strategy of resistance to Great Britain that
they would follow until Independence. For the new leaders who engineered this
policy, however, the community's resolution of July was only the beginning of
months of strenuous efforts to secure their victory. Both the elite and the populace
were caught up in that radicalizing of thought and action needed to oppose Great
Britain, but their loyalty and zeal could not be assumed. It had continuously to be
cultivated. The Assembly, moreover, had yet to be converted. To keep Pennsylvanians to their resolve, to win over, or silence, their opponents, and to build more
regular political machinery for the resistance became the goals of Pennsylvania's
radical leaders.[2] They had to legitimize their new committees by winning the endorsement of more powerful and prestigious political bodies, by fixing their own
identity in the public mind through regular elections, and by taking on the regulatory functions of constituted governments.

---

1. To Dennis DeBerdt, Sept. 26, 1774, Letter-Book, 1772–74, p. 109, Reed Papers, N.-Y.
Hist. Soc.

2. In the period September 1774–March 1775, I label those Philadelphians "radical" who
favored a strong, vocal support of the First Continental Congress and a strict enforcement of
its nonimportation Association. These men would not permit any considerations of personal
inconvenience or any temporary loss of commercial opportunity by Philadelphia's tradesmen
to interfere with the implementation of the Continental Association. These radicals also waged
a vigorous propaganda campaign against the consumption of British imports, and supported a
movement to develop American manufactures. The most radical committeemen even favored
arming Pennsylvania in January 1775, but they were outvoted by several committeemen who
were radical on other issues, and by "moderates" who favored an easier enforcement of the
Association. The radicals continued to develop a leadership that grew steadily more comprehensive in socio-economic terms, while moderates continued to favor leadership by the
mercantile-professional elite. "Conservatives" remained antiboycott, and anti-Congress.

THE RADICALS BROADEN THE RESISTANCE

August 1774 was a quiet month in Philadelphia. The fundamental issue of the resistance, intercolonial unity, was settled, and most Philadelphians gladly left decisions of strategy to the congress. All understood the central question, the adoption of a comprehensive, enforceable boycott of British imports until America's grievances were redressed. City moderates hoped that the congress would reject this measure, while the radicals were confident of its approval, but the absence of extended commentary in the press and the inactivity of the Forty-Three suggest that the commanders on each side, although not always their followers, agreed that the general public was not the proper body to make this decision.[3]

But while most Pennsylvanians now looked to the congress for a sound resistance policy, radical spokesmen treated this new body in a different manner from their opponents. Joseph Galloway assumed that congressmen from most other colonies would, like him, be constitutionally conservative and tactically cautious, and as delegates arrived in Philadelphia, neither he nor Pennsylvania's other conservative congressmen sought out their new colleagues to present their views.[4] The radicals were not so foolish; the congress would decide America's resistance strategy, so they determined to persuade its members to adopt vigorous measures. Although Galloway's Assembly had shut most of their leaders out of this grand deliberative body, the radicals still had two entrees into congressional circles. Thomas Mifflin, Pennsylvania's only radical congressman, held several dinner parties for eastern and southern delegates, a useful political device that his conservative colleagues ignored.[5] Fully as effective was John Dickinson. He and other Philadelphia radicals were better known outside Pennsylvania than Galloway, who now began to pay for his cool indifference over the past decade to other colonial legislatures. Most congressmen had heard of the celebrated "Pennsylvania Farmer," and several knew of the organizing work of his friends George Clymer, Thomas Mifflin, Joseph Reed, and Charles Thomson. A few delegates had already corresponded with these men; all wanted to meet them. The "Farmer" and his colleagues did not disappoint their old friends or miss any opportunity to make new ones.[6]

The amiable diplomacy of Philadelphia's radicals, together with the zealous temper of New England and Virginia congressmen, quickly won a series of brilliant victories that altered Pennsylvania politics. On September 5, Congress chose the Forty-Three's home quarters, Carpenters' Hall, as its meeting place in preference to Galloway's State House, and elected Charles Thomson the body's secretary over the opposition of moderate New Yorkers and Pennsylvanians. Galloway was appointed to the important committee on colonial rights, but

---

3. Moderate pieces appearing in August include those by "A Moderate Man," Aug. 8, and "A Tradesman of Philadelphia" [John Drinker], Aug. 17, *Pa. Jour.*; and "A Zealous Friend," *Pa. Gaz.*, Aug. 31, 1774. Notable radical pieces on congressional policy were by "A Philadelphian" and "A. B.," *Pa. Gaz.*, Aug. 17; "Sydney," *Pa. Jour.*, Aug. 29; "An Artisan," Aug. 31, and "A Mechanic," Sept. 5, 1774, *Pa. Gaz.*

4. William H. Nelson, *The American Tory* (1961), pp. 47–63; Edmund Cody Burnett, *The Continental Congress* (1941), p. 27.

5. Burnett, *Continental Congress*, p. 27; H. James Henderson, *Party Politics in the Continental Congress* (1974), p. 35.

6. Burnett, *Continental Congress*, p. 27; Henderson, *Party Politics*, p. 22; Force, ed., *American Archives*, 4th Ser., I: 406–7, 434, 725; Mifflin to Samuel Adams, May 21, 1774, Samuel Adams Papers, New York Public Library.

Thomas Mifflin secured seats on both the rights and commerce committees.[7] It quickly became clear that most congressmen preferred to confer with Mifflin, Thomson, and even Dickinson, who was outside the chamber, rather than with Galloway and his friends.

In the third and fourth weeks of its deliberations, Congress's essentially radical policy took shape. Following their approval of the spirited Suffolk Resolves on September 17, the delegates announced their intention to boycott British imports starting on December 1, and on September 28, they voted to postpone the consideration of Galloway's conciliatory Plan of Union.[8] By October 1, Congress had given Pennsylvania's radicals the essential foundation on which to erect a strong resistance organization: a uniform continental boycott of British imports. What the radicals still required from Congress was an explicit grant to local committees of broad regulatory powers over commerce.[9] To advance their congressional goals, however, they briefly turned their attention to their own city, where they had a splendid opportunity to further their cause while Congress was still in session. It was election day in Philadelphia.

The year of 1774 had not been kind to Pennsylvania's Quaker party. In June, Philadelphia's freemen had questioned the Assembly's traditional claim to be the sole voice of the people; in July, leaders from every part of the province had presumed to instruct their legislators on resistance policy; and in September, Congress had ignored Speaker Galloway in favor of the Quaker party apostates Dickinson and Thomson. By October the province should have been ripe for an electoral revolution.

But Pennsylvania politics still did not work that way. What was needed was not the retirement, but the conversion, of the House. Seven of the thirty-eight seats changed occupants in county elections in October, but in five turnovers, which were probably uncontested, there was no apparent ideological shift.[10] The election in Chester County of the zealous young Anglican Anthony Wayne in place of an older Quaker was more important, but Chester's voters were probably not voicing unhappiness with the Quaker party. Anthony's father Isaac had been a Quaker party assemblyman in the 1760s; his opponent had already tried to retire from the House; and many well-known moderate men of old families had joined the committee of correspondence in Chester County.[11]

The seventh turnover told a different story. Philadelphia County elected John Dickinson to the House. Even Dickinson's victory may not have been the outcome of a conservative-radical contest, because shortly before election day, Samuel Miles, a freshman legislator and member of the Forty-Three, announced his wish

---

7. *Journals,* I: 14, 28–29, 41; Burnett, *Continental Congress,* p. 34; Henderson, *Party Politics,* pp. 34–35. Hereafter, I shall use the term "Congress" for this now-existing institution.

8. *Journals,* I: 39, 43–52.

9. Becker argues persuasively (*History of Political Parties,* pp. 143, 151–56) that the question of the boycott committees' regulatory powers was the essential issue at the First Continental Congress, because it determined whether the colonies would, in effect, establish an independent government or only a negotiating convention in 1774.

10. Three seats turned over in Bucks County, one changed in York County, and one in Bedford. Compare *Votes and Proceedings,* VIII: 7023 and 7148 for a list of the assemblymen newly elected in 1774.

11. Samuel W. Pennypacker, "Anthony Wayne," *PMHB,* XXXII (1908): 258; *Pa. Gaz.,* Sept. 26, 1771 (withdrawal notice of Wayne's predecessor, John Minshall).

to retire from the Assembly. Pennsylvania's voters rarely turned out a legislator, and Miles' fortunate but perhaps not fortuitous withdrawal enabled Dickinson to stand for election without opposing an incumbent, a considerable advantage even for the famous "Farmer."[12] The importance of Dickinson's election was not the addition of another vote for the resistance, because Miles was also a radical, but the entrance into the House of an eloquent, widely respected resistance leader, a role that was uniquely his. Pennsylvania's Assembly, like Virginia's Burgesses, Massachusetts' House, and even Britain's House of Commons, all "partyless" bodies in the twentieth-century sense of party, was filled with backbenchers who looked to a handful of talented orators, writers, and parliamentarians for guidance.[13] Dickinson gave the cause of resistance in the Assembly the strength of a half dozen radical cyphers. He was the indispensable bridge between the economically and socially conservative past to which the legislators clung tenaciously, and the politically and constitutionally radical present in which they found themselves.

The radicals' greatest electoral triumph, however, was filling an empty House seat. On October 3, the freemen of the City of Philadelphia elected two burgesses. This produced the only known electoral contest for the Assembly in 1774. The incumbents were Thomas Mifflin and Benjamin Franklin, who, although living in London, had as a singular mark of honor been elected in 1773. In 1774, however, Philadelphians decided that they wanted both burgesses present and voting. Mifflin, a Quaker, a merchant, and an ardent patriot, was invincible. The radicals paired him with Charles Thomson, whose natural constituencies were the mechanic, young merchant, and Presbyterian voters. More moderate Philadelphians ran two other candidates, the great Anglican merchant Thomas Willing and the prosperous Quaker sugar-baker Edward Penington. All four contestants were members of the Forty-Three. At the close of the poll, Mifflin had won the favor of 83 percent of the voters; Thomson took Franklin's seat with 50 percent; Willing lost with 47 percent; and Penington received only 20 percent.[14] The Quaker machine had collapsed in the City. "The Samuel Adams of Philadelphia" and his friend the "Pennsylvania Farmer" ended their long years in the political wilderness and entered the provincial Assembly.

The election of only three new proresistance spokesmen, two of whom were unopposed, was no landslide victory for the radicals. Yet it furthered their strategy effectively. The radical goal in October was not to sweep out several archconservative assemblymen, most of whom held safe seats in Bucks and Chester counties, but to bring over a handful of moderate Quaker party men who were not firmly under Galloway's control. If they could radicalize Edward Biddle of Berks, George Ross of Lancaster, John Morton and Isaac Pearson of Chester, William Rodman of Bucks, and Michael Hillegas of Philadelphia, resistance leaders could break

---

12. *Pa. Packet,* Sept. 19, 1774 (Miles' withdrawal notice).

13. See Jack P. Greene, "Foundations of Political Power in the Virginia House of Burgesses, 1720–1776," *WMQ,* 3d Ser., XVI (1959): 485–506; Zemsky, *Merchants, Farmers, and River Gods*; and Lewis Namier, *The Structure of Politics at the Accession of George III* (1929); and *England in the Age of the American Revolution* (1930).

14. Henry Drinker to Benjamin Booth, Oct. 4, 1774, Henry Drinker Letter-Book (domestic), HSP, reports the tally. Each voter could write the names of two men; thus the voters more commonly paired Willing with Mifflin than with Penington, indicating disorganization and division among moderate and conservative Philadelphians.

Galloway's power. Dickinson was the one Pennsylvanian personally able to do this, while Thomson's victory over Willing must have persuaded many legislators that a vigorous opposition to British imperial policy had finally gained wide public approval.

When the new House met to organize for the coming year, Joseph Galloway, who had easily won reelection in Bucks County, did not appear, and the chamber chose Edward Biddle to be speaker, the first "westerner" to hold that post. On the following day, the legislature added John Dickinson to its congressional delegation. More thorough alterations in the organization of the House, however, still lay in the future. The membership of the Assembly's standing committees changed little; the same men dominated the chamber as before.[15] Yet they behaved differently with Galloway absent, and Dickinson present. No doubt, too, Biddle and his colleagues realized that Pennsylvania was in a radically different position than it had been one year earlier. The old party policies would no longer work; to survive politically, the legislators had to discover new ones.

While the Assembly was reassessing its future, Joseph Galloway continued to fix his attention upon Congress. All his hopes depended upon the approval of his Plan of Union, which centered on the principle of noncoercive negotiations with Great Britain to settle the imperial crisis.[16] Yet the week that Galloway stayed away from his old Assembly not only saw the rejection of his policies there, but brought catastrophe in Congress. Pennsylvania's resistance strategists, now including Speaker Biddle and assemblyman George Ross,[17] took firm control of the Assembly's relationship with Congress to bring their province solidly behind determined intercolonial opposition to Britain. Dickinson entered Congress on October 17, and was immediately set to work drafting the appeal to the King. On October 20, the delegates completed their great achievement, the Continental Association; on the twenty-second, Galloway's Plan of Union was expunged from the records.[18] Commercial warfare had annihilated noncoercive negotiation. In six months Pennsylvania's radicals, with considerable help from Congress, had turned the tables on their opponents.

The Continental Association amply justified the Philadelphia radicals' resistance strategy of 1774. Understanding their people's deep conservatism and sensing that several colonies were more zealous in sentiment, Pennsylvania's resistance leaders had worked since May to perfect their province's willing participation in a continental congress. When this body convened in Philadelphia, cautious townsmen saw the wealthiest, most respectable leaders from other colonies propose the strongest measures to secure colonial rights. This performance won over the city, the province, and the Assembly.

---

15. *Votes and Proceedings,* VIII: 7148 (Biddle), 7152 (Dickinson). Although he sat for Berks, a "western" county, Biddle had the usual qualifications for the speakership; he was an Anglican lawyer descended from an established Pennsylvania and New Jersey Quaker family. Dickinson was the only new legislator to receive a standing committee seat (*Vote and Proceedings,* VIII: 7150).

16. Here I have found Nelson's portrait of Galloway (*American Tory,* pp. 47–63, esp. p. 48) most persuasive.

17. Thomson to Drayton, N.-Y. Hist. Soc., *Colls.,* XI: 280–81; Galloway to Governor William Franklin, Mar. 26, 1775, *NJA,* X: 574, 583.

18. *Journals,* I: 74–80. See Nelson, *American Tory,* pp. 47–63; and David Ammerman, *In the Common Cause: American Response to the Coercive Acts of 1774* (1974), pp. 57–60.

Yet no leader could quite appreciate the effect that the Continental Association would have upon Pennsylvania. This concise plan laid out the basic framework for commercial relations with the British Empire that the colonies would follow between December 1774 and Independence. Its main provisions were the cessation of all imports from the British Isles after December 1, 1774, and of all exports to the British Isles and the British West Indies after September 10, 1775.[19] For internal American politics, however, the most important part of this plan was its implementing mechanism. Article 11 directed that committees be chosen in "every county, city, and town, by those who are qualified to vote for representatives in the legislature." These boards were to examine every import shipment arriving after December 1, and supervise the reshipment, storage, or sale of all goods in accordance with the Association's provisions, and they received the power to publish accounts of all violations of the Association in the local papers so that all might condemn their perpetrators "as the enemies of American liberty."[20]

The Continental Association threatened every recalcitrant colonist with economic and social ostracism, whether or not he agreed to the compact, and even provided for the boycotting of whole colonies. In taking this unprecedented step, the Congress had created new governments, both national and local.[21] Yet even Pennsylvania's conservative Assembly, searching desperately for political security in a disintegrating empire, was grateful for the creation of a national power with its coordinated set of local powers, all beyond Parliamentary control. On the evening of October 20, the assemblymen gave a banquet for the Congress; the tireless entertainer Thomas Mifflin managed the affair. Six days later the Congress, having approved Dickinson's memorial to George III, adjourned to May 10, 1775.[22] The burden—and the opportunity—of directing the resistance fell once again upon local leaders and their committees.

THE TRIUMPH OF THE RADICAL-MECHANIC FACTION

Since May 20, the more radical mercantile and professional resistance leaders of Philadelphia had allied with moderate men of their class in support of an intercolonial congress, but as the political tide flowing from Congress turned public opinion in the radicals' favor, the usefulness of this coalition to them ended. The competitive October 3 city election marked its dissolution and signaled the formation of a new, radical alliance of politically ambitious young merchants and lawyers and aspiring young mechanics. In November both moderate and radical public figures accepted the Continental Association and set to work creating the Committee of Observation and Inspection that would give the Association life in their community. Now, however, Philadelphia's two broad factions worked not in tandem, but in opposition.

It was the radicals who welcomed the Association's call for committee elections most eagerly. On November 2, in the same issue of the *Gazette* in which the

19. *Journals,* I: 75–80, gives the text of the Association.
20. *Journals,* I: 79.
21. See Becker, *History of Political Parties,* pp. 154–56; and Ammerman, *In the Common Cause,* pp. 83–86, 103–24.
22. *Votes and Proceedings,* VIII: 7152; Burnett, *Continental Congress,* p. 27; *Journals,* I: 81–121.

Forty-Three scheduled the election for one committee for the city and county of Philadelphia for November 12, a number of young merchants and mechanics proposed the creation of two separate boards, one for the city and its suburbs, the other for the county's rural townships. Although they offered several technical reasons for dividing the existing city-county board, the goal of these Philadelphians was to bar from city politics the conservative county voters who had opposed them on June 18. On November 7, "a respectable number of [city] inhabitants," surely including the mechanics who had protested against merchant moderation in the summer, assembled and resolved that a new committee of sixty members chosen by secret ballot should represent the city alone.[23] During the following week, the radical-mechanic faction drew up its committee ticket, followed apparently by its moderate opposition.

The mechanics' ticket was thoroughly radical in character. Every leading conservative on the Forty-Three was excluded from this list, including Dr. William Smith and Thomas Wharton, Sr. Heading the ticket were over a dozen committee veterans, ranging from moderate activists like Robert Morris and John Nixon to the radical core—Dickinson, Mifflin, Reed, and Thomson, George Clymer, John Cox, and William Bradford. Completing the slate were several artisans and Germans and a host of minor merchants and shopkeepers. The ticket, unlike every committee that the city had elected before, was not dominated by major merchants, but embraced a broad occupational cross section of Philadelphia's inhabitants. The slate also included fewer Quakers, more Presbyterians, and many more Anglicans than the Forty-Three. It was a young committee, and less affluent than any the city had ever chosen.[24]

The opposing moderate-conservative ticket was of a fundamentally different kind. Twenty-one men on this list also appeared on the radical-mechanic ticket, including moderates like Robert Morris and the more established radicals Dickinson and Mifflin; but Bradford, Clymer, Cox, Reed, and Thomson were left off. The slate included many prosperous merchants and a few artisans, together representing most of the major religious denominations in the city. Yet it was the inclusion of several prominent major merchants and manufacturers who had long retarded the resistance movement, men like Thomas Penrose and the influential Quakers Thomas Fisher, Reese Meredith, James Pemberton, John Reynell, and Samuel Shoemaker, that revealed the ticket's true character. Presbyterians were almost entirely excluded, and the average assessed wealth of those candidates nominated by the moderates only was 71 percent greater than that of the mechanics' exclusive entries.[25]

---

23. *Pa. Gaz.,* Nov. 9, 1774.

24. This broadside ticket (Evans No. 13534.1) is in the Philadelphia Library Company (960.F.52). I employ the terms "mechanics'" ticket and "radical-mechanic" ticket here both because this was the first committee slate to include many artisans and shopkeepers and because the victorious committee ticket of August 16, 1775, the obvious successor to this November 12 slate, was labeled the "mechanicks'" ticket by a contemporary. The term "radical-mechanic faction" used in the text is intended to indicate a correlation sensed by contemporaries and demonstrable through the group-biographical analysis of the large committees of 1774–76 presented in chapter 8 below. It is not my intention to argue that all mechanics were radical; more to the point, radicals were by no means all mechanics.

25. Broadside, Evans No. 13534.2, Philadelphia Library Company, 960.F.53. This list is discussed in chapter 8 below, where the coalition suggested by the term "moderate-conservative ticket" is analyzed in detail.

Had Philadelphia's moderate leaders been better able to assess their chances for victory, they perhaps would not have gone to the trouble of composing a ticket. On November 12, according to a later tory account, 499 persons favored the radical slate, while only 18 backed the moderates! Fully as significant is the low total vote, probably between one-fourth and one-third of that usually cast for assemblymen in the urban area.[26] These figures do not reflect the true state of Philadelphia's support for the moderate and radical approaches to the imperial crisis. They suggest instead the prevalence of the feeling that the proponents of congressionally led commercial resistance to British authority were invincible. The zealous had thoroughly cowed the cautious.

Despite the lopsided proportions of their victory, however, the fund of lasting support that November 12 generated for the radicals was no unearned good fortune. The radical-mechanic ticket was composed with consumate skill and bore every mark of Charles Thomson's policy of achieving consensus by enlisting representatives of several economic and social groups. The slate carefully balanced the city's major denominations, recruited many young Quakers who were new to politics, and included several Germans. Its selection gave every occupational group and every class above the level of unskilled laborer a direct and significant voice in political affairs for the first time in Philadelphia's history.[27]

The construction of the opposing ticket could not have been more different. Moderate and conservative strategists, whether unable or unwilling to compose a broadly inclusive slate, were surprisingly casual and insensitive in their work. Where the radicals placed eighteen veterans of the Forty-Three and several recognized leaders of the mechanics and Germans at the top of their slate, the moderates entered only ten of the Forty-Three, while awarding valuable places to James Pemberton, who had refused committee service in June, and to Thomas Fisher, John Reynell, and William West, who had deserted and then attacked nonimportation in 1770. The inclusion of these ultraconservatives and the random scattering of committee veterans, including their best drawing cards, Dickinson and Willing, far down the slate, suggests that the moderates worked in haste and lacked the political skill needed to win. The most prominent men on their ticket either opposed Congress or, like Dickinson and Mifflin, opposed the moderates, and it was highly unlikely that their strict Quaker candidates would have accepted committee service if elected.[28] Such a board could hardly inspire public confidence that the Association would be well administered and Pennsylvania firmly united with the other colonies. Over such weak opposition did the radical-mechanic faction ride to victory.

Congressional approval and regular elections greatly promoted effective resistance committees in Pennsylvania, but they could not alone assure committee life.

---

26. *Pa. Ledger*, Mar. 16, 1776, piece by "Tiberius." The October 3, 1774, vote in the corporate City of Philadelphia was over 1,300. Adding the suburban voters of Northern Liberties and Southwark, one would expect that a good turnout for the area that the new committee was to represent would run to nearly 2,000 voters.

27. Compare tables 5 and 6 in chapter 4, with tables 12 and 13 in chapter 8.

28. See Appendix K and chapter 8 below. For pronouncements by the Society of Friends against political involvement, see *Pa. Gaz.*, June 1, 1774; "Minutes of the Philadelphia Monthly Meeting, 1771–1777," pp. 253, 266, Friends Historical Library, Swarthmore College; and Bauman, *For the Reputation of Truth*, esp. chap. 9.

Only the active cooperation of the provincial legislature could provide such support. But the Assembly, which had parted from the Congress on such cordial terms in late October, now began to have second thoughts. There was a majority for congressional policy in the House, but it was a narrow one. Had conservative Quaker party legislators been more aggressive in December, the Assembly might have dealt the resistance effort a severe setback. But those who were disturbed by congressional policy, though numerous in the House, were in a weak position. Joseph Galloway, after spending several weeks following the adjournment of Congress commiserating with conservatives in New York and then relaxing on his country estate, arrived in Philadelphia too late to block the Assembly's endorsement of Congress's *Journal*.[29] The most prominent Quaker party leader after Galloway, John Morton of Chester County, evidently approved of congressional policy.[30] Nevertheless, the radicals attained their primary goal of the December session only with difficulty. On December 10, after two days of debate, the legislators approved the work of Congress and recommended to their constituents "a strict Attention to, and inviolable Observation of, the several Matters . . . contained in the Journal of the Congress."[31]

Three days later Joseph Galloway entered the House, and immediately his more cautious colleagues rallied around him. Denouncing the Assembly's endorsement of the *Journal,* Galloway discoursed at length on the errors of congressional policy and opposed his own reappointment to Congress's next session in May.[32] But the House insisted on renaming him and then directed several of its members to draw up instructions for its congressmen. Radical legislators, led by Charles Thomson, were well represented on this board, but when they reported a draft, the House referred it "to further Consideration." On December 24, Galloway scored a significant victory: the Assembly, unable to agree on the proposed instructions, deferred the question to their February meeting.[33]

At the close of 1774, Pennsylvania's conservative leaders, inspired by Joseph Galloway, began to overcome their timidity of late October. They now realized how deeply the policy of Congress threatened their political world. Many conservative legislators, however, were quite dependent upon a strong leader, and Galloway's own recovery from his political setback in October came too late to turn the Assembly back to its pre-Congress ways. Galloway himself, while he believed that Pennsylvanians of property wished to oppose the policies of Congress, conceded that they would not do so "until the measures of Parliament are known, and they can hope to be protected in their upright conduct."[34] Conservative timidity kept the initiative with the radicals as the crisis deepened. The Assembly's approval of Congress's *Journal* on December 10 was crucial to their cause. Pennsylvania's House was the first colonial legislature to debate the work of Congress, and its endorsement of the *Journal* undoubtedly encouraged a similar approval in New

29. Galloway to Samuel Verplanck, Dec. 7, 1774, "Some Letters of Joseph Galloway, 1774–1775," *PMHB*, XXI (1897): 478; *Votes and Proceedings*, VIII: 7163.

30. Morton signed the Continental Association in Congress (*Journals*, I: 80), and in 1775 and 1776 supported armed rebellion and independence.

31. *Votes and Proceedings*, VIII: 7162.

32. *Votes and Proceedings*, VIII: 7163; Galloway to Verplanck, Jan. 14, 1774 [1775], "Galloway Letters," *PMHB*, XXI: 477–78.

33. *Votes and Proceedings*, VIII: 7167–68, 7180.

34. Galloway to Verplanck, Jan. 14, 1774 [1775], "Galloway Letters," *PMHB*, XXI: 478.

Jersey and perhaps elsewhere in the middle colonies. Only the New York Assembly refused to follow Pennsylvania's lead.[35] More important, the Assembly's recommendation of the Continental Association to Pennsylvania's inhabitants guaranteed the resistance committees the authority to pursue congressional strategy for several months without obstruction.

THE COMMITTEES REGULATE COMMERCIAL LIFE

Immediately after their election, Philadelphia's sixty radical merchant and mechanic committeemen received petitions from Southwark and Kensington that claimed those districts were underrepresented, whereupon they added six suburban merchants, shipwrights, and carpenters to the board.[36] The Sixty-Six then formally organized as Philadelphia's Committee of Observation and Inspection and chose their officers. With Dickinson, Mifflin, and Thomson deeply involved in legislative and congressional duties, the board elected three relative newcomers to politics: Joseph Reed became their chairman, and John Bayard Smith and John Benezet their secretaries.[37] The full board met every Monday in the hall of the American Philosophical Society, and on December 5, the members divided into six district subcommittees. These small bodies supervised commercial activity in the several parts of the city, assigning at least one of their number each day to inspect all ships docking in their district and to be available at Bradford's London Coffee House, the city's commercial center, between 10 A.M. and 1 P.M. to register every import and assign it for sale, storage, or reshipment in accordance with the rules of the Association.[38]

The official duties of the Sixty-Six were complex and time-consuming, and probably not very interesting to the committeemen, but a brief consideration of their execution is essential to an understanding of the resistance in Philadelphia. The board's district subcommittees were soon busy inspecting and registering cargoes, but Congress's September 22 request that importers cancel all orders for English goods was so effective that most merchandise arriving by mid-December was from the West Indies.[39] Importers of British manufactures, however, were not happy with the committee's strict execution of its duty. Abel James and Henry Drinker had not expected nonimportation to begin so soon, and when they learned in early October that Congress would set December 1 as the date for ending the sale of new imports for a profit, they realized that they had been caught short.[40] The early

---

35. See Force, ed., *American Archives,* 4th Ser., I: 1286–1313, *passim,* for the transactions of the New York Assembly, January–March 1775.

36. *Pa. Packet,* Nov. 14; *Pa. Gaz.,* Nov. 23, 1774. See chapter 8 below for portrait data on these men.

37. See *Pa. Gaz.,* Dec. 21, 1774; and Joseph Reed to the Baltimore Committee of Observation and Inspection, Feb. 2, 1775, Gratz Collection, HSP, for the officers.

38. *Pa. Gaz.,* Nov. 16, 23, 30, Dec. 7, 14, 21, 28, 1774; *Pa. Packet,* Dec. 12, 1774; and subcommittee transaction booklets for districts 1 (Northern Liberties), 3 (between Arch and Chestnut streets), and 4 (between Chestnut and Spruce streets), Am 817, nos. 1–4, and Am 3079, HSP. See also APS, #973.2.M31, vol. 2, p. 33. I have been unable to find records for districts 2 (between Vine and Arch streets), 5 (between Spruce and South streets), and 6 (Southwark).

39. See the subcommittee booklets cited in note 38 above.

40. Henry Drinker to Thomas Pearsall, Oct. 1, to Benjamin Booth, Oct. 8, and to Pigou & Booth (New York), Nov. 13, 1774, Letter-Book (domestic); and James & Drinker to L. Cowper, Nov. 5, 1774, Henry Drinker Letter-Book (foreign), HSP.

cutoff date affected several other conservative importers, too, and all expected the committee to make allowances for ships that had sailed from England as early as September but were unable to reach Philadelphia before December 1 because of unfavorable weather.[41]

The Sixty-Six, however, would permit no exceptions to the Association. Soon over £1,000 worth of James & Drinker's goods alone rested in the warehouses rented by the committee. The importers could sell their stock until March 1, but could keep only costs plus shipping charges; any profit went to the relief of Boston. Although the committee did have difficulty holding prices down after March 1775, when all imports had ceased, its control of trade in the winter months was both strict and successful.[42] So thorough was the support given the Sixty-Six by Philadelphia's inhabitants that neither the district subcommittee records nor the board's occasional press releases indicate any resistance to the Association before the battle of Lexington-Concord. Only in their private correspondence, in declarations of local Quaker meetings, and through occasional communications to James Rivington's *New-York Gazetteer* did Philadelphia's conservative merchants reveal their bitter hatred of the resistance.

Nonconsumption, the pledge of patriots to eat, drink, and wear only what America could produce itself, appeared to be equally successful in Philadelphia. The Sixty-Six did issue occasional reminders to the public to stop eating mutton in order to increase native wool production, and to beware of English tea and East India products entering the city from the Dutch West Indies, but the only violation recorded was one butcher's attempt to sell ewe mutton in the city market. The Bradfords' *Journal* remarked with obvious relish that the butcher "soon found that his best way was to send [the mutton] to the prisoners, and thought himself happy that he got off at so small a price. Probably the next may not get off so well."[43] The intensity of popular commitment to checking British power insured that few Philadelphians would seriously consider violating even one of the more hortatory provisions of the Association.[44]

Finally, the last important element of the committee enforcement system in Pennsylvania, the rural committee network, quickly reached completion. Philadelphia County elected its own committee in November, and although it was more conservative than the Sixty-Six, its commitment to the Association was never in doubt.[45] In December and early January, Berks, Lancaster, York, Chester, Northampton, Cumberland, and even Bucks counties chose boards to enforce congres-

41. Henry Drinker to Pigou & Booth (New York), Nov. 3, 1774, Letter-Book (domestic); and James & Drinker to Jones & Campbell, Dec. 7, 1774, and to L. Cowper, Feb. 23, 1775, Henry Drinker Letter-Book (foreign), HSP.

42. James & Drinker to Pigou & Booth (London), Jan. 18, 1775, Henry Drinker Letter-Book (foreign), and Henry Drinker to Samuel Cornell, Apr. 22, 1775, Letter-Book (domestic), HSP; Schlesinger, *Colonial Merchants*, pp. 499–500; *Rivington's N.-Y. Gaz.*, Mar. 30, 1775.

43. *Pa. Gaz.*, Dec. 21, 1774; Mar. 1, and Apr. 5, 1775; and *Pa. Jour.*, Jan. 4, 1775, p. 3 (quote).

44. See the Sixty-Six to New York City's committee, Feb. 16, 1775, *N.-Y. Gazette*, Mar. 31, 1775, and Force, ed., *American Archives*, 4th Ser., I: 1243, quoted in Schlesinger, *Colonial Merchants*, pp. 498–99; Penn to Dartmouth, Dec. 31, 1774, *American Archives*, I: 1081; "An Englishman in New York to the Committee of Correspondence in Philadelphia, March 28 [1775]," *American Archives*, II: 238–42, cited in Schlesinger, pp. 498–99; and letters in the James and Drinker Correspondence for this period. A good summary of the enforcement of committee policy throughout the colonies is Ammerman, *In the Common Cause*, pp. 119–22.

45. *Pa. Gaz.*, Nov. 14, 30, 1774.

sional policy.[46] The election of a committee in Bucks County was a particularly impressive testament to the breadth of the resistance in Pennsylvania. The great Bucks landowner Joseph Galloway complained that the board was chosen "by a few warm People of neither Property or [sic] significance among us," but several prosperous Quaker farmers of old families were selected for committee service, as was Galloway himself, and most performed that service at least until Lexington-Concord.[47] The Bucks committee was unusually conservative for a local revolutionary board, but it did support the Association, and its election completed Pennsylvania's mechanism for commercial regulation in accordance with the policy of Congress.

COMMERCIAL VERSUS ARMED RESISTANCE: PENNSYLVANIA'S SECOND PROVINCIAL CONVENTION

The Continental Association's dramatic alteration of the imperial relationship and of the state of intercolonial unity in British North America has been apparent since the agreement's execution, but the impact of that agreement upon the internal politics of Pennsylvania and other provinces has seldom been appreciated.[48] Shortly after their election, the Sixty-Six decided that it was essential to perfect the popular dedication to the nonimportation and, especially, to the nonconsumption objectives of the Association. On December 22, the board invited rural committeemen to a second provincial convention, to meet in Philadelphia on January 23, 1775.[49]

Yet the desire to revitalize the feeling of solidarity among Pennsylvania's several local committees by promoting nonconsumption that was stated in the invitation was not the only motive behind this decision. Many of the Sixty-Six, observing that Virginia, Maryland, and Delaware were arming themselves and training for war, determined that Pennsylvania must not be left behind.[50] In late December, the militants appeared to be close to a majority of the committee, and the rural response to the circular letter was enthusiastic even though the martial plans of the ultraradicals were evidently widely known. Joseph Reed, chairman of the Sixty-Six, greatly feared their victory.[51] But in the month between the invitation and the

---

46. Committee elections were held on December 15 in Berks (*Pa. Packet,* Dec. 12), and Lancaster ("Committee of Safety, Lancaster County," volume of MS minutes, Peter Force Collection, Library of Congress); in York on December 16 (*Pa. Gaz.,* Dec. 28); in Chester on December 20 (*Pa. Packet,* Dec. 26); in Northampton on December 21 (*Pa. Jour.,* Jan. 18); in Cumberland on January 4 (*Pa. Jour.,* Jan. 18); and in Bucks, also on December 15 (*Pa. Packet,* Dec. 19).

47. Galloway to Verplanck, Jan. 14, 1774 [1775], "Galloway Letters," *PMHB,* XXI: 478. At least ten of the twenty-nine Bucks committeemen were almost certainly Quaker, based upon last names and upon the withdrawal of eight members in the summer of 1775 due to the inauguration of military activity in Pennsylvania (see "Minutes of the Committee of Safety of Bucks County, Pennsylvania, 1774–1776," *PMHB,* XV [1891]: 259).

48. An exception is Becker, *History of Political Parties,* chap. 6.

49. *Pa. Gaz.,* Dec. 28, 1774.

50. Joseph Reed to Dartmouth, Dec. 24, 1774, W. B. Reed, *Life of Reed,* p. 90; and Force, ed., *American Archives,* 4th Ser., I: 1066, in which a Philadelphian declared (Dec. 24): "the Province of Pennsylvania will follow [Virginia's and Maryland's] example; in a few weeks our Militia will amount to no less than sixty thousand men."

51. *Pa. Gaz.,* Feb. 23, 1775 (Bedford committee letter); *Pa. Gaz.,* Jan. 18, 1775 (York committee letter); Reed to [Charles Pettit], Jan. 4, 1775, Reed Papers, N.-Y. Hist. Soc.; Reed to Dartmouth, Dec. 24, 1774, cited in note 50 above. The identity of the militants, unfortunately, is not known.

convention, many Pennsylvanians expressed strong reservations about arming the province.[52] Bucks County's committeemen flatly refused to participate, observing that they could not "conceive from any information we have had, the necessity of such Provincial Convention, or that any good effects can be produced thereby, towards carrying into execution the Association so clearly pointed out to us by the Continental Congress."[53]

Pennsylvania's committees could not ignore Bucks County's dissent. Moderate and conservative Pennsylvanians, becoming bolder, were determined that if they could not undo the work of Congress, and many did not want to, they must prevent the zealous from driving the province one step beyond the policy of that body.[54] Veteran resistance leaders, sensing this mood, worked to prevent the convention from dividing the province. Mifflin and Thomson, who knew that their efforts to redirect Assembly policy would founder if the convention were to play too radical a part, joined the gathering and persuaded John Dickinson, who was becoming deeply disturbed by the radical temper of the Sixty-Six, to put in a belated appearance for the sake of unity.[55] Assemblymen George Gray and Anthony Wayne and Speaker Edward Biddle also attended. Their presence and the moderation of many rural delegates had a powerful influence upon the convention's deliberations, while Joseph Reed's exercise of parliamentary powers as convention president allowed him to control the ultraradical delegates from his own committee.[56]

Yet the January convention, called without an agenda and held in the dead of winter, was an impressive testimony to the province's desire to strengthen its resolve and reaffirm its policies. It presented an excellent opportunity to perfect the unity of the resistance, if only the delegates could hit on the proper proportion of bold initiative and a sober regard for the many moderate patriots in the province. As in July 1774, the city committee dominated the provincial gathering with 55 members in attendance, but Berks, Chester, Lancaster, Philadelphia, and York counties all sent large delegations. Only 31 of the 105 members had attended the July convention, and on several delegations new men were not only more numerous but probably more influential than veteran conventioneers. These delegates made the January convention distinctly more radical than its predecessor in July.[57]

When the convention opened, however, veteran city leaders, with the aid of several rural delegations, gained the upper hand more easily than they had anticipated.[58] As chairman of the Sixty-Six, Joseph Reed set the tone of the sessions in the opening address by calling for unity and a more perfect commitment to nonconsumption, while ignoring the demand for a provincial militia. The conven-

52. Galloway to Verplanck, Jan. 14, 1774 [1775], "Galloway Letters," *PMHB*, XXI: 478; Thomas Wharton, Sr. to Joseph Wharton, Jan. 18; and to Samuel Wharton, Jan. 31, 1775, Thomas Wharton, Sr. Letter-Book, HSP; Reed to Dartmouth, Feb. 10, 1775, W. B. Reed, *Life of Reed,* p. 94; and Force, ed., *American Archives,* 4th Ser., I: 1180 (Jan. 25, 1775).

53. *Pa. Gaz.,* Jan. 25, 1775.

54. See the letters cited in note 52 above.

55. Duane, ed., *Passages from Marshall,* p. 15 (Jan. 27, 1775); Force, ed., *American Archives,* 4th Ser., I: 1211 (Feb. 4, 1775); and Reed to [Charles Pettit], Jan. 14, 1775, Reed Papers, N.-Y. Hist. Soc.

56. Reed to Dennis DeBerdt, Feb. 13, 1775, Reed Letter-Book, 1772–74, N.-Y. Hist. Soc. See also Reed to DeBerdt, Dec. 24, 1774, Reed Letter-Book.

57. *Pa. Gaz.,* Feb. 1, 1775, for full transactions; and compare *Pa. Gaz.,* July 27, 1774, postscript. No minutes or detailed personal accounts of the gathering appear to have survived.

58. See the letters cited in note 52 above, and esp. Force, ed., *American Archives,* 4th Ser., I: 1180.

tion then named its officers and passed twenty-seven resolves, all "unanimously." The proposal to raise a militia, which was probably sponsored by scattered members rather than by any full delegation, was rejected without extensive discussion.[59]

The majority of the convention's resolves dealt only with the Association's call for nonconsumption, but even this goal provided ample opportunity for strengthening the resistance. The delegates pledged that each committee would aid every other in executing the Association against all opposition, and resolved that if Great Britain were to enforce her arbitrary acts by arms, "we hold it our indispensible duty to resist such force, and at every hazard to defend the rights and liberties of America." Subsequent resolutions called for a largely self-sufficient economy that could survive an extended loss of imports. The members exhorted Pennsylvanians to make their own textiles, steel, paper, printer's type, liquors, and salt. In a sterner temper, they called for the production of saltpeter and gunpowder. Their most productive resolve recommended the establishment of local societies to encourage the manufacture of these several commodities. This appeal would yield important results, both industrial and political, in the next few months.

Conservative Pennsylvanians warmly congratulated each other on the failure of the convention's ultraradicals to establish a militia, clear proof, they believed, that the political tide had at last turned their way.[60] But the convention's work hardly favored their cause. Leaders from throughout the province had traveled through winter snows to pledge their loyalty to one another, to the Continental Association, and to nonconsumption, which they made the central symbolic expression of patriotic virtue in Pennsylvania. The committees' promise to support one another against all opposition, to resist force with force (in far more explicit terms than the July convention had dared use), and to promote the production of gunpowder looked toward a province that could defend itself even if it was not actively training its citizens for war.

The January convention's resolves formed a vital extension of the resistance strategy of 1774, and when moderate and radical committee veterans had defeated the ultraradical newcomers' plan for a militia, the two wings of the resistance closed ranks to face their anticongressional opponents. Dickinson and his colleagues could now enter the February Assembly session confident that their committee allies had not alienated moderate legislators and endangered the policy of Congress. But more conservative Pennsylvanians were alarmed and began a counterattack against the resistance.

THE STRUGGLE TO PRESERVE A CONSENSUS
FOR THE RESISTANCE

In the fall of 1774, the Philadelphia press printed almost no political opinion.[61] Local radicals worked quietly to reduce the local circulation of James Rivington's

---

59. Force, ed., *American Archives,* 4th Ser., I: 1180; Reed to Dartmouth, Feb. 10, 1775, W. B. Reed, *Life of Reed,* p. 94.

60. Henry Drinker to Pigou & Booth (New York), Jan. 31, 1775, Drinker Letter-Book (domestic), HSP; Galloway to Verplanck, Feb. 14, 1775, "Galloway Letters," *PMHB,* XXI: 481; Galloway to Governor William Franklin, Feb. 28, 1775, *NJA,* X: 573; and Thomas Wharton, Sr. to Samuel Wharton, Jan. 31, 1775, Wharton Letter-Book, HSP.

61. But see "Political Observations, Without Order; Addressed to the People of America," *Pa. Packet,* Nov. 14, 1774. This was reprinted in *Rivington's N.-Y. Gaz.,* Dec. 1, 1774, with critiques by "Nestor" and "M."

tory newspaper and of several conservative pamphlets emanating from New York, but the Sixty-Six as an institution characteristically kept clear of this suppression.[62] With the new year, however, appeared the first public essay in Philadelphia to criticize the work of Congress. By attacking the unexpectedly sudden initiation of the Continental Association, "An Anxious By-Stander" hoped to arouse public opinion and force both the Sixty-Six and Congress to award some compensation to merchants who had suffered losses because of congressional policy.[63] Rising to the defense of Congress, "Philadelphus" contended that the Association was fair to all merchants, and persuasively argued the necessity of every American's remaining loyal to Congress and accepting without public debate the resistance strategy that Congress had carefully considered and adopted.[64] This first public exchange over congressional policy effectively placed the protection of a strong public consensus for the resistance at the center of the American cause in Philadelphia. Other critics were now ready to test the movement's resolve to defend itself.

The Society of Friends had opposed committee involvement for its members since May 1774, but its first declarations persuaded only a few wealthy Quaker merchants to abandon committee service.[65] In December, the Society's elders decided to impose their sect's strict discipline to bring younger members back to the doctrine of nonresistance and to prevent Quaker assemblymen from supporting congressional policy. In January, they recommended to Pennsylvania's local monthly meetings that all Friends serving on committees be admonished by the meeting's elders and, if they proved recalcitrant, that they be disowned.[66] Some two dozen Quaker elders, not content simply to purify their own house, then turned to the broader public. On January 24, they published a "testimony," which attacked Congress and branded all radical activity as a usurpation of legitimate authority.[67] The declaration was clearly intended to counter the effect of the second provincial convention then in session, and to influence the upcoming meeting of the Assembly. It closed with the request that the Assembly petition George III directly for a redress of grievances, rather than rely upon John Dickinson's congressional memorial to the monarch.

By issuing this direct challenge to congressional leadership, Philadelphia's Quaker elite seriously undercut their Society's apolitical image.[68] The elders' first reason for publishing the testimony was religious: they hoped to free their pacifist sect from the snare of involvement in violence by shaming their activist youth into a sense of their duty. But the testimony had its political motivation as well. In

---

62. *Rivington's N.-Y. Gaz.,* Dec. 8, 1774, and Mar. 30, 1775; and Force, ed., *American Archives,* 4th Ser., I: 1011.

63. *Pa. Gaz.,* Jan. 4, 18, Feb. 1, 15, 1775.

64. *Pa. Gaz.,* Jan. 11, 25, Feb. 8, 1775.

65. See chapter 3 above, and note 28 in this chapter. Quakers who had withdrawn from political activity were James Pemberton in June and Jeremiah Warder, Jr., Edward Penington, and Thomas Wharton, Sr. in November.

66. Schlesinger, *Colonial Merchants,* pp. 496–97; "Minutes of the Philadelphia Monthly Meeting, 1771–1777," pp. 285, 292, Friends Historical Library, Swarthmore College. See also Bauman, *For the Reputation of Truth,* pp. 147–53.

67. "The Testimony of the People Called Quakers, Given Forth . . . at Philadelphia the Twenty-fourth Day of the First Month, 1775," (broadside, Evans No. 14052), reprinted in *Pa. Gaz.,* Feb. 23, 1775. See also "An extract of a letter from Philadelphia, to a gentleman in New-York," Feb. 27, 1775, Force, ed., *American Archives,* 4th Ser., I: 1270.

68. For criticism of this testimony by influential London Friends, see Isaac Sharpless, *A History of Quaker Government in Pennsylvania,* II, *The Quakers in the Revolution* (1900), pp. 113–14, 118.

early 1775, Friends still held considerable political power in Pennsylvania, and they vividly remembered the days when their power had been even greater. The Revolution was by its nature a threat to the political, economic, and social dominance of this minority. Because of the nonresistant character of the Quaker faith, it was ultimately an unanswerable threat. Older, more prominent Quakers had to express their bitter opposition to Pennsylvania's new future, even though their testimony invited dangerous attacks upon both their powerful political position and their freedom to hold their religious convictions without harrassment.[69]

For all their courage, however, Quaker leaders inflicted no apparent damage upon the resistance and drew little radical response.[70] But the elders' insistence on taking a hard line with their youth inflicted immediate damage upon the unity of their own Society. Joseph Reed privately observed their distress with undisguised pleasure: "The Quakers had like to have given themselves a deadly Wound by a publication of theirs . . . respecting the Congress or rather the present Publick Measures, wherein the Doctrines of passive Obedience, and Non Resistance were pretty strongly inculcated. It occasioned such Division among them that Proposals were made and signed by great Numbers to set up an independent Meeting, . . . by great Application and coaxing they have endeavoured to draw the Mutineers to their Colours again, but I believe they will be very cautious how they issue any more Bulls of this Kind."[71]

The January testimony so strongly polarized the Society of Friends that the elders issued no more public protests in 1775. Yet the Quaker leadership was not as frightened by the power of resistance sentiment as Reed had hoped. Philadelphia's monthly meetings immediately initiated proceedings against several of their members for serving on the Sixty-Six, and in March, Thomas Mifflin, Benjamin Marshall, and Owen Biddle were charged with "promoting Measures pursued by the People for asserting their Civil Privileges in such Manner as are [*sic*] inconsistent with our Peaceable Profession and Principles."[72] Thus began the reprimands, contrite confessions, and disownments that would swell to a flood of Quaker soul-searching and disorder in the next twelve months.

The absence of public commentary on the Society's troubles argues that resistance leaders made a conscious decision to stay clear of this discord. Philadelphia's Quakers, in their inner turmoil, were developing ever-stronger religious convictions, but their political power in the larger community now declined precipitously.[73] An attack upon the Society would have effected nothing for the resistance;

---

69. Tolles, *Meeting House and Counting House,* p. 235, argues that Friends had no desire to dominate Pennsylvania's political life after 1757, but even a cursory reading of Quaker letters and diaries of the 1770s refutes that claim. See Bauman, *For the Reputation of Truth,* chaps. 4–5, 7–9, for a most effective reply to Tolles' argument.

70. For a brief radical-Quaker exchange, see *Pa. Jour.,* Feb. 1, 8, 15, 1775.

71. Reed to Charles Pettit, Jan. 31, 1775, Reed Papers, N.-Y. Hist. Soc.

72. Bauman, *For the Reputation of Truth,* pp. 153–55; "Minutes of the Southern District Monthly Meeting, 1772–1778," pp. 82–83, and "Minutes of the Philadelphia Monthly Meeting, 1771–1777," pp. 298–99 (quote), Friends Historical Library, Swarthmore College.

73. In the February 15 issue of the *Journal,* the editors stated that the reply by one "B. L." to a Quaker critic of "B. L's" earlier attack on the "Testimony" (*Pa. Jour.,* Feb. 1, 8, 1775), intended for the February 15 issue, was laid aside "at the desire of the author." It was probably pressure from the radical leadership, however, that terminated the exchange. On the impact of the crisis on the Quakers' religious convictions, see Tolles, *Meeting House and Counting House,* pp. 230–39; and Bauman, *For the Reputation of Truth,* chaps. 7–10.

condemnation by non-Quakers could only have worked to restore Quaker unity and reduce the number of young Friends willing to embrace the resistance. The radicals' bland refusal to admit any inconsistency between congressional policy and Quaker principles put Friends in the peculiarly uncomfortable position of attacking an enemy who refused to retaliate. In this battle the only wounds that the Quakers could inflict were, as Joseph Reed observed, upon themselves.

The dissension in Quaker ranks sapped the will of Philadelphia's conservatives to attack their opponents just as they sensed a fresh opportunity to recover their influence in public counsels.[74] Congress and its Association committees provided them the institutional targets that they had lacked in the early fall, and the rapidly expanding Philadelphia press was now more open to their opinion.[75] In February, conservative propaganda from New England and Joseph Galloway's *A Candid Examination of the Mutual Claims of Great-Britain and the Colonies,* published in New York, reached Philadelphia, affording local conservatives the opportunity to consider real alternatives to the policy of Congress.[76] But in succeeding weeks they failed to mount an attack of their own. When radical propagandists attacked the conservative essays coming from the north, Philadelphia's conservatives made no attempt to defend their friends.[77] The few essays that Philadelphia's tories wrote themselves were timid and defeatist, and they appeared only after the important political struggle in the winter Assembly session had ended.[78]

It was in their relationship with the New York press that Philadelphia's conservative writers most fully revealed their weakness. Just as tories in every colony looked to England for aid rather than making allies at home,[79] so Philadelphia's tories looked to New York's James Rivington to print information and opinion that they did not dare to publish in Philadelphia. They privately excused their passivity by saying that Philadelphia's press was not free, but both the recently established *Ledger* and the *Gazette* carried critiques of congressional and committee policy. After mid-February, however, nearly all conservative opinion appeared in Rivington's *Gazetteer.* This paper was a poor substitute for local journals: its Philadelphia circulation had recently declined, and it was as partisan as Philadel-

---

74. Galloway to Verplanck, Feb. 14, 1775, "Galloway Letters," *PMHB,* XXI: 481; Henry Drinker to Pigou & Booth (New York), Jan. 31, 1775, Letter-Book (domestic), HSP; and [Abel James?] to Pigou & Booth (New York), Feb. 8, 1775, Am 30795 [typescript], James and Drinker Correspondence, HSP.

75. Nelson, *American Tory,* p. 64; Henry Drinker to John Clitherall, Oct. 11, 1774, Letter-Book (domestic), HSP; advertisement for the *Pennsylvania Ledger,* in *Pa. Gaz.,* Jan. 11, 1775; Joseph Reed to Charles Pettit, Jan. 14, 1775, Reed Papers, N.-Y. Hist. Soc.; [Abel James?] to Pigou & Booth, Feb. 8, 1775, cited in note 74 above; and, on the editor of the new *Pennsylvania Mercury,* Enoch Story, see James & Drinker to Coleineon & Sandwith, May 9, 1769, Henry Drinker Letter-Book, HSP.

76. *Pa. Gaz.,* Feb. 15, 1775; *A Candid Examination* (New York, 1775 [Evans No. 14059]). Rivington printed the *Examination;* see the announcement of publication in *Rivington's N.-Y. Gaz.,* Feb. 23, 1775.

77. The radicals' essays were by "Camillus," Feb. 22, and "A Lover of English Liberty," Mar. 1, 8, 1775, *Pa. Gaz.;* and a Dickinson-Thomson letter attacking *A Candid Examination* in *Pa. Jour.,* Mar. 8, 1775. See also Galloway to Verplanck, Apr. 1, 1775, "Galloway Letters," *PMHB,* XXI: 481–82; Julian P. Boyd, *Anglo-American Union: Joseph Galloway's Plans to Preserve the British Empire* (1941), pp. 45–50; and Thomas R. Adams, *American Independence, The Growth of an Idea* (1965), pp. 125–26.

78. *Pa. Gaz.,* Mar. 22; *Pa. Mercury,* Apr. 28, 1775.

79. See Nelson, *American Tory,* pp. 19–20.

phia's radical *Journal* and *Evening Post.*[80] Rivington's bias may have encouraged Philadelphia's conservatives to substitute vague charges and heated denunciations for compelling arguments against radical policy; his paper certainly damaged their arguments by carrying them alongside the strongest New York tory invective.

In the absence of a face-to-face dialogue, tory attacks launched from New York upon radicals in Philadelphia became increasingly bitter and misdirected, and the conservatives' mood changed from moderate optimism in January to desperation by late March. In mid-January, Rivington's *Gazetteer* claimed that "the violent party" in Philadelphia was losing supporters daily and that John Dickinson had deserted the cause.[81] There was enough truth in these charges to justify a broader propaganda effort, but nothing more appeared for two weeks. Then, after the Sixty-Six had again secured Dickinson's allegiance and the provincial convention had strengthened Pennsylvania's commitment to the resistance, Rivington's anonymous correspondents reiterated the "Farmer's" defection and dismissed the convention as a meaningless show of enthusiasm.[82] On February 16, another letter to Rivington reported that the Sixty-Six was behaving arrogantly and had earned the disapproval of a recent "high Whig," who now condemned the board and described its members as bankrupt republicans, smugglers, 1770 nonimportation-breakers (!), illiterates, and nobodies who had been elected by less than one-sixth of Philadelphia's voters.[83]

There was still time for a strong and sustained conservative assault: Pennsylvania's cautious, uncertain assemblymen were about to convene, and the city press was relatively open. But the author of the February 16 letter failed to name the recent "high Whig" or produce damaging criticisms of committee practices, so nothing transpired from this promising beginning. The only full critique of Philadelphia's resistance movement in early 1775 did not appear until March 30, three weeks after the radicals had stemmed the conservative tide by defeating Joseph Galloway and his supporters in the Assembly.[84] By then the conservatives' propaganda campaign had failed dismally. The oblique and surreptitious character of their criticism killed whatever chance they had to undermine Pennsylvania's support for congressional policy. And they had had a rare opportunity to sway their province in the winter of 1775. Pennsylvania's assemblymen came close to qualifying their support for Congress; any significant alteration in public opinion might well have changed their policy.

But public opinion did not change, for several reasons. First, conservative writers mistakenly assumed that any news from England could only help their cause and waited too long to attack their opponents directly. Second, the Sixty-Six

80. Benjamin Booth to James & Drinker, Aug. 8, 1774, Am 30795 [typescript], James and Drinker Correspondence, HSP.

81. Jan. 19, 1775, p. 3, under "New York, January 19" (general news), but headed "Extract of a letter from Philadelphia, dated January 10."

82. *Rivington's N.-Y. Gaz.*, Feb. 2, 1775, also in Force, ed., *American Archives*, 4th Ser., I: 1180; and "Extract of a letter from Philadelphia to James Rivington, New York, dated February 4, 1775," *American Archives*, 4th Ser., I: 1211.

83. *Rivington's N.-Y. Gaz.*, Feb. 23, 1775. The 517 persons who voted on November 12, 1774, were probably more nearly one-fourth of the regular voters than one-sixth (see note 26 above). For the Sixty-Six's formal defense of its city's patriotism to New York's Committee of Observation, also dated Feb. 16, 1775, see *New-York Journal*, and Force, ed., *American Archives*, 4th Ser., I: 1243.

84. *Rivington's N.-Y. Gaz.*, signed "An Englishman."

played a cautious game. Their strategy centered on their strict execution of the Continental Association without favoritism, their summoning of a second provincial convention to encourage Pennsylvanians to support nonconsumption and economic independence, and their refusal to recognize the existence of either institutional or individual opponents. Fully as effective was the behavior of radical writers. They replied to all criticism of the resistance in a vigorous style that eschewed personal invective, and when they declined to attack Philadelphia's Quakers by name or implication, they left the Society of Friends without a good target to strike.

The restraint of radical strategists and penmen was essential to protect the resistance in early 1775. Pennsylvanians waited on every packet from England and every post from Boston for clues to their future. In this awkward hiatus, some erosion of the province's patriotic zeal was unavoidable. To hold the community to its determination to resist the British ministry, resistance leaders employed all of their patience and subtlety and directed public attacks only at those writers who questioned the depth of the community's commitment to the resistance. Their cool self-control and the timidity of their opponents together preserved the dedication of ordinary Pennsylvanians and their assemblymen to the cause. The lawmakers' commitment to the resistance, however, withstood an even sharper challenge in this winter of 1775.

JOSEPH GALLOWAY'S LAST STAND

When the Pennsylvania Assembly convened on February 20, it faced two critical tasks. First, the legislators considered their instructions to their congressmen, which they had put aside at Galloway's insistence in December. Moderate and radical delegates sought to issue brief, open guidelines, but conservative members blocked all instructions in the hope that Pennsylvania would withdraw its support from Congress. Unable to settle their differences, the lawmakers again postponed drafting the instructions to their spring session, only to face a more serious problem. This was Governor Penn's recommendation that the House petition George III for a redress of Pennsylvania's grievances. In the fall, Britain's Colonial Secretary, Lord Dartmouth, in an attempt to shatter the united colonial support for Congress, had instructed each governor to urge his assembly to send its own petition to the Crown. Both Governor Franklin of New Jersey and Governor Colden of New York had already exhorted their legislatures to take this step, although only Colden was successful.[85] The issue, then, was no less than the unity of the colonies.

The defenders of congressional policy enjoyed important advantages as the debate on Penn's message began. With the continued support of public opinion, they could still count on a majority of the legislators; and congressionally led resistance also had friends in another quarter. Neither Governor Penn nor most of his councilors were deeply hostile to Congress, but they were thoroughly alarmed by the imperial crisis. Unsure of how to preserve their power and privileges, proprietary leaders preferred to do nothing. Joseph Galloway charged that Penn had deliberately put off advising the Assembly to petition the Crown, and that only the

---

85. *Votes and Proceedings*, VIII: 7185–86; Force, ed., *American Archives*, 4th Ser., I: 1286–87, 1289, 1290, 1313 (New York Assembly transactions of January–March 1775).

example set by Governors Franklin and Colden had forced him, on February 20, to ask the opinion of his Council on submitting such a message.[86] The Council split evenly on the question, with most younger members opposing any action, until the late arrival of the venerable James Hamilton broke the deadlock in favor of submission. Penn sent his address to the House on the following day, but the force of his request was much softened when his father-in-law, the proprietary leader and assemblyman William Allen, declared in the House that the message "meant no more than to save Appearances."[87]

Joseph Galloway was now in such poor health that Joseph Reed had "hopes of his not existing to increase and continue public confusions much longer."[88] But Galloway's growing conviction that most proprietary leaders really supported the rebellious Congress so outraged him that he determined to make one last attempt to check the resistance movement in the Assembly. In two days of heated debate, he implored the House to petition the King, and he made some converts, although he was opposed on the floor by William Allen, John Dickinson, Thomas Mifflin, George Ross, and Charles Thomson. When he found that he could not carry the point, Galloway requested that the issue be deferred. The radical leadership vigorously opposed this delay, but on February 25, the House agreed by a single vote to postpone considering its reply to Penn until March 8.[89]

While Galloway was undoubtedly grateful for this respite, he sensed that it would be too brief. He believed that both the Assembly and the people were coming around to his view of congressional resistance, but he feared that if a vote were taken before April, the House would decide either not to send a message to the Crown or to send one that would not be "consistent with the dignity of [the British] Government to receive."[90] Thus it was particularly unfortunate for the conservative cause that in this ten-day hiatus Philadelphia's tories failed to place one effective critique of congressional policy in the city press. Yet on March 4, Galloway was unexpectedly encouraged to hope that enough votes were swinging to him when his opponents, "despairing of success in preventing a petition to his Majesty, moved that the Doors should be thrown open [for public viewing of the March 8 debates], and the Mob let in upon me." This maneuver was soundly defeated, and Joseph Galloway prepared for what he expected would be one of the greatest triumphs of his career.[91]

On March 8, however, those favoring a petition to George III were still roughly

86. Galloway to Governor Franklin, Feb. 28, Mar. 26, 1775, *NJA*, X: 572–86; and see Thomas Wharton, Sr. to Samuel Wharton, Jan. 31, 1775, Letter-Book, p. 142, HSP. Penn, writing to Dartmouth on Dec. 31, 1774, Force, ed., *American Archives*, I: 1081, said that the Assembly had approved the transactions of Congress "to my great surprise," so it is possible that Penn was merely less diligent than Colden and Franklin in dealing with his legislature on imperial issues.

87. Galloway to Franklin, Mar. 26, 1775, *NJA*, X: 580.

88. Reed to Charles Pettit, Feb. 25, 1775, Reed Papers, N.-Y. Hist. Soc.; Galloway to Verplanck, Feb. 14, June 24, 1775, "Galloway Letters," *PMHB*, XXI: 480, 483.

89. Galloway to Franklin, Feb. 28, 1775, *NJA*, X: 573–74 (also "Extract of a letter from Philadelphia, to Mr. Rivington, New-York, dated February 28, 1775," *Rivington's N.-Y. Gaz.*, Mar. 2, 1775). Also see Joseph Reed to Charles Pettit, Feb. 25, 1775, Reed Papers, N.-Y. Hist. Soc., who gives a different account of this vote; and *Votes and Proceedings*, VIII: 7193.

90. Galloway to Franklin, Feb. 28, 1775, *NJA*, X: 574.

91. Galloway to Franklin, Mar. 26, 1775, *NJA*, X: 581–82; *Votes and Proceedings*, VIII: 7202.

four votes short of a majority. Galloway then proposed that the House inform Governor Penn that it would consider his request further and reply in its spring session, shortly before Congress was to reconvene. To the radicals' dismay, this motion carried, and Speaker Biddle named several members to prepare a reply to Penn based upon Galloway's proposal and an amendment suggested by Dickinson. But according to Galloway, Biddle departed from proper legislative procedure by appointing a committee that was decidedly unsympathetic to Galloway's plan.[92] Galloway also charged that George Ross and Charles Thomson, with Dickinson's connivance, called an unscheduled meeting of the committee and drew up their own answer in his absence. By whatever process, the committee did compose a bland rejection of Penn's request and reported this draft back to the full House that same afternoon.[93]

Galloway and his friends now met with a catastrophic stroke of misfortune, but it was a misfortune that their own lack of understanding of the dynamics of the imperial crisis had invited. Conservative leaders had assumed that any news of Great Britain's response to colonial resistance strategy, whether the response was mild or repressive, would hurt Congress; time, they were sure, would work to their advantage.[94] But about noon on March 8, the Bristol packet arrived with a letter from the Assembly's London agent, Benjamin Franklin, who wrote that Congress's petition to the Crown, when presented to George III by Lord Dartmouth, "was very graciously received, and . . . his Majesty had been pleased to say, it was of so great Importance, that he should, as soon as they met, lay it before his two Houses of Parliament."[95]

This news was a disaster for Joseph Galloway. Everywhere the cry went up that Congress had saved America. Galloway correctly foresaw the ministry's eventual cool reaction to Congress's petition, but several undecided legislators were impressed with the memorial's apparent success, which compared so favorably with the failure of their own House, under Galloway's leadership, to gain any favor with either Crown or Parliament.[96] Seizing the advantage, the radicals secured the votes of several wavering Chester and Philadelphia county assemblymen and, in Galloway's absence, rammed their reply to Penn through first and second readings on the afternoon of the eighth.

The next morning Galloway entered the House and charged the committee with dishonorable behavior in excluding him by deception from taking part in drafting the reply to Penn, and in ignoring his proposal, which the full chamber had just endorsed, that the final answer to Penn be deferred to the spring. But when he moved to recommit the draft, the Assembly rejected his request 22 to 15, and then

92. Galloway to Franklin, Mar. 26, 1775, *NJA*, X: 582–83; and *Votes and Proceedings*, VIII: 7210. Galloway says that fourteen members were appointed, of whom twelve opposed his motion, but the *Votes*, while confirming Galloway's proportions, list only thirteen members of the committee. No record of Dickinson's amendment appears to have survived, and the details of this day's maneuvers remain rather obscure.

93. Galloway to Franklin, Mar. 26, 1775, *NJA*, X: 583; *Votes and Proceedings*, VIII: 7211–12.

94. See Galloway to Verplanck, Jan. 14, 1774 [1775], "Galloway Letters," *PMHB*, XXI: 478, and to Franklin, Mar. 26, 1775, *NJA*, X: 579, 586.

95. *Votes and Proceedings*, VIII: 7216; Galloway to Franklin, Mar. 26, 1775, *NJA*, X: 583.

96. Galloway to Franklin, Mar. 26, 1775, *NJA*, X: 579. On Galloway's poor record with Crown and Parliament, see Hutson, *Pennsylvania Politics*, chap. 4.

approved the third reading of the radicals' answer to Penn by the same margin. Immediately the House transcribed its answer and delivered it to the governor. The reply blandly stated the legislators' great hopes that Congress's petition to the Crown would help to settle the present crisis and assured him that they would "always pursue such Measures, as shall appear to them necessary, for securing the Liberties of America, and establishing Peace, Confidence, and Harmony between Great Britain and her Colonies."[97]

The Assembly decision of March 9 was a crucial one for the resistance. It continued the division of the Quaker party into two hostile camps, which had begun in October, and terminated Joseph Galloway's career in the legislature. Galloway promptly withdrew from Assembly debates and again asked to be excused from service in Congress. In May the House granted his request.[98] His departure left Pennsylvania's most conservative lawmakers without a strong leader; thereafter they either reluctantly followed moderate patriot spokesmen or became pure obstructionists, a role that many were to have ample occasion to play when the Assembly, which rose in mid-March, reconvened on May 1.

The two roll call votes of March 9 are also a remarkably accurate indicator of the Assembly's resistance temper in early 1775. Galloway informs us that whenever he proposed a measure that was openly hostile to Congress, he lost by a margin of about 25 to 15, but that whenever he suggested deferring a commitment to congressional leadership, he won by roughly the same margin. He further remarks that between the mornings of March 8 and 9, he lost the support of several "weak and irresolute" delegates from Chester and Philadelphia counties. The House *Votes* gives the roll calls for the latter date.[99] Whenever conservative assemblymen were poorly led, which was whenever Joseph Galloway was absent, the radicals' resolves passed "unanimously," that is, by a margin of 25 to 15 or more, with the conservatives declining to ask for a roll call to record the division. When the conservatives were well led, however, neither a strong endorsement nor an emphatic rejection of congressional leadership was as popular as a postponement of the issue.

A detailed picture of the chamber's internal divisions makes this behavior more comprehensible. All eight Bucks County delegates, four more from Philadelphia County, two from Lancaster County, and one from Chester County were hard line conservatives (fifteen members). All nine voting frontier delegates (Speaker Biddle did not vote, except in a tie), both City burgesses, George Ross of Lancaster, Benjamin Bartholomew and Anthony Wayne of Chester, and John Dickinson and Joseph Parker of Philadelphia County consistently supported Congress (sixteen members). Two Philadelphia County delegates, five Chester County representatives, and one Lancaster County delegate were swing voters, men with a foot in both camps, open to rhetorical argument and easily swayed by the latest news from any quarter (see table 7).

An aggressive conservative leadership might have turned these divisions to advantage by taking the offensive, but Pennsylvania's conservative spokesmen never seized this opportunity. Their campaign to win over public opinion was too

97. Galloway to Franklin, Mar. 26, 1775, *NJA,* X: 583–84; *Votes and Proceedings,* VIII: 7211–12 (quotation).

98. *Votes and Proceedings,* VIII: 7234.

99. Galloway to Franklin, Mar. 26, 1775, *NJA,* X: 582, 584 (quotation); *Votes and Proceedings,* VIII: 7211–12.

TABLE 7

Assemblymen Classified According to Their Support for the Program of the First Continental Congress, March 1775

Pro-Congress		Swing Voters		Anti-Congress	
T. Mifflin	} City	G. Gray	} Philadelphia County	*I. Jacobs*	
C. Thomson		M. Hillegas		*H. Pawling*	} Philadelphia County
J. Dickinson	} Philadelphia County			*S. Rhoads*	
J. Parker		*J. Gibbons*		*J. Roberts*	
B. Bartholomew	} Chester	*C. Humphreys*	} Chester	*J. Pennock*	Chester
A. Wayne		*J. Jacobs*			
		I. Pearson		*J. Ferree*	} Lancaster
G. Ross	Lancaster	*J. Morton*		*J. Webb*	
J. Ewing	} York	M. Slough	Lancaster	*J. Brown*	
M. Swoope				B. Chapman	
W. Allen	} Cumberland			*J. Foulke*	
J. Montgomery				*J. Galloway*	} Bucks
(E. Biddle, speaker)	} Berks			*J. Heany*	
H. Chreist				*R. Kirkbride*	
W. Edmonds	Northampton			*W. Rodman*	
B. Daugherty	Bedford			G. Wynkoop	
S. Hunter	Northumberland				
W. Thompson	Westmoreland				
16 votes (not counting the speaker)		**8 votes**		**15 votes**	

Note: This table is based upon the roll call votes of March 4 and March 9, 1775, and upon the remarks of Joseph Galloway to William Franklin and Samuel Verplanck. Quakers in good standing, men of Quaker background and behavior, and men probably of Quaker background are italicized.

111

timid and ill timed to affect legislative action. Moreover, prominent conservatives proved incapable of capitalizing on John Dickinson's brief attack of doubt about the direction of the resistance in mid-January, perhaps because so few of them were personally close to him.[100] By February the "Farmer" had renewed his determination to resist the British ministry, and in the legislative battles of February 23–25 and March 8–9, he headed the radical forces. But in the final analysis, Pennsylvania's conservatives lacked strong leaders. Joseph Galloway was the only Pennsylvanian to play this role; one must assume that other conservative figures did not have the necessary courage. When Joseph Galloway made his last stand, he stood alone.

The decision of Pennsylvania's Assembly on March 9 to reject the conservative demand for an independent petition to the Crown in favor of continued support for Congress drove the last nail but one into tory hopes for the collapse of congressionally directed resistance in Pennsylvania; the last would be the news of the battles at Lexington and Concord. The initiative now lay entirely with the radicals. These zealots, though they could not yet join their compatriots to the north and south in public training for war, were finding other ways to increase their solidarity and intensify their patriotic ardor.

PATRIOT DEVOTION, RADICAL FORESHADOWING: THE AMERICAN MANUFACTORY

The Continental Association and the resolves of the provincial convention of January 1775 excited a keen interest in domestic manufactures in Pennsylvania, and beginning in March, political news and opinion in Philadelphia's newspapers yielded space to essays on manufacturing ventures and announcements of prizes to be awarded by local committees of inspection for establishing them.[101] Save as an emotional substitute for the military activity denied the zealous in January, however, these manufacturing endeavors were of little political importance, with one exception—the United Company of Philadelphia for Promoting American Manufactures.

The American Manufactory was an ambitious venture that raised substantial capital through subscription and employed several hundred persons idled by nonimportation in the spinning of coarse textiles.[102] This commercial concern apparently also served as an entryway into Philadelphia politics for several important ultraradical leaders in the Revolutionary movement. The Manufactory did not at

---

100. Dickinson is not known to have been personally hostile to any conservative leader except Galloway—a major exception to be sure; but although he was probably worshipping with the Quakers at this time (see Dickinson to ?, Aug. 25, 1776 [draft], p. 1, R. R. Logan Collection, HSP), there is no indication that he was especially friendly with any Quaker party Assembly leaders, or with Thomas Wharton, Sr., Dr. William Smith, Abel James, Henry Drinker, Samuel Shoemaker, or the Pembertons. His political friends were still radicals or moderates; his only close personal friend, apparently, was Charles Thomson.

101. *Pa. Gaz.,* Mar. 8, 15, and Apr. 5, 1775. Also see Schlesinger, *Colonial Merchants,* pp. 500–502.

102. Force, ed., *American Archives,* 4th Ser., II: 140–44; *Pa. Jour.,* Feb. 22; *Pa. Packet,* Mar. 6; *Pa. Gaz.,* Mar. 22; *Pa. Evening Post,* Apr. 11, 13, and Sept. 19, 1775; Schlesinger, *Colonial Merchants,* p. 502; Ammerman, *In the Common Cause,* p. 115.

first appear to be politicized; at the time of its formation only two of its officers sat on the Sixty-Six, and the majority of its directors had never been involved in formal political activity. But the subsequent careers of several of these men suggest that the United Company somehow functioned as much more than a patriotic commercial venture.

The Company held its first public meeting on March 16, at which time the subscribers evidently chose as their president Daniel Roberdeau, who delivered a speech on the virtues and advantages of domestic industry. The shareholders also named Joseph Stiles treasurer and James Cannon secretary, and elected twelve managers. There is no easy way to characterize this small group. Its members ranged in age from thirty to sixty-six; they included several Quakers, an Anglican, a Presbyterian, a Lutheran, and a Baptist; their assessed wealth covered nearly the whole spectrum of city taxpayers; and among their number were minor merchants, a brewer, a schoolmaster, a college mathematics professor, and a retired druggist. Yet the economic and social dimensions of this board of directors were unusual for either a major business firm or a public venture. Although few of these men were young or poor, fewer were either wealthy men themselves or members of wealthy Philadelphia families. Only Robert Strettel Jones could claim both family and fortune. Most of the Company's officers occupied a modest position in Philadelphia society; they were secure without being in any way prominent. Only six of the fifteen had ever been active in politics, and their political roles had been minor. There was little about these fifteen men to suggest that they would become important resistance figures (see table 8).[103]

Yet within the next eighteen months, Daniel Roberdeau was elected commander of the Pennsylvania militia and James Cannon became secretary of the ultraradical Committee of Privates, in which Joseph Stiles also figured prominently. Robert Strettel Jones was named a secretary of the city Committees of Observation and Inspection elected in August 1775 and February 1776, the most radical civilian boards chosen in the course of the resistance. Four other Manufactory directors—Isaac Howell, Frederick Kuhl, Christopher Ludwig, and Christopher Marshall, Sr.—also served on those civilian committees, all fairly prominently. Kuhl ran for the Assembly on the proindependence ticket in the May 1, 1776, by-election. Ludwig and Marshall were delegates to the June 1776 provincial conference that arranged for the termination of Pennsylvania's Constitution of 1701, and Kuhl and Cannon were delegates to the Constitutional Convention of 1776. James Cannon became the most important radical penman in Pennsylvania after Thomas Paine,

---

103. *Pa. Ledger,* Mar. 18, *Pa. Gaz.,* Mar. 22, 1775; Force, ed., *American Archives,* 4th Ser., II: 140. Several scholars, relying on a MS copy of the opening address in the Wetherill Papers, University of Pennsylvania, have claimed that Benjamin Rush was chosen president of the Manufactory (William R. Bagnall, *The Textile Industries of the United States* [1893], p. 64; Nathan G. Goodman, *Benjamin Rush: Physician and Citizen, 1746–1813* [1934], pp. 46–47; Lyman H. Butterfield, ed., *The Letters of Benjamin Rush* [1951], I: 90; and David Freeman Hawke, *Benjamin Rush, Revolutionary Gadfly* [1971], pp. 128–29). None of these scholars, however, acknowledges the evidentiary problem presented by the account in Force, *American Archives,* II: 140, which says that it was Roberdeau who was chosen president and gave the March 16 address. This writer, like Schlesinger and Ammerman before him (see note 102 above), follow Force's account of the Company's organization. If the prominent radical penman and strategist Benjamin Rush were in fact president, however, that would hardly damage the present argument.

TABLE 8

Officers of the American Manufactory, March 16, 1775

(See Table of Symbols, p. xi)

	Age	Occupation	Religion	1774 Tax Assessment	Prior Service 1774–75	Future Service 1775–76
President						
Roberdeau, Daniel	48	merchant	P?	£59		CS, militia colonel
Treasurer						
Stiles, Joseph		schoolmaster	Q	5		
Secretary						
Cannon, James	35	college teacher	A	25		1776 Convention
Managers						
Gray, Isaac	28	grocer	Q	1		
Howell, Isaac		brewer	Q	25	43	
Humphreys, Richard[a]		silversmith	Q	50		100,[1] 100[2]
Jones, Robert Strettel	30	merchant	B	104		100,[1] 100[2]
Kuhl, Frederick	47	gentleman		204		100,[1] 100,[2] 1776 Convention
Ludwig, Christopher	55	baker	L	99	43, 66	100,[1] 100[2]
Marshall, Christopher, Sr.	66	druggist (retired)	Q[disowned]	70		100,[1] 100[2]
Popham, James				?		
Tilbury, Thomas		shopkeeper		60		
Wells, Richard	41	merchant?		50		
Wetherill, Samuel, Jr.		shopkeeper	Q	6		
Winey, Jacob		merchant		35	66	

a. Or possibly Richard Humphreys, tailor, assessed £40 in 1772.

writing both the proindependence "Cassandra" letters and a large part of the radically democratic Pennsylvania Constitution of 1776.[104]

It is not clear why the American Manufactory served as an entry into Pennsylvania's resistance movement for these eight men, but the involvement of so many prominent young radicals in the American Manufactory at the outset of their political careers suggests two observations about the character of the resistance movement in Pennsylvania. First, the role of patriotic commercial associations in the coming of the Revolution may well deserve the attention commonly accorded political clubs and factions. Second, although Philadelphia politics between December 1774 and March 1775 centered largely on implementing a fully developed resistance strategy and lacked the crucial decisions and high drama of the months preceding and following it, the period ended in the formation of a commercial venture that had important political dimensions. This event points to the continuing operation of basic revolutionary processes in Philadelphia during this apparent hiatus. Behind the immediately apparent propaganda war and the debates in the Assembly lay more local and informal proceedings of the highest importance. As Pennsylvanians moved from commercial warfare to armed resistance, this spontaneous local political activity would take on a central role in the Revolution.

---

104. See chapters 6, 7, and 9 below. Hawke, *Midst of a Revolution*, pp. 102–6, identifies six men as the core of an essentially conspiratorial revolution in May–July 1776, of whom two, Cannon and Marshall (and possibly a third, Benjamin Rush), were officers of the American Manufactory.

Chapter

6

Pennsylvanians Take up Arms

. . . in a State of Political Society and Government all Men, by their original Compact and Agreement, are obligated to unite in defending themselves.[1]

The Philadelphia Committee of Observation
October 31, 1775

On the evening of April 24, 1775, the news of the battles at Lexington and Concord reached the City of Brotherly Love. The first reports of these conflicts, everywhere electrifying, were doubly so in Philadelphia. Alone among American colonists, Pennsylvanians had never known compulsory military service.[2] For this reason, the political transformation that occurred in the next six months was among the most comprehensive in Pennsylvania's history. The Assembly put the province on a thorough defense footing, legislating militia service and voting large sums for war. Public discussion of public policy subsided at once, and for the first time active dissent from the majority will approached the status of a high crime.

This transformation could only subject Pennsylvanians to great emotional stress. The mutual resentment existing between strict Quakers and zealous patriots quickly grew more bitter as each side, discovering that it could no longer afford to ignore the behavior of the other, turned from espousing distinctive resistance strategies to advocating diametrically opposed views of the proper goals for civil society. At the same time, however, their deepening antagonisms were increasingly repressed as an exuberant display of patriotic ardor terminated public controversy. All opposition to congressionally directed armed resistance became covert—and treasonable. The rational, voluntary unity of 1774 yielded in 1775 to the mandatory zeal of the true patriot.

PENNSYLVANIA PREPARES FOR WAR

On April 25, 1775, several thousand Philadelphians gathered in the State House Yard and agreed to associate in neighborhood militia units to defend their rights,

---

1. *Votes and Proceedings,* VIII: 7336.
2. The Pennsylvania Assembly had authorized the raising of voluntary militia forces in the 1740s and 1750s to engage the French and their Indian allies.

property, and lives. No identification of this assembly's leaders has survived, but the Philadelphia Committee of Observation—the Sixty-Six—was deeply involved in organizing Philadelphia's militia from the outset and probably called the meeting.[3] Although Philadelphia's armed forces had no legal foundation, their growth was rapid. The associators immediately began martial exercises, and expenses mounted rapidly; in early May, Philadelphians petitioned the Assembly for the emission of £50,000 in paper currency for Pennsylvania's defense, and the Sixty-Six sought reimbursement from the legislature for military expenses already incurred.[4] By May 10, over thirty companies had formed, including one of young Quakers who trained in the yard of the American Manufactory.[5] The response in rural Pennsylvania was equally zealous. Berks County boasted two companies as early as April 26, and Lancaster County associated on May 1. In the next three weeks, Philadelphia, Bucks, Bedford, Chester, Westmoreland, and Northampton counties associated, and Cumberland's farmers voted the astonishing sum of £27,000 for their county's defense.[6]

When the Assembly convened on May 1, an extraconstitutional army was springing up all around it and demanding to be legitimized and funded. The House was now under the leadership of John Morton, a moderate Quaker party veteran from Chester County, who had replaced the ailing Edward Biddle as speaker in mid-March. Morton and his colleagues were not eager to fund an armed force, but both the news of Lexington-Concord and Franklin's most recent letter to the lawmakers, which recounted the ministry's contemptuous treatment of Congress's petition to the King, shattered their illusions of a quick and peaceful settlement of the imperial crisis. To Joseph Galloway's chagrin, this rebuff only stiffened the Assembly's resolve to support Congress.[7]

On May 2, Governor Penn, at Dartmouth's behest, recommended to the House Lord North's new plan of accommodation, whereby each colony might, by making an annual contribution to the British treasury that was satisfactory to both Crown and Parliament, secure an exemption from all imperial taxes.[8] After brief debate, the House returned a cool rejection of North's offer, written by John Dickinson. Their aim in resisting the claims of Parliament, the lawmakers asserted, had ever been to establish the right "that all Aids from them should be their own free and voluntary Gifts, not taken by Force, nor extorted by Fear. Under which of these Descriptions [the ministry's proposal] deserves to be classed, we chuse rather to submit to the Determination of your Honour's good Sense, than to attempt proving by the Ennumeration of notorious Facts, or the Repetition of obvious Reasons."[9]

---

3. See *Pa. Gaz.,* Apr. 26, 1775; *Pa. Evening Post,* Apr. 29, 1775; *Votes and Proceedings,* VIII: 7232–33; and *Pa. Archives,* 2d Ser., III: 655.

4. *Votes and Proceedings,* VIII: 7230, 7232–33.

5. *Pa. Jour.,* May 10, 1775; Duane, ed., *Passages from Marshall,* p. 25 (May 3).

6. *Pa. Jour.,* May 3 (Berks); "Committee of Safety, Lancaster County," MS volume of minutes, Force Collection, Library of Congress, p. 20; *Pa. Jour.,* May 10 (Cumberland); *Pa. Gaz.,* May 3 (Philadelphia and Bucks counties); *Pa. Jour.,* June 14 (Bedford); *Pa. Gaz.,* May 10 (Chester); *Pa. Gaz.,* Aug. 9 (Westmoreland notice dated May 16); and *Pa. Evening Post,* June 10, 1775 (Northampton). The first meetings of associators in York and Northumberland counties were not reported in the press, but they definitely occurred in May.

7. On Morton's election, see *Votes and Proceedings,* VIII: 7217 (Mar. 14–15, 1775); on the February 5, 1775, letter from the Assembly's agents, ibid., pp. 7221–23.

8. *Votes and Proceedings,* VIII: 7223–25.

9. *Votes and Proceedings,* VIII: 7226–30, quotation on p. 7228.

Whatever effect this reply may have had upon the earl of Dartmouth or Lord North, it convinced John Penn. In the remaining fourteen months before Independence, the governor never referred to the imperial crisis. Contenting himself with performing his usual executive functions on every occasion the House afforded him, he simply ignored the legislators' unconstitutional seizure of extraordinary executive powers for themselves.

The Assembly confirmed its decision to stand with Congress by making three additions to its congressional delegation on May 6. Benjamin Franklin, now a firm patriot, had arrived from England on the previous day; Thomas Willing and James Wilson had been proposed to the Galloway House as congressmen nine months earlier by the first provincial congress. Their appointment and the Assembly's vote the following week to excuse Galloway from service in Congress put Pennsylvania's delegation firmly in the resistance camp.[10] And on May 9, the House at last approved instructions to their congressmen. This brief directive, although nearly identical to the one issued in 1774, no longer spoke of avoiding "every Thing indecent or disrespectful to the Mother State."[11]

This still heavily Quaker legislature was less eager to involve itself directly in armed resistance. The Philadelphians' petition for a £50,000 currency issue and the Sixty-Six's request that it be reimbursed for military expenses occasioned several days of debate. Finally the House allocated small amounts for military expenses that would not require the emission of new bills of credit, granting the Sixty-Six £2,000, and empowering an unusually radical committee of legislators to spend up to £5,000 for essential supplies.[12] On the next day, May 13, the assemblymen adjourned for six weeks, during which time the House leadership hoped to assess Pennsylvania's military needs more accurately.

Even before the Assembly adjourned, Philadelphia's militia had organized into thirty-one companies, grouped into three battalions and an artillery unit, and elected over one hundred and fifty officers. The associators named twenty-nine members of the Sixty-Six to this first officers' corps on May 10, and these committee leaders dominated the upper ranks of the corps, supplying thirteen of the twenty-eight infantry captains, five of the six majors, and four of the six lieutenant colonels and colonels. Joseph Reed, chairman of the Sixty-Six until late June, and John Nixon, who presided over the committee in Reed's absence in July, both became lieutenant colonels, and John Cox, John Bayard, Thomas Mifflin, and Samuel Meredith, all committee leaders, became majors (see table 9).[13] This close identity between the civilian and military leadership of the resistance insured that the Committee of Observation and the Committee of Officers of the Military Association would work smoothly together.

Despite a widespread popular commitment to resist the ministry by all necessary means, however, the prospects for Pennsylvania's defense remained uncertain in May and early June. The militia had neither firm rules to guide it nor assured financial support. Moreover, scarcely more than a third of the able-bodied men in

---

10. *Votes and Proceedings,* VIII: 7231, 7234.
11. *Votes and Proceedings,* VIII: 7232–33; compare pp. 7100–01.
12. *Votes and Proceedings,* VIII: 7230–34. The committee included Dickinson, Mifflin, Thomson, Anthony Wayne, and seven other radicals from the western and frontier counties.
13. See the Peters Papers, vol. 8, pp. 44, 71, HSP.

TABLE 9

Militia Officers and Members of the Sixty-six, May 10, 1775

Colonels	*Lieutenant Colonels*
1. *Dickinson, John*	1. Chevalier, John
2. Roberdeau, Daniel	2. *Reed, Joseph*
3. *Cadwalader, John*	3. *Nixon, John*

Majors

1. Morgan, Jacob
   Coats, William
2. *Cox, John*
   Bayard, John
3. *Mifflin, Thomas*
   Meredith, Samuel

Captains

1. *Irvine, James*	
Hassenclever, Francis	
Williams, John	
Leib, George	
Goodman, George	3. Morgan, George
Wood, Joseph	Willing, Richard
Eyres, Emmanuel	Sprout, David
Williams, Enion	*Knox, Robert*
Copperthwaite, Joseph	Wharton, John
2. *Prior, Thomas*	*Cadwalader, Lambert*
Shee, John	*Gurney, Francis*
Wilcocks, John	*Clymer, George*
Bradford, William	Faulkner, John
Furman, Moore	
Wade, Francis	
Peters, Richard	
Todd, William	
Semple, William	
Keppele, John	

Ensigns in Chief	*Artillery Officers*
1. Jones, Robert Strettel	Mifflin, [John?]
2. Allen, William	*Loxley, Benjamin*
3. Tilghman, Richard	Moulder, [John?]
	Biddle, [?]

Note: All officers are listed in the order in which they appear in the Peters Papers, VIII, ff. 44 and 71, HSP, with their respective battalions, of which there were three in May 1775. All members of the Sixty-Six are italicized.

Philadelphia had associated.[14] Civilian and militia leaders alike believed that the solution to these problems would come only with a full awakening to the military challenge by the two bodies upon which Pennsylvanians were still emotionally dependent for leadership, the Congress and the Assembly.

The rapid escalation of tension and violence in New England soon settled this issue, for Congress was forced to act. For their part, Philadelphia's associators encouraged Congress's commitment to armed resistance by staging military reviews for the members. Congress responded in mid-June by voting to raise eight rifle battalions in Pennsylvania for a new Continental Army, appointing George Washington Commander-in-Chief of that army, and resolving to issue two million dollars in paper currency to finance their forces.[15] These measures could not have been better timed to transform Pennsylvania's military condition. The Assembly, which convened on June 19 to reassess Pennsylvania's defense, received Congress's request for rifle battalions on June 24. At the same time the legislators learned of the battle of Bunker Hill, which dispelled any lingering hopes that Great Britain would not suppress armed resistance with determination.[16]

Seizing the advantage, the Sixty-Six immediately asked the Assembly to guarantee Pennsylvania's military associators pay for active service in opposing any invading force, to fortify Philadelphia against attack by warships, and to empower several House members to act as a "Committee of Safety and Defense." This standing executive board would supervise the entire province's military preparations and conduct. Several officers of the Philadelphia militia promptly endorsed this petition.[17] The combined pressure of Philadelphia's Committee of Observation, the city's militia, and Congress was of critical importance because the House seemed still to be inclined to temporize. But Governor Penn's veto of a special £22,000 money bill, which the Assembly may have designed to raise covert funds for war, together with local and congressional demands, at last forced the legislators to realize an obvious fact.[18] If they wanted to have the guiding role in defending Pennsylvania, they would have to raise large amounts of money openly and spend it through an executive of their own creation. On June 27, after lengthy debate on the Sixty-Six's petition urging this policy, the House appointed ten legislators to frame the necessary resolves. On June 30, following two more days of debate, the drafting committee's program passed intact.[19]

---

14. The *Pennsylvania Gazette* of May 3 predicted that Philadelphia would soon have 4,000 men under arms, but only about 1,800 participated in the review of June 10, the first in the presence of Congress (*Pa. Packet,* June 12, 1775). By the most conservative population estimate for the city and suburbs (Warner, *Private City,* p. 12), there must have been at least 5,000 men able to bear arms in Philadelphia in 1775.

15. Burnett, *Continental Congress,* pp. 67–73, 75, 76, 82; *Journals,* II: 89, 91, 103, 104. The Philadelphia militia staged reviews for Congress on June 10, 12, and 20 (*Pa. Ledger,* June 10; *Pa. Packet,* June 12; *Pa. Gaz.,* June 21, 1775).

16. *Votes and Proceedings,* VIII: 7241; Burnett, *Continental Congress,* p. 83.

17. *Votes and Proceedings,* VIII: 7237–40, 7241.

18. *Votes and Proceedings,* VIII: 7236–37, 7240, 7242, 7243. Because it was unusual for the Assembly to pass a money bill on short notice in the spring, and because the notes were to be funded by an excise tax on liquors, a device which the House had earlier used to create large amounts of unrestricted revenue (see James H. Hutson, "Benjamin Franklin and Pennsylvania Politics, 1751–1755: A Reappraisal," *PMHB,* XCIII [1969]: 322), it seems likely that the bill's purpose was to help fund defense expenses.

19. *Votes and Proceedings,* VIII: 7242–49. The committee included the radical leaders John Dickinson, Charles Thomson, Anthony Wayne, and George Ross; the moderates George

Pennsylvania's first comprehensive plan for defense explicitly endorsed the local military associations, promised to pay all soldiers who defended Pennsylvania from invasion by land or sea, and ordered that 4,500 muskets be made for a corps of minutemen. The program made specific provision for the defense of the Delaware River, offered bounties for saltpeter production, and authorized the emission of £35,000 in paper currency that would be funded by new taxes on all real and personal estates. But the Assembly's most important political action was the appointment of twenty-five persons to form a Committee of Safety. This body would be Pennsylvania's real executive branch for the next eighteen months.

The Committee's initial membership illustrates the relative strengths of moderate and radical elements at the highest level of the resistance in 1775, and of the degree of cooperation between them.[20] The board was almost evenly divided between assemblymen from throughout the province and prominent local leaders from Philadelphia and Chester, the two towns of prime concern in any plan of defense. The House named one assemblyman from each interior county and two each from Philadelphia and Chester; all were moderate to radical on imperial issues, and most were already prominent resistance leaders. John Dickinson and George Gray spoke for Philadelphia County; the young zealots Anthony Wayne and Benjamin Bartholomew represented Chester; and George Ross and Edward Biddle sat for Lancaster and Berks (see table 10).[21]

The twelve nonassemblymen were a more varied collection of moderates and radicals, but all were firmly committed to armed resistance, and all had excellent qualifications for service. The congressman, merchant prince, and Pennsylvania Supreme Court justice Thomas Willing and Attorney General Andrew Allen were leaders of the proprietary faction, whose adherence to the cause was considered essential. Elder statesman Benjamin Franklin was both a congressman and the most widely respected man in Pennsylvania. Daniel Roberdeau and John Cadwalader commanded Philadelphia's second and third militia battalions. Francis Johnston and Richard Reiley were resistance leaders in the borough of Chester, which Pennsylvanians feared would be a prime target for British warships. Samuel Morris, Jr. and Thomas Wharton, Jr. were prominent Quaker merchants who had amply demonstrated their devotion to the cause, Morris by joining Philadelphia's elite First City Troop of cavalry upon its formation in November 1774, Wharton through service on the Nineteen and the Forty-Three. Robert Morris, Willing's business partner, had served on both the Forty-Three and the Sixty-Six. Owen

---

Gray and Michael Hillegas, Philadelphia County veterans, who had acquired considerable expertise in managing the province's finances; and Isaac Pearson and William Rodman, conservative Quaker veterans from Chester and Bucks counties, who were becoming convinced of the necessity of armed resistance. The *Votes* does not record the proposal of any amendments to the committee's plan; therefore it was probably accepted whole.

20. For the period April–November 1775, I label those Philadelphians "radical" who favored a vigorous armed resistance against British authority in America, who worked to create an effective war machine in Pennsylvania, who concurred in the popular demand to silence local tories by public ostracism and intimidation, and who, in October 1775, insisted on the inauguration of compulsory militia service throughout Pennsylvania. In addition, radical merchants continued to welcome new leaders from the mechanic classes, as they had done in June and November 1774, and to test established merchant and professional leaders for the intensity of their commitment to the resistance. Many "moderates" opposed compulsory militia service, and all adhered to older, elitist leadership patterns. "Conservatives" increasingly became disaffected tories, who were forced into silence by community pressure.

21. *Votes and Proceedings,* VIII: 7247.

TABLE 10

The First Committee of Safety, Appointed June 30, 1775

(See Table of Symbols, p. xi)

	Age	Occupation	Religion	1774 Tax Assessment (City Only)	Prior Service (Since 1773)
Assemblymen					
Bartholomew, Benjamin (Chester)	23	farmer	B		?
Biddle, Edward (Berks)	37	lawyer	A		Berks committees
Daugherty, Bernhard (Bedford)	?	?	?		j.p.
Dickinson, John (Philadelphia)	43	lawyer	Q[lapsed]	£710	19, 43, 66, militia colonel
Edmunds, William (Northampton)	?	farmer	Moravian?		Northampton committees
Gray, George (Philadelphia)	49	ferry-owner	A	389	43, Philadelphia County committee
Hunter, Samuel (Northumberland)	?	?	?		?
Montgomery, John (Cumberland)	?	farmer	P		Cumberland committees
Ross, George (Lancaster)	45	lawyer	A		Lancaster committees
Swoope, Michael (York)	?	?	?		York committees
Thompson, William (Westmoreland)	?	?	?		?
Wayne, Anthony (Chester)	30	tanner	A		Chester committees
Wynkoop, Henry (Bucks)	28	?	Dutch P		?
City of Philadelphia and Borough of Chester					
Allen, Andrew	35	lawyer	P	290	attorney general, Gov. Council
Biddle, Owen	28	merchant	Q	8	66
Cadwalader, John	33	merchant	A	143	66, militia colonel
Franklin, Benjamin	69	public servant	Deist	330	Congress
Johnston, Francis (Chester)	27	lawyer	P?	116	Chester committees
Morris, Robert	41	merchant	A	152	43, 66
Morris, Samuel, Jr.	41	merchant	Q		?
Reiley, Richard (Chester)	?	shopkeeper	?		Chester committees
Roberdeau, Daniel	48	merchant	P?	59	militia colonel
Wharton, Thomas, Jr.	40	merchant	Q[disowned]	86	19, 66
White, Robert[a]	ca. 35–40	mariner	A	8	tea committee?
Willing, Thomas	44	merchant	A	533	43, Congress, Justice of Pa. Supreme Court

a. Also Whyte; this is probably the same man who served on the 1773 tea committee.

123

Biddle and Robert White, the only men without fortune on the board, were also useful, Biddle as a zealous Quaker watchmaker and petty merchant, White as a ship captain with a sound knowledge of the naval problems facing the board.

Pennsylvania's Committee of Safety was an eminently respectable body; its members were established leaders of the province's component local elites rather than young men without family or fortune, like those who were playing so prominent a role on the Sixty-Six and in the militia. Moreover, the board included several moderate figures, notably Thomas Willing, Andrew Allen, Robert Morris, and the increasingly cautious John Dickinson. In June 1775, the Committee's socially elitist and ideologically inclusive character was of the greatest importance. The board's several members together had excellent connections with every important socio-economic group in the province and with men of every widely held attitude toward the resistance, with the exception of the strict Quakers.

The Assembly's initial defense plan provided all that its constituents had requested and all that Pennsylvania appeared to need for its security, so the lawmakers adjourned to September. In two respects, however, their work remained unfinished. They had not offered adequate compensation for military service in the field, thereby causing those citizens without substantial means to decline active duty; and the militia that they did fund was voluntary. No penalties were applied against those who chose not to bear arms. Instead, the legislators recommended to the associators "that they bear a tender and brotherly Regard towards [all pacifists]; and to these conscientious People it is also recommended, that they chearfully assist, in Proportion to their Abilities, such Associators as cannot spend their Time and Subsistence in the public Service without great injury to themselves and Families."[22]

In the summer of 1775, Pennsylvania's legislators were still hoping to defend their province without offending or inconveniencing the Quakers. On June 30, they believed that their strategy was sound. Their achievement was unquestionably remarkable. For the first time since the onset of the imperial crisis a decade before, all elements of Pennsylvania's government were working smoothly together, with the full cooperation of the great majority of the province's citizens.

THE APPEARANCE OF DISUNITY IN THE RESISTANCE

The dramatic outpouring of patriotic zeal following Lexington-Concord insured that routine resistance activities would proceed smoothly in Philadelphia. Committee vigilance and public outrage easily frustrated attempts by local Quaker firms and English merchants to break the boycott in June and July, and the transition from nonimportation to Congress's total embargo of Anglo-American trade in September was without incident.[23] And Philadelphia's radicals discovered that

---

22. *Votes and Proceedings,* VIII: 7249.

23. *Pa. Gaz.,* May 3, 31, June 14, 28, July 7, Aug. 31, 1775; Duane, ed., *Passages from Marshall,* p. 24 (Apr. 29); letters of James & Drinker to several foreign firms, dated Apr. 29, May 27, 29, June 1, 5, 1775, Henry Drinker Letter-Book (foreign), HSP; Burnett, *Continental Congress,* pp. 93–94; *Journals,* II: 123–25, 173, 177, 184, 185, 200–201, 202, 238–39. The committee's only failure was its inability to hold down the price of scarce commodities (see Schlesinger, *Colonial Merchants,* p. 500).

the expression of anti-Congress opinion was as easy to check as commercial individualism. On April 29, Jabez Fisher, a bold and disaffected young Quaker, was publicly humiliated for submitting a letter to the *Pennsylvania Ledger* that questioned the commitment of a county in neighboring Delaware to congressional policy; shortly thereafter, Fisher, James Rivington's best local correspondent, left for England, never to return. Soon other critics of the resistance made contrite apologies for their sins, and local conservative journals grew quiet.[24] The Quakers, too, were silent. The Society of Friends now turned from conservative public testimonies to the charitable relief of all those suffering from the war in New England. Many young Friends rushed to arms, but here the elders stood firm; quiet disownment proceedings soon severed hundreds of Quakers from their ancestral faith, beginning with Thomas Mifflin in July.[25] Quaker pacifism now became a more private affair, however; for several months Philadelphia's Friends would issue no more of the public "bulls" that had excited Joseph Reed's scorn in January.

Behind Philadelphia's evident unanimity for the cause, however, certain quiet alterations in committee leadership marked the appearance of deep divisions within the resistance. The actors in this shadowy conflict were as reticent about contention in their ranks as anyone familiar with the history of resistance activity would expect them to be. Yet the surface turbulence generated by their deep struggle suggests the character of the conflict. In late June, the Sixty-Six lost Thomas Mifflin and Joseph Reed to the new Continental Army. John Dickinson and Charles Thomson, the elder statesmen of the resistance, had already turned away from Philadelphia affairs to the Assembly and to Congress. By July, new leaders were directing the resistance in Philadelphia. George Clymer and John Nixon, who had been active committeemen since the tea affair, chaired the Sixty-Six. Also prominent were John Bayard, John Cox, and John Bayard Smith, all veterans of the summer of 1774, and John Benezet and Samuel Meredith, who had become committeemen only in November.

The particular circumstances surrounding Reed's departure, and certain events in the summer and fall, however, point not to an orderly transition in resistance leadership, but to a series of decisive shakeups. Only days after signing the Sixty-Six's petition to the June Assembly session for financial support for the militia, the most important committee document since December 1774, the board's chairman Joseph Reed startled the entire city by accepting an appointment as George Washington's secretary. Leaving Philadelphia in a military escort for the general on June 23, Reed planned to return that same day, but he accepted Washington's offer en route and continued straight to New England, where he remained

---

24. Duane, ed., *Passages from Marshall*, pp. 24 (Apr. 29), 24–25 (May 2), 35 (July 17); Miers Fisher to Jabez Fisher, May 14, 1775, Joshua Francis Fisher Papers, HSP; *Pa. Gaz.*, July 19, Aug. 16, 1775. Jabez Fisher's correspondence with loyalists in other colonies, and especially with Rivington, was strongly suspected by Philadelphia's radicals as early as February 1775 (see Force, ed., *American Archives*, 4th Ser., I: 1270). On the letter that Fisher received from Kent County, Delaware, and published, see *Pa. Ledger*, Feb. 11; *Pa. Gaz.*, Feb. 23; *Rivington's N.-Y. Gaz.*, Feb. 23; and *American Archives*, 4th Ser., I: 1231–32, 1233.

25. Duane, ed., *Passages from Marshall*, p. 35 (July 9); *Pa. Jour.*, July 12; *Pa. Gaz.*, July 19; *Pa. Ledger*, July 22, 1775; "Minutes of the Philadelphia Monthly Meeting, 1771–1777," pp. 319–20, and "Minutes of the Southern District Monthly Meeting, 1772–1777," p. 102, Friends Historical Library, Swarthmore College.

until October. His correspondence with his closest friends explains his last-minute decision: sometime in the spring he had led a quiet purge of certain leaders of the Sixty-Six, who now harbored strong resentments against him. Service in the Continental Army provided an honorable escape from a position which this sensitive leader found uncomfortable.[26] Yet Reed did not totally surrender his power in Philadelphia; through his friends John Bayard and John Cox he remained a vital presence in committee politics. Two subsequent events suggest the continuation of divisions within the committee movement. In the election for a new city committee in August, the public had at least three tickets from which to choose, each presenting candidates of a distinct socio-economic and ideological character.[27] And in October the radicals ran Charles Thomson and Thomas Pryor, a wealthy but politically obscure city committeeman, against the well-known moderates Samuel Miles and Robert Morris for two Assembly seats being vacated by Quakers in moderate Philadelphia County.[28]

The character of these events marks the summer of 1775 as a turning point in Pennsylvania's Revolutionary movement. As resistance leaders triumphed over their opponents to fill the entire political horizon, they began to lose the cohesion that had insured their victory. The arming of the province created or strengthened a host of institutions that had both overlapping memberships and distinct political, economic, and social characteristics. By mid-summer, the Assembly, the Committee of Safety, local committees of observation, committees of militia officers, and committees of militia privates all competed for the loyalties of patriotic Pennsylvanians. These institutional conflicts, however, masked a much larger struggle. By 1775, cautious elder leaders were fighting to retain that ultimate political authority sought so aggressively by radical young zealots; moderate and radical clusters within the movement became quietly warring factions. Disinterested patriot leaders were caught in the middle, trying to preserve a united resistance as all old political alliances began to disintegrate. The conflict between largely civilian elites of different character was one origin of Pennsylvania's growing factional controversy; the other was the sudden appearance of bitter dissent in the militia rank and file, which quickly developed both cultural and class targets.

The Assembly's June 30 defense resolves created a military machine that grew rapidly in power, refinement, and complexity. The Sixty-Six immediately organized a saltpeter manufactory, while the purchase of gunpowder, the defense of the city's waterfront, and the procurement of arms and medical supplies proceeded

---

26. John Cox to Reed, July 26, Charles Pettit to Reed, Aug. 10, 17, and Cox to Reed, Sept. 9, 1775, Reed Papers, N.-Y. Hist. Soc.; and Reed to Elias Boudinot, Aug. 13, 1775, Gratz Collection, HSP. Pettit (Aug. 10) mentioned a campaign to damage Reed's reputation by revealing his correspondence of December 1773–February 1775 with the earl of Dartmouth. "I know not where to fix the Malice of this Attempt," Pettit wrote, "but it seemed to be strongly tinctured with Buttonwood Balls—perhaps it is the Produce of some that fell when you shook the [this?] Tree so hard some Time ago." Unfortunately, Pettit does not explain his cryptic remark. Reed's uneasiness over his political role in the Sixty-Six earlier in the year appears in Reed to [Pettit?], Feb. 25, 1775, Reed Papers, N.-Y. Hist. Soc.

27. Broadside tickets, Philadelphia Library Company, catalogued Am 1775 Phi Com, 962.F.70, 71, 73 (Evans No. 14385). These tickets will be discussed below.

28. *Pa. Evening Post,* Oct. 3, 1775; Duane, ed., *Passages from Marshall,* pp. 49–50 (Oct. 3, 4); Marshall to "S. H.," Oct. 31, 1775, Marshall Letter-Book, p. 151, HSP; Henry Drinker to Benjamin Booth, Oct. 3, 1775, Drinker Letter-Book (domestic), HSP.

smoothly under the guidance of the energetic Committee of Safety.[29] Congress gave Pennsylvanians needed reassurance and direction by issuing its "Declaration of the Causes and Necessities of Taking Up Arms," and by publishing general rules for military service, a common plan for the militia and minutemen in every province, and a pay scale for the Continental Army, which nicely complemented the brief provisions made by the Assembly.[30]

In this atmosphere of enthusiastic cooperation between continental, provincial, and local bodies, Philadelphia's newly formed Committee of Officers of the Military Association sought to perfect the organization of its forces by securing every associator's pledge to observe the new congressional militia plan. To involve the entire community, the city's militia commanders held a meeting of all officers in both the city and the surrounding county, and of all committeemen on both city and county boards. On July 22, with the Sixty-Six's Lieutenant Colonel John Nixon in the chair, and the great majority of the officers and at least half of each civilian committee in attendance, the gathering resolved to submit Congress's militia plan to the associators at once.[31] Under this plan, every male between the ages of sixteen and fifty was urged, but not required, to associate under arms. One-fourth of the associators were required to train constantly so they would always be ready to take the field, but they received no pay for training.[32] The July 22 meeting directed each captain in the city and county to poll his men to determine their allegiance to these provisions and to report the results to his colonel. The officers and committeemen agreed to meet again on July 31, when each colonel would report his battalion's decision.

The secretary of the Committee of Officers, Captain Richard Peters, Jr., began the survey by polling his company, but every man refused Congress's terms, claiming that the plan neither provided for the sacrifice in time which regular training demanded—and which poor men could not afford—nor supported the associators' families while their breadwinners were away on campaign. In the next few days, every company rejected the plan, most of them unanimously.[33] On July 31, the assembled officers and committeemen concluded that Philadelphia's military association must fail unless they could secure fresh articles of association tailored to their specific needs.

Yet the officers did not seek more funds to pay the associators for training and to support their families during an invasion, although that alone appeared to be a likely remedy for the militia's unrest. Probably they believed that there was little hope of calling the House into irregular session to appropriate funds before September, and while they apparently considered calling another provincial convention to do something, they quickly dropped this notion. Instead, they elected to use their great political and social authority and that of the Committee of Safety

---

29. *Pa. Gaz.,* July 5, 1775; Committee of Safety proceedings in *Minutes of the Provincial Council,* vol. X of *Colonial Records* (Harrisburg, Pa., 1852), immediately following the Council Minutes, 277 ff. (hereafter *Minutes*). The transactions for July 10–August 15 appear on pp. 285–305.

30. *Journals,* II: 128–57 ("Causes of . . . Taking Up Arms"), pp. 111–22 (rules for military service), pp. 187–90 (the militia plan), p. 220 (the pay scale).

31. *Pa. Gaz.,* July 19, 1775; Peters Papers, vol. 8, p. 65, HSP (this lists all of the civilian committeemen and many of the officers who attended this meeting).

32. *Journals,* II: 187–90, 220.

33. Peters Papers, vol. 8, pp. 54–64; HSP.

to recommend to the associators a set of militia rules, newly prepared by the Committee of Safety, without a pay plan.[34] These rules, while necessary, totally ignored the economic grievances of the associators. Yet another, more explosive issue, which few companies voiced in July but which many associators probably felt this early, was the demand that militia service be required of all citizens, with monetary fines for those who refused to bear arms. But in July, the associators did not push this demand, so obviously liable to create bitter conflicts with the Quakers, and their officers ignored it, only to have to face squarely both this grievance and the general problem of compensation for training in the fall.[35] Thus matters stood as the city faced another grand committee election to shape the direction of the resistance for the next six months.

ANOTHER STEP TO THE LEFT: THE FIRST ONE HUNDRED

In November 1774 the Sixty-Six had been elected to serve until the next adjournment of Congress, when a new committee would be chosen. Congress rose on August 2, 1775; five days later, the Sixty-Six announced that its successor would be elected on August 16 and recommended the creation of an expanded board of one hundred members, seventy-six for the corporate City and twelve each for the Northern Liberties and Southwark.[36] Vigorous politicking filled the nine days following this notice. On August 10, "Mentor," writing in the *Evening Post* on behalf of "a great number of the inhabitants," asked that "lists of the persons proposed [for committee service] may be printed and distributed two or three days before the election, that they may have leisure to deliberate thereon, and make such alterations as may be thought necessary." Both this suggestion and a request by Southwark that its residents be allowed to ballot for their twelve delegates separately were heeded, and at least three different tickets quickly appeared.[37]

The winning list, named the "mechanics' ticket" by a contemporary, was the obvious successor to the radical-mechanic slate of November 1774.[38] Of its eighty-eight nominees, only three suffered defeat, apparently through widespread altera-

34. The transactions of July 31 appear in Peters Papers, vol. 8, p. 65. At the bottom of p. 43 in the same volume is an undated draft motion to request the Committee of Observation of Philadelphia (the Sixty-Six) to call another provincial convention. This motion was probably made at the July 31 meeting of officers, or possibly at some unrecorded meeting about this time. The work of the Committee of Safety on the militia rules appears in *Minutes,* pp. 297–98 (Aug. 3, 4, 1775). Also see Peters Papers, vol. 8, p. 66.

35. Of the thirteen companies whose votes have survived in Peters' records, only two are mentioned as giving the relatively small number of citizens who had associated as a reason for refusing to subscribe to the congressional plan (Peters Papers, vol. 8, pp. 59, 63).

36. *Pa. Gaz.,* Nov. 9, 1774, Aug. 9, 1775.

37. *Pa. Gaz.,* Aug. 16, 1775 (committee transactions of August 15). Southwark apparently asked for the exclusive right to vote for her twelve committee seats, letting the corporate City and the Northern Liberties vote jointly for the other eighty-eight. Both the "radical-mechanic" and the "conservative" tickets omitted candidates for Southwark (see notes 38–40, 42 in this chapter, and chapter 8 below).

38. "Committee/ For the City of Philadelphia, to be and continue until the 16th/ day of February A.D. 1776, and no longer" [broadside, Evans No. 14385], Library Company, Am 1775 Phi Com, 962.F.70. In manuscript at the bottom appears "This is called the mechanicks' Ticket." For the full ticket, see Appendix L. This and the other tickets are discussed in considerable detail in chapter 8 below.

tions made by hand in the printed ticket. Although this slate was manifestly the work of the same alliance of radical merchants and artisans that had won in November, it was almost certainly not composed by the Sixty-Six itself, because twenty-two veterans of that board were left off the list. While the majority of those dropped were obscure figures, one deletion was significant: the mechanics chose not to support the Sixty-Six's acting chairman, Lieutenant Colonel John Nixon. Nixon had the reputation of being a moderate, yet the radicals retained other prominent moderates, like Robert Morris and John Allen, suggesting that Nixon had suffered a particular fall from their favor. But the men added to this ticket were more indicative of its character than any who were deleted. Most of these newcomers appeared only on the mechanics' list and included several persons who were soon to be important radical leaders, most notably Robert Strettel Jones and Timothy Matlack. Two more key radical recruits, Christopher Marshall, Sr. and Isaac Howell, also appeared on the most conservative ticket, and three others, Thomas Wharton, Jr., Samuel Morris, Jr., and Delaware's congressman Thomas McKean, appeared on all three lists.

Moderate and conservative political leaders in Philadelphia, despite their defeat in the winter and spring, were far better organized in August than they had been the previous November: in a single week, two distinct sets of Philadelphia leaders produced carefully composed slates of candidates to counter the radical-mechanic ticket. The first ticket to appear was the work of moderate resistance leaders.[39] Its sponsors, evidently satisfied with the Sixty-Six, omitted only three members of that body who appeared on the other tickets. To the fifty-seven veterans thus continued, they added ten new men carried by both other lists, and at least twenty-two more favored by the conservatives, but only four advanced by the mechanics, and no more than seven new men under their own aegis.[40] The twenty-nine men on the moderate ticket who were not nominated by the mechanics included nine major proprietary faction supporters, including provincial councilor Andrew Allen, as well as several prominent moderate merchants.[41] The moderates' new candidates were far wealthier and more politically prominent than the new men who appeared on the mechanics' ticket. The proprietary faction was especially well represented, as was the military elite. This slate retained every important militia officer on the Sixty-Six, including John Nixon, and it added Lieutenant Colonel John Chevalier, Captain Richard Peters, and several lieutenants and ensigns. This was the status quo ticket, the officers' ticket, and even the proprietary ticket.

---

39. "Committee,/ For the City of Philadelphia, District of Southwark/ and Northern Liberties," [broadside], Library Company, Am 1775 Phi Com, 962.F.71. This slate, labeled the "moderate" ticket, appears in Appendix L. Since this ticket alone gives candidates for Southwark, it probably appeared before the mechanics' and conservative tickets, giving further indication that Philadelphia's more moderate forces were better organized in 1775 than they had been in 1774.

40. Some of these figures must be qualified by "at least" or "no more than" because the list of conservative candidates for Southwark has not survived for comparison with the moderates' and the mechanics' nominees for that district. (The mechanics' nominees were, presumably, the committeemen actually elected for Southwark).

41. The other proprietary figures were James Allen, Tench Francis, John Gibson, John Maxwell Nesbit, Captain Richard Peters, Richard Tilghman, Tench Tilghman, and Alexander Wilcocks. The merchants were Colonel John Chevalier, Peter Knight, and Carpenter, James, and John Wharton.

The third slate was a shrewdly planned rejection of the current radical leadership and bore an unmistakably conservative stamp.[42] Its composers did not strike off the most prominent and popular radical leaders—Mifflin, Thomson, Bradford, Clymer, Reed, Cox, or Bayard—but they did drop thirty other veterans of the Sixty-Six, including moderates dedicated to vigorous armed resistance like Robert Morris and John Nixon, and radical stalwarts of the second rank like James Mease, James Milligan, and Benjamin Loxley. The conservatives then filled their fifty-two vacant slots with ten nominees run by both the moderates and the mechanics, nearly every prominent figure on the moderate ticket, six men placed by the mechanics, and thirteen persons of their exclusive choice. This last contingent revealed the slate's essential character. These thirteen deeply conservative leaders probably supported the current policy of Congress only reluctantly. Heading this group was Thomas Willing, a far more cautious leader than his business partner Robert Morris, and Jabez Fisher's older brother Samuel, who was so adamantly opposed to the resistance that his name must have been entered on the ticket without his consent. This slate was not as hostile to Congress as the more conservative of the two tickets of November 1774, however. The ongoing radicalization of Philadelphia's politics had affected all persons still active in public affairs; the extreme conservatives of 1774 were no longer politically active by mid-1775.

No description of the August 16 election has survived, but the mechanics' nominees were chosen.[43] Two days later, forty-nine of the victors gathered to elect the absent Joseph Reed, and George Clymer, Thomas McKean, and Samuel Meredith their chairmen, in that order of precedence. John Bayard Smith was again named secretary, but the committee passed over his assistant, John Benezet, in favor of Robert Strettel Jones and Peter Z. Lloyd. On the following day, the board divided itself into six district subcommittees on the same plan as that observed by the Sixty-Six.[44] The radicals had survived the spring shakeup in their leadership, Joseph Reed's surprise departure for New England, and the resurgence of conservative forces in August to take even firmer control of the resistance.

Philadelphia's new Committee of Observation resembled its predecessor in social composition more closely than any other two successive boards. Although the mechanics had dropped nearly two dozen veterans, they did not make men of any particular economic or social background the target of their deletions; and in the committee tradition of working to mobilize all elements of the community, they chose new men who covered a broad religious, economic, and social spectrum. The persistence of committee veterans was quite high; where the Sixty-Six had included only about 40 percent of the preceding Forty-Three, the August 1775 election restored that continuity of membership which had prevailed in the summer of 1774. Just over two-thirds of the Sixty-Six sat on the First One Hun-

---

42. "Committee/ For the City of Philadelphia and Northern/ Liberties. To continue for Six Months" [broadside], Library Company, Am 1775 Phi Com, 962.F.73. This slate, labeled the "conservative" ticket, is in Appendix L.

43. Three obscure new mechanics' candidates were rejected by the voters in favor of a veteran of the Sixty-Six omitted by the radical-mechanic leadership, Joseph Deane, and two other new recruits. All three winners had been nominated by both the moderates and the conservatives. Compare the election returns in *Pa. Gaz.*, Aug. 23, 1775, with the three tickets, reproduced in Appendix L.

44. Duane, ed., *Passages from Marshall*, p. 42 (Aug. 18); *Pa. Gaz.*, Aug. 30. 1775.

dred, a pattern repeated in February 1776, when sixty-nine committeemen were reelected.[45] The age structure of the board changed little, and the proportion of Quakers and Anglicans serving was unchanged, while the role of the Presbyterians actually decreased in favor of German sectarians.

Yet the First One Hundred was not simply an overgrown Sixty-Six; important alterations shaped its distinctive character. The board members were again of more modest fortune than their predecessors, although this change was not so great as it had been in November 1774. Another objective dimension of the new committee changed dramatically: the number of committeemen described as artisans and retailers, or "mechanics," which had risen steeply in November, again increased sharply.[46] But the most important differences between the Sixty-Six and the First One Hundred were immediately political. With the voluntary departure of the cautious radical leader Joseph Reed and the forced retirement of the moderate John Nixon, the upper-class radicals George Clymer and Thomas McKean rose to power in August. By October, however, they were joined on the committee's inner councils by the socially less distinguished but even more zealous Christopher Marshall, Sr. and Timothy Matlack. Committee membership had changed only modestly in August, but committee leadership soon took another step to the left.

THE SUPPRESSION OF DISSENT

Philadelphia's First One Hundred, like the Sixty-Six, was nominally elected to enforce the Continental Association, but by August 1775 the focus of committee activity had shifted from regulating commerce to suppressing dissent and preparing for war. Insofar as the committee was still concerned with the Association, it directed its attention toward the nonconsumption of British imports that remained unsold and the control of the prices of scarce goods. Yet it was the First One Hundred's enforcement of nonconsumption that sparked the only open defiance of committee authority in Philadelphia. The incident began when a dry goods retailer, reprimanded by a committeeman for trying to sell linen contrary to the Association, secured attorney Isaac Hunt to defend him. Hunt, who had written a conservative pamphlet the previous winter, boldly challenged the board's right to regulate commerce, and the case dragged on for two weeks in both district subcommittee and plenary sessions of the First One Hundred. At last succumbing to popular pressure, Hunt agreed to make a public apology for questioning the authority of the committee.[47]

On September 6, the day set for Hunt's confession, the affair took an unexpected turn. As thirty militiamen escorted him around town in a cart to make his contrite declarations of error to orderly groups of townsmen, they happened by the house of Dr. Kearsley, an archtory, who threw up a window sash and fired a

45. For a comparison of the Sixty-Six, the First One Hundred, and the Second One Hundred, see table 12, chapter 8 below.

46. For the quantitative data upon which the analysis in this paragraph is based, see table 12, chapter 8 below, and Appendix M.

47. See *Pa. Gaz.,* Sept. 6, 1775; Duane, ed., *Passages from Marshall,* pp. 43, 44, 45, 46 (Aug. 19, 22, 26, 28, 1775). On Hunt's pamphlet, see Adams, *American Independence,* p. 132.

pistol into the crowd. The militiamen rushed into the doctor's house, seized him, put him in the cart in place of Hunt, whom they released, and conducted him about the town, allowing the populace to heap abuse upon him. At the height of the furor, Philadelphia's mayor, Samuel Rhoads, asked Major John Bayard to call out his militia battalion to disperse the mob at the London Coffee House, but Bayard ignored him.[48]

Hunt and Kearsley were the only Philadelphians ever to defy the resistance openly; their intransigence incited the city's only display of mob violence between the burning of Hutchinson and Wedderburn in effigy in May 1774 and Independence. For the next several months, opposition to the resistance would again be covert and largely innocuous, but some Philadelphians were not content to express their hatred of the Revolution privately. Early in October, Dr. Kearsley and two associates sent letters attacking the local resistance movement to England with a Christopher Carter, but word of the letters leaked out, and Carter was seized and removed from an outbound vessel at Chester.

On October 7, a special subcommittee of the First One Hundred met to hear the charges against Kearsley and his associates, whom the full committee had arrested the day before, and to search for other papers that contained "base and cruel invectives against the liberties of America." This was done without any legal authority, yet with the full cooperation of the county sheriff and the jailer. Before the subcommittee could proceed, however, Pennsylvania's Committee of Safety informed the First One Hundred that on the previous day Congress had placed all cases of treason under the exclusive jurisdiction of province-wide committees of safety, conventions, and assemblies within the several colonies, and of Congress itself. The city board reluctantly handed over the prisoners and all papers to the Committee of Safety. But the superior board did not exclude the First One Hundred from the case; recognizing the Philadelphians' investigative work on the incident, they selected fifteen city committeemen to assist them in trying the disaffected correspondents. Their hearing ended in the Committee of Safety's sentencing Dr. Kearsley and one colleague to indefinite terms in Pennsylvania jails.[49]

The adventures of Dr. Kearsley had exposed a new, more ugly public mood toward opponents of the resistance in Philadelphia. Revolutionary leaders responded to this temper by adopting measures to control both dissidents and the public that they disturbed so deeply. On September 19, the First One Hundred directed Philadelphians to desist from persecuting their tory neighbors and to bring to the committee all charges against individuals whom they judged disloyal to America.[50] But Congress, upon hearing of the arrest of Dr. Kearsley and his colleagues, decided that the authority to deal with treason should not be entrusted to local boards.

The Revolutionary movement entered a new phase with Congress's October 6

48. *Pa. Jour.,* Sept. 20, 1775; Duane, ed., *Passages from Marshall,* pp. 46–47 (Sept. 6, 8, 1775); Christopher Marshall, Sr. to "S. H.," Sept. 30, 1775, Letter-Book, pp. 141–42, 146, HSP.

49. *Pa. Jour.,* Oct. 11, 1775; Duane, ed., *Passages from Marshall,* pp. 50–52 (Oct. 6–9, 1775); Marshall to "S. H.," Oct. 31, 1775, Marshall Letter-Book, pp. 153–54, HSP; *Minutes,* pp. 357–59, 360–62, 367, 371–73 (Oct. 7, 9, 10, 14, 18, 19, 1775).

50. *Pa. Gaz.,* Sept. 27, 1775.

decision. The resistance had at last acquired the status of official policy; the "Cause of America" took on the authority of the state, and any dissent became a punishable crime. With the rapid suppression of all opposition to the resistance, the First One Hundred and the Committee of Safety once again turned their attention to the military problems facing Pennsylvania. But now their mood—and even more the mood of the militia that they sought to control—was one of uncompromising, righteous zeal.

THE MILITIA ENTERS POLITICS

Toward the end of August, the Committee of Safety approved Articles of Association, and Rules for Establishing Rank and Precedence, both based on the report of a subcommittee that the board had directed to draft militia rules on August 3, at the request of Philadelphia's Committee of Officers. The Committee of Safety forwarded copies of this new plan to militia colonels throughout the province for submission to the associators for approval.[51] Pennsylvania's new rules did resolve serious problems of military order and discipline, but they did not touch two larger issues: securing adequate financial support for minutemen and obligating all able-bodied men to serve in the militia. For this reason, the associators rejected the Committee's Articles and Rules as soundly as they had the minuteman proposal in July.

But the associators now went far beyond their earlier position; they made new demands for militia reform, developed an effective critique of the Committee of Safety's proposals, and founded a new organization to support their own program. Their essential argument probably originated in July; a few companies had then given as reasons for spurning Congress's minuteman plan their distaste for being labeled mercenaries and their resentment over the great number of Philadelphians who had yet to associate. On August 21, an essay in the *Pennsylvania Packet* asserted that a militia force that was kept in paid service in the field for long periods and that included only a small part of the population able to bear arms was a standing army. And a mercenary force, "Caractacus" reminded his readers, was always destructive of the people's liberties; any body of men that fought for pay, no matter what its origin, would soon fall into corruption and become a ready instrument for aspiring tyrants. The only remedy was to require all to associate and to fine those who would not do so, although "Caractacus" apparently favored leaving sincere pacifists undisturbed.

By September, Philadelphia's associators shared "Caractacus's" conviction that they were being maneuvered into the despised role of mercenaries by an appointed committee of privileged elites that boldly claimed unlawful powers, and when they were presented with the Committee of Safety's Articles, they responded by forming their own Committee of Privates. This body of elected representatives of Philadelphia's militia companies named William Adcock, James Cannon, John Chaloner, Samuel Simpson, Joseph Stiles, and William Thorne its leaders. Al-

---

51. *Minutes*, pp. 307, 308–12, 315, 316–22, 323–27, 329, 330, 335–36 (Aug. 17–19, 25, 26, 29, Sept. 1, 4, 15, 16, 1775).

though Cannon, the new committee's secretary, and Stiles had been central figures in organizing the American Manufactory in March, all six men were obscure artisans or schoolteachers who had never played a visible role in Philadelphia politics.[52] On September 27, the Committee of Privates issued its first public declaration.

The privates' "Address" to their officers, a skillfully composed piece written by a well-educated penman, asserted that no law that obligated one part of the community to perform a duty that benefited the whole, while freeing another part from that obligation, was consistent with a free government.[53] Therefore, they would not agree to articles that might make them a standing mercenary force, but instead requested short enlistment terms for those willing and able to enter full-time service. In the best Anglo-American constitutional tradition, they denied the Committee of Safety's right to legislate militia rules, arguing that only the people generally and the Assembly in particular had the authority to do this; and they roundly condemned the attempt of an appointed body, which included persons whom they had not elected and whom they could not control, to dictate to them. The "Address" closed with the privates' pledge never to submit to any militia law that did not apply equally to all; if any were to be exempted from service, the opportunity to claim an exemption must be extended to all, and the monetary fee charged for that exemption must be proportional to the exempted man's property.

The privates' "Address" finally convinced the Committee of Officers of the Philadelphia militia that it must petition the Assembly for the solution to its military problems. It was clear that the Committee of Safety's attempt to legislate articles of association was as deeply resented as its inability to deliver what the associators really wanted: more adequate funding and a general militia law. Once they understood the temper of their men, the officers moved swiftly. On September 27, the day they received the "Address," the officers reported to the Assembly the associators' refusal to accept the Committee of Safety's militia articles, endorsed their reasons for refusing, and argued that many Philadelphians were using religious scruples as a convenient excuse to escape obligations that ought to fall upon all citizens. If the Assembly would pass a general militia law, however, the officers felt confident that every associator would make great sacrifices to defend the province.[54] On September 29, a concurring petition from the Committee of Safety asserted that a general law that would exempt men from bearing arms only on the condition that "a Rate or Assessment be laid on their estates equivalent to the Expense and loss of Time incurred by the Associators" would quickly resolve Pennsylvania's military difficulties.[55]

---

52. On the formation and early activities of the Committee of Privates, see *Pa. Evening Post,* Sept. 14, 19, 28; *Pa. Gaz.,* Oct. 11, 18, Nov. 1, 15, 1775; Duane, ed., *Passages from Marshall,* pp. 53–54 (Oct. 17, 20, 1775); and Marshall to "S. H.," Sept. 30, 1775, Marshall Letter-Book, HSP. Unfortunately, no full membership list of this body appears to be extant. Stiles and Thorne were schoolmasters, and Cannon was professor of mathematics at the College of Philadelphia. Simpson was a well-established shoemaker; Adcock was a shopkeeper.

53. The text of the "Address" is in *Pa. Evening Post,* Sept. 28, and *Pa. Gaz.,* Oct. 11, 1775. James Cannon was by far the most literate and best educated of these men, and was the probable author of the "Address" and a likely author of the newspaper essay by "Caractacus" as well.

54. *Votes and Proceedings,* VIII: 7259–60.

55. *Votes and Proceedings,* VIII: 7261–62.

ELECTION DAY, OCTOBER 1775

The haste with which Philadelphia's militia officers and the Committee of Safety referred their difficulties to the Assembly upon receiving the associators' "Address" was a product of the legislature's traditional schedule and its members' cautious deliberation. In their brief September session, the lawmakers settled Pennsylvania's annual accounts, as they had each September.[56] They also heard several petitions requesting that they meet the province's most urgent military needs.[57] The real target of these memorials, however, was the first session of the next Assembly in October. September sessions were short affairs, and no general legislation except routine money bills emerged from them. The petitioners' problem was that the Assembly's organizational sessions in October were even briefer: the newly elected legislators chose their speaker, established procedural rules, appointed standing committees, and occasionally heard, but did not discuss, a few petitions.[58] The aim of the September petitioners was to insert their urgent requests into the Assembly's minutes in order to force the new House to hold a long October session and relieve Pennsylvania's pressing military problems before winter. Having submitted their memorials, the petitioners turned their attention to the annual balloting for legislators and local officials.

The election of October 2, 1775, was the most hotly contested in Philadelphia since the Quaker-proprietary battles of 1764 and 1765. An unprecedented number of aspirants stood for sheriff and for coroner, and at least ten candidates ran for Philadelphia County's eight Assembly seats.[59] Contests in the rural counties were less numerous, but the steadily deteriorating state of the empire, which had had a rather slight effect on the 1774 election, now had a major impact upon the settled traditions of Pennsylvania politics. In Bucks County, two conservative Friends succeeded Joseph Galloway and a Quaker colleague, who had probably withdrawn from the election. The replacement of the zealous Colonel Anthony Wayne by a conservative Friend in Chester County balanced a conservative lawmaker's retirement from a Lancaster County seat, which the patriotic Colonel Curtis Grubb won. Only the addition of a new seat for Northampton County gave the resistance a net gain of one vote outside the City and County of Philadelphia.[60]

It was in elections in and around Philadelphia that the Revolution made its first great impact upon the Pennsylvania Assembly. Nearly every candidate for the legislature in Philadelphia County was an ardent patriot, and several committee-

---

56. *Votes and Proceedings,* VIII: 7252–53, 7255–57, 7296–97.

57. *Votes and Proceedings,* VIII: 7251–52, 7256, 7258–62. Petitions from York County and Philadelphia's battalion leaders asked for money; Chester County requested money and militia rules; the Philadelphia Committee of Officers' petition already mentioned asked for rules and a general militia law; the Committee of Safety's memorial made many requests.

58. See Leonard, "Organization of the Assembly," pp. 220–21, 223.

59. See the September issues of the *Gazette* and *Evening Post* for withdrawal notices; Duane, ed., *Passages from Marshall,* pp. 49–50 (Oct. 2–4, 1775); Marshall to "S. H.," Oct. 31, 1775, Marshall Letter-Book, HSP; and Henry Drinker to Benjamin Booth, Oct. 3, 1775, Drinker Letter-Book (domestic), HSP.

60. Lawmakers leaving the House were Galloway, Wayne, Robert Kirkbride (Bucks), Joseph Ferree (Lancaster), and William Edmonds (Northampton). Entering were Thomas Jenks and David Twining (Bucks), Joseph Pyle (Chester), Curtis Grubb (Lancaster), and Peter Kachlein and George Taylor (Northampton). Jenks, Twining, and Pyle were Quakers and conservatives; Grubb, Taylor, and Kachlein strongly supported the resistance (*Votes and Proceedings,* VIII: 7148, 7301–2; and Appendix B for portrait data).

men stood for county sheriff or coroner, although they were outpolled by the more moderate incumbents, who also supported the resistance.[61] In the Assembly race, Henry Pawling and Israel Jacobs, a Quaker, formally withdrew. A spirited contest for these two seats developed at once, and for a third as well, because Mayor Samuel Rhoads, also a Quaker, either announced his withdrawal verbally or was simply beaten. The three moderate candidates for the seats, who were elected, were Colonel Thomas Potts, member of a prominent county iron-forge family, Colonel Samuel Miles, who had served in the 1773–74 Assembly and was the county's most prominent militia officer, and the energetic Committee of Safety member Robert Morris.

The election of these three men would insure a more activist House, but the city's radicals rashly decided to test their strength in a wider field by running Charles Thomson and the radical Quaker city committeeman Thomas Pryor for county seats. They probably hoped to defeat the conservative Quaker incumbent, Jonathan Roberts, and the moderate challenger, Robert Morris, but their nominees were not the best. Thomson, a sure winner in the city, had the now-anachronistic reputation among county moderates of being a firebrand and was far too busy in Congress to attend Assembly sessions. Pryor, although a wealthy flour merchant, was politically too radical, and too obscure, for the county; even in the city there were a dozen better-known zealots. The radicals probably hoped that Pryor's Quaker background would overcome these obstacles, but they should have known better.[62]

At least one radical, however, was not content with supporting Pryor and Thomson. Writing as "A Citizen," he departed from the politics of consensus laid down by the radicals' old master, Thomson, to assault moderate patriot candidates.[63] Passing quickly over the obviously undesirable characters who had ever spoken or written unfavorably of American liberties, he focused his attack upon those persons who, though of sound understanding and noble intentions, lacked the courage to act on their convictions. No possible target of these charges loomed so large as the increasingly cautious John Dickinson, who stood for re-election. But if "A Citizen" did intend to destroy Dickinson's popularity, he failed completely. The returns fully vindicated the Farmer's resistance policy— a vigorous military opposition to the ministry combined with dutiful, optimistic petitions to the King—among the voters of Philadelphia County. Dickinson himself led the poll, followed closely by the moderate incumbents, Michael Hillegas and George Gray, and then Colonels Potts and Miles. The more radical Joseph Parker was just a few votes behind. Robert Morris, who was probably hurt by Thomson and Pryor in the city, and who may not have been well known in the

61. Aspirants for sheriff were John Bull, a prominent county committee member and militia colonel, Francis Wade, member of the Sixty-Six and First One Hundred and a militia captain, and William Masters of the First One Hundred. William Moulder, a veteran of the Forty-Three, ran for coroner. See *Pa. Ledger,* Aug. 26; *Pa. Evening Post,* Aug. 31, Sept. 23, 30, Oct. 3; and *Pa. Gaz.,* Sept. 20, 27, 1775.

62. Henry Drinker to Benjamin Booth, Oct. 3, 1775, Drinker Letter-Book (domestic), HSP, is the only source for the candidacy of Thomson and Pryor, and contends that they ran specifically against Potts and Morris. The heavy vote cast for Potts, however, suggests that he received both moderate and radical support, while Roberts, who ran last, probably attracted moderate voters only. This argues that Roberts, not Potts, was the radicals' target. See also Christopher Marshall, Sr. to "S. H.," Oct. 31, 1775, Marshall Letter-Book, HSP.

63. *Pa. Jour.,* Sept. 13, 1775.

rural townships, trailed badly but secured the seventh seat. Finally, Friend Jonathan Roberts' courage paid off. The elders of his meeting had urged him to withdraw, but many Quaker voters must have rallied to his defense, because he won a close contest against heavy odds.[64] The radicals suffered a serious setback and learned that they were a long way from taking over the Pennsylvania Assembly.

The election for City burgesses, which had been such a triumph for the radicals in 1774, should again have given the resistance two strong spokesmen in the chamber, but resistance leaders, by nominating Dr. Franklin and Thomas Mifflin, bungled this contest as well. Franklin was so busy with congressional duties that he was finding it difficult even to chair Committee of Safety meetings, and there was no indication that Mifflin was tiring of the war in New England. But although the two were really ineligible, they were invincible; almost certainly they were unopposed. With the vote for burgesses off nearly 50 percent from 1774, the resistance secured two seats that it had little immediate prospect of filling. While gaining four seats in the countryside, strong supporters of congressional resistance in effect threw away two in the City.[65]

The election of 1775 was a major triumph for the resistance; the victory of Miles, Morris, and Potts drew the Committee of Safety and the officers of the military association into much tighter unity with the Assembly. But the triumph went to resistance moderates, not to the more radical leaders, who, with the defeat of Thomson and Wayne, the absence of Mifflin, and the growing caution of Dickinson, were left with few capable spokesmen in the House.[66] Pennsylvania's commitment to current congressional policy was assured; the new House of forty-one members had at least nineteen steady supporters of Congress, twelve swing voters, including Speaker John Morton, and ten firm conservatives (see table 11 below). The Assembly's activist-conservative balance remained fairly close, however; any measure that broke sharply with tradition, like a law requiring militia service, would face strong criticism in the chamber. A more decisive change, like leaving the British Empire, would have no chance in this house.

The view that the 1775 elections placed the Assembly more firmly behind armed resistance, and yet made quite limited changes in that body's character, finds ample confirmation in the legislature's selection of leaders in mid-October.

---

64. The poll appears in *Pa. Evening Post*, Oct. 3, 1775 (evidently the first newspaper issue in over twenty years to give voting statistics—for winners only—in a Pennsylvania election), and in Duane, ed., *Passages from Marshall*, pp. 49–50 (Oct. 3, 1775), and stood:

John Dickinson	3,122	Samuel Miles	3,098
Michael Hillegas	3,111	Joseph Parker	3,077
George Gray	3,107	Robert Morris	1,882
Thomas Potts	3,103	Jonathan Roberts	1,700

On Roberts' difficulties with his Quaker meeting, see Philip Shriver Klein, "Memoirs of a Senator from Pennsylvania, Jonathan Roberts, 1771–1854," *PMHB*, LXI (1937): 469–70.

65. Duane, ed., *Passages from Marshall*, p. 50 (Oct. 4, 1775), gives the vote as: Franklin, 775; Mifflin, 724. The vote cast in October 1774 for City burgesses stood at about 1,300 (see chapter 5, note 14 above).

66. Anthony Wayne, I am arguing, ran and was defeated, although he may have withdrawn from the election. Wayne was a prominent radical orator in the House, and his seat was taken by a conservative Friend, indicating an ideological change that one must, in the absence of counterevidence, presume resulted from an electoral contest. It is quite possible that Wayne's defeat was due to the rumor in Chester County, vehemently denied by the county's Committee of Observation, of which Wayne was chairman, that local committeemen and military associators were working toward independence (see *Pa. Gaz.*, Sept. 27, 1775, noticed dated Sept. 25).

John Morton, speaker since March, secured unanimous reelection to the chair. Morton, in filling the Assembly's important standing committees, largely adhered to those principles of seniority, ability, and geographical distribution followed by Joseph Galloway through October 1773.[67] The personnel of these boards changed little; no legislator was removed from a standing committee for his politics, and few were added for that reason. The continuity of veteran leaders, both activist and conservative, remained high. As in 1774, however, the legislators themselves had changed. The retirement of Joseph Galloway and his firm ally Samuel Rhoads, and the radicalization of several Quaker party regulars still in the chamber, especially Hillegas, Gray, Morton, and Pearson, determined that the Pennsylvania Assembly of 1775–76 would both carry on the work of its predecessor and be prepared to go a little further in resisting the British ministry.

THE ASSEMBLY VOTES A MILITIA LAW

Immediately upon organizing their chamber, Pennsylvania's lawmakers confronted the most divisive political issue of 1775: would the province require militia service of every freeman and fine all those who would not bear arms? For the next forty days, the legislators directed most of their energies to settling this issue, while the Committee of Safety, the First One Hundred, several bodies of militia officers, Philadelphia's Committee of Privates, and the Quaker Yearly Meeting all sought to influence their decision. But those favoring a new militia law had first to convince the Assembly to hold a long fall session. Some radicals believed that the legislators planned to adjourn quickly to avoid the issue, but this fear was probably without foundation. The September petitions had achieved their aim, and on October 20, the House resolved to discuss the state of the province within the week. From this day forward, the Assembly never waivered in its commitment to finding a better solution to its militia problems.[68]

Pennsylvania's militant radicals, however, were still unsure of the new Assembly's enthusiasm for required militia service, so they deluged the House with adamant new demands for a military establishment. The legislators heard fresh arguments for mandatory militia service from Philadelphia's First One Hundred (October 20) and Committee of Privates (October 21), which had collaborated closely in framing their memorials, and from the Chester County Committee of Observation (October 26). Each petition advised that a special assessment be levied against all conscientious objectors "adequate to the many difficult and dangerous Services of those who are willing to hazard their Lives and Fortunes in defense of their Country. . . ."[69] These addresses thoroughly alarmed Pennsyl-

---

67. *Votes and Proceedings,* VIII: 7304, 7313, and 7385 on Morton; and for the names of members leaving and those taking up standing committee seats, compare *Votes and Proceedings,* VIII: 7026, 7150, and 7304. The last standing committee list under Galloway, for 1773–74, is given in Appendix C.

68. Duane, ed., *Passages from Marshall,* p. 54 (Oct. 20, 1775); *Votes and Proceedings,* VIII: 7306.

69. *Votes and Proceedings,* VIII: 7311–12, 7312–13, 7323–25. The quote is from the Committee of Privates' petition, p. 7313. Compare the phrasing of this memorial with that of the First One Hundred, presented to the Assembly on the previous day; and see Duane, ed., *Passages from Marshall,* pp. 53–54 (Oct. 17, 1775), for the cooperation between the Committee of Privates and the First One Hundred in securing a new militia law.

vania's Quakers. Since February, Friends had kept clear of political activity, but they could not ignore this threat to their pacific practice. On October 27, spokesmen for the Society presented an "Address" to the House, which argued that any special assessment upon pacifists in place of militia service would infringe upon their liberty of conscience and violate the religious toleration granted by William Penn in the province's 1701 charter.[70]

The "Address" sparked the only direct confrontation between resistance leaders and the Society of Friends before Independence. Three resistance bodies immediately drew up rebuttals to the Quakers' argument and submitted them to the House. Philadelphia's Committee of Officers and Committee of Privates naturally advanced harsh critiques of the pacific "Address," but fully as devastating an assault came from the civilian First One Hundred.[71] The city committee appointed officers George Clymer, Thomas McKean, John Bayard Smith, and Robert Strettel Jones and members Sharp Delaney, John Wilcocks, and Timothy Matlack to draft this petition, and on October 31, sixty-six committeemen marched two by two, with Clymer and McKean at their head, to the State House and presented their memorial.[72] This procession vividly calls to mind July 21, 1774, when seventy-five members of Pennsylvania's first provincial convention had approached the Galloway House for aid. But how different were the circumstances fifteen months later! In 1774 resistance leaders were firmly shut out from power in the Assembly; in 1775 men favoring armed resistance led the chamber, and the First One Hundred and its allies enjoyed equal access with Pennsylvania's Friends to the ear of their legislature.

The First One Hundred's "Petition and Remonstrance" opened with a harsh condemnation of the Quakers' attempt to withhold support from the resistance. The committee asserted that if "the Patrons and Friends of Liberty succeed in the present glorious Struggle, [the Quakers] and their Posterity will enjoy all the Advantages derived from it, equally with those who procured them, without contributing a single Penny, and with Safety to their Persons. [But if] the Friends of Liberty fail, [the Quakers] will risk no Forfeitures, but be entitled by their Behavior to Protection and Countenance from the British Ministry, and will probably be promoted to Office." This last possibility, the committee remarked caustically, "they seem to desire and expect."[73] The "Remonstrance" utterly denied the Quakers' claim that Penn's 1701 charter granted them an exemption from military service and monetary sacrifice in the defense of the community.[74] But the First One Hundred's strongest arguments arose from its view of English history and especially of natural law. "Self-preservation," the "Remonstrance" declared, "is the first Principle of Nature, . . . in a State of political Society . . . all Men, by their original Compact and Agreement, are obligated to unite in defending themselves and those of the same Community against such as shall attempt unlawfully to deprive them of their just Rights and Liberties . . ."[75]

---

70. *Votes and Proceedings,* VIII: 7326–30.
71. *Votes and Proceedings,* VIII: 7337–39 (Committee of Officers), 7339–43 (Committee of Privates), 7334–37 (First One Hundred).
72. Duane, ed., *Passages from Marshall,* pp. 55–56 (Oct. 29–31, 1775).
73. *Votes and Proceedings,* VIII: 7334.
74. *Votes and Proceedings,* VIII: 7335. The Committee of Officers' memorial made this point even more persuasively.
75. *Votes and Proceedings,* VIII: 7336.

This argument, the powerful new institutions that advanced it, and the compelling need for a strong militia must all have impressed Pennsylvania's legislators. A chamber that still had a dozen strict Friends and several other members who were solicitous of the welfare of Pennsylvania's Quakers, however, could not resolve militia policy easily. The lawmakers debated for a week before agreeing upon the bare outline of a modest defense program, and when they took occasional respites to consider easier questions, their solutions to them displayed their old talent for skillfully blending decisive resistance measures with moderate political decisions.

The first important political act of the fall session was the appointment of a new Committee of Safety. The existing board had been both a zealous and a socially respectable resistance body, and the Assembly reappointed all but three of its members. At the same time the House added ten new men, including the former city committeemen John Nixon and Samuel Howell, the newly elected legislator Samuel Miles, and the prominent young Philadelphia lawyer Alexander Wilcocks, all popularly identified as resistance moderates, and three radical leaders of the First One Hundred, George Clymer, James Mease, and Joseph Reed, who would soon return to Philadelphia from New England. The new members further strengthened the already dominant role on that board of Philadelphians from outside the legislature.[76]

More important decisions were the Assembly's choice of congressional delegates for the coming year, and its composition of instructions for them. Here the lawmakers acted an even more moderate part. For their new role as resistance leaders, Pennsylvania's legislators had a new hero, who influenced their every decision as powerfully as had his great rival just over a year earlier. Retaining his central position in Congress as the leading spokesman for the more cautious delegates from the middle colonies, John Dickinson now reached the pinnacle of his prestige with the moderate legislators and voters who still dominated the constituted government of Pennsylvania. And with each passing month he became more alarmed at the growing bitterness of the resistance movement against Great Britain. Dickinson could not accept a permanent break with Britain, and his growing moderation, which became apparent to all when he insisted that Congress send one final "Olive Branch" petition to the Crown in July 1775, soon alienated radical leaders. Pennsylvania's new congressional delegation, appointed on November 4, would firmly support Dickinson's approach to the imperial crisis until Independence. The House dropped congressmen Thomas Mifflin and George Ross, but reappointed the more conservative Charles Humphreys, John Morton, Thomas Willing, and Dickinson himself. Edward Biddle and James Wilson were perhaps more zealous, but the only radical veteran retained was Dr. Franklin. To these seven, the Assembly added the moderate leaders Robert Morris and Andrew Allen.[77]

The character of the committee chosen to draft instructions for the new con-

---

76. *Votes and Proceedings,* VIII: 7310–11. Of those deleted, William Thompson and Thomas Willing had not attended the board's meetings, while William Edmonds was no longer an assemblyman.

77. *Votes and Proceedings,* VIII: 7347. Characterizations of the assemblymen in this paragraph as conservative, moderate, or radical on resistance issues rest on their roll call records in the House, discussed in chapter 5 above, and below in this chapter (see table 11).

gressmen revealed Dickinson's influence even more starkly. When Speaker Morton named Dickinson himself to that committee, the "Pennsylvania Farmer" received the rare privilege of framing directives for himself. Assisting him were four safely moderate legislators and three more ardent frontier delegates.[78] Under Dickinson's guidance, the committee reported out the existing instructions, to which they added a clause that directed Pennsylvania's congressmen to "dissent from and utterly reject, any Propositions, should such be made, that may cause, or lead to, a Separation from our Mother Country, or a Change of the Form of this Government."[79] Alarmed by growing talk of independence throughout the colonies and fearful that George III's contemptuous rejection of Dickinson's "Olive Branch" petition of July, of which they had just learned, might transform these private conversations into public debate, the legislators approved these instructions on November 9.[80]

On November 8, immediately after naming members to draft instructions for its congressmen, the Assembly framed eight resolves that outlined its military policy for the coming year. The most important provisions urged all men between the ages of sixteen and fifty to associate, committed the legislature to issue £80,000 in paper currency to finance the province's defense, and, in a sharp break with tradition, declared that all men who would not associate "ought to contribute an Equivalent to the Time spent by the Associators in acquiring the military Discipline. . . ."[81] These resolves afforded the solution, in principle, to every difficulty of which Pennsylvania's militia organizations had complained. Their adoption had not been easy; the fifth resolve, by which the House, for the first time in its history, committed itself to penalize strict pacifists for refusing to bear arms, must have caused much soul-searching. But the assemblymen now had a course of action to follow, and they quickly appointed several of their number to prepare militia rules and a plan for taxing nonassociators. Named to this committee were the radicals Joseph Parker of Philadelphia and Benjamin Bartholomew of Chester, four ardent resistance leaders from the frontier, the moderate activists Dickinson and Morris, and four even more cautious legislators.[82] In creating an ideologically balanced, geographically inclusive drafting committee, the Assembly showed its determination to maintain unity while considering potentially explosive yet finally unavoidable issues.

On November 15, the committee reported out militia rules and a taxation bill, and the full House directed Dickinson, Michael Hillegas, Isaac Pearson, and Speaker Morton to prepare its £80,000 currency bill.[83] Debate on the militia rules began the next day and reached critical roll calls on November 17, when the lawmakers had to set the minimum number of muster days. This question was no mere technicality, because the fines levied on nonassociators would be proportional to

---

78. *Votes and Proceedings,* VIII: 7350.

79. *Votes and Proceedings,* VIII: 7353.

80. See *Votes and Proceedings,* VIII: 7350, 7352.

81. *Votes and Proceedings,* VIII: 7351–52.

82. *Votes and Proceedings,* VIII: 7352. Again, these members are placed upon a radical-to-conservative spectrum on the basis of roll call votes in the Assembly and literary testimony about their positions on resistance to Great Britain.

83. *Votes and Proceedings,* VIII: 7356.

the number of days on which associators would be required to exercise.[84] The two roll calls determined whether there would be twenty-two or only twenty such days in the coming year, and each vote was a tie. Speaker Morton voted against twenty-two and for twenty days, which consequently passed.[85]

The November 17 roll calls finely delineate the alignment within the House over the larger question of required militia service. While these ayes and nays fit well with the division of the chamber into nineteen active supporters of armed resistance, twelve swing voters, and ten conservatives advanced above, they suggest an important qualification to that pattern. If attendance was low on any given day, conservative assemblymen, who lived in counties near Philadelphia and were most likely to attend every session, could block resistance legislation favored by the full House. Thus the roll calls' indication that the forces opposing the resistance were of roughly equal strength with those favoring the cause is misleading. On November 17, all but two conservative and swing voters were present, but nine activists were away (see table 11).[86]

The roll calls of November 17 saw the last determined attempt to oppose a general militia law; thereafter the House quickly completed its defense program. On November 18, the £80,000 currency bill passed the House. On the twentieth and twenty-first, the Assembly approved "Rules and Regulations for the better Government of the military Association" and "Articles of Association." Two days later, the lawmakers agreed to a "Mode of levying Taxes on Non-Associators," and on November 25, they approved a transcription of the entire plan and released it for publication.[87] On the previous day the legislators had disposed of two other politically important matters. The House honored Thomas Mifflin's request that he be excused from Assembly service by directing Speaker Morton to arrange a by-election for Mifflin's seat; and in response to a petition from Philadelphia's Committee of Observation, which reported that many Pennsylvanians were not accepting the provincial currency voted in June, the House resolved that anyone who refused its bills ought "to be deemed inimical to the Liberties of America."[88] This vote implicitly granted local committees of observation the license to apply public ostracism against any pacifists who scrupled at handling the money that fed Pennsylvania's new war machine. With the completion of these matters, and of its first militia law, the Pennsylvania Assembly adjourned to February 1776, ending the longest and most important fall session in its history.

The Assembly's new militia law was an important victory for the resistance. While its plan generally followed the rules and organization adopted by Congress and then by the Committee of Safety, it made several innovations designed to

---

84. See *Votes and Proceedings,* VIII: 7377, clause 9, where the penalty for nonattendance at any muster is set at two shillings and sixpence (2/6); and p. 7382, clause 8, where the annual assessment for nonassociating is set at £2.10.0 (2/6 times twenty days).

85. *Votes and Proceedings,* VIII: 7357–58.

86. The conservatives absent were James Gibbons and Joseph Pennock of Chester County. The absent radicals were Franklin and Mifflin, who never sat in the 1775–76 House, the frontier delegates Hunter and Thompson, who would not appear until February, and George Ross and Curtis Grubb (Lancaster), Edward Biddle and Henry Chreist (Berks), and William Allen (Cumberland), who were absent for reasons unknown. Biddle, however, was probably ill, and William Allen seems to have retired from public life at just this time.

87. *Votes and Proceedings,* VIII: 7358–61, 7362–63, 7365–66. Full texts of the plan's provisions are given on pages 7369–84.

88. *Votes and Proceedings,* VIII: 7361, 7366 (Mifflin); pp. 7363, 7365 (quotation).

TABLE 11

Assemblymen Classified According to their General Support for Armed Resistance and the Program of the Second Congress, October 1775–April 1776

Activists, Moderate and Radical		Swing Voters		Conservatives	
J. Reed[a]	City	G. Gray	County	J. Roberts[b]	County
D. Rittenhouse[a]	City	M. Hillegas	County	J. Brown	County
J. Dickinson	County	S. Miles	County	B. Chapman	Bucks
R. Morris	County	T. Potts	County	J. Foulke	Bucks
J. Parker	County	W. Rodman	Bucks	J. Haney	Bucks
B. Bartholomew	Chester	G. Wynkoop	Bucks	T. Jenks	Bucks
C. Grubb	Lancaster	J. Gibbons	Chester	D. Twining	Bucks
G. Ross	Lancaster	C. Humphreys	Chester	J. Pennock	Chester
J. Ewing	York	J. Jacobs	Chester	J. Pyle	Chester
M. Swoope	York	J. Morton, Sp.	Chester	J. Webb	Lancaster
W. Allen[a]	Cumberland	I. Pearson	Chester		
J. Montgomery	Cumberland	M. Slough	Lancaster		
E. Biddle[a]	Berks				
H. Chreist	Berks				
G. Taylor	Northampton				
P. Kachlein	Northampton				
B. Dougherty	Bedford				
S. Hunter	Northumberland				
W. Thompson	Westmoreland				
19 votes (17 usually present)		12 votes		10 votes	

Note: This table is based upon the roll call votes of October 30, and November 17, 1775, and March 13 and 14, 1776 [Votes and Proceedings, VIII: 7333, 7357–58, 7444, 7446].

a. Reed entered the House only on February 16, and Rittenhouse on March 5, 1776, to replace Franklin and Mifflin, who never took their seats but were also strong supporters of Congress. Before these dates, the City seats were not occupied. William Allen was probably not in the House long after October 30, when he was present and voting. Biddle was very ill and missed many sessions.

b. Quakers in good standing, men of Quaker background and behavior, and probable Quakers are italicized.

overcome the unpopularity of that earlier arrangement. The passage of a militia law providing for compulsory service under arms was the greatest innovation, but significant new provisions appeared in each of the plan's three parts. The "Rules and Regulations" directed that every associator attend twenty Monday drills in the early spring and late summer, each to run no more than six hours, encouraged further exercise for any units that felt the need of it, and most important, promised that whenever an associator who was called into active service left a family that could not support itself, local officials would make immediate provision for its maintainance out of the funds for poor relief.[89] The "Articles of Association" levied a fine of two shillings and sixpence for every muster day missed, set up a military-court system with judges chosen from among both the rank and file and the officers' corps, and put all troops called into active service by the Assembly or by the Committee of Safety under the rules Congress had devised for Continental troops.[90] Finally, the "Mode of levying Taxes" provided that a full census of non-associators be completed by the spring, and that any persons who chose not to associate by June 1 be assessed £2.10.0 over and above all usual rates and taxes in the province.[91]

By their own lights, the lawmakers had performed their duties courageously, with skill and sound judgment. They had voted unprecedented sums for defense, and guaranteed support for the families of poor associators who were away on campaigns. The only militia demand that they had failed to meet was the request that the fines levied for nonassociating be in proportion to each nonassociator's wealth. But were any pacifists actually required to make a significant sacrifice to support Pennsylvania's military machine? It is true that the £2.10.0 annual fine charged to every nonassociator under fifty equalled the property tax paid by persons assessed at least £33 in 1774, a high assessment in Philadelphia, and a very high one in the province's rural districts.[92] Moreover, the Assembly's decision to issue £35,000 in new bills in June and £80,000 in November insured that several wealthy Philadelphia Quakers over the age of required military service could not avoid substantial contributions to the resistance.[93] Routine militia service, however, would run far more than £2.10.0 per associator in equipment costs—the new currency issues voted by the Assembly were insufficient to arm and outfit more than a fraction of the associators—and in lost time for routine training. Each associator who went on active duty would be making a far greater sacrifice.[94]

---

89. *Votes and Proceedings*, VIII: 7372 (Rule 27); p. 7374 (Rule 35).

90. *Votes and Proceedings*, VIII: 7377 (Article 9); pp. 7377–78 (Articles 15–18); p. 7380 (Article 31).

91. *Votes and Proceedings*, VIII: 7380 (Resolution 1); pp. 7381–82 (Resolutions 7–8).

92. Compare the assessments laid on Philadelphia County farms in 1774 in "A Transcript of the Assessment of the Seventeenth 18 d. Provincial Tax laid the 8th Day of April 1774 on the Inhabitants of the City and County of Philadelphia," MS, pp. 196–514, Pennsylvania Historical and Museum Commission, Harrisburg (on film). This list is published, with some errors, in *Pa. Archives*, 3d Ser., vol. XIV.

93. Wealthy, strict Quakers over the age of military service included Israel, James, and John Pemberton (assessed £950, £358, and £430 respectively in 1774), Owen Jones (£500), Jeremiah Warder, Sr. (£440), Samuel Rhoads (£381), Joshua Fisher (£325), Abel James (£240), Thomas Wharton, Sr. (£166), John Reynell (£140), and Samuel Shoemaker (£135). The provincial currency issues of £35,000 and £80,000 were to be sunk by a 7½ percent tax on all estates; thus these Friends would be compelled to pay from £10 to £70 whenever an assessment was laid.

94. Daily wages for agricultural workers in this period were probably about 3s., but wages

It was not at all clear, in November 1775, that the Assembly had effectively calmed the new egalitarian zeal of the militia and insured a sound provincial defense for the coming year. And the House compounded the public uncertainty generated by its still insufficiently funded militia plan with a grievous error. The lawmakers' decision to go on record against independence well before it became an unavoidable issue, and to link the form of Pennsylvania's government with a continued dependence upon the Crown, when this connection was in several respects not essential, would eventually cost them dear. But as their fall session drew to a close, there was little indication that the legislators' decision was unwise, or that their militia plan might prove inadequate. Pennsylvania's assemblymen retired to their homes for the winter believing that they had done their legislative duty well and retained the full confidence of their constituents.

MILITANT PATRIOTISM AND THE RADICALIZATION OF THE COMMUNITY

Each major assault upon Pennsylvania's autonomy by Great Britain and, beginning in 1774, each attack upon another colony with threatening implications for Pennsylvania radicalized the policies that local and provincial leaders were willing to adopt to protect their community's liberties. The succession of local challenges to imperial authority in 1765, 1769, 1773, and 1774, in response to these British assaults, gradually acquired a powerful momentum. After the battles at Lexington and Concord, this momentum reached a critical level, radicalizing community thought and action in a way that was new in kind rather than in degree; Pennsylvanians in arms developed a militant patriotism that they could not achieve when their weapons were strictly commercial. The growth of this patriotic temper illuminates the process by which the majority of Pennsylvanians developed that deep commitment to a rapidly changing and increasingly cohesive community that marks the emergence of a revolutionary mentality. But that commitment also divided the community: all who opposed their community's transformation, resisted its growing cohesiveness, or denied that it was in grave peril were branded as unconscionably individualistic. These dissenters quickly became a despised and then a repressed minority.

Political radicalism in Pennsylvania's resistance movement was always closely linked to appeals for self-sacrifice in the name of civic virtue. This was the lesson that John Dickinson and Charles Thomson had taught their city in a decade of exhortation. But as the zealous mechanics assured Dickinson in 1774, some Philadelphians (whom the mechanics identified as avaricious merchants and proprietary appointees) could never be converted to the common cause; to attempt this was as "vain as to try to make them Lovers of their Country, or to give up their

---

for skilled labor ranged upward from 3s. 6d. per day for journeyman tailors to 6–8s. or more per day for ship carpenters, and were higher in several luxury crafts (Richard B. Morris, *Government and Labor in Early America* [1946], pp. 94, 96, 194, 196). Thus the twenty Mondays spent voluntarily and without pay in militia training by associators, which nonassociators had to pay only 2s. 6d. per day to escape, were seen as an unfair economic sacrifice on the part of the associators, particularly if they were skilled journeymen or master craftsmen in urban trades.

Prospects of rising on our Ruin."[95] By the fall of 1775, the patriot vision of Pennsylvania's radicals was complete: patriots think first of their community and make personal sacrifices for its security; the unpatriotic wait quietly for the patriotic to stumble and fall so that they may augment their personal power and profit. In the months before Lexington and Concord, however, Pennsylvania's zealots gloried in the voluntary character of patriot virtue; all who did not feel that virtue were left quietly in their own corrupt sloth.

This mood soon changed when Pennsylvanians took up arms. The militia afforded a patriotic role in which every man could display his civic virtue. The radical conviction that every man should associate quickly split the community into militant patriots and their conservative and often pacifist opponents. The ensuing political conflicts wrought certain changes in the socio-economic background of both military and civilian leadership by retiring several cautious members of the ruling elite and replacing them with zealous Pennsylvanians of a more modest social status. These contests culminated in the bitter battle over requiring militia service by law, which widened the gulf between the more cautious, pacific Pennsylvanians and their activist neighbors and prepared the way for a sharp, intense propaganda war over independence and a long and anguished struggle over a new constitution.

The Pennsylvania community split most fundamentally over the patriot demand that in times of peril every citizen's social obligations expand, that each individual sacrifice his time, money, and even safety for the good of the whole. This debate began in June 1775, when those who had joined the militia clamored for mandatory service to force their backward neighbors to make common cause with them. They denounced as elitist selfishness all attempts by the officers' corps and the Committee of Safety to calm their outrage; and finally they converted their superiors, achieving in the early fall, for one brief moment, a simple division between all Pennsylvanians who were active in the resistance, of whatever subcommunity, class, or degree of radical zeal, and all pacifists. By October, local committees of observation, committees of militia officers and of privates, and the provincial Committee of Safety all asserted that every Pennsylvanian must defend the liberties of his community.

For their part, the common associators made this demand because they harbored the darkest suspicions of their neighbors' motives for declining militia service. "Caractacus" had suggested in August that Pennsylvania's ruling elite hoped to make its underpaid, undersubscribed voluntary militia into a standing army, ripe for corruption and tyranny. In early October, the Committee of Privates voiced the same fear, while the Committee of Observation openly charged that those who were unwilling to join or support the militia were not merely selfish individualists, but self-serving enemies of their country.[96] The character of the associators' arguments, when set beside the patriots' call to "civic virtue" voiced earlier in the year, suggests that their fears grew not only out of the eighteenth-century mind's traditional association of standing armies with corruption and tyranny, but also out of their personal conviction that their nonassociating neigh-

---

95. The mechanics to John Dickinson, June 27, 1774, P.S. July 4, 1774, item #156, Dickinson material, R. R. Logan Collection, HSP.
96. *Pa. Jour.,* Aug. 21, 1775; *Pa. Gaz.,* Oct. 11, 1775; *Votes and Proceedings,* VIII: 7334.

bors wished to rob them of their civic virtue and reduce them to pawns in a game played by an unprincipled elite, which fully intended, no matter how the Revolution ended, to come out on top. The Committee of Privates expressed the new egalitarian and communal ethic of Pennsylvania's militant resisters particularly well, declaring that "the true distinction between liberty and despotism consists in this, that in a free state every member thereof is subject to every law of the land, but in despotic states one part is bound while the other is free, and by this means the party bound is always considered as slaves to the party which is free."[97]

The sharp split in the Pennsylvania community in 1775 was the product of a long process, first gradual, then accelerating to a critical velocity. As the conflict with Great Britain escalated, the patriot worldview became starkly dichotomous: all mankind was locked in a struggle between liberty and power; there were no neutrals, no noncombatants.[98] This belief transformed the radicals' concept of self-sacrifice from a moral imperative in the January provincial convention to a statutory obligation in the November Assembly session.

Pennsylvania's new patriot ethic was of indispensable psychological value in preparing its citizens for their Revolution. In 1775, Pennsylvanians, like other colonists, felt deeply wronged by Great Britain and believed that a just God would favor their cause. Yet they also knew that they were politically divided, industrially feeble, and militarily unprepared. The only strong element of their capacity to resist Great Britain was their will. Extraordinary self-sacrifice *would* make them powerful, visible sacrifice *would* unify them. When thousands of patriots publicly cast their timid self-interest aside, they reinforced the courage of all, and earned the right to expect the aid of divine Providence. Only through this mutual self-congratulation could the weak, the dubious, and even the cowardly gain the strength to prevail. This was the psychological—and hence the political—impact of Pennsylvania's rush to arms.

---

97. *Pa. Gaz.,* Oct. 11, 1775.
98. The classic statement of this theme in the thought of the American Revolution is Bailyn, *Ideological Origins,* chaps. 3–4.

The "Wordy War" for Independence

Simple:	Gentlemen, we really ought to sit upon this matter.
Brazen:	That is not a business that comes before the committee, sir.
Tackabout:	The committee, sir, begging your pardon, have a right to take up what business they please; and to give any opinion.[1]

ROBERT MUNFORD, *The Patriots*

The November 1775 Assembly adjournment initiated several quiet weeks during which Pennsylvanians could soberly reflect upon what their legislators had done, where Congress was leading them, and what Great Britain's recent decision to crush America's rebellion throughout the colonies by arms would mean to them.[2] As befitted a time when current resistance policy had long been accepted while the factors that would determine future policy were still obscure, Philadelphia's Committee of Observation had little to do. Its military and commercial duties, while still important, were routine; the board was acting largely as the local agent for the Assembly, the Congress, or Pennsylvania's military machine.[3] The First One Hundred sought no alterations in policy and had no official reaction to the Assembly's categorical rejection of independence.

Like the longer "quiet period" throughout the American colonies a few years earlier, however, this brief hiatus in Pennsylvania's resistance movement thinly covered over deep seated tensions that would shortly erupt into serious conflict between the province's citizens. Three broad causes shaped this new round of political contention. First, the political struggle over arming the province throughout 1775 had intensified the resentments of two groups of Pennsylvanians against

---

1. *WMQ,* 3d Ser., VI (1949): 479. *The Patriots* was probably written in 1776 or 1777. Munford (ca. 1735–84) was a Virginia gentleman, and a distinctly conservative patriot.

2. See Force, ed., *American Archives,* 4th Ser., III: 240 (George III's proclamation against the rebelling colonies, August 23, 1775); 627 (the letter from Richard Penn and Arthur Lee to the Congress, dated September 2, 1775, announcing the King's refusal to reply to Congress's "Olive Branch" petition); and 1792 (the reading of the Penn-Lee letter in Congress, November 9, 1775). Important related documents appear in Force, III: 6, 241, 255, 256, 435, 655, 776, 812, 940, 944, 985, and 1013.

3. For the Philadelphia committee's routine activities from November 1775 to January 1776, see Duane, ed., *Passages from Marshall,* pp. 60–62 (Dec. 10, 21, 1775, Jan. 6, 1776); *Pa. Gaz.,* Dec. 27, 1775, Jan. 10, Feb. 5, 1776; *Pa. Jour.,* Jan. 10, 1776; *Votes and Proceedings,* VIII: 7363, 7365; and *Journals,* IV: 49–50.

the resistance: Quaker pacifists, who had lost the first battle over compulsory militia service, and prominent moderate patriots. Pennsylvania's traditional leadership elite, now largely driven from power on the First One Hundred and having only a tenuous control over the militia, had regrouped in the Committee of Safety and in the Assembly. Second, the battle over the militia was far from over; the Assembly's November plan did not satisfy the associators, and they would soon demand rules of association that were more favorable to them—and more offensive to pacifists and moderate leaders alike. Finally, the Assembly's instructions to its congressmen, far from settling the question of independence, opened it up for the most contentious public discussion.

THE DIALOGUE OVER INDEPENDENCE BEGINS

The Philadelphia press, quiet on resistance issues since May, opened the public discussion of the Assembly's November 9 instructions to its congressmen in late November. On November 22, "A Lover of Order" began this dialogue in the *Journal* with the assertion that Pennsylvania's voters had permitted the Assembly to appoint delegates to Congress simply as a matter of convenience, never intending that the legislators regard the congressmen as representing themselves rather than the people. He then advised Pennsylvania's congressmen to act "continentally" according to their best judgment, not "provincially" according to Assembly instructions.[4] Three days later, "A Pennsylvania Associator" attacked "A Lover of Order" in the *Ledger,* charging that his adversary had no real objection to the Assembly's power to instruct its delegates, but only to the substance of the November 9 instructions, because his goal was independence. Pennsylvania's congressmen, the "Associator" declared, were still free under the new instructions to carry on a stout resistance to Britain's imperial policy, which had always been Congress's stated goal.

In the *Journal's* next issue, a third contender, an "Independent Whig," advanced several important ideas.[5] He agreed that the principal objection of "A Lover of Order" to the instructions was their content, but countered that "A Pennsylvania Associator" was more alarmed by his opponent's inclination toward independence than by his argument about the Assembly's proper powers. Then, as openly as any Pennsylvanian at this date, he endorsed independence, saying that the colonists appeared to have little choice. The "Independent Whig" was not entirely clear on this point; he seemed to regard independence either as a mere tactic to force Britain into concessions or as a necessary policy after Britain's defeat by the colonies (of which he was quite confident). He did insist, however, that the Assembly's decision to reject a break with England in principle was an egregious tactical error.

The following week, "A Lover of Order," now signing himself "A Continental

---

4. On the growing distinction between the people and their representatives made by Revolutionary-era Americans, see Buel, "Democracy and the American Revolution," pp. 165–90; Bailyn, *Ideological Origins,* chaps. 5–6; and Wood, *Creation of the American Republic,* chaps. 2, 5, 8–9. Unfortunately, the identities of "A Lover of Order" and most other Philadelphia newspaper propagandists are not known.

5. Nov. 29, 1775.

Farmer," closed this brief interchange with the most penetrating assessment of the challenge facing the colonies yet advanced in Philadelphia.[6] Congressmen who were instructed to avoid anything "which might lead to a separation" from England, he argued, would be reduced to a state of paralysis. Both the past and current policy of Congress and of the Assembly, whether petitioning Britain long after petitions had proven useless or prosecuting a war, could lead to that total separation. The instructions were "ill judged"; every policy ought to have a fair hearing, and none ought to be rejected out of hand. The goal of resistance leaders was to "promote the good and happiness of the whole continent, and not for a day or two, but lastingly so," and either dependence or independence might be consistent with this goal.

This brief public exchange raises two points of the first importance in understanding Pennsylvania's independence movement. The scope of the attack upon the Assembly's instructions was actually quite limited; neither of the two radical penmen endorsed independence unequivocally, and no public body would comment on the instructions.[7] Nevertheless, the substance of the criticism directed at the Assembly by "A Lover of Order"/ "A Continental Farmer" and "Independent Whig" should have given Pennsylvania's legislators pause for reflection. The remarks of "A Lover of Order" particularly suggest that the Assembly's claim to unquestioned authority in speaking for its constituents was not universally accepted. At least some Pennsylvanians believed in the absolute sovereignty of the people, whereby the legislature was reduced to a mere convenient instrument of government. This sentiment had surfaced before, in July 1774, when Galloway's Assembly had sought to monopolize Pennsylvania's participation in the resistance movement; its reappearance in late 1775 signaled that the Assembly was again losing contact with its constituents.[8]

The second aspect of this criticism was of greater immediate significance. In late 1775, independence was not yet a measure that Pennsylvanians could discuss openly; all reference to it had to be indirect. At the same time, several local leaders were beginning to appreciate a fact of immense importance. The entire direction of the resistance effort and all of its achievements up to December 1775 pointed

---

6. *Pa. Jour.*, Dec. 6, 1775. The pen name "A Continental Farmer" may well have been an intentional dig at John Dickinson, who, after the Assembly's November 9 instructions, must have appeared to this propagandist as an old-fashioned, "provincial" farmer, a mere shadow of the "Pennsylvania Farmer" of 1767–68.

7. In the period November 1775–April 1776, one key issue set all Philadelphia "radicals" off from their neighbors—independence. For the months of November and December 1775, I label "radicals" all those who were willing to consider seriously an immediate break with Great Britain; beginning in January 1776, "radicals" are those who openly favored that break. Radicals were also distinguished by their demand for a stronger compulsory militia law than the one passed by the Assembly in November 1775, and by their insistence that if the Assembly would not support independence and a stronger militia, it must be immediately reformed. As before, radical merchant committeemen continued to ally with new leaders from the mechanic classes and to allow mechanic leaders more power and responsibility in the resistance movement than ever before. All "moderates" opposed both independence and any precipitate reform of the Assembly; and they clung to a traditional, elite leadership model, as they had throughout the resistance movement. "Conservatives" were by this period nearly all loyalists or nonresistant Quakers with strong loyalist sympathies.

8. The first such argument, appearing in the *New-York Journal*, July 14, 1774, was a critique of the June 28, 1774, letter from the Pennsylvania Assembly's correspondence committee to the correspondence committee of the Massachusetts House of Representatives (see chapter 3 above). It did not appear in the Philadelphia press, however.

toward a separation from Great Britain. "A Continental Farmer" saw this clearly, despite his reluctance to champion independence directly. Appealing to the first principle of the resistance, the promotion of the lasting "happiness of the whole continent," he suggested that to secure this end the colonists had cautiously chosen the minimum necessary tactical weapon to check each new imperial design, only to find the possibility of separation from Britain growing with every step taken. Thus the argument stood in mid-December, just prior to the first attempts of radical penmen to tackle the issue of independence head on.

A complete separation from Great Britain must have been considered by at least a few Philadelphians as early as 1774, but the initial development of this idea remains as obscure in Pennsylvania as in every other colony. Patriot leaders, even in their private correspondence, betrayed little interest in the matter, and public comment on the issue before the appearance of *Common Sense* was characteristically tentative and ambivalent.[9] When Thomas Paine, as "Humanus," published a brief essay in mid-October 1775 that closed with his fervent belief that "the Almighty will finally separate America from Britain," he was still far to the left of the patriot mainstream.[10] More typical is the Chester County Committee of Observation's indignant denial that it sought a separation from England.[11] The failure of this sincere disclaimer to achieve its most probable object, the reelection of Chester County's radical committee chairman, Anthony Wayne, to the Assembly in the October 2, 1775 polling, argues that many Pennsylvanians were now thinking about independence, and dreading it.

Radical leaders, too, were reluctant to face this issue, even in private. In early October, Joseph Reed wrote to his brother-in-law, Charles Pettit, that he still favored remaining in the British Empire on the terms that had prevailed before 1763, although he doubted that such an arrangement could now be made.[12] And, as we have seen, Philadelphia's most zealous patriot writers could not bring themselves to demand independence as the only solution to the colonists' dilemma, even after learning of George III's rude rejection of the "Olive Branch Petition." They could only recommend separation as a reasonable alternative that the colonists might soon have to consider, an alternative that should not be rejected arbitrarily by the provincial Assembly. What was lacking in these arguments was a sense of immediacy, a conviction that the colonists must make independence the central question in their plans for the future.

All this began to change with the appearance of the first letter of "Salus Populi" in the *Pennsylvania Journal* on December 27, 1775. The author declared that all persons who sincerely wished to see peace restored to the colonies, with their liberties intact, could be divided into those favoring independence "as the only state in which they can perceive any security for our liberty and privileges, . . . And those who, overlooking the possibility of Lord North's motion [of February 1775, that each colony be allowed to clear all its imperial obligations with an

9. Early references to independence published in Philadelphia or written privately by Philadelphians appear in "Political Observations, Without Order," *Pa. Packet,* Nov. 14, 1774 (also in *Rivington's N.-Y. Gaz.,* Dec. 1, 1774); the essay by "Caractacus," *Pa. Packet,* Aug. 21, 1775; and Joseph Reed to Charles Pettit, Aug. 29, 1775, Reed Papers, N.-Y. Hist. Soc.

10. *Pa. Jour.,* Oct. 18, 1775, also in Moncure Daniel Conway, ed., *The Writings of Thomas Paine* (New York, 1894–96; reprinted, 1967), pp. 66–67 (hereafter Paine, *Writings*).

11. *Pa. Gaz.,* Sept. 27, 1775.

12. Reed to Charles Pettit, Oct. 8, 1775, Reed Papers, N.-Y. Hist. Soc.

annual grant to the Crown] being a political manoeuvre to lull us to rest, . . . think it not impossible that Britain and America may yet be united." Whichever viewpoint was sounder, he continued (as if he had not suggested which was sounder), the colonists should take one step immediately—the foundation of a strong government uniting the thirteen colonies. If the colonies became independent, unity would be essential to preserve peace among them; and if they did strike a good settlement with Britain, they would still need a continental union to hold Britain's untrustworthy ministers and monarchs, present and future, to that agreement.

A way was clearly opening up in the press for a deliberate assault upon the prevailing notion that independence was an undesirable last resort. Resentment and frustration over George III's rejection of the "Olive Branch Petition" and the lack of any favorable signs from Britain were mounting in Philadelphia. But the public was still so confused and indecisive that even radical committees kept quiet on the issue. On January 10, however, two events finally shattered this mood of awkward hesitation: a copy of George III's hard-line address to Parliament, delivered on October 27, 1775, reached Philadelphia and immediately appeared in print; and Thomas Paine's *Common Sense* went on sale.[13]

Paine's famous tract needs no extensive commentary here, but an appreciation of its effect upon Philadelphia politics, within the context of local opinion, is essential. In Pennsylvania and throughout the middle colonies, where the independence movement was particularly in need of ammunition, certain features of this essay were particularly effective in changing public attitudes. Philadelphians already believed that George III and his ministers were flawed and even pernicious. What they needed to be told was that monarchy, aristocracy, and the British constitution were useless. What was required was a bold figure who would declare that their veneration for an ideal British political system was erroneous and anachronistic.

The author of *Common Sense* was just that figure. The burden of Paine's argument was not that George III was a tyrant, but that kings were tyrants; not that the British constitution was deteriorating, but that it had been decayed and useless for centuries; not that Britain was currently harsh and arbitrary with her colonies because of some temporary aberration, but that her natural interests were, always had been, and always would be utterly incompatible with the interests of the colonies. Paine foresaw that opponents of independence would not attempt to deny the cruel folly of present imperial policy, but would stress the general benefits of a tie with Great Britain and assert the impossibility of erecting a stable government in a large country without a king. It was his genius to sense that these widely held beliefs were in fact vulnerable, that the colonists were now unsure of these long-cherished axioms of their political world. By entering the field first—and *Common Sense* was the first public piece in Philadelphia to espouse the desirability of independence—Paine turned the tables on moderate patriots who wished to remain within the British Empire. Monarchy, not republicanism, had now to be defended; the domination of a vast and virtuous continent by a small and corrupt island had now to be explained.

Common Sense caused a great stir in Philadelphia and sold briskly; on January 27, a second edition appeared, and in mid-February a third edition, which included

---

13. For these two pieces, and commentary on their exact dating, see *Pa. Jour.*, Jan. 10, 1776 (supplement); Duane, ed., *Passages from Marshall*, p. 62 (Jan. 8, 1776); Paine, *Writings*, pp. 67–112, esp. 67n and 112; and Evans Index, No. 14954.

a commentary on the King's October 27 speech to Parliament and an "Epistle to Quakers."[14] The "Epistle" was a response to the first strong attack upon independence in Philadelphia. The Society of Friends had been most circumspect in their public pronouncements since their January 1775 testimony, which had caused such serious dissensions within their own ranks, but the specter of independence was too much for them to accept meekly. On January 20, 1776, the Society's elders issued their "ANCIENT TESTIMONY . . . addressed to the PEOPLE IN GENERAL," which explained that "the setting up and putting down kings and governments, is God's peculiar prerogative; for causes best known to himself: And it is not our business to have any hand or contrivance therein; . . . but to pray for the king, and safety of our nation, and good of all men: That we may live a quiet and peaceable life, in all godliness and honesty; *under the government which God is pleased to set over us.*"[15]

The Quakers' rejection of a break with England did not elicit an immediate reply. Leading radicals probably wished to avoid any confrontation with a religious body, and while Paine had finally made independence a public issue, the battle had yet to be fully joined. But sentiment for separation was growing rapidly. "Salus Populi's" second essay, appearing only a few days after the Quaker's "Testimony," argued that no secure reconciliation with Britain was now to be expected. The following week Samuel Adams, writing as "Candidus" in the radical *Evening Post,* praised *Common Sense* and coldly rebuked the Friends' "Testimony" by expressing the hope that if Pennsylvania's Quakers did not relish "putting down kings," at least they would not continue to "support tyrants."[16]

This first stage in Philadelphia's propaganda war for independence came to a fitting climax in mid-February with the publication of three important essays within three days. In his "Epistle to Quakers," Thomas Paine, himself of Quaker background, admonished Philadelphia's Friends for abandoning their nonresistant principles by publishing a defense of the status quo. If they wanted nothing to do with "the setting up and putting down kings and governments," they should remain entirely neutral, and be silent.[17] The Quakers' defense of dependence, however, hardly needed to be demolished. Their otherworldly passivity in the face of obnoxious worldly developments had little appeal outside their Society and continued to cause division within it.[18] After Paine's rebuke, Independent writers turned to more pressing issues.[19]

---

14. Paine, *Writings,* pp. 112–20 (on George III's speech) and pp. 121–26 ("Epistle to Quakers").

15. Early American Imprints (microcard), Evans Index Nos. 14765–66.

16. *Pa. Jour.,* Jan. 24, 1776; *Pa. Evening Post,* Feb. 3, 1776. Adams is identified as "Candidus" by William V. Wells, *The Life and Public Services of Samuel Adams* (Boston, 1865), II: 360–63. This essay marks the beginning of Adams' direct and soon widely known participation in Pennsylvania politics.

17. Paine, *Writings,* pp. 121–26.

18. Between September and December 1775, twelve Philadelphia Friends were expelled from the Society for warlike activity. To this number the Society added sixty-one more between January and June 1776. Twelve of these disowned Friends were committeemen, and their committee activity was often cited in Society records as one reason for their expulsion ("Minutes of the Philadelphia Monthly Meeting, 1771–1777," ff. 319–88 *passim;* "Northern District Minutes, 1772–1781," ff. 165–213 *passim;* and "Southern District Minutes, 1772–1780," ff. 102–42 *passim;* all on film, Friends Historical Library, Swarthmore, Pa.).

19. In this chapter and in chapter 9 below, I will frequently employ the term "Independent," both as adjective and noun, singular and plural, to denote those propagandists, strategists, and

On February 14, the day on which Paine issued his third edition of *Common Sense* with its "Epistle," the *Journal* published "Salus Populi's" third letter, which advanced a strong argument that anticipated and answered the main line of defense soon to be developed by Philadelphia's anti-Independent publicists. "Salus Populi" asserted that while it was perhaps true that the colonists "enjoyed happiness *in* a state of dependence" they did not enjoy it *"from* that state," but from their own effort and virtue, and from the fertility of the American soil. Three days later the *Evening Post* published unsigned "Questions and Answers," a comprehensive and dispassionate consideration of the practical benefits of independence. Building an argument at once judicious and sanguine, the author considered the future of American trade, defense, finances, foreign alliances, political stability, and liberty in a state of independence, and concluded that although the war needed to secure the separation would be costly, it was certain to succeed and would not be a high price to pay to establish America's freedom.

By late February, the propaganda war for independence had made phenomenal progress. Seizing the initiative, the Independents had advanced all of their central arguments and developed them in detail, with clarity and style. Remarkably, they had yet to encounter strong opposition. This success surely owed something to the radical bias of the *Journal, Packet,* and *Evening Post,* but the *Packet* and *Post* soon ran a few anti-Independent pieces, and the moderate *Gazette* and conservative *Ledger* would shortly print several essays that attacked separation from Britain. The explanation for the moderates' failure, before the end of February, to produce anything beyond the Quakers' "Testimony" and a bit of satiric verse[20] was probably the familiar one—they were again surprised and outmaneuvered by the bold initiative of the radicals.

THE RADICAL RESISTANCE ON THE OFFENSIVE: THE SECOND ONE HUNDRED

While radical penmen were opening their campaign for independence, radical organizers were engineering a decisive victory over moderate patriots through direct political action. The coalition of moderates and radicals put together by John Dickinson and Charles Thomson in the summer of 1774 had begun to splinter as early as October of that year. By the summer of 1775 further partisan contention threatened the unity of the resistance as the radicals, who had seized control of the movement the previous November, themselves began to split into moderate radical and ultraradical camps. The first signs of this schism were the

---

rank-and-file Pennsylvanians who, between January and June 1776, sought a complete separation from Great Britain. This term was first taken by a proindependence writer as his pen name on March 18, 1776 (*Pa. Packet*), and by May was used by several radical writers with pride. I label all those leaders and writers who worked to stay in the British Empire in these same months "anti-Independents." The term is awkward, but any other term is probably too inaccurate to be useful. To call these men tories or loyalists would imply a degree of fidelity to Great Britain that many opponents of independence did not feel. To call them "dependents," as Thomas Paine and other radicals did in May 1776 (meaning, among other things, that they were *proprietary* dependents), would be both prejorative and inaccurate, because many anti-Independents neither had nor sought proprietary or Crown connections, and were thus not demonstrably more dependent on others for their livelihoods than their Independent neighbors.

20. *Pa. Evening Post,* Feb. 6, 1776.

election of the First One Hundred in August and the Assembly election in October. November and December had been quiet, but friction between the great patriot importers and the more radical young merchants, retailers, and artisans persisted; the controversy over independence and continuing militia dissatisfaction with the Assembly's military leadership brought this conflict to a head.

With the new year, the First One Hundred again turned to open political activity. By January 25, when the board announced that the new committee to succeed it would be elected on February 16, a few "friends of America" had already met to begin composing a ticket for that election.[21] This was apparently a gathering of the most radical leaders in Philadelphia, both on and off the committee. At the same time, the whole First One Hundred was engaged in some nominating work of its own; on the morning of January 26, the day set for the by-election to fill Thomas Mifflin's Assembly seat, the First One Hundred named its candidate for the post. Joseph Reed, who had recently returned to Philadelphia from the army in New England and who still enjoyed strong support on the committee, won the nomination over George Clymer, who had been acting chairman of the First One Hundred in Reed's absence. Reed and Clymer do not appear to have held very different political views, but the contest must have expressed a real political division on the committee, because when a new Second One Hundred was chosen on February 16, Reed was on it, but Clymer was not. However secured, the First One Hundred's endorsement in the Assembly by-election carried weight with City voters; Joseph Reed was elected to the House on January 26, 1776.[22]

What occurred during the next three weeks in Philadelphia will possibly always remain obscure, but on February 16, the radical-mechanic faction had a ticket ready. The "mechanics' ticket" is the only one extant and may have run unopposed, but whether or not the moderates offered a slate, the dimensions of their defeat are clear. In several respects the Second One Hundred was not very different from its predecessor, and not nearly so different as the Sixty-Six had been from the Forty-Three. Sixty-nine committeemen had been returned, in addition to four men who had served on earlier boards. But a closer examination shows that important changes in committee composition had again occurred. The new board's members were the least affluent and most obscure committeemen since the beginning of the resistance. For the first time, retailers and artisans outnumbered merchants; the number of members with high tax assessments dropped sharply, and two-thirds of the new board had been assessed less than £45 in 1774, a certain indication of careers that either were in their early stages or were not especially prosperous. And for the first time since the tea affair in Philadelphia, the proportion of Quakers in the whole fell below one-quarter.[23]

Remarkably, these dramatic changes involved a turnover of only thirty-one out of one hundred members. Those deleted included several leading Quaker and Anglican merchants, notably George Clymer, Lambert Cadwalader, Benjamin Marshall, Robert Morris, and Thomas Wharton, Jr. A few of these deletions were not the product of radical opposition; Benjamin Marshall, for example, was a

---

21. *Pa. Gaz.*, Feb. 14, 1776; Duane, ed., *Passages from Marshall*, p. 65 (Jan. 20).

22. *Votes and Proceedings*, VIII: 7361, 7366; Duane, ed., *Passages from Marshall*, pp. 66, 67 (Jan. 26, 27).

23. See chapter 8 below, and tables 12 and 15, for a quantitative comparison of these several committees and a full discussion of the composition of the Second One Hundred.

pious Quaker who finally yielded to pressure from his sect to retire from public life.[24] The omission of Clymer, Wharton, and Robert Morris, however, must have been deliberately partisan. These men were not excluded from political activity after February 16, however, for they were active members of the Committee of Safety, a body that was thoroughly under the control of moderate patriots. It may well have been friction between the Committee of Safety and the First One Hundred over the issue of militia reform that led to their exclusion from the new city committee.[25] The deleted veterans were replaced by relatively obscure Philadelphians, who were almost without exception artisans and retailers of modest fortune or young merchants just beginning their careers. Most would remain obscure, even in radical politics, but two of the newcomers were or soon would be prominent leaders. Samuel Simpson headed Philadelphia's Committee of Privates, which was at the center of the city's ultraradical political activities, and Dr. Benjamin Rush, a close friend of Thomas Paine, would play a key role in bringing both independence and the Constitution of 1776 to Pennsylvania.

The new committee perfected its internal organization on February 26 by assigning eighty-eight members to its six district subcommittees. The twelve remaining committeemen were chosen as officers; six of them had led the First One Hundred—secretaries John Bayard Smith, Robert Strettel Jones, and Peter Z. Lloyd, and chairmen Joseph Reed, Samuel Meredith, and Thomas McKean. The other six—John Bayard, Sharp Delaney, and James Searles, and the renegade Quakers Isaac Howell, Timothy Matlack, and Samuel Cadwalader Morris—completed the board's new correspondence subcommittee, a select policy-making body.[26] The new roster of officers suggests little change from the previous board, but the leadership structure of the committee was in fact changing. Three board members who were not given special assignments, Christopher Marshall, Sr., Dr. Benjamin Rush, and Samuel Simpson, would soon join Timothy Matlack, and several noncommitteemen, to exercise as great an influence upon committee policy as that of the board's officers. Equally important, events would soon show that Thomas McKean, the radical congressman from Delaware, had now become the committee's real leader, while Joseph Reed and Samuel Meredith, George Clymer's business partner, had lost power. The sudden decline in Reed's ability to deter the committee from what he considered rash endeavors in the winter of 1776, an ability that he had exercised so effectively in January 1775, was especially significant.

---

24. "Minutes of the Philadelphia Monthly Meeting, 1771–1777," ff. 299, 314, 330, 335–36, 344–45, 357, 385–86, 393.

25. See table 15 on the background of the members deleted and added, *Pa. Gazette,* Feb. 21, for a list of the committeemen, and Appendix M for portrait data on each of them. Of the veterans not included on the new committee, six were Committee of Safety members: Owen Biddle, George Clymer, James Mease, Robert Morris, Samuel Morris, Jr., and Thomas Wharton, Jr. The Committee of Safety members retained on the Second One Hundred were John Dickinson and Benjamin Franklin, who were no longer active on either board, and John Cadwalader, Joseph Parker, and Joseph Reed. On the city committee's disagreements with the Committee of Safety, see its circular letter to the counties, *Pa. Packet,* Mar. 5, 1776 (to be discussed shortly below).

26. "List of the Sub-Committees, appointed by the committee for the city and liberties of Philadelphia, . . ." (Feb. 26, 1776) [Evans No. 15012]. This list also includes six men, not elected on February 16, who were to inspect commerce in Moyamensing and Passayunk, two suburbs south and west of Southwark. The role of the new correspondence subcommittee, whose membership does not appear in the sources but has been inferred, is established by Christopher Marshall, Sr., Duane, ed., *Passages from Marshall,* p. 69 (Mar. 4, 1776).

The primary objectives of the Second One Hundred, from the moment of its election, were to force the Assembly to alter its militia rules to make nonservice costlier and less attractive, and to revise its instructions to Pennsylvania's congressmen to allow them to vote for independence.[27] Within the committee, however, there were sharp differences of opinion over the proper strategy for achieving these goals. The more moderate members of this most radical committee, led by Joseph Reed, advocated working through traditional channels. Local committees, militia groups, and ordinary citizens would petition the House to change its policies, and activist assemblymen, led by Reed himself, would carry on the struggle within the chamber.[28] The ultraradicals, led by Thomas McKean, Timothy Matlack, and Christopher Marshall, Sr., favored calling a provincial convention that would force the Assembly to grant the newer counties more seats in the legislature, alter the membership of its delegation to Congress and of the Committee of Safety, frame new militia rules, and permit its congressmen to support independence.[29]

The Assembly opened its winter session only the day before the Second One Hundred was elected, and the legislators had hardly begun their work when, on February 28, the new committee voted to call a provincial convention to force their hand.[30] In its circular letter to Pennsylvania's county committees released on March 5, the Second One Hundred explained why it had rejected the committee moderates' proposal to await the results of the petition campaign among the voters, then in progress, to effect Assembly reforms. First, the board was concerned over the recent news that Britain was sending commissioners to treat with the colonies; from this overture the committeemen expected nothing but British treachery and colonial division. Furthermore, the city committee had long been unhappy with a provincial Committee of Safety composed largely of "members not having the authority of the people"—that is, nonassemblymen like George Clymer and others recently deleted from the city committee—as well as with the nonassembly delegates to Congress, conservatives Andrew Allen and Thomas Willing.[31] In addition,

---

27. In pursuing its routine duties, the Second One Hundred followed traditional practices. The board worked for the acceptance of Continental currency by printing the names of all who refused it in the press, continued to oversee shipping, and tried, largely unsuccessfully, to control the prices of goods that were or appeared to be scarce. But while the more radical board members lost their battle for stricter commercial regulation, the contest was a relatively minor one at this time. Commercial regulation aroused little apparent public interest in early 1776, in sharp contrast to the emotions it would stir up later in Philadelphia. It was instead a nagging chore for a political body that was far more interested in political issues than in its commercial duties. See Duane, ed., *Passages from Marshall*, pp. 68–70, 74, 84; *Journals*, IV: 133, 172; *Pa. Gaz.*, Mar. 13 ("Cato" Letter I, and "Luke, the Physician"), June 5, 6, 1776; *Pa. Evening Post*, Mar. 7 ("An Enemy to Monopolizing"), Mar. 28, Apr. 4, 6. For an interpretation that argues that economic tensions did powerfully shape political contention in early 1776, see Warner, *Private City*, chap. 2.

28. See Reed to Charles Pettit, Mar. 3, 1776, Reed Papers, N.-Y. Hist. Soc.

29. Christopher Marshall, Sr. identifies McKean and Matlack as leaders of the radicals in March–June 1776. Allied with them in this period, and probably as early as February, were James Cannon, secretary of the Committee of Privates, Thomas Paine, Dr. Thomas Young, and other noncommitteemen (Duane, ed., *Passages from Marshall*, pp. 71, 73, 75, 79, 80, 83, 84). Marshall establishes his own involvement with these ultraradicals in the same diary entries.

30. *Votes and Proceedings*, VIII: 7384–85; Duane, ed., *Passages from Marshall*, p. 69 (Feb. 28).

31. The circular letter appeared in *Pa. Packet*, Mar. 11, 1776. For related arguments in the press at this time, see essays in the *Pa. Evening Post* by "The Apologist," Feb. 29, and by "The Censor," Mar. 5, 1776.

the Second One Hundred had probably heard rumors that the several voter petitions of February 22, 23, and 27, which asked for a revision of the militia rules
and the levying of extra taxes on nonassociators, had been cooly received by the
House, despite the legislators' decision of February 28 to appoint a subcommittee
to revise the militia rules. For these particular reasons, but ultimately because of
their growing disillusionment with the Assembly and its increasingly conservative
leader, John Dickinson, Philadelphia's committeemen voted to issue their invitation
to a new provincial convention at once.[32]

Joseph Reed was most upset by this decision. His campaign to alter the policy
of the House from within was well under way; Philadelphia's committeemen, he
was convinced, were spoiling his efforts by their impetuosity.[33] Reed had good
reasons for believing that he could carry his reform program in the chamber. On
February 27, Benjamin Franklin resigned the Assembly seat he had never occupied,
and the House called a by-election for March 2, giving the radicals a fine opportunity to gain another vote in the legislature. This they did by electing the mathe-
matician, astronomer, and political zealot David Rittenhouse.[34] And on February
28, the same day on which the Second One Hundred first resolved to call a convention, Bedford, Berks, Cumberland, Northumberland, and York counties, in an
unprecedented and obviously well-coordinated move, petitioned the Assembly for
more seats in the chamber.[35]

Did not these events suggest that the redress of the radicals' grievances through
established channels was imminent? Reed firmly believed so, and on March 4, a
delegation of assemblymen met with the Second One Hundred and persuaded that
body to postpone its summons for a convention and await the Assembly's decisions
concerning representation, the militia, the Committee of Safety, and its instructions
to Pennsylvania's congressmen.[36] In its letter to the county committees, the Second
One Hundred first fully explained each part of the dissatisfaction with the Assembly
that had led it to decide to call a convention, for it had no intention of letting up
the pressure on the lawmakers. The committeemen then stated that they had
decided to delay calling a convention only after receiving strong assurances that
the House would vote the reforms that they sought. In the meantime, the committee
had framed petitions for more equal representation for the City of Philadelphia in
the House.[37] The ball was now in the other court; with the publication of the
Second One Hundred's circular letter and the appearance of several important
petitions to the Assembly, public attention turned from the committee to Pennsylvania's legislators.

---

32. Duane, ed., *Passages from Marshall*, p. 69 (Feb. 28, 29).
33. Reed to Pettit, Mar. 3, 1776, Reed Papers, N.-Y. Hist. Soc.
34. *Votes and Proceedings*, VIII: 7410, 7428.
35. *Votes and Proceedings*, VIII: 7412.
36. See the Second One Hundred's circular letter to the counties (dated Mar. 5), *Pa. Packet*,
Mar. 11, 1776. The members of this delegation are not known, but Reed may well have been
their leader.
37. *Pa. Packet*, Mar. 11, 1776; *Votes and Proceedings*, VIII: 7436. In their circular letter,
the committeemen did not recall their invitation, but postponed it indefinitely. The board only
decided to drop its convention plans on March 13, after the Assembly had framed its bill to
expand the size of the House by giving Philadelphia and the newer counties more seats. See
Selsam, *Pennsylvania Constitution*, p. 99n; "Cato," Letter III, *Pa. Gaz.*, Mar. 20, 1776; and
"No Enemy," *Pa. Evening Post*, Mar. 21, 1776.

RESISTANCE, BUT NOT REVOLUTION:
THE PENNSYLVANIA ASSEMBLY

On February 15, the Pennsylvania Assembly began its winter session. In late November, the moderate legislators who led the House had probably believed that they had quieted Pennsylvania's zealots and put the province on a sound defensive footing with their instructions to their congressmen and their militia law. It is unlikely that they were so sanguine by mid-February. The propaganda war for independence dominated the press, and dissatisfaction with the new militia law, although less publicized, was widespread. These two issues were among the most explosive in the Assembly's history. Most assemblymen believed that independence could only bring about major alterations in the provincial government, which they were determined not to make. Equally important, a denial of the needs of the militia would antagonize thousands of men who, although to a large extent without the franchise, could wield great power in wartime. The military associators could, by deliberate inaction, threaten the security of a polity that they could hardly influence as poor civilians under more peaceful circumstances.

Most Pennsylvania lawmakers, however, simply did not recognize the danger that they faced. The numerous Quaker and Quaker-party veterans were adamantly opposed to major change, and worked to protect strict Friends from the sacrifices of military mobilization. The legislators as a whole were determined to retain power in their own hands, and genuinely believed that they could both resist independence while other colonies sought it, and deny their militia its vital needs without disrupting the resistance effort. Having controlled the province securely and fended off the strongest challenges to their power for half a century, Pennsylvania's assemblymen appeared to be incapable of realizing how suddenly that power might now be torn from their grasp.

The Assembly's first task was to defuse the anger of Pennsylvania's military associators over its November militia rules. From the day of the legislature's fall adjournment, Philadelphia's Committee of Privates had held frequent meetings to discuss the new rules and frame its policy regarding them, and several rural militia groups and civilian committees had been equally active.[38] Everywhere the rules were received with disfavor, and everywhere the objections were much the same. The plan did not provide enough muster days to perfect military training, or enough arms for those who were too poor to arm themselves. The financial support voted for the families of poor associators on active duty was insufficient, and because it would be channeled through poor-relief officials, it was demeaning. Pennsylvania's numerous nonassociators were too lightly fined for declining to serve, and the provision exempting all men over fifty from service permitted many able-bodied wealthy individuals to evade any contribution to the common defense. Pennsylvania's associators concluded that under the Assembly's plan a few mostly poorer men were to bear the entire burden of protecting the province, while many

---

38. The Philadelphia committee met on November 25 and 30, December 4, 16, 20, 23, and 27, 1775, January 15, 27, and 30, and February 5 and 10, 1776 (*Pa. Gaz.,* Nov. 22, 29, Dec. 27, 1775, Feb. 7, 14, 1776; *Pa. Packet,* Dec. 4, 18, 1775, Jan. 15, 22, 1776; *Pa. Ledger,* Dec. 16, 23, 1775; *Pa. Evening Post,* Dec. 19, 1775). On the rural response, see *Pa. Jour.,* Jan. 3 (Chester County committee resolve), and Feb. 7, 1776 (Berks County committee resolve); and the petitions cited in note 39 below.

wealthy Pennsylvanians who could not claim the slightest attachment to sincere pacifist principles could avoid military service for the trifling sum of fifty shillings.[39]

In meetings held in December and January, Philadelphia's Committee of Privates worked out a strategy to secure militia reform, and on January 30, the board released at least a part of its plan for publication. Recommending that all associators sign the November rules, even though they were clearly defective, the committee at the same time expressed its confidence that the House would soon make the necessary alterations in the articles.[40] But Philadelphia's Committee of Privates had no intention of leaving legislative action either to chance or to the good will of the lawmakers. In its January 30 public letter, which it evidently circulated to every county, the committee announced the formation of a nine-man subcommittee of correspondence to which rural associators were encouraged to communicate their suggestions for changing the militia rules.[41]

Although no accounts of coordinated planning between Philadelphia's Committee of Privates and any rural bodies have survived, the circumstantial evidence for this activity is persuasive. On February 23, four groups presented petitions to the Assembly that called for an alteration of the militia rules: Philadelphia's Committee of Privates, the city's Committee of Officers, the Committee of Observation and the field officers of Berks County, and the Committee of Observation of Chester County. One week later, Bucks County's Committee of Observation and Pennsylvania's Committee of Safety followed suit.[42] All the petitions were in fundamental agreement: the Assembly must vote more money for the associators, more muster days, more light arms for poor militiamen, and more fines and taxes for nonassociators.

The Second One Hundred did not present a petition seeking these ends, but city radicals supported the objectives of their associators as zealously as did their country allies. Joseph Reed and other moderate city committeemen had as their prime objective the immediate alteration of Assembly policy concerning both independence and militia rules. Moreover, on February 28, five western counties petitioned for more seats in the legislature.[43] The coordinating work behind this

---

39. See the petitions of the Berks County Committee of Observation and Field Officers (*Votes and Proceedings,* VIII: 7396–7401); Philadelphia (city) Committee of Privates (pp. 7402–7); Philadelphia (city) Committee of Officers (pp. 7407–9); Chester County Committee of Observation (pp. 7409–10); Bucks County Committee of Observation (pp. 7422–23); Pennsylvania Committee of Safety (p. 7426); Cumberland County, First Battalion, Privates (pp. 7438–40); Whitehall and Salisbury Townships, Northampton County (p. 7443); and a second Philadelphia Committee of Privates petition, reporting the objections of Chester County, Elk Battalion, Committee of Privates, and Lancaster County, Colonel Galbreath's Battalion (pp. 7448–49).

40. *Pa. Evening Post,* Feb. 1, *Pa. Gaz.,* Feb. 7, 1776. I say "at least a part of its plan" because it is probable that the committee's strategy also included encouraging the back counties to seek greater representation in the Assembly. The committee's likely role in this effort will be considered shortly below.

41. *Pa. Gaz.,* Feb. 7, 1776. Internal evidence and the appointment of a subcommittee of correspondence indicate that this document was a circular letter. Those appointed to the correspondence subcommittee were William Adcock, chairman of the full Committee of Privates, Robert Bell, the printer of *Common Sense,* James Cannon, secretary of the full committee, Frederick Hagener, Patrick Logan, George Nelson, Andrew Porter, Edward Ryves, and Michael Schubert, a member of the Second One Hundred. For one result of this subcommittee's work, see the Committee of Privates' petition in *Votes and Proceedings,* VIII: 7448–49.

42. *Votes and Proceedings,* VIII: 7396–7410, 7422–23, 7426.

43. *Votes and Proceedings,* VIII: 7412.

unprecedented move must have originated in Philadelphia, whether in a group of backcountry delegates collaborating with Joseph Reed, in the Committee of Privates, in the Second One Hundred itself, or perhaps in all three groups working together. At first there was not perfect agreement between Philadelphia and the rural counties over the best means to secure reform; on the same day that the petitions for more representatives were presented by the western counties, the Second One Hundred resolved to call a provincial convention. After a delegation of lawmakers persuaded the Second One Hundred to suspend its invitation, however, city and county worked together smoothly to secure reform of the Assembly's program through a reform of the chamber's composition.

The demand for expanded representation in the Assembly for the backcountry, and for the City of Philadelphia, which petitioned the legislature on March 8,[44] was a shrewd strategy for securing the reform of Assembly policy. The newer counties were underrepresented, and radical leaders did resent this. Nevertheless, the simultaneous demand of five counties for more seats on February 28 was entirely unexpected; some directing group of radicals, seeking a way to apply massive pressure on the Assembly, had hit upon an ingenious scheme. The House could not deny a widespread demand for more equitable representation without risking serious dissension within the province; yet to comply with this demand would go far to radicalize the legislature. Whether Joseph Reed and moderate members of the Second One Hundred or James Cannon and his Committee of Privates devised this maneuver, expanded representation was not the foremost goal of Pennsylvania's Revolutionary movement at this time. The more equal representation that is often viewed as a major objective of Pennsylvania's Revolutionary movement was, in March 1776, the means whereby Pennsylvania's radicals might achieve their vital objectives.[45] It would not be long, however, before a reformed legislature would be regarded as a necessary and significant achievement of the Revolution in Pennsylvania.

Initially the Assembly's moderate majority probably had no intention of yielding to the radicals on either independence or the militia articles, or even on representation, but the Second One Hundred's precipitate decision to call a provincial convention left the lawmakers little choice. Nevertheless, they understood that the demand for greater representation was primarily the radicals' means to achieve the substantive reform that the Assembly hoped to avoid, and they decided to take a gamble. Believing that Pennsylvanians desired neither independence nor a coercive militia system, the legislators immediately agreed to create several new seats in the House but deferred committing themselves to specific alterations in the militia law.

On March 8, the Assembly voted to add seventeen new seats to the chamber. The new places were distributed among the City of Philadelphia and all eight counties created since 1700, leaving only Bucks, Chester, and Philadelphia counties with unenlarged delegations.[46] The legislators transformed this major resolve into

---

44. *Votes and Proceedings,* VIII: 7436.

45. See Lincoln, *Revolutionary Movement,* pp. 42–52; Selsam, *Pennsylvania Constitution,* pp. 31–39, 99–100; and Hawke, *Midst of a Revolution,* p. 20.

46. *Pa. Packet,* Mar. 11, 1776; *Votes and Proceedings,* VIII: 7428 (Mar. 5), 7436 (Mar. 8). The City received four additional seats; Lancaster, York, Cumberland, Berks, and Northampton counties each gained two; and Bedford, Northumberland, and Westmoreland counties each acquired one.

law with unwonted speed. The expansion bill was reported out of committee and survived its first reading on March 11, and passed its second and third readings on March 13 and 14 by large majorities. The roll calls, ranging from 21 to 23 affirmative votes, against only 8 to 11 opposed, saw from eight to ten moderates from Bucks, Chester, and Philadelphia counties support the measure, which insured the weakening of their counties' influence in the legislature as well as the reduction of both moderate and Quaker power.[47] Nor did Governor Penn hesitate. On March 15, after one day's consideration, he announced his willingness to sign the expansion bill, which he did on March 23, thereby setting in motion preparations for a most important by-election on May 1, 1776.[48] By late March, Assembly moderates were irrevocably committed to their great gamble; they had staked their political future on their ability to retain control of the legislature in the May 1 by-election. Governor Penn probably approved the measure with the same hope; two of his brothers-in-law, both moderates who opposed independence, stood for newly created Assembly seats in May—and won.[49]

Having passed the expansion bill, however, the Assembly regarded its obligation to move with the times as largely fulfilled, at least for the present. The lawmakers still intended to pass much vital legislation, and they understood that to survive politically they could not entirely avoid a revision of the militia articles. But on principles there would be no change. The full House heard nine petitions concerning the militia articles between February 23 and March 15, and on February 28 named a subcommittee to consider all such petitions and prepare recommendations for revising the militia law. Although seven backcountry delegates and Joseph Reed could have formed an activist majority of one on this subcommittee, John Dickinson and six other moderate veterans apparently dominated its proceedings.[50]

While this subcommittee was weighing the petitions for militia reform, the Assembly tackled other important military matters. The legislators handled several of these problems energetically, for while they hoped to avoid a revolution, they

---

47. *Votes and Proceedings,* VIII: 7437, 7443–44, 7446. The respective votes on an amendment setting a date for the election and on the second and third readings stood 21 to 11, 23 to 8, and 21 to 9. Delegates from the three oldest counties supporting the bill were Michael Hillegas, Thomas Potts, Samuel Miles, Joseph Parker, and Robert Morris (Philadelphia County), William Rodman and Gerardus Wynkoop (Bucks), and Benjamin Bartholomew (Chester) on all three votes, and George Gray (Philadelphia) and John Jacobs (Chester) on the second and third readings. Parker, Rodman, and Jacobs were Quakers. All opponents of the bill were Quakers from the oldest counties.

48. *Votes and Proceedings,* VIII: 7449, 7456.

49. Penn's victorious relatives were Andrew Allen and his younger brother James (see chapter 9 below). For a representative of the King to sign a bill expanding a legislature that was in rebellion in the spring of 1776 was certainly daring, and perhaps irresponsible, but Penn could argue plausibly that his veto would merely have accelerated the movement toward full-scale revolution. Moreover, it is possible that John Penn had ceased to think like a Crown official entirely by 1776, and was operating only as the proprietor of Pennsylvania, desperately seeking to protect his property. Both his heart and his pocketbook had been in Pennsylvania for years (see Leonard, "Organization of the Assembly," pp. 406–7, and n.116), and he had to insure his position with Pennsylvanians, who now exercised all local power, and take his chances with George III, who had none for the present and might never again.

50. *Votes and Proceedings,* VIII, 7412–13. See note 39 above for exact citations of the petitions. The strongest supporters of the resistance on this subcommittee, based on Assembly roll calls, were Reed, Ross (Lancaster), Ewing (York), Montgomery (Cumberland), Chreist (Berks), Kachlein (Northampton), Dougherty (Bedford), and Hunter (Northumberland). Moderates were Dickinson and Gray (Philadelphia County), Rodman and Brown (Bucks), Pearson and Humphreys (Chester), and probably Slough (Lancaster).

were still committed to a vigorous defense of the province. On February 29, they listened to several resolves of Congress on military subjects and appointed sub-committees to investigate the delay in producing the muskets that they had ordered in June 1775, and to frame rules for punishing those who harbored deserters.[51] On March 1, they heard the Committee of Safety recommend the raising of 2,000 active duty soldiers to defend the province; on March 5, they voted to recruit 1,500 men.[52] On March 11, they ordered the completion of the civilian census that was to be the basis for identifying nonassociators. This census had been legislated in November 1775, but had been delayed by the reluctance of Quaker or Quaker-sympathizing county officials to enumerate the population.[53] On March 15, they listened to a request from Congress that they disarm all those who were dis-affected or who would not associate.[54] And between March 26 and their adjourn-ment on April 6, they tied up loose ends, approving penalties for those sheltering deserters, rules for disarming the disaffected, and military articles for the 1,500 active-duty troops, as well as voting £85,000 in bills of credit to finance Pennsyl-vania's new military activities.[55] The enactment of these measures must have caused much soul-searching on the part of many members. Friends and many former Friends could hardly condemn either deserters and their protectors or the disaffected, who were often their own coreligionists. The civilian census was also a sore point. Yet some concessions to reality could hardly be avoided.

By the last week of the session, however, the lawmakers had exhausted their capacity for compromise. The report of the subcommittee on militia rules, brought in on March 29, occasioned a full week of debate, and the draft upon which the Assembly finally agreed was a major triumph for those who opposed compulsory militia service with meaningful penalties for noncompliance and sufficient support for poor associators.[56] Military and civilian committees in all parts of the province had requested over a dozen alterations in the November 1775 law, but the House made only four important changes: those associators who could not afford to leave their families for active service could send a substitute; active duty was to be divided up among companies so that no community would be temporarily depopu-lated; militia fines were earmarked to aid associators who were wounded in battle and the families of those who were killed; and masters who refused to allow their apprentices to serve were to pay the usual fine for nonassociation.[57] Each of these changes had been requested by one or another of the petitions, but the first provi-

---

51. *Votes and Proceedings,* VIII: 7413–18 (resolves of Congress), 7420 (arms, deserters).

52. *Votes and Proceedings,* VIII: 7425–26 (Mar. 1), 7429–32 (Mar. 5). A vote on a key amendment to this resolve ended in a tie, which was broken by Speaker Morton, who favored an activist position on the question. This was the closest vote mentioned in the minutes of this session; unfortunately, the roll was not called.

53. *Votes and Proceedings,* VIII: 7438.

54. *Votes and Proceedings,* VIII: 7447–48.

55. *Votes and Proceedings,* VIII: 7457 (deserters), 7467, 7505–7 (the disaffected), 7491–7503 (rules for the troops), 7509–13 (funds).

56. I am here assuming that the full House, by a narrow margin, voted the policy outlined in this and the following paragraph. It is possible, however, that a stronger militia bill could have passed in a full House, and was defeated only because several western delegates had left the session early. This was suggested by "A Friend to Government by Assembly," *Pa. Evening Post,* Apr. 4, 1776.

57. *Votes and Proceedings,* VIII: 7479, article 35 (compare p. 7374, art. 34) on substitutes; p. 7479, art. 38 (cp. p. 7374, art. 37) on dividing up active duty; p. 7480, art. 39 (cp. p. 7375, art. 38) on the use of fines; and p. 7487, rule 9, on apprentices.

sion was most helpful to those who enjoyed at least a moderate income, and the last put a burden on the masters of apprentices, while the more affluent masters of indentured servants and slaves could escape entirely, a matter of concern in at least one county.[58]

At the same time, the more important goals of the petitioners were ignored. The request that indigent families of associators on active duty be honorably supported out of a special fund, rather than receive humiliating handouts from the Overseers of the Poor, effected only a nominal change; the Overseers were henceforth to pay these families from an "Out Pension" fund.[59] The Assembly, asked to elevate Germans and other disfranchised military associators to full civic status, merely recommended this step to succeeding legislative sessions.[60] Requests for the annual election of officers and for the apportionment of an equal number of officers and privates to military courts were rejected, as were suggestions for higher penalties for county officials who refused to take the census of able-bodied men voted by the Assembly the previous November.[61] Active-duty service remained without any maximum limitation, while the number of official training musters, to which the fines of nonassociators were geared, was kept at twenty days per year, although fifty or more had been requested.[62] Finally, the Assembly refused to open the public coffers any wider to fund the militia adequately, or to provide more arms for poor associators.[63]

These decisions accorded well with the lawmakers' quite moderate amendments to the plan for taxing nonassociators. As in November, the legislators made no attempt to reduce the number of nonassociators by requiring an oath or affirmation of conscientious objection, and they kept the maximum age of liability at fifty years.[64] The Assembly did raise the fine levied for nonassociation, but only to £3.10.0 per year, far below the amount that several petitions had implied would be proper; and the legislators declined to lay extra taxes against the property of nonassociators.[65]

---

58. Only Berks County asked for the right to send substitutes on active duty (*Votes and Proceedings*, VIII: 7398). Chester County's Committee of Observation claimed that the November articles favored the wealthy because their indentured servants and slaves were not subject to the military association, while apprentices, who worked for less-affluent men, were (ibid., p. 7409). Philadelphia's Committee of Privates, however, sought to make the militia obligations of apprentices and their masters more explicit (ibid., p. 7405). This difference of opinion should caution us that not all zealous patriots thought alike or saw their interests in the same way, and the Assembly's compliance with the request of one radical group might frustrate the desires of another.

59. *Votes and Proceedings*, VIII: 7479.

60. *Votes and Proceedings*, VIII: 7490.

61. *Votes and Proceedings*, VIII: 7483, rules 16–17 (military courts); p. 7486, rule 2, and p. 7488, rule 10 (county officials).

62. *Votes and Proceedings*, VIII: 7478–80, arts. 34–38 (active duty); p. 7477, art. 28 (muster days).

63. *Votes and Proceedings*, VIII: 7476, art. 19, and pp. 7476–77, arts. 25–26.

64. *Votes and Proceedings*, VIII: 7485–86, rule 1 (age fifty); p. 7487, rule 8 (no oath). Several of the petitions had sought a maximum age of sixty for service so that affluent, able-bodied men in their fifties would have to contribute either themselves or a part of their fortunes to the defense of the community.

65. *Votes and Proceedings*, VIII: 7487, rule 8. None of the petitioners stated what they thought the fine for nonassociation should be, but all thought that it was too low. Several petitions asked for weekly musters; if this had been granted, and if the fine for nonassociation had remained geared to muster days, the annual fine would have been £6.10.0 at the November rate of 2s. 6d. per muster, or £9.2.0 at the rate of 3s. 6d. set in April.

The Assembly had now finished all of its necessary business and was ready to adjourn, but one optional task remained. On March 20, after the petitioning campaign to alter the militia rules had ended and the expansion bill had secured Assembly approval, the Second One Hundred voted, with only one dissent, to ask the Assembly to lift the ban against independence in its instructions to Pennsylvania's congressmen.[66] This memorial was read in the House and tabled on March 23, and the assemblymen could easily have deferred the matter to their next meeting, but on the last day of the session a member raised the matter again, and "after a Debate of considerable Length," a vote to alter the instructions "carried in the Negative by a great Majority."[67] On April 5 and 6, 1776, the Pennsylvania Assembly, its capacity for accommodation exhausted, threw out the challenge to the radicals: neither compulsory militia service nor independence would be permitted by the established government. The issues were clearly drawn; the battle was set for May 1; the ballots would decide.

THE "WORDY WAR" FOR INDEPENDENCE

The increasingly open conflict between Pennsylvania's moderate and radical patriots, following eighteen months of uneasy cooperation, found its most dramatic expression in the winter of 1776 in the Assembly, and in the press. Just as Pennsylvania's lawmakers were tackling, or dodging, the major issues of this season, Philadelphia's propagandists began what Joseph Reed called their "wordy war" over independence.[68] The character of this debate suggests what the escalating Revolutionary contest meant in one major city and colony; in the columns of the weekly press, one discovers the hopes and fears of Pennsylvanians on the eve of Independence.

From mid-February, the question of independence forced every other public issue into the background. A few writers made suggestions for the efficient organization of the militia, the just contribution of nonassociators, or the proper structure of government, but these vital issues meant little when separated from independence. Even discussions of the proper role of the Assembly or of the desirability of holding a provincial convention were subordinated to the grand question.[69] From February to May, writers sought to convince the electors of the virtues of dependence or independence; they made little mention of specific persons or parties, even in the most indirect of hints, until a few days before the May 1 by-election. Yet Philadelphia writers did not treat independence abstractly; local propagandists showed little interest in discussing the ideal form of human government, for example. Perhaps most Philadelphians were satisfied with Thomas Paine's vigorous answer to that question. What they apparently wanted to know,

---

66. Duane, ed., *Passages from Marshall*, p. 74 (Mar. 20); John Adams to James Warren, Mar. 21, 1776, "Warren-Adams Letters," *Massachusetts Historical Society Collections*, LXXXII (1917): 213.

67. *Votes and Proceedings*, VIII: 7455 (Mar. 23); 7513 (Apr. 6).

68. Joseph Reed to Charles Pettit, Mar. 30, 1776, Reed Papers, N.-Y. Hist. Soc.

69. See "Proposals, . . ." *Pa. Evening Post*, Mar. 5, 1776; "Cato," Letter I, *Pa. Ledger*, Mar. 9, and *Pa. Gaz.*, Mar. 13, 1776; [Questions and Answers concerning Government], *Pa. Evening Post*, Mar. 16, 1776; and "A Friend to Government by Assembly," *Pa. Evening Post*, Apr. 4, 1776.

and what every propagandist was eager to tell them, was not whether republicanism was ideally superior to monarchy (most apparently believed that it was), but whether Pennsylvania, in 1776, needed a republic, or could still afford to live under George III. Not a single writer doubted that independence must usher in republicanism; all agreed, whether euphorically or despondently, that a break with Great Britain meant revolution.[70]

Philadelphia's propagandists sought to determine the desirability of independence by answering two broad questions: was the present British ministry a candid adversary whose words could be trusted, and could Britain permanently guarantee any liberties that the colonists might win through immediate concessions? The first question became of immediate concern early in March, when Philadelphians learned that Lord North planned to send commissioners to treat with America. No one knew who these commissioners would be, whom they were to see, or what instructions and powers they were to have, but the Independents were sure that they understood the reason for their visit. On March 2, James Cannon, the ultra-radical secretary of the Committee of Privates, writing as "Cassandra" in the *Evening Post,* suggested that the commissioners, on reaching America, be taken into custody by the army and conveyed incommunicado to Congress, which should negotiate with them only after they had ordered all English fleets and armies home.[71] An even starker distrust of British intentions infused the remarks of "Dialogus," who declared that the commissioners' visit was only the opening sally in a long campaign to lull America into helplessness, after which a naked military despotism would begin.[72]

The commissioners' only defender in the Philadelphia press was "Cato," the veteran publicist and moderate patriot spokesman Dr. William Smith, who denounced "Cassandra's" plan for receiving the emissaries as barbaric, and expressed confidence in Britain's sincerity in seeking negotiations. "Cassandra," he said, had drunk too deeply of "the cup of independence" to welcome reconciliation on any terms.[73] This charge would have been more telling if Cannon had made the least attempt to conceal his ardent desire for separation from Great Britain. But Dr. Smith's rejoinder did encourage the radicals to spell out their fullest fears of the commissioners' arrival, and their replies showed that for many Philadelphians the question of independence was beginning to cut close to home.

"Independent," writing in the *Packet,* insisted that the commissioners should not be permitted to speak to anyone but Congress; and "Cassandra" told "Cato," whose identity and moderate political activity in the patriot cause he knew well, that he (Smith) would never become "the first American D---t--y [Deputy?], if you are not permitted to shake hands with the Commissioners, and allowed the opportunity of explaining your mysterious conduct."[74] The radicals' hostility

---

70. On monarchy versus republicanism, see Paine, *Common Sense* (Jan. 10); "Salus Populi," Letter V, *Pa. Jour.,* Mar. 13; "Cato" [Dr. William Smith], Letters V–VIII, *Pa. Ledger,* Mar. 30, *Pa. Gaz.,* Apr. 10, 24; "Civis," *Pa. Ledger,* Apr. 6; and "Eudoxus," *Pa. Packet,* Apr. 22, all 1776; and the analyses in Wood, *Creation of the American Republic,* chaps. 2–3; and Maier, *From Resistance to Revolution,* chap. 9, and "The Beginnings of American Republicanism, 1765–1776," in *The Development of a Revolutionary Mentality* (Library of Congress Symposium on the Revolution, 1972).

71. *Pa. Evening Post,* Mar. 2, 1776 (reprinted in *Pa. Packet,* Mar. 25, 1776).

72. *Pa. Evening Post,* Mar. 9, 1776. Also see "Candidus," *Pa. Gaz.,* Mar. 6, 1776.

73. *Pa. Gaz.,* Mar. 13, 1776.

74. *Pa. Packet,* Mar. 18; "Cassandra to Cato," *Pa. Gaz.,* Mar. 20, 1776.

toward the commissioners, clearly, arose not only from a fear of the emissaries' treachery, but also from their anxiety over the secretly disaffected colonists whom they might contact. In an atmosphere so charged with mutual distrust, this debate could proceed no further, but "Cato" expressed his faith that the conflict between Britain and America was still open to reconciliation and would remain so as long as neither side called in foreign troops, a move that Britain, he was sure, would never make.[75]

The Independents, however, not only remained unconvinced of British candor but quickly concluded that the colonies could never be safe in the British Empire. One "A. B.," building upon arguments advanced by Thomas Paine and Samuel Adams in January and February, contended early in the "wordy war" that no mere change of administrations could resolve the conflict, not simply because George III had now shown himself to be a tyrant, but primarily because of inherent differences of interest between England and the colonies.[76] Again the only defender of continued dependence was Dr. William Smith. In "Cato's" third letter, by far the most impressive anti-Independent newspaper essay in the independence controversy, Smith frankly admitted that Britain had never protected America out of parental affection or altruistic sentiment, but simply to further her own interests. But why, he asked, should this fact make that protection any less necessary, valuable, or secure? America had only to resist stoutly to vindicate her claims, "Cato" continued, and if Britain were to renew her unreasonable demands at a later date, America could again, and more easily, bring her back to reason.[77]

Four days after the Assembly's spring adjournment, Thomas Paine, as "The Forester," savagely attacked "Cato's" advice, arguing that there could be little security for American liberties in the British Empire if even anti-Independent apologists talked about the greater ease of conducting a second resistance, should it become necessary.[78] But the most succinct statement of the Independent position appeared on April 27, just five days before the Assembly by-election. James Cannon, in "Cassandra's" last letter, issued to "Cato" a clear challenge. "I call upon you to prove that Great-Britain can offer *any plan* of *constitutional dependence* which will not leave the future enjoyment of our liberties to *hope, hazard,* and *uncertainty.* . . . By the constitution of Great-Britain the present Parliament can make no law which shall bind any future one. . . . Is it wisdom then, or is there *safety* in entering upon terms of accommodation with a power which cannot stipulate for the performance of *its* engagements?"[79]

---

75. *Pa. Ledger,* Mar. 30, 1776. Smith was making a thinly veiled reference to the Independents' hopes for an alliance with France; he knew nothing of the treaties that George III had just signed with the rulers of Brunswick, Hesse-Cassel, and other German principalities to hire 30,000 mercenaries for service in America.

76. *Pa. Jour.,* Feb. 28, 1776.

77. *Pa. Gaz.,* Mar. 20, 1776. "Cato" may have been—but probably was not—implying that 1776 was not *the time* to leave the British Empire because the colonies were still too weak and immature. This sentiment was widespread among moderate Pennsylvanians, and another anti-Independent spokesman, "Moderator," developed this argument explicitly while admitting the eventual need for independence (*Pa. Ledger,* Apr. 27, 1776).

78. *Pa. Gaz.,* Apr. 10, 1776. Paine virtually admitted his authorship of "The Forester's" letters in *Pa. Evening Post,* Apr. 30, 1776, but this was already widely known (John Adams to Abigail Adams, Apr. 28, 1776, in Lyman Butterfield, ed., *Adams Family Correspondence* [1963], I: 400), just as Smith's authorship of "Cato's" letters was an open secret by the beginning of April (*Pa. Gaz.,* "The Forester," Letter I, Apr. 3, 1776).

79. *Pa. Ledger,* Apr. 27, 1776. The phrase "leave the future enjoyment of our liberties to hope, hazard, and uncertainty," was Paine's, and "Cassandra" thanked "The Forester" for it.

The arguments of Philadelphia's Independent penmen clearly reveal the goals toward which local radicals were working in the early spring of 1776. These patriots had no lingering doubts about the grand question; unimpressed by the glories of monarchy and unable to trust the current British ministry or to believe that Britain could ever grant them secure liberties under its hallowed Constitution, they cried out to leave the empire. To achieve that end, they demanded two immediate changes in local government. First, the conservative Assembly's exclusive right to appoint members of the Committee of Safety, and to appoint and instruct Pennsylvania's congressmen, would have to end. Second, the Assembly would have to be radicalized by removing treacherous legislators who acted only according to "avarice, ambition, and servility," and replacing them with new leaders who, like committeemen and conventioneers, would become the voice of the people.[80] The Independents defended these alterations on the grounds that committees, conventions and the Congress were the only true instruments of popular will,[81] but in their exchanges with "Cato," another motive for their determination is even more starkly evident. By March 1776, Philadelphia's Independents had become deeply suspicious of their opponents' fundamental allegiance to America's welfare, and they quickly concluded that until the power of Pennsylvania's moderate patriots was totally crushed, their province would be in the gravest peril.

"Cato" vigorously denounced the Independents' arguments for local constitutional change, and pointed out that the Assembly had no constitutional right either to change Pennsylvania's 1701 constitution or to terminate the province's allegiance to the British Crown.[82] Many Independents, however, believed that existing oaths and constitutional checks were only shields behind which cautious legislators were hiding from essential public duties that they found personally repugnant; and one radical argued that both the British Constitution and Pennsylvania's Constitution of 1701 had become dangerous to the public safety.[83] In the struggle for independence, radical strategists and writers developed a two-pronged attack on the Assembly. All urged the radicalization of that body, implicitly through the regular election process; but in the event that such radicalization failed, the more extreme Independent propagandists simultaneously advanced justifications for the circumvention of the Assembly by direct popular action, that is, by a provincial convention.[84]

Several influential Independents, like Joseph Reed, strongly favored working through the established government and could not imagine circumventing the Assembly, but in the propaganda campaign of March and April it was the most zealous patriots who dominated the press. Two observations establish the overwhelmingly ultraradical character of Independent propaganda. First, Independent

---

80. "Serious Questions . . . to Congress," *Pa. Evening Post,* Apr. 16, 1776.

81. "A Lover of Order," *Pa. Evening Post,* Mar. 9, 1776.

82. Letter III, *Pa. Gaz.,* Mar. 20, 1776.

83. "Queries . . . to . . . Cato," *Pa. Evening Post,* Mar. 14, 1776.

84. In addition to the essays cited in notes 80–83 above, see "The Censor," *Pa. Evening Post,* Mar. 5; "Cato," Letter I, *Pa. Ledger,* Mar. 9; "Cassandra to Cato," *Pa. Gaz.,* Mar. 20; "The Forester," Letters I–III, *Pa. Gaz.,* Apr. 3, 10, 24; and "Reasons for . . . Independence," *Pa. Evening Post,* Apr. 20 (all 1776). The two-pronged radical strategy described here is nowhere explicitly stated; indeed, few political essays referred to either the May 1 by-election or a provincial convention. But remarks made about the Assembly and the local radical committees leave little doubt that the radical Independents intended to pursue their ends through the Assembly if possible, around or over it if necessary (see immediately below in this chapter).

writers rarely paid the slightest respect to either the Assembly or other pre-Revolutionary institutions, but instead contended that established forms—oaths and constitutions—and established leaders had become obstructions to liberty. Second, the only Independent authors whom one can identify were ultraradicals who would participate in the overthrow of Assembly power in the late spring and summer.[85] The propaganda campaign for independence was a massive assault by a half dozen or more spirited ultraradicals upon half as many anti-Independents; it was also an assault upon the Assembly by supporters of committee power, an attack upon the establishment by practitioners of the new politics. At the heart of the ultraradicals' message was not their exhortation to elect proindependence men on May 1, but their thinly veiled accusation that Pennsylvania's moderate patriot establishment—the Assembly of John Dickinson and Speaker John Morton, and the proprietary dependents led by the Allen brothers and Dr. Smith—was an immediate threat to the public safety.

This is where the Independents' "wordy war" was going, but what of its immediate goal? Did radical propagandists win over the people of Philadelphia to independence? In fact, their success is hard to determine. They outwrote their opponents two to one in published essays, and may have enjoyed an even greater advantage in the number of authors and newspapers favorable to them.[86] Quality is harder to measure, but here, too, the Independents appear to have outclassed their opponents. Only one seasoned anti-Independent writer kept to his desk throughout the contest—Dr. William Smith. Arrayed against him were several extensively serialized Independents: the journalistic activity of James Cannon and Thomas Paine was widely known, and Dr. Benjamin Rush apparently also wrote several Independent essays. In addition, Samuel Adams, and perhaps Christopher Marshall, Sr. and Dr. Thomas Young contributed occasional radical pieces. Smith himself was acutely aware of the odds against him and tried to make light of them in a bit of comic verse at the head of "Cato's" fourth letter (March 27):

> . . . Who would endure this Pain,
> This foul discharge of wrath from Adam's sons
> Marshall'd in dread array, both old and Young,
> Their pop-guns here, and there their heavy Cannon,
> Our labor's pages deem'd not worth a Rush.[87]

Yet Smith's strong defense of the British Empire was overwhelmed conclusively only after the May 1 by-election, less by his many able opponents than by the deeds of Great Britain, which he felt obliged to defend. "Cato" could never make the Mother Country appear either lovable or admirable; he may not even have

---

85. "Cassandra to Cato," *Pa. Gaz.,* Mar. 20, 1776; "A Lover of Order," Mar. 9, "Queries . . . to . . . Cato," Mar. 14, and "Serious Questions . . . to Congress," Apr. 16, 1776, all *Pa. Evening Post.*

86. In the period February 28–April 27, 1776, twenty-seven pieces appeared in Philadelphia newspapers which explicitly or implicitly favored independence. There were fourteen anti-Independent pieces, eight of which were by "Cato." Eight other items, mostly radical, made no reference to independence. Prior to late February, and again after late April, radical and Independent pieces were even more dominant in the press. Of Philadelphia's five newspapers in 1776, the *Journal, Packet,* and *Evening Post* had a strong Independent bias, the cautious *Gazette* was fairly neutral, and the *Ledger* was anti-Independent.

87. *Pa. Gaz.,* Mar. 27, 1776.

made the mighty empire more feared and hence more respected. Soon he was reduced to arguing that the time had not yet come for independence.[88] Even this claim was dependent upon a momentary lull in the continuing flood of bad news from Great Britain: harsh speeches from the Throne, fresh punitive Parliamentary statutes, and above all the hiring of foreign mercenaries. Had certain confirmation of this last event broken in April rather than in May, the strongest remaining anti-Independent argument—the continuing existence of a minimum level of British respect and affection for her errant colonies—would have been destroyed.

THE REVOLUTION DELAYED: THE MAY 1 BY-ELECTION

In the last week of April, the character of Philadelphia's propaganda war suddenly changed as the discussion of the broad advantages of dependence versus independence yielded to arguments that focused directly on the May 1 by-election and exhorted the voters to support particular candidates. Yet one theme of the "wordy war" remained prominent: the Independents' election pieces displayed an ever darker suspicion of their opponents' motives.

The first election piece to appear was a satirical note in the *Evening Post* that observed that elections had at least one virtue: they forced the elite to speak familiarly with their less affluent neighbors for a few days each year. The author singled out the sheriff of Philadelphia County and one "J____ _____" (perhaps John Dickinson) as notably friendlier at election time.[89] In a more extended effort in the April 29 *Packet,* "An Elector" made the radically divisive suggestion that all who insisted on dependence be excluded from the election, while propertyless militia associators who were normally disfranchised be admitted. Election officials ignored this advice in April, but its appearance is noteworthy because the radicals would carry out this plan when they framed the Pennsylvania Constitution of 1776. Four radical pieces appearing on April 30 and May 1 were more personally partisan. All attacked anti-Independent candidates Andrew Allen, Thomas Willing, and Alexander Wilcocks as proprietary aristocrats who would rather secure their own high political positions than save their country from destruction, and one author asserted that anti-Independent support came largely from Philadelphia's wealthiest merchants, who alone could afford the long years of trade restrictions, monopolies, and high prices that resisting Britain without declaring independence would entail.[90]

On the same two days, two pieces defending the anti-Independent cause appeared in the press. The first calmly advised the voters to exercise moderation and suggested that during the five months that the by-election victors would serve (until October 1), it would probably become clear whether independence was really necessary. A second piece, by "Civis," mounted a spirited attack on "An Elector's" recommendation that anti-Independents be barred from voting. The opponents of independence, he argued, were "the true whigs, who are for pre-

---

88. "Cato," Letters III and V, *Pa. Gaz.,* Mar. 20, *Pa. Ledger,* Mar. 30, 1776; and see "Moderator," *Pa. Ledger,* Apr. 27, 1776.

89. Apr. 27, 1776.

90. Two unsigned items, and a piece, "To the Tories," by "Old Trusty," all *Pa. Evening Post,* Apr. 30, 1776; and an unsigned item in *Pa. Jour.,* May 1, 1776.

serving the constitution, as well as [*sic*] against the secret machinations of ambitious innovators, as against the open attacks of the British parliament. . . ."[91]

No election of the past decade had generated so many pointed appeals to the voters. Every Philadelphian knew this would be a hard-fought contest, and both the Independents and their opponents began composing their election tickets at least two weeks before the poll. Groups of anti-Independents, probably led by the Allen brothers, Dr. William Smith, Thomas Willing, and perhaps John Dickinson, held several meetings prior to April 21. The new coalition that emerged from these gatherings drew its principal strength from proprietary faction leaders, from major merchants with proprietary ties, and from those Quakers who were still worldly enough to support and vote for political candidates. The alliance of Quaker party and proprietary faction leaders, in the making for several years, was the most important development in conservative politics in Pennsylvania in over a decade.[92]

Sometime prior to April 30, the anti-Independents chose their four nominees. Samuel Howell was a major merchant and a disowned Quaker who had been active on Philadelphia's resistance committees; as the only moderate nominee not connected with the old proprietary faction, he enjoyed the widest popularity among the anti-Independent candidates. Alexander Wilcocks was a prominent young lawyer and a member of the City corporation. Thomas Willing was perhaps Philadelphia's wealthiest merchant, a justice of the Supreme Court of Pennsylvania, and a congressman. The most distinguished anti-Independent nominee, however, was Andrew Allen—congressman, attorney general of Pennsylvania, brother-in-law of Governor Penn, and provincial councilor until April, when he resigned his seat to run for the Assembly. Allen was the perfect symbol of everything that the ultraradicals hated and feared: inherited money and power, family connections, and perhaps even hidden, sinister plans laid by the proprietors and the British Crown.[93]

The Independents began organizing at about the same time as their opponents. Their most notable supporters were congressmen Samuel and John Adams, Thomas McKean, Delaware congressman and current chairman of Philadelphia's Second One Hundred, and the great majority of the Second One Hundred's members. Joseph Reed may have aided them.[94] Two less prominent but more extreme radicals presided over the meetings that composed the radical ticket, however: Christopher Marshall, Sr. and James Cannon. They were assisted by about fifteen

---

91. *Pa. Evening Post,* Apr. 30, 1776; *Pa. Gaz.,* May 1, 1776 (quotation). "An Elector" replied to "Civis," *Pa. Gaz.,* May 13, 1776.

92. Duane, ed., *Passages from Marshall,* pp. 75, 76; *Pa. Evening Post,* Apr. 30, 1776; Hutson, *Pennsylvania Politics,* chap. 4; and G. B. Warden, "The Proprietary Group in Pennsylvania, 1755–1765," *WMQ,* 3d Ser., XXI (1964): 367–89.

93. See the item on Allen, and "To the Tories," by "Old Trusty," *Pa. Evening Post,* Apr. 30, 1776; and *Pa. Jour.,* May 1, 1776. The contention of these writers that Allen, Willing, and (by implication) Governor Penn were in collusion with the British ministry was certainly false, but such fears were, on the part of many radicals, undoubtedly genuine.

In addition to their four City candidates, the anti-Independents ran Andrew Allen's brother James in Northampton County, and may have been behind the candidacy of the Quaker James Rankin in York County.

94. Reed probably did not play an active role in the election; he continued to be troubled by indecisiveness and to express his distaste for partisan politics. See Reed to Charles Pettit, Mar. 30, 1776, and Reed to Esther Reed [May–June? 1776], Reed Papers, N.-Y. Hist. Soc.

members of the Second One Hundred, by spokesmen from the Committee of Privates and the zealous, mechanic-dominated Patriotic Society, and probably by several close friends, such as the publicist Thomas Paine, as well. Beginning their deliberations at least as early as April 18, the Independents soon completed their slate, but resolved not to reveal it until April 29.[95]

Heading the Independent ticket was George Clymer, a wealthy young Anglican merchant and a prominent radical since the tea affair in 1773. By his candidacy he would appear to have regained the high position in radical circles that he had lost in January 1776. Colonel Daniel Roberdeau, a Presbyterian merchant, was perhaps the most popular militia chieftain in Philadelphia. Owen Biddle was a recently disowned Quaker, a minor merchant, and an active resistance leader. Frederick Kuhl was politically more obscure than his colleagues, but his appeal to the German vote was a sufficient qualification for his candidacy.

The May 1 by-election, one radical observed, was "one of the sharpest contests, yet peaceable, that has been for a number of years. . . ."[96] A minor altercation arose when the proprietary faction merchant Joseph Swift made aspersions on the voting qualifications of certain Germans; and a crowd of voters, angry over Sheriff Dewees' decision to suspend the balloting early in the evening and to continue the following morning, forced him to reopen the polls until after 10 P.M., when the election was terminated. But there was no violence. The returns, however, were bitterly disappointing to the radicals. The anti-Independent winners were Samuel Howell (941 votes), Andrew Allen (923), and Alexander Wilcocks (921), while the Independents elected only George Clymer (923). Willing lost narrowly (911), outpolling Kuhl (904), Biddle (903), and Roberdeau (890). Discounting a few anti-Independent/Independent combinations, whose number cannot be determined, the average anti-Independent vote was 924, or 50.5 percent of the votes cast, and the average Independent vote was 905.[97]

The by-election vote is as precise an indication of the political attitudes of Philadelphians on May 1, 1776, as one will ever have. Thomas Paine attributed the Independents' defeat to the number of Philadelphians serving in the army in Canada, to the disqualification of many Germans who had not been naturalized, and to Sheriff Dewees' brief closing of the polls in the evening, which fooled several voters into going home, expecting to return and cast their ballots the next morning.[98] The number of Independents kept from balloting in these ways could indeed have swung the election to the radicals. On the anti-Independent side, however, several Quakers may have decided to sit out the election, although most

---

95. Duane, ed., *Passages from Marshall*, pp. 74–75 (Apr. 18, 19, 20, 25). Marshall was chairman of the nominating meetings; Cannon was secretary. See chapter 2 above on the formation and character of the Patriotic Society.

96. Duane, ed., *Passages from Marshall*, p. 76 (May 1).

97. Duane, ed., *Passages from Marshall*, pp. 76–77 (May 1); William Bradford, Jr., "A Memorandum Book and Register for the months of May and June 1776," p. 4, Col. William Bradford Papers, HSP; "The Forester," Letter IV, *Pa. Jour.*, May 8, 1776. The total number of votes for all eight candidates was 7,316; as each voter could select four men, roughly 1,829 persons voted, a heavy turnout.

98. *Pa. Jour.*, May 8, 1776, "The Forester," Letter IV. In this essay, Paine labeled the anti-Independent forces "the dependent faction," and "the dependent side." These terms were based partly upon his view that three of the four anti-Independent candidates were proprietary men, while "Mr. Samuel Howell, though in their ticket, was never considered by us a proprietary dependent" (see Paine, *Writings*, pp. 155, 158, 159).

Friends probably voted in a contest that was so critical to their interests. The radical leader Christopher Marshall evidently believed that the election was fair, and only lamented the fact that proprietary and Quaker leaders, who had been bitter enemies for over a generation, had finally joined forces to keep the province under the control of the moderate elite.[99] This was the key to the anti-Independent victory.

The most important message of the election returns, however, may simply have been that on May 1, Philadelphians were almost evenly divided over the question of independence. In January and February independence was a new, radical idea; by early May it had persuaded nearly a majority of the City's voters. The anti-Independents were still in nominal control of both Philadelphia and the province, but their hold on the populace was precarious. Nor was their control of the legislature itself secure. They had won three seats in the City, one in Northampton County, and one in York County, but it would appear that Independents had gained the remaining twelve places, leaving the anti-Independents with the slightest of majorities in the chamber.[100] And the Assembly was the last political institution upon which Pennsylvania's anti-Independents could rely; local resistance committees, militia officers and soldiers, and the Congress were all dominated by men who either favored independence on May 1 or would certainly favor that final measure if Britain were to take any further hostile action against America.

Nevertheless, the moderates did have the Assembly. The radicals' attempt to take over that body had failed, and to them the House now appeared to be an immovable obstruction. The radicals had already given every indication that if the chamber were to continue its opposition to independence, they would work to destroy the power of the current legislators and seize full control of the province. And this is exactly what happened in the next two months. Before considering how and why radical Pennsylvanians overthrew the old Assembly, however, it may be helpful to review their achievement in the preceding several months.

PENNSYLVANIA ON THE EVE OF REVOLUTION

Pennsylvania's eventual break with Great Britain was in part the achievement of radical propagandists who, early in 1776, successfully indicted both Britain's intransigent rejection of the authority and the peace overtures of Congress, and its escalation of the military conflict in America. In their propaganda campaign, they attained three objectives. First, they made independence an intellectually and emotionally acceptable proposition. Second, they rent the veil of sanctity that had traditionally enveloped limited monarchy and the British Constitution. Finally, they raised the disturbing possibility that the primary goal of the resistance—the security of American liberties—was simply not compatible with membership in

---

99. Duane, ed., *Passages from Marshall*, pp. 76–77 (May 1).
100. In addition to Clymer's victory, the Independents probably took one of the two new seats in Northampton, one of the two in York, and all of the new seats in Lancaster (2), Cumberland (2), Berks (2), Bedford (1), Northumberland (1), and Westmoreland (1). For a view that gives the anti-Independents more seats, see Hawke, *Midst of a Revolution,* pp. 61–62 and n.8, and the commentary on his argument in chapter 9 below.

the British Empire. By May 1, just under half of Philadelphia's voters and a large minority in the Assembly believed the Independents. If Britain were to pursue her plans to suppress America's rebellion by armed force, a majority for independence would form automatically.

But sentiment is not action, and in the winter and early spring the Independents did not neglect institutions through which they could act on their convictions. On February 16, they further radicalized Philadelphia's Committee of Observation, and between February 28 and March 5, that body laid the groundwork for calling a new provincial convention and then held a summons to that convention as a threat over the Assembly. In April, radical Philadelphians elected a new Committee of Privates.[101] And in the by-elections of January, March, and May, they put over a dozen new radical spokesmen into the Assembly. Nevertheless, in the early spring even the most zealous Independents were willing to work through the established government if they could achieve their goals by doing so. Only the Assembly's adamant refusal to admit the possibility of independence and to compel Pennsylvania's nonassociators to help defend the society that protected them, and then the Independents' failure to take over the chamber in the May 1 by-election, explain the decision of radical leaders in mid-May to proceed in a more revolutionary fashion.

The necessary condition for a fully developed revolution—an abrupt alteration in the structure and personnel of government and a radical transformation in the practice of politics—was the widespread alienation of Pennsylvanians from their long-accepted established order. This was initially the achievement of the obstructionist legislators themselves. Their cautious policy outraged their radical opponents, who saw their behavior as the last desperate effort of a privileged elite to cling to power; and the radicals soon infected others with their anger and developed it into a public expression of bitter disillusionment with the House. But while a growing estrangement from the established government was evident in the early spring, a spark was needed, some dramatic event that would demonstrate to all that the Assembly's policy was a failure and must lead to a disaster for the community that only revolutionary change could avoid.

Before discussing the explosive climax to Pennsylvania's resistance movement, however, one may profitably examine more closely the Philadelphia leaders behind that explosion to discover what their selection by their fellow citizens reveals about the Revolutionary transformation of Pennsylvania politics. In their economic and social backgrounds, Philadelphia's new radical leaders were themselves a major cause of revolutionary change. A group portrait of these men shows how they differed from leaders of the old order, and suggests why they were so hostile toward the established elite—and so capable of destroying it.

---

101. *Pa. Packet,* Apr. 1, 1776.

Chapter

8

The Revolution
of the Middle Classes

Now the establishment of this extra-legal machinery was the open door through which the common freeholder and the unfranchised mechanic and artisan pushed their way into the political arena.[1]

CARL LOTUS BECKER

Between the adjournment of the First Continental Congress and the Declaration of Independence, a new political world took shape in Pennsylvania around a new extraconstitutional government. This government, a vigorous system of local committees of observation, inspection, and correspondence, quickly became quasi-official; and with the severing of each remaining imperial bond, it grew mightily in authority, efficiency, and size. By the spring of 1775, all provincial commerce was under its control; by the fall, it was a power in Pennsylvania's defense establishment. By the spring of 1776, it had become an alternative source of authority coequal with the established government; in the summer, the committee movement seized control of the province from that establishment's vital core, the Assembly.

This chain of events culminated in a full political revolution, in which Pennsylvania experienced a sudden dislocation in the source of governmental authority and a rapid transformation of the means of exercising that authority. The emotional and ideological underpinnings of the province's public life, too, were so badly damaged in the break with Great Britain that they had to be thoroughly restructured before they could support a new polity.[2] Were there accompanying revolutionary shifts in the personnel of government in Pennsylvania as well? Put another way, did the new elite that formed between 1770 and 1774 to take power from their elders—elders often in the most literal sense of that word—hold that power securely; or was this new elite in turn challenged by yet another group of leaders, by different men who came from the newly aggressive middle classes?

---

1. Becker, *History of Political Parties,* p. 22.

2. See the definition of revolution offered by Eugene Kamenka, "Revolution—The History of an Idea," in Kamenka, ed., *A World in Revolution? The University Lectures 1970* (1970), p. 6, quoted in chapter 10 below. This definition also appears in Kamenka, "The Concept of a Political Revolution," in Carl J. Friedrich, ed., *Nomos VIII—Revolution* (1966). On the ideological restructuring of the American polity, see Bailyn, *Ideological Origins,* chap. 5; and Wood, *Creation of the American Republic.*

The answer to this question, for Pennsylvania and for the other colonies, may determine, in large measure, how revolutionary one feels the American Revolution to have been. A full portrait of those men who brought Pennsylvania out of the British Empire and restructured its political life lies at the heart of any inquiry into the meaning of the Revolution in this pivotal province.

COMMITTEE ELECTIONS AND THE NEW POLITICS

A most important factor shaping the character of Philadelphia's Revolutionary committees after the First Continental Congress was the method of their election. The increasing momentum of the resistance and the quasi-governmental status that committees acquired under the Continental Association encouraged Philadelphia's more zealous resistance leaders, while pressing local moderates very hard. Moreover, the moderate-radical alliance of May–June 1774 was already badly shaken by the Assembly election contest in October, when Mifflin and Thomson defeated Penington and Willing. All four men had been leaders of the alliance. But it was Philadelphia's decision to elect new committees by secret ballot that most effectively encouraged the city's moderates and radicals to split apart.

The change from nominating committeemen in open-air gatherings to selecting them by secret ballot was significant precisely because the second method encouraged a more open, yet orderly, contention of persons, factions, policies, and ideas. To appreciate the full import of this fact, one must understand the eighteenth-century Anglo-American mind's deep uneasiness with political conflict. Before Independence, Americans widely assumed that all community decisions must be reached by sober, rational, and unrecorded discussion, followed by the unanimous selection of one policy. Men viewed not only rancor and recrimination, but any public display or even any public memory of division, as threatening to the very fabric of the social order.[3] This conviction was heightened when the contested issues became more important, particularly when the community had to defend its decisions to, or against, hostile outside forces. Eighteenth-century Americans did not always come to perfect agreements, but they did become upset when they failed to reach a harmonious consensus, especially whenever any public record preserved an account of that failure and thereby destroyed the elaborate fictions that they had developed to mask dissension and bury its memory. They lived before that era when society would accept the value of issues and men contending openly for the support of a simple majority. In this most basic sense, democracy did not and could not exist in pre-Revolutionary America.[4]

At first glance, secret-ballot elections may appear to have little to do with this

---

3. An effective development of this theme is Michael Zuckerman, *Peaceable Kingdoms: New England Towns in the Eighteenth Century* (1970). Although Zuckerman exaggerates the degree to which Massachusetts towns *were* harmonious and consensual, he powerfully demonstrates how deeply they hungered for this consensus.

4. This is a major reason why one cannot equate widespread voting, whether in Massachusetts (Brown, *Middle-Class Democracy*) or Pennsylvania, with democracy. It was not only deference, but also the whole highly moral purpose of elections (see note 5 below), which separate pre-Revolutionary from nineteenth- and twentieth-century American politics. This is probably also the reason why the Pennsylvania Assembly seldom recorded roll call votes before the Revolution, and why the press rarely published election figures before 1775, and then for the victors only (see *Pa. Evening Post*, Oct. 3, 1775).

attitude. Elections in eighteenth-century America were regarded as vital tests for the selection of morally upright representatives, not as referenda on public issues.[5] But even before 1765 in Pennsylvania, and undoubtedly elsewhere in the colonies as well, this was often a fiction. Competing election tickets, which were really alliances of candidates committed to the interests of one region, religious sect, or class, or even to a specific policy, clashed openly in several Assembly elections.[6] Thus the secret-ballot committee election of November 1774 permitted resistance radicals to break with their moderate allies and oppose them directly. Yet this contest would appear, at least officially, to be like any other selection of representatives on the basis of their intellectual and moral fitness for public office. Had one or two thousand Philadelphia freemen assembled in the State House Yard in November to vote by voice for candidates to fill a large Committee of Observation, however, one of three things, all harmful to the radical resistance, would probably have occurred. First, the crowd might have voted on a single prepared ticket, as it had in June. This procedure would elect many moderates, who, the radicals feared, would support Congress and the resistance with little energy or enthusiasm. Second, the crowd might have voted for each candidate separately until the several dozen seats were filled, a terribly confusing process, which would probably become bitterly personal. Finally, the voters could have chosen between two or more prepared tickets, thereby raising in a public meeting the abhorrent spectacle of contentious interest- and issue-centered appeals to a simple majority.

Philadelphia's decision to elect its Committee of Observation by secret ballot avoided this dilemma. Politically active Philadelphians, both moderate and radical, composed slates of candidates in two relatively small, partisan meetings, and presented their work to the public in the form of printed ballots. After the voters had chosen one slate over the other, no one published either voting figures or a description of the voting. The winning ticket simply appeared in the *Gazette* as though it were the unanimous choice of the city.[7]

The real impact of the November 1774 committee election and of those that followed it in 1775 and 1776, however, bore little relationship to the public appearance of those contests. Distinct tickets were brought out of nomination, and the freemen repeatedly preferred one kind of slate over all others. These electoral decisions sharply altered political life in Philadelphia by completing the transformation of the local resistance committee, which had first been an instrument of one occupational class (1765), and then a traditionally elitist representative of the whole community (June 1774), into a new, aggressive advocate drawn from, and speaking for, the middle classes that would soon politically dominate the whole community. In a microcosm that was both spatial and chronological, this transformation embraced America's gradual evolution from the corporate, class-based politics of the colonial era to the more egalitarian, individualistic politics of majoritarian democracy in the new nation.

---

5. See Buel, "Democracy and the American Revolution," pp. 165–90; and Charles Sydnor, *Gentlemen Freeholders: Political Practices in Washington's Virginia* (1952).

6. Contested elections were the rule in Pennsylvania from 1700 to about 1725, and occurred again from time to time, most notably in 1742 and in 1764–66. See Nash, *Quakers and Politics*; Leonard, "Elections in Colonial Pennsylvania," pp. 385–401; and Hutson, *Pennsylvania Politics*, chaps. 3–4.

7. See *Pa. Gaz.*, Nov. 16, 1774. Only in 1776, in a political essay, were the voting figures made public for this election (see "Tiberius," *Pa. Ledger*, Mar. 16, 1776).

THE CHANGING CHARACTER OF THE
PHILADELPHIA COMMITTEE

One hundred and fifty Philadelphians served on one or more city Committees of Observation between the First Continental Congress and Independence. To determine when and how these men came to differ so markedly from the committeemen who served before the Congress, one may pose the same seven questions already asked of their predecessors. To what extent did the same men serve on one committee after another? What was their economic status within the community? How old were the committeemen at the time of their service? How did they make their living? From what countries or colonies did they, or their immediate ancestors, come? To what religious denominations did they belong? Finally, do the answers to these questions change during the two years before Independence, and if they do so, is that change indicative of a significant, or even purposeful, alteration in the pattern of leadership recruitment?

Persistency and Continuity of Service.   After the adjournment of Congress, just as before that event, many names recurred on Philadelphia's successive committee lists. The extent of this carry-over, however, was not even from committee to committee, and a sharp break in continuity marks November 1774 as a point at which a major change occurred in the selection of committee leaders. Only 42 percent of the Forty-Three secured seats on the Sixty-Six, and only 35 percent of the Sixty-Six had served on any important committees since 1765. Some part of this and later alterations was inevitable simply because Philadelphia's committees continued to grow until 1776, but in relative terms the committees grew more slowly after the First Continental Congress—from forty-three to sixty-six, and in 1775 to one hundred—than they had in the summer of 1774, when committee size more than doubled.[8] In fact, the numerical growth of the committee hardly begins to explain the magnitude of the interruption in continuity of November 1774. Seventeen members of the Nineteen had continued on the Forty-Three in June 1774, and 58 percent of the Forty-Three were committee veterans; moreover, the continuity that had been an increasingly prominent feature of the committee movement quickly revived in 1775 and 1776 (see table 12).

The November 1774 interruption in continuity suggests that the Sixty-Six, like the tea committee of 1773, was somehow different from its immediate predecessors. A portrait of the committeemen themselves confirms this view; but rather than show that the Sixty-Six was unlike the committees that came after it, as was true with the tea committee, all other data argue that the Sixty-Six set the pattern for its successors, a pattern that was the culmination of a decade of radical political mobilization in Philadelphia.

Wealth.   After May 1774, one earlier feature of the economic status of Philadelphia's committeemen disappeared. No longer were there fluctuations in their average wealth from committee to committee, but only a steady downward slope. The marked decline in the average tax assessment of Philadelphia's committeemen

---

8. Strictly speaking, committee growth did not end in 1775, for the February 1776 board had 106 members; but the six seats were added for representatives of Moyamensing and Passayunk, two semirural areas south and west of Southwark, which had not been represented before on the city committee. To add these men to the portrait would distort the quantitative analysis of Philadelphia's committeemen; for their names, see "List of the Sub-Committees, appointed by the Committee for . . . Philadelphia, . . ." (Philadelphia, Feb. 26, 1776 [broadside]), and Appendix M.

TABLE 12

Philadelphia's Committeemen, 1774–76

	May 1774	June 1774	November 1774	August 1775	February 1776
Number of members	19	43	66	100	100
Persistency	89%	42%	68%	69%	—
Long-term continuity	68%	58%	35%	49%	73%
1774 Tax Assessment					
£200+	3	5	6	9	7
100–199	7	13	12	14	10
45–99	3	10	12	20	16
0–44	6	15	35	54	63
Unknown	—	—	1	3	4
Average	£155	£113	£82	£73	£64
Median	£100	£92	£40	£40	£34
Age					
20–29	—	—	6	3	4
30–39	7	17	22	25	23
40–49	11	16	8	15	13
50+	1	6	7	11	11
Unknown and Uncertain	—	4	23	46	49
Average	41.8	41.9	39.6	41.0	41.4
(Base)	(16)	(35)	(43)	(54)	(51)
Occupation					
Merchants	11	23	30	33	28
Manufacturers	4	12	13	21	19
Mechanics	1	3	17	34	40
Professionals	3	3	5	7	8
Others	—	2	—	4	4
Unknown	—	—	1	1	1
Religion					
Quakers					
total[a]	8	13	17	30	22
in good standing[b]	(5)	(10)	(11)	(20)	(14)
Anglicans	5	9	19	28	28
Presbyterians	5	12	18	17	22
Baptists	1	3	1	3	3
Lutherans	—	2	4	2	2
Others	—	1	1	—	1
Unknown and Uncertain	—	3	6	20	22

a. This category includes several Quakers who had been disowned by the Society of Friends between 1750 and 1770, but who had not joined another denomination.

b. This category includes all Quakers who were in good standing until at least the summer of 1775, when the Society began disowning men for committee or military service.

in June 1774 preceded an equally precipitous drop in November. Thereafter the decline slowed, but was still pronounced even after the committee stopped expanding. Moreover, as successive committees expanded in size, the distribution of their seats among the wealthy and well–to–do (here over £100), the comfortable (£45–99), and finally those men who were either still in the early stages of prosperous careers or who were of modest means and prospects (under £45) form an even clearer, more significant pattern. In November, despite the increase in committee size, the number of men in the upper assessment brackets barely changed. In 1775, their numbers again grew modestly, but in 1776, when committee size stabilized, the higher assessment groups declined in size. The number of members assessed less than £45, however, men of the most varied life styles and future promise, but generally with limited means at hand, rose dramatically. They formed only 35 percent of the Forty-Three, but at least 53 percent of the Sixty-Six, 54 percent of the First One Hundred, and 63 percent of the Second One Hundred (see table 12 and figure 1).[9]

Where do these figures place the great majority of Philadelphia's committeemen within their economic community? Certainly most were not poor; in 1774 only one Philadelphia taxpayer in ten was assessed even £45. Equally important, however, few were wealthy; nearly all of the later committeemen were far less affluent than provincial legislators, major import-export merchants, most professionals, and most committeemen of May and June 1774. The chronological pattern of declining committee wealth, however, is more interesting. The greatest increase in committeemen assessed less than £45 occurred in November 1774, when Philadelphians turned from nominating to electing their committees, and both moderate and radical leaders ran competing committee tickets. Notable increments to the already large base of less affluent committeemen, however, came as late as February 1776, when the city chose the committee that engineered the overthrow of the Assembly and led Pennsylvania out of the British Empire (see table 12). A correlation between declining average wealth and a rising commitment to the radical resistance—to Congress, commercial and armed warfare, and finally independence—is certainly plausible for Philadelphia's committeemen. Again, however, as at an earlier stage of the analysis of committee membership, one must ask two independent questions: were the less affluent committeemen really the more radical, and were less affluent committeemen simply younger relatives of the pre-Congress committee elite? A persuasive answer to the first question requires an assessment of committee election tickets and of individuals and groups within the full committees; this analysis will be presented shortly. The second question calls for a brief discussion of the ages of the new committeemen.

Age. As with Philadelphia's early resistance leaders, age is the most elusive information about committeemen who served after the Congress. The ages of a large proportion of the committeemen cannot be determined at all. Even the known ages, however, give suggestive clues to the dynamics of committee recruitment. First, successive average ages strongly confirm the hypothesis that November 1774 was the point of greatest change in the personnel of the committees. The

---

9. Because a few men assessed at less than £45 had respectable fortunes that were not liable to the particular provisions of the 1774 tax, or had lucrative incomes but little property, I use the expression "*generally* with limited means at hand." I use the phrase "*at least* 53 [and 54 and 63] percent" here because for a few committeemen no assessments could be found. It is likely that most of these men, as obscure figures, were of modest fortune.

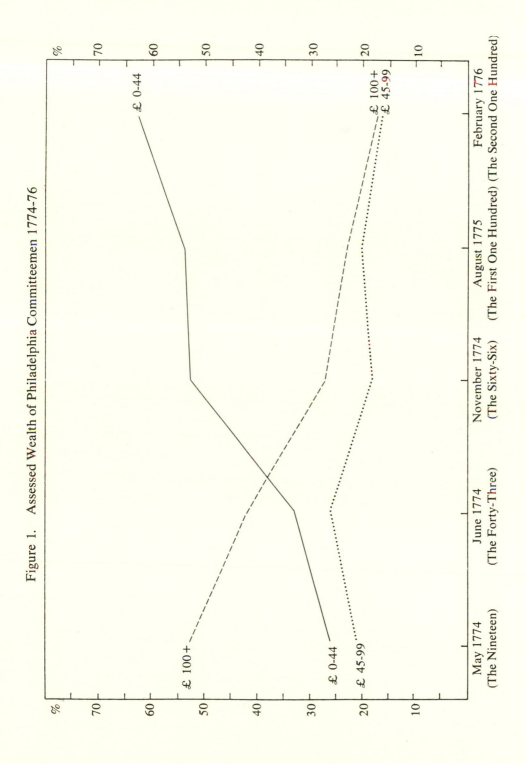

Figure 1. Assessed Wealth of Philadelphia Committeemen 1774-76

average known age on the Sixty-Six was over two years lower than on the Forty-Three; the number of members in their forties declined as the number in their thirties rose, and for the first time since the tea affair, a few men in their twenties served as well. In 1775, however, the average known age rose nearly one and one-half years, and in 1776 it rose again, although only by about five months. Two factors worked to increase the 1775 and 1776 averages. First, as the persistency and long-term continuity of service recovered from the sharp interruption of November 1774, the rise in the average age of the veterans whose ages are known becomes significant. Second, in 1775 the number of committeemen of unknown or uncertain age, many of whom as obscure men were probably also relatively young men, becomes for the first time very large—46 percent. By this same reasoning, the apparently modest increase in the 1776 average obscures an influx of generally younger newcomers. Forty-one veterans of the First One Hundred whose exact ages are known, now counted as one year older than in August 1775, sharply raised the new committee's average age, and the number of unknowns remained almost unchanged; yet the youthfulness of ten newcomers whose ages are known nearly stabilized the average known age of the whole board (see table 12).

The modest range of these fluctuations in known age suggests three important points about committee recruitment after the Congress. First, it reinforces the impression made by the indices of persistency and continuity that a stable new political establishment was emerging in 1775 and 1776. Second, the average decline in the ages of the committeemen is far too small to indicate that the new committeemen were of a different generation than the pre-Congress elite. Except in those rare cases where a 1774–76 committeeman is positively known to have been a younger, less affluent relative of a wealthy member of the early committees, the sharp decline in committee wealth and the modest level of that wealth compared with the fortunes of the early committeemen cannot be explained by changes in the age of the new committeemen. Finally, the very slight increase in average age on the Second One Hundred, despite a high carry-over of veterans from 1775, argues that the creation of a new committee establishment did not seriously retard the recruitment of young men into radical politics. Combined with the continuing fall in average assessed wealth, the age data suggest that the 1776 committee, the most radical of all in both word and deed, was a product of a continuing recruitment of young, economically obscure committeemen. If this is so, the post-Congress period saw two major alterations in the pattern of committee selection, the sharp, obvious break of November 1774, and a more subtle change five months before Independence. To confirm this hypothesis, one must consider other dimensions of Philadelphia's resistance leaders.

Occupation.　Before the Congress, age and wealth changes on the committees were often accompanied by changes in occupation that broadened the representative character of these new institutions. The same trend continued after the Congress, and for some of the same reasons. As the resistance faced more complex commercial, political, and finally military challenges, manufacturers, shopkeepers, builders, lawyers, and ship captains, as well as merchants, all had particular talents to contribute to the cause. And all could help to generate support among their several occupational groups for opposing Great Britain.

In the fall of 1774, however, the occupational structure of the committees began to show a more radical change. The number of craftsmen, shopkeepers, and petty retailers—the "mechanics"—swelled so greatly that it first cut into the strength of merchant committeemen, and then into that of the manufacturers and large-scale retailers.[10] As long as the committees were still growing, merchant and manufacturer representation only declined relative to that of the mechanics, but in 1776 the number of merchant and manufacturer committeemen declined absolutely. The "mechanics'" tickets of 1774, 1775, and 1776 were both instruments to express mechanic and radical views, and vehicles on which craftsmen and shopkeepers, who for the first time were effectively organized to participate in public life, "pushed their way into the political arena" of Revolutionary politics.[11]

The magnitude and pacing of this change point up its true significance. Merchants held 58 percent of the committee seats in May 1774. In June, after the recruitment of many manufacturers and large-scale retailers, the merchants were still a majority at 53 percent. Immediately after the Congress, however, their share of committee places fell to 45 percent, then in 1775 to 33 percent, and in 1776 to only 28 percent. Manufacturers and large-scale retailers increased their share of committee places from 21 percent in May to 28 percent in June 1774, but they were never again so prominent, holding just one-fifth of all committee seats between the Congress and Independence. Both groups lost seats to the mechanics—Philadelphia's brewers, grocers, tanners, carpenters, joiners, tailors, metal workers, druggists, chandlers, shipwrights, sailmakers, and other petty tradesmen. These Philadelphians held 5 percent of the committee places in May and 7 percent in June 1774, but the victory of the first "mechanics'" ticket in November increased their participation to 26 percent. In 1775 they secured 34 percent of the places, barely exceeding the number of merchants, and in 1776 they took a commanding lead in occupational representation with 40 percent of all committee seats (see table 12 and figure 2).

Between 1774 and 1776, Philadelphia's committees experienced a "mechanic revolution." No other change in the background of Philadelphia's committeemen was as dramatic as this, and perhaps none was more important. In June 1774, Philadelphia chose a resistance committee that reflected, however imperfectly, the diversity of its economy (see chapter 4). In February 1776, the city created a public body that directly incorporated a large part of that diversity. By Independence, Philadelphia's radical leadership not only spoke for the city's middle-class tradesmen, it began to speak through them.[12]

Ethnic Origins and Birthplaces.   Two closely related aspects of committee

---

10. As in chapter 4 above, I have labeled as "merchants" all committeemen who were called merchants in the sources and who were given no other trade there. "Manufacturers" and the "large-scale retailers" grouped with them on the tables are any men of trade who were assessed £45 or more, and were not labeled in the sources as merchants only. "Mechanics" are any men of trade who were assessed less than £45 and were not labeled as exclusively merchants. On table 12, "professionals" includes lawyers, doctors, ministers, teachers, and ship captains. "Others" includes gentlemen without known occupations, gentlemen-public servants (like Benjamin Franklin), retired businessmen (like Christopher Marshall, Sr.) and, in June 1774, two men of rural occupations.

11. Becker, *History of Political Parties,* p. 22. See chapters 2–3 above; and Olton, *Artisans for Independence.*

12. One must always remember two things about this socio-economic expansion of committee service, however. First, Philadelphia's Revolutionary committees never became exclusively middle class; indeed, major merchants were always overrepresented in terms of their numbers in the total business community, even when they were in a minority on the committees. Second, the lower classes were not represented at all, even in 1776: no porters, stevedores, domestics, journeymen, apprentices, women, or blacks sat on the committees.

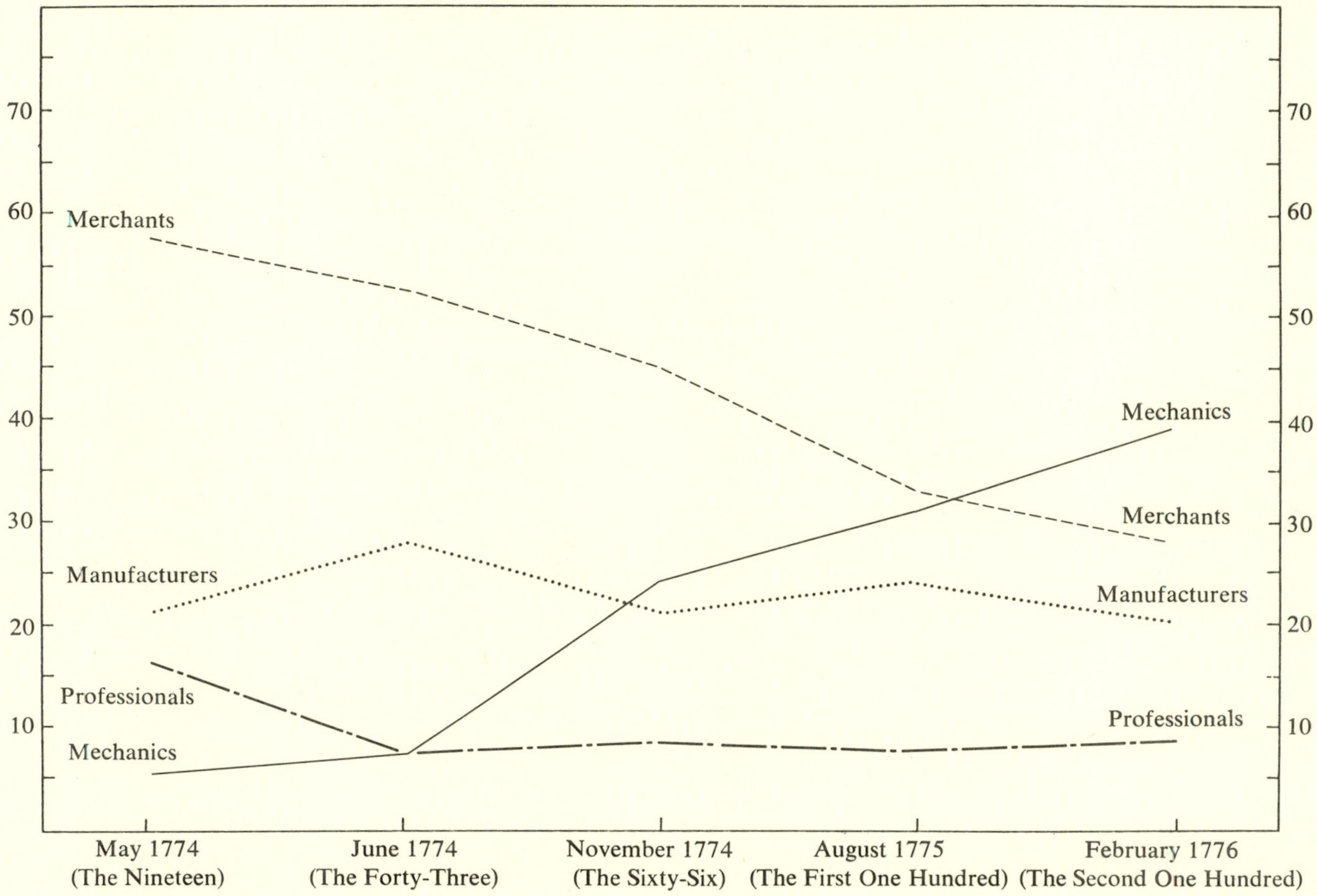

Figure 2. Percentages of Merchants, Manufacturers, Mechanics, and Professionals on Philadelphia Committees, 1774–76

composition showed little change after the Congress. The proportion of German committeemen, which had risen from almost nothing to a range of from 10 to 15 percent by the summer of 1774, remained steady until Independence. In the back-country, Pennsylvania's Germans were taking an ever-greater role in resistance politics, but in Philadelphia they did not become noticeably more prominent, either individually or collectively, after 1774. Nor did men born outside of Pennsylvania become more active in city politics. Between the Congress and Independence, a few Scottish and English immigrants became leaders, but hardly more than before the Congress. Men who were culturally either quite foreign—the Germans—or mildly so—English, Scottish, and Scotch-Irish immigrants and men from other colonies—continued to play a prominent role in Pennsylvania's resistance movement, but that role was no larger after 1774 than it had been before. Pennsylvanians in the Revolution did enjoy a political culture in which an outsider could make his mark, but except for rural Germans, for whom the Revolution was a political liberation, and for the already active rural Scotch-Irish, this was apparently no more true in the mid-1770s than it had been for decades.

Religion.   Increasingly, Philadelphia's resistance leaders were younger, less affluent, and far more likely to follow a manual occupation or retail trade than either members of the established government or early participants in the committee movement. Before 1774, these were tendencies among the resistance leadership; thereafter, they became a coherent trend. In religion, too, committeemen differed from more established leaders; they were less likely to be Quaker, and more likely to be Presbyterian. Yet even after 1769, when the Society of Friends first officially disapproved of its members' involvement in resistance politics, Anglicans, Presbyterians, and Quakers were usually about equally numerous on committees, and in May 1774, Charles Thomson persuaded the radical leadership to adopt a policy of denominational balance (see chapters 3 and 4).

A portrait of the committeemen after the Congress suggests that the radical leadership had learned this lesson particularly well. While the growing number of committeemen whose religious affiliation is not known—20 percent by 1775—makes an accurate assessment of the degree of denominational balance difficult, the known affiliations form a clear pattern.[13] Presbyterians, who became so numerous in Pennsylvania's new government after Independence, do not seem to have played an increasing role in Philadelphia's committees immediately prior to that event.[14] Quakers and all those of a strong Quaker heritage, however, held a remarkably stable position on Philadelphia's committees between June 1774 and the end of 1775. This stability is apparent whether all committeemen of Quaker background or only those who were Friends in good standing until 1775 are considered. Only in 1776 did Quaker participation in resistance politics drop sharply, under

---

13. This sudden upsurge in committeemen who are not mentioned in denominational sources may itself be significant; unchurched colonials may well have been of a lower economic and social status than their affiliated neighbors.

14. On the sudden explosion of Presbyterian participation in Pennsylvania's Revolutionary government in 1776, see Bockelman and Ireland, "Internal Revolution," pp. 124–59. I say the Presbyterians "do not seem" to have played a greater role in this period because with so many committeemen of unknown denomination in 1775 and 1776, it is possible that more committeemen were Presbyterians than Anglicans or Quakers.

heavy pressure from the Society of Friends.[15] Finally, in the twenty months before Independence, it was the Anglicans who emerged as Philadelphia's most active denomination in radical politics (see figure 3).

Religion had long been a divisive factor in Pennsylvania politics, and it remained so in the late 1770s and in the 1780s.[16] From 1774 to 1776, however, radical leaders struggled to overcome these basic divisions, which involved deep national and historical, as well as theological, antagonisms. In Philadelphia's committee politics, they were remarkably successful in achieving their goal. Even as the Society of Friends pressured Quaker committee veterans to withdraw from a public activity that was offensive to its peaceable convictions, new Quaker recruits entered the radical fold. A few of the newcomers were renegade Quakers of some notoriety, like Christopher Marshall, Sr. and Timothy Matlack, but others, like Owen Biddle, Thomas Pryor, and members of the Morris clan, had been respectable, if often worldly, Friends.[17] Indeed, new committeemen with a strong Quaker background who achieved some political prominence in 1775 and 1776 quite outnumbered the new Presbyterian members, of whom only the Delaware congressman Thomas McKean and Dr. Benjamin Rush became well known. Anglican newcomers, too, played a far more prominent role than the Presbyterian recruits, and included such leaders as Sharp Delaney, Richard Willing, and Samuel Simpson, a power in the Committee of Privates.

Change and Development. The overall structure of the religious affiliation of the committeemen, like every other portrait index except their static ethnic backgrounds and places of birth, continued to evolve in the same direction after the First Continental Congress as before. Together these indices show as close a balance of different groups as do the pre-Congress committees, together with an even greater pluralism and a further dilution of the originally ultraelitist character of Philadelphia's resistance leadership. The crucial question is how and why these patterns emerged. The suggestion advanced for the pre-Congress committees, that younger, poorer men who were not members of any economic, social, or political establishment felt that they had less to lose in defying imperial authority than more established leaders, should be as valid for 1775 as for 1770. At best, however, this only explains a predisposition to rebel against the established order in a negative way, by drawing attention to the environmental factors that did not impede Phila-

---

15. To qualify as a Quaker in good standing, either in table 12, in figure 3, or in Appendix M, a committeeman must not have been disowned by the Society of Friends before 1775. Thereafter, nearly all Quaker committeemen who persisted in resistance activity were disowned; technically, few committeemen were Quakers by Independence. Yet these disowned men were popularly regarded outside Quaker circles as Friends and, in a few cases, as pious, strict Friends who sincerely defended their right to fight a defensive war. To call these men anything but Quakers between 1774 and 1776 would be to misunderstand the purpose of balanced denominational leadership recruitment in Revolutionary Philadelphia. For many worldly Quakers, disowned Quakers, and men of Quaker background, and for all non-Quakers, the essential basis of Quaker identification was not membership in the Society of Friends, but the living of a Quaker life, the holding of many Quaker attitudes toward politics and society, and, in many cases, the commitment to defending the Society of Friends in times of stress and maintaining Quaker influence in Pennsylvania society.

16. Hutson, *Pennsylvania Politics,* chaps. 3–4; Bockelman and Ireland, "Internal Revolution," pp. 124–59; Ireland, "Ethnic-Religious Dimension of Pennsylvania Politics," pp. 423–48.

17. Marshall had been disowned in 1751 for counterfeiting provincial currency and remained bitter about his disownment for the rest of his life. Matlack had been disowned in 1765, after sorely trying the patience of the Society, whose members had repeatedly bailed him out of business difficulties.

Figure 3. Percentage of Philadelphia Committeemen known to have been
Quakers, Anglicans, or Presbyterians 1774-76

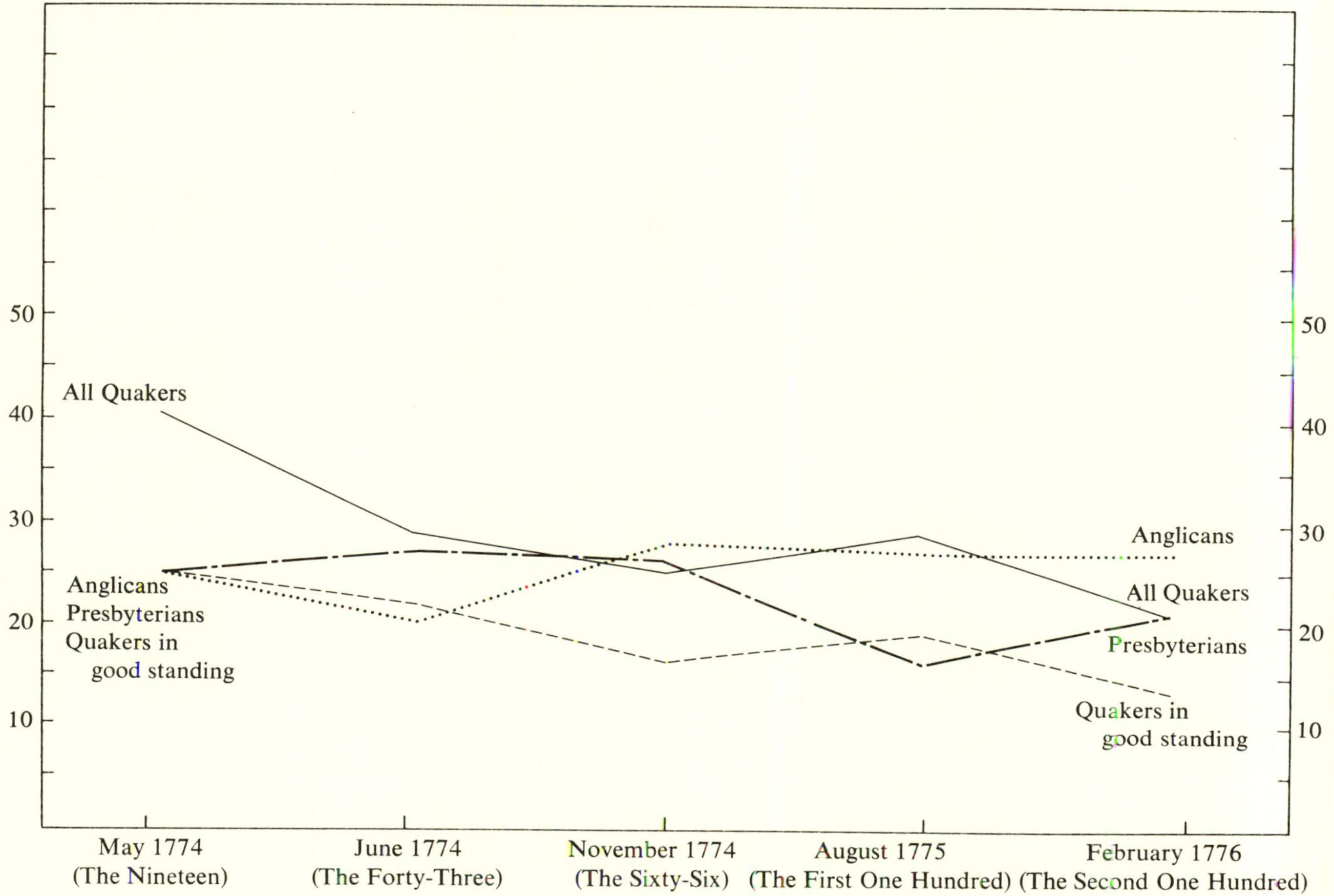

delphia's revolutionaries from acting. What were the positive social and collective motives that impelled younger merchants and professionals of modest fortune, craftsmen and shopkeepers, and heretofore quiet Anglicans, Presbyterians, Germans, and even young Quakers to step forward, to put a career, a social and cultural environment, and perhaps even a life on the line?

Put another way, one wishes to know not only those forces which permitted, but also those which encouraged the revolution of the middle classes. Between 1765 and 1774, an older, mercantile, Quaker elite, the central element in Pennsylvania's established order, lost control of city politics to a new, young elite, also largely mercantile and both Quaker and Anglican in origin, but more open and pluralistic than its predecessor. Between 1774 and 1776, Philadelphia's middle classes successfully challenged the domination of this second elite. The result was a new leadership, which drew from the entire upper and middle ranges of Philadelphia society but which finally centered on the aggressive, rising men of the middle classes, who were held together by youth, economic ambition, and a relative lack of the "unearned" advantages, as they saw them—wealth, family, and social status—of nearly all earlier political leaders. To measure this process, however, is not to understand it. This revolution of the middle classes did not just happen; it had its ways, and its reasons. These now command our attention.

LARGE-SCALE COMMITTEE RECRUITMENT: THE SECOND RADICAL DESIGN OF POLITICAL MOBILIZATION

November 1774. In the fall of 1774, radical young merchants and aggressive mechanics vividly remembered their recent victories—and their many defeats. In May, they had accepted an alliance with city moderates to launch the local movement for a continental congress. In June, mechanic attempts to radicalize the city committee and force it into a unilateral commitment to nonimportation had failed when conservative rural voters supported the mercantile aristocracy led by the moderate committeemen Thomas Willing, Thomas Wharton, Sr., and Dr. William Smith. In July, the Galloway Assembly had frustrated the moderate-radical alliance by sending a most conservative delegation to the new Congress. Only in October did radical young merchants and mechanics have their first revenge, when Thomas Mifflin and Charles Thomson soundly defeated Edward Penington and Thomas Willing to become assemblymen representing the corporate City. After their victory, the more zealous resistance leaders, who were committed not only to nonimportation but also to nonconsumption and even to preparations for war, had no wish to see their accelerating movement to radicalize Philadelphia blunted by hundreds of conservative rural voters, as it had been on June 18.

It was at this point that perceptive young merchants and leaders of the mechanics saw their grand opportunity. Philadelphia's moderate-radical alliance, embracing both city and county, still existed, embodied in the Forty-Three. After their June 18 defeat in a city and county gathering and their October victory in the corporate City alone, however, the radical merchants understood the key to securing control of the resistance. In early November, they suddenly broke with the moderates and allied openly with the mechanics, who now dominated electoral politics in Philadelphia.

On November 2, the Forty-Three announced in the *Gazette* that the election for the new committee to administer the Continental Association would be held on November 12. Immediately following that announcement, however, was a proposal by "a number of the citizens of Philadelphia" to elect separate city and county committees. The unknown authors gave several sensible reasons for this alteration, but subsequent events suggest that they were motivated by far stronger considerations. On November 7, a gathering of concerned Philadelphians—including several mechanics' leaders and probably several radical members of the Forty-Three as well—met to plan for the committee election. It was this body that first decided to use the secret ballot; because this practice was traditional in Pennsylvania, however, this decision would likely have been made by any large gathering of freemen. The meeting then voted to have separate city and county bodies, thus insuring that the secret-ballot election would work in their favor.[18]

The November 7 meeting completed its work by selecting twenty-four men to supervise a preliminary poll on November 10 to choose inspectors for the November 12 election.[19] For anyone who cared to look, the backgrounds of the supervisors chosen on November 7 clearly marked out the direction that city politics was taking. Fifteen of the supervisors had been or would become involved in the committee movement. One of these fifteen had played a conservative role in previous committee decisions, the other fourteen had participated or would participate in the radical resistance and would support independence. Nine were merchants, but the majority of these whose denominations are known were Presbyterian, and none was wealthy. Seven supervisors were shopkeepers or craftsmen, one was an innkeeper, and four were manufacturers. Twenty-one whose 1772 or 1774 tax assessments are known averaged £40. Five were Presbyterian, four were Anglican, two were Quakers. Significantly, only two sat on the Forty-Three, the radical young merchant John Bayard and the conservative shipbuilder Thomas Penrose—but four had been among the spokesmen chosen by the mechanics and Germans in June.[20] The November 7 supervisors were the first wave of that great alliance of young merchant and rising mechanic radicals that would soon sweep into committee politics.

Once the November 7 meeting had set the election procedure, if not before, politically active Philadelphians quickly split into two competing clusters to select candidates. Their meetings were probably not public, and nothing is known of them beyond the tickets they produced. Yet evidence within the lists suggests who joined these meetings and how they went about selecting their candidates. These brief glimpses into the political process permit some speculation about how Philadelphia's leaders perceived the political realities of their day.

It is likely that the more radical forces issued their slate, which one may conveniently label the radical-mechanic ticket, first. Twenty-one persons on that slate also appeared on the moderates' card, but while they are scattered all over the radical ticket, seventeen of the twenty-one head the moderate ticket without

18. *Pa. Packet,* Nov. 7, 1774; *Pa. Gaz.,* Nov. 9, 1774.

19. See *Pa. Gaz.,* Nov. 9, 1774; and compare the election procedures in *Pa. Gaz.,* Aug. 9, 1775, and Feb. 14, 1776.

20. Thomas Penrose, an Anglican who worshipped with the Quakers because of an argument with his rector, was the only known conservative in this group (see chapters 2–3 above). For the data on the inspectors, see Appendix J below.

interruption and in nearly the same order as they appear on the radical ticket, suggesting that moderate and conservative strategists began selecting their candidates by picking from the radicals' card anyone whom they liked, or any popular figure whom they could tolerate.[21]

The radicals had demonstrated a growing commitment to religious pluralism in politics since 1773, yet a detailed study of their November 1774 ticket suggests that the increasing official Quaker opposition to the resistance had some power to frustrate the full realization of that commitment. Thus both Anglicans and Presbyterians significantly outnumbered Quakers on the full radical ticket. This imbalance was even more pronounced among the thirty-nine candidates run by the radicals only, although if the radical ticket appeared first, there is no reason to distinguish between overlappers and other candidates as far as radical strategy is concerned. The radicals did nominate fifteen craftsmen and shopkeepers, however, a marked increase over the Forty-Three. The new radical slate was also younger and less affluent (£83 average assessment) than the Forty-Three (£113). A summary view of this ticket might characterize it as an alliance of radical young merchants—some of them rich, most of them not—and of mechanics, in roughly a two-to-one ratio, with large-scale manufacturers and retailers forming a third occupational force. This was, then, a radical (merchant)-mechanic ticket (see table 13).

Despite this occupational label for the radical ticket, however, the moderate and conservative candidates did not differ so greatly from their opponents in their occupations as they did in their previous political careers, in their wealth and age, and in their religious affiliations. Indeed, the occupational breakdowns of the two slates appear to be nearly identical. How, then, can one justify the label "mechanic" for one ticket and not for the other? Two reasons are persuasive. First, in addition to its craftsmen, the moderate-conservative slate listed five merchants who had openly opposed the nonimportation policy favored by organized mechanic meetings in 1770, but only two merchants who had prominently supported that boycott. The radical-mechanic ticket ran eight prominent supporters of the 1770 boycott, but only one known opponent. The latter slate also listed men who were prominent in the tea affair, and leaders of the mechanic meetings of June 1774.[22] Second, if the moderate-conservative ticket did appear after the radical slate, its occupational inclusiveness may have been a response to its competition. Mechanics had been gaining political power steadily in Philadelphia since 1770; for moderate and conservative merchants to rebuff them openly now, as they had long done behind the scenes, would be to invite disaster. By November 1774, resistance leaders who had reservations about Congress, nonimportation, and committee

---

21. See the italicized names in Appendix K. I use the term "moderate-conservative" ticket here to indicate the wide diversity of outlook and prior political careers represented on this ticket, from strict Quaker to ardent Presbyterian, from 1770 boycott-breaker to 1773 endorser of the Boston Tea Party. Also, this label will set this ticket off from the distinct "moderate" and "conservative" tickets of 1775.

22. Those who had opposed the 1770 boycott were Owen Biddle, who also ran on the mechanics' ticket and would soon become a prominent radical, and Philip Benezet, Thomas Fisher, John Reynell, and William West. Those who had supported the boycott were Samuel Howell and Thomas Mifflin, who appeared on both tickets, and John Cadwalader, George Clymer, Benjamin Loxley, James Mease, John Shee, and Charles Thomson on the mechanics' ticket. See chapter 2 above on the men and the event.

TABLE 13

Committee Tickets of November 12, 1774

	Thirty-nine men on the "mechanics'" ticket only	The whole "mechanics'" ticket	Twenty-one on both tickets	The whole moderate-conservative ticket	Thirty-nine men on the moderate-conservative ticket only
1774 Tax Assessment					
£200+	3	6	3	8	5
100–199	6	10	4	14	10
45–99	9	12	3	12	9
0–44	21	31	10	25	15
Unknown	—	1	1	1	—
Average	£59	£83	£114	£105	£101
Age					
20–29	3	4	1	2	1
30–39	13	20	7	13	6
40–49	5	7	2	9	7
50+	5	7	2	14	12
Unknown or uncertain	13	22	9	22	13
Average[a]	39.8	39.6	39.2	41.9	43.3
Occupation					
Merchants	19	28	9	30	21
Manufacturers	9	12	3	10	7
Mechanics	7	15	8	13	5
Professionals	4	5	1	3	2
Others	—	—	—	1	1
Unknown	—	—	—	3	3
Religion					
Quaker	6[b]	13	7[c]	21	14[d]
Anglican	10[e]	18	8[f]	22	14[g]
Presbyterian	14	17	3	3	—
Baptist	1	1	—	3	3
Lutheran	2	3	1	1	—
Other	1	2	1	1	—
Unknown	5	6	1	9	8

a. These averages are calculated on exact known ages only. The decennial breakdowns, however, include a few known *minimum* ages in the 50+ category.
b. Includes one disowned Quaker, and two uncertain attributions.
c. Includes three disowned Quakers.
d. Includes one uncertain attribution.
e. Includes two uncertain attributions.
f. Includes two uncertain attributions.
g. Includes three uncertain attributions.

activity itself were nevertheless learning something about popular politics—they now had their mechanics, too.[23]

If this was a conscious concession to the new politics, however, it was the only one that moderate and conservative strategists were willing to make. They stoutly resisted any economic leveling of political leadership by composing a slate that, despite its artisans, was nearly as affluent (£105 average assessment) as the Forty-Three (£113). Moreover, its candidates were noticeably older than their radical opponents, with fully a dozen of the thirty-nine men whom they alone nominated in their fifties and sixties. (On a late-appearing moderate-conservative ticket, the characteristics of its core, as distinct from the twenty-one overlappers, are significant for understanding its composers' ideas about political mobilization.)

The greater age of the moderate-conservative candidates may relate to another characteristic of their ticket, its pronounced religious imbalance. The whole slate included twenty-one members of the Society of Friends, which traditionally favored its elder members as leaders, and twenty-two Anglicans, but only three Presbyterians. The radical-mechanic slate ran only thirteen Quakers, of whom four had been disowned before the current troubles with Great Britain, eighteen Anglicans, and seventeen Presbyterians. The three Presbyterians who did appear on the moderate-conservative ticket also appeared on the radical slate; the moderates did not nominate a single Presbyterian on their own account. The heart of the moderate-conservative ticket, then, was a group of wealthy elder Quaker and Anglican merchants; the young, the less affluent, and members of Philadelphia's less prestigious religious faiths found no home there (see table 13).

A comparison of the two tickets points up the ways in which each group hoped to win favor for its approach to the imperial crisis. Radical strategists, committed to that aggressive and uncompromising opposition to British imperial policy which most mechanics had favored since 1770, ran an unprecedented number of artisans and retailers, thereby pressuring more conservative leaders to recruit their own mechanics. Equally important, the radicals continued to draw new leaders from each of the three major religious faiths, although it was becoming harder to bring strict Quakers into the cause. Moderate and conservative forces that were dedicated to the more cautious approaches to settling the imperial crisis which the elder mercantile elite had supported since 1765 stood by older leadership patterns. They made little attempt to recruit younger, less affluent merchants, and they were either uninterested in or averse to balancing religious and ethnic candidates in order to reach Presbyterian and German voters.

The November 12 election was a sweeping victory for the radical-mechanic alliance. On the basis of the election tickets alone, the radical triumph seems to confirm the lesson that Charles Thomson had taught his followers so well—the central role of religious balance in Philadelphia's new politics. But there were other reasons for the radical victory. On November 7, moderate and conservative strategists were forced to enter an election run by their opponents and restricted

---

23. An earlier example of the political use of Philadelphia's mechanics by conservative politicians may well have been Joseph Galloway's mobilization of Philadelphia's shipwrights in 1765 to protect Stamp Agent John Hughes and the Quaker party from pressure by anti-Quaker party and anti-Stamp Act crowds. See Hutson, *Pennsylvania Politics,* chap. 4, and "White Oaks," pp. 3–25. As was probably true of the "White Oaks" in 1765, most mechanics on the moderate-conservative ticket were Quakers or Anglicans.

to the city. Moreover, their way of selecting candidates was not only stiff-necked and obsolete, it was inept. They chose as standard-bearers several strict Quakers, who probably would not have accepted committee office, and put the popular John Dickinson far down their list instead of at its head. Their work shows not only haste, but also ignorance about what political mobilization required in 1774. Outnumbered and outmaneuvered, most moderates and conservatives apparently gave up hope before the poll. On election day, if a later tory account is correct, 499 Philadelphians favored the radical ticket; only 18 voted for the moderate-conservative slate.[24]

August 1775. The next committee election in Philadelphia, held on August 16, 1775, to choose an expanded board of one hundred members, dramatically demonstrated the success of the November 1774 revolution in electioneering. The mechanisms of selecting election officials and conducting the poll followed the pattern of November, and the mechanics probably again dominated this procedure.[25] What was different in 1775, and quite remarkable, was the degree to which the radicals' concept of ticket building was accepted by their opponents.

For 1775 there are three extant committee tickets. Each presented Philadelphians with a distinct approach to conducting the resistance, yet the differences among the three slates were far more subtle than those between the two tickets of November 1774.[26] The immediate reason for this is the extensive duplication of names on the 1775 tickets. In 1774, only twenty-one men held places on both sixty-candidate slates. In 1775, forty-three men appeared on all three slates. In addition, the "mechanics' " ticket shared twelve more men with the "moderate" ticket, and another six with the "conservative" ticket, while running only thirty-nine men of its own. Yet the mechanics were more venturesome than their opponents. The moderates shared fifty-five men with the mechanics, and sixty-nine with the conservatives, running only nineteen men on their own. The conservatives shared forty-nine candidates with the mechanics, and sixty-nine with the moderates, running only thirteen candidates of their own. This extensive sharing of candidates is of the greatest importance in the development of committee politics in Philadelphia. By 1775 an established leadership had emerged that was so powerful that it could not be directly challenged. Indeed, Philadelphia's moderates made no attempt to challenge it: their slate included fifty-seven members of the existing Sixty-Six. Theirs was properly the committee establishment ticket. The other slates were more novel: the mechanics ran only forty-four of the Sixty-

24. Essay by "Tiberius," *Pa. Ledger,* Mar. 16, 1776.

25. *Pa. Gaz.,* Aug. 9, 16, 1775.

26. The three tickets, printed in broadside, may be found in the Philadelphia Library Company, catalogued as Am 1775 Phi Com, 962.F.70, 71, and 73. It is difficult to make exact comparisons between these slates, because the "mechanics' " slate (962.F.70) lists eighty-eight names for the City and Northern Liberties, to which the twelve men actually elected for Southwark have been added here, on the assumption that in the separate election which that suburb had requested (*Pa. Gaz.,* Aug. 16, 1775), the victorious candidates were local nominees of the radical-mechanic alliance. The "moderate" ticket (962.F.71) gives all one hundred candidates. The "conservative" slate (962.F.73), however, only gives eighty-eight men; the twelve for Southwark, if our assumption about that election is correct, are not now known. Thus the numbers of candidates that the conservative faction shared with the moderates and mechanics may have been higher than those given in the text.

The fact that the conservative slate is twelve names shorter than its two competitors must be kept in mind, particularly when comparing the portrait data figures for the tickets in table 14.

Six, and the conservatives continued only thirty-six. Yet both slates listed a higher proportion of veterans than either ticket of November 1774.[27]

With their extensive overlapping, the 1775 tickets had to resemble one another more closely than the 1774 slates had done, but the degree of this similarity is still striking. The first major index, the distribution of assessed wealth among the candidates, shows no appreciable differences among the three tickets. The age distribution on the tickets did vary, but the ticket of the radical-mechanic alliance was apparently not the youngest; that distinction went to the moderates. And although the conservatives ran the oldest candidates, the age difference between them and the mechanic nominees is too slight to have any significance (see table 14).[28] The impact of the radical-mechanic victory of 1774 is unmistakable here. In 1775, all political contenders accepted two major radical premises: successful resistance committees must include all the upper and middle economic classes in the community, and they must be young.

There are two important quantitative differences between the tickets, however. First, the "mechanics'" slate—the first Philadelphia committee election ticket to be so labeled by a contemporary—did list many more mechanics, and a few more manufacturers and large-scale retailers, than either the moderate or the conservative cards.[29] And the moderate and conservative tickets ran more merchants and more professionals than did the mechanics' ticket. One can best express this difference by observing that the moderates maintained existing mechanic strength on the committee at about one-quarter of the whole, while the mechanic ticket increased mechanic strength to one-third of the committee (compare tables 13 and 14). By 1775, Philadelphia's moderates and conservatives were nominating young merchants, lawyers, and doctors of modest fortune, but the radical-mechanic alliance was backing young artisan candidates even more strongly than they had in 1774.

The second major difference between the tickets is surprising. The mechanics advanced as many Friends in good standing as the conservatives, and a few more disowned Quakers, but they also nominated fewer Presbyterians than did the conservatives, and far fewer than the moderates.[30] While the moderate ticket had many fewer Quakers than Presbyterians, the radical-mechanic alliance reversed this pattern. All three tickets were balanced—or unbalanced—to roughly the same degree (see table 14). The religious composition of the mechanic ticket argues that the radical-mechanic alliance was more successful in recruiting young Quaker merchants and craftsmen than it had been in November; and because this ticket

---

27. The radical-mechanic slate of 1774 ran eighteen of the Forty-Three; the moderate-conservative slate ran ten.

28. If the unusually large number of men of unknown age on the mechanic ticket were relatively young, as is likely, the mechanics' slate may in fact have been the youngest, but no indeterminable variables can make the moderates' nominees into elder statesmen.

29. At the bottom of the Library Company copy of this ticket (962.F.70) appears the handwritten sentence "This is called the mechanicks' Ticket." Brief comments in the same hand appear on the moderate and conservative tickets, and on the sole extant ticket for February 1776.

30. Because the mechnics' ticket has the largest number of candidates whose religion could not be determined, the radicals might have run many more Presbyterians than the sixteen given in table 14. It is highly unlikely, however, that any adjustment would give them as many Presbyterians as the moderates endorsed, particularly because the moderates had several candidates of unknown religion as well.

TABLE 14

Committee Tickets of August 16, 1775

	"Mechanics'" ticket— 100 names[a]	Moderate ticket— 100 names	Conservative ticket— 88 names
1774 Tax Assessment			
£200+	9	11	8
100–199	15	15	13
45–99	17	15	16
0–44	56	57	50
Unknown	3	2	1
Age in 1775			
20–29	4	8	2
30–39	24	31	30
40–49	15	19	18
50+	11	11	13
Unknown and Uncertain	46	31	25
Average	41.0	39.7	41.3
Occupation			
Merchants	33	38	39
Manufacturers	22	18	11
Mechanics	33	24	21
Professionals	7	15	12
Others	4	2	3
Unknown	1	3	2
Religion			
Quakers	31	23	27
Disowned Quakers	(10)	(7)	(6)
Anglicans	30	28	26
Presbyterians	16	29	20
Baptists	3	1	1
Lutherans	2	2	2
Others	—	2	1
Unknown and Uncertain	18	15	11

a. The "mechanic's ticket" given here is actually a combination of the ticket proper, with its eighty-eight names, and the twelve victorious members for Southwark who, I assume, were run on a coordinate ticket, allied with the main slate of radical-mechanic nominees.

was constructed in the midst of Philadelphia's first preparations for war, this was an astonishing triumph for the radicals' policy of balanced denominational recruitment. That policy does not explain why the moderates so greatly outrecruited the radicals among the Presbyterians, but a consideration of the broader character of the August election tickets does suggest one reason for the high number of Presbyterians on the moderate slate.

The three tickets of 1775 evidently represent three political factions which had distinctive approaches to the imperial crisis but which had accepted the lessons taught by radical activists in 1774. All resistance leaders had learned that effective committees must bring together the upper and middle economic classes, merchants of all kinds, manufacturers and large-scale retailers, craftsmen and shopkeepers, lawyers, doctors, and ship captains, Quakers, Anglicans, and Presbyterians. And the committeemen must be relatively young, preferably averaging in their late thirties, to identify most effectively with the thousands of younger Philadelphians who were actively carrying out nonimportation and nonconsumption and filling up the ranks of the militia.

It was within these guidelines that the three factions expressed their individuality. One can argue plausibly that either the "mechanics'" or the "moderate" ticket was the natural successor to the Sixty-Six. It was the moderates who filled their slate with fifty-seven of the Sixty-Six and nominated every prominent militia commander in the city. This was the party of the new patriot establishment. It was "moderate" in not wanting further change, and although nearly all of its members would accept independence, most would oppose Pennsylvania's radical Constitution of 1776. The ticket also presented a patriot vehicle for young proprietary faction leaders like the Allen and Tilghman brothers, who had entered the resistance late but still hoped to retain their political influence in a new Pennsylvania. It is this proprietary faction orientation that may explain the moderate ticket's high number of Presbyterians, for most members of that denomination had favored the proprietary cause before the rise of the radical resistance, and several still retained that loyalty. The low number of Quakers on the moderate slate probably arose from the same cause; most Quakers were still wary of the proprietary interest. Viewed in this light, the moderate and conservative tickets represent the last separate electioneering of proprietary faction and Quaker party leaders. In May 1776, these leaders would join to oppose constitutional revolution.[31]

The other "successor" to Philadelphia's tradition of committee leadership was the ticket that did in fact succeed—the "mechanics'" slate. Three considerations mark this set of candidates as more radical than its moderate opposition. The radical-mechanic leaders did not stand still with respect to recent changes in committee recruitment, like the moderates, but ran still more mechanics and—something that wealth profiles do not show—more young men who lacked a prominent family background. Thus the mechanics' ticket followed the established direction of change in committee personnel. Where the moderate ticket was the static successor to the Sixty-Six, the mechanics' ticket was the dynamic successor. Second, the moderate ticket included two men who had been active in committee politics

---

31. Prominent proprietary faction men who appeared on the moderate ticket but not on the mechanics' slate include Andrew and James Allen, Tench Francis, John Gibson, John Maxwell Nesbit, Richard Peters, Jr., Richard and Tench Tilghman, and Alexander Wilcocks.

as early as 1769, but who then played a moderate or conservative role.[32] The mechanics ran no such figures. Finally, several mechanics' candidates who were not on the moderate ticket would become prominent supporters of a radical new constitution for Pennsylvania in 1776, while several moderates not on the mechanic ticket would oppose that change. Thus 1775 was both the last time that Quaker party and proprietary faction supporters operated independently and the first time that the ideological differences between the Constitutionalists (radicals) and the Republicans (moderates) of the fall of 1776 begin, however dimly, to take shape in distinct political combinations.

February 1776. The election of colonial Philadelphia's last Committee of Observation was the culmination of the patterns of leadership recruitment that had characterized the resistance since 1774. Because no committee tickets have survived for 1776, it is not known whether the victorious candidates, who again were sponsored by the radical-mechanic alliance, were opposed.[33] But a comparison of the First and Second One Hundred makes clear both the direction and the dimensions of the last alterations in resistance committee composition in Philadelphia, and suggests some reasons for them.

Two important differences between the Second One Hundred and its predecessor followed established patterns: the new committee was less affluent, and it had fewer merchants and more mechanics. A third difference was more novel, and perhaps more significant: the number of Quaker committeemen fell sharply. The Society of Friends' threat of disownment against Quakers who served on the committees seems to have driven a few out of resistance politics, and perhaps discouraged others from entering.[34] What is remarkable about these alterations in the wealth, occupation, and religion of the committeemen is that they involved a turnover of only thirty-one of the one hundred seats on the board. Among the relatively few members moving off of and on to the committee, these alterations were extensive and dramatic. Thirteen men assessed over £45 left committee service, but only four such men joined the new board; the assessments of those leaving averaged £61, of those entering, £28. Eleven departing mechanics were replaced by seventeen new ones. Ten departing Quakers were succeeded by only three (see table 15).

It is unlikely that all of these alterations were part of a radical-mechanic grand design; the loss of Quaker leadership was too damaging to the image of resistance unanimity to have been planned by radical strategists. Yet the continuing transition from prosperous merchant to obscure mechanic committeemen was probably entangled with a deliberate and partisan alteration in committee leadership. As the military and political crisis in Pennsylvania mounted in 1775 and early 1776, the city committee increasingly favored the demand made by the Committee of

---

32. Tench Francis opposed nonimportation in 1770; Peter Knight did not sign the Philadelphia tea committee's letter of December 25, 1773, to Boston, condoning that town's Tea Party.

33. As in 1774 and 1775, the radical-mechanic alliance firmly controlled election procedures in 1776. The First One Hundred itself took the first step toward setting up the committee election (see *Pa. Gaz.,* Feb. 14, 1776).

34. Especially notable was the plight of Benjamin Marshall, who declined further committee service in February 1776 to avoid disownment by the Society, but was soon disowned anyway because he would not make a proper repentance for his committee service. See "Minutes of the Philadelphia Monthly Meeting, 1771–1777," ff. 357, 375, 385–86, 393, Friends Historical Library, Swarthmore.

TABLE 15

Changes in the Committee

February 16, 1776

	Deletions	*Additions*
1774 Tax Assessment		
£200+	2	—
100–199	4	1
45–99	7	3
0–44	17	25
Unknown	1	2
Average	£61	£28
Occupation		
Merchants	12	8
Manufacturers	6	3
Mechanics	11	17
Professionals	2	3
Religion		
Quakers	10	3
(Disowned Quakers)	(3)	—
Anglicans	9	9
Presbyterians	3	8
Others	—	1
Unknown and Uncertain	9	10

Privates for a well-funded militia based on compulsory service. Several members of the Committee of Safety, however, continued to support the Assembly's cautious, badly funded, and almost voluntary militia plan. This disagreement, and perhaps others, led to friction between the First One Hundred and the Committee of Safety.[35] Just as in November 1774, when the radical-mechanic alliance excluded conservative committeemen like Thomas Willing from their ticket, and in 1775, when the mechanics left off the moderate John Nixon, so in 1776 the reigning coalition did not renominate several widely known committee veterans. Of eleven Committee of Safety members on the First One Hundred, five were continued on the Second One Hundred, but only one of these members attended sessions of the Committee of Safety frequently.[36] The six men who were dropped, however, were among the most active members of the Committee of Safety. Five of the six were

---

35. See chapters 6 and 7 above; and the circular letter of the Second One Hundred to the county committees, dated March 5, 1776, in *Pa. Evening Post,* Mar. 9, and *Pa. Packet,* Mar. 11, 1776.

36. Those continued were John Dickinson and Benjamin Franklin, who almost never attended Committee of Safety sessions; Joseph Parker and Joseph Reed, who attended sporadically; and John Cadwalader, who attended about half of the sessions.

also major merchants, and it was their departure that finally tipped the occupational balance of the Philadelphia committee strongly toward the mechanics.[37]

The constant search for new resistance leaders in Philadelphia ended in 1776 much as it had begun six years earlier. With each new disagreement within the leadership the most venturesome and uncompromising strategists cut their ties with their more moderate colleagues and sought fresh allies who were not identified with any established interest, whether it be the old Quaker party or proprietary faction, the merchant aristocracy, or the provincial Assembly's Committee of Safety. This process of recurrent exclusion and inclusion moved at an uneven rate and became more or less conscious and dramatic as challenges to the resistance rose and fell or changed in character. It peaked dramatically in November 1774, subsided in 1775, and then rallied to effect one last redefinition of Philadelphia's resistance movement in 1776. That its final casualty, the Committee of Safety member and former Committee of Observation chairman, George Clymer, had been one of its most brilliant early recruits is both ironic and rather uncharacteristic of the American Revolutionary movement, either in Philadelphia or elsewhere in the colonies. But it should not surprise us. Clymer would soon gain back the favor of the radicals, and then again lose it, but his personal experience was only an early sign of a growing division among radical Philadelphians over what a total rejection of the British Empire must finally mean for Pennsylvania. Never before had this proud, nearly autonomous community faced the necessity of charting out its own independent future.

Each of Philadelphia's three committee elections held between the adjournment of the First Continental Congress and Independence had distinctive characteristics, but their common pattern provides a clear picture of leadership recruitment and political mobilization in Revolutionary America's largest community. One cannot know what made particular Philadelphians run for committee office. No study of the election tickets and voting returns can discover the unique blend of patriotic ardor, personal ambition, reluctant acceptance of a call to duty, or a dozen other motives that animated the city's resistance leaders, either individually or collectively. Nor can one know, in most instances, who wanted to be nominated and was not, or who wished to avoid political involvement but agreed to serve. What one can discover are both the socio-economic backgrounds that were considered useful or appealing in a resistance leader, and the probable motives of major groups within the community in expressing their choice for committeemen. Young merchants and newly mobile mechanics independently developed a strong desire to serve Philadelphia in its gravest crisis—and doubtless to protect the economic interests of their occupational class. Each group independently saw the

---

37. These six men were too prominent in the resistance to have been omitted by oversight, and too dedicated to have declined committee election. Owen Biddle, James Mease, Robert Morris, and Thomas Wharton, Jr. had been at the center of the opposition to Britain for years. But the most persuasive case is that of George Clymer. A veteran of every Philadelphia resistance committee since 1770, and the acting chairman of the First One Hundred in the summer and early fall of 1775, Clymer would rise again in radical circles to run for the Assembly on the proindependence ticket on May 1, 1776, and then to serve in the constitutional convention in July. Clymer was also the Committee of Safety's best attender and probably its most influential member in the spring of 1776; he missed only 30 out of 259 sessions between October 1775 and July 1776. For portrait data on Biddle, Clymer, Mease, Robert Morris, Samuel Morris, Jr., and Thomas Wharton, Jr., see Appendix M.

advantages of allying with the other. The young merchants had political experience, social status, and the prospect of economic success. The mechanics had the numbers to swing elections. So while the individual political motives of hundreds of resistance leaders are now obscure, the leaders' collective concepts of effective political mobilization are reasonably clear. We cannot know why particular men decided to become local revolutionary leaders; we can get a sure sense of why particular men were asked.

THE REVOLUTION OF PHILADELPHIA'S MIDDLE CLASSES AND THE BIRTH OF MODERN AMERICAN POLITICS

In February 1775, James Rivington's *New-York Gazetteer* printed a letter from a Philadelphia correspondent that caustically described that city's new committee of Sixty-Six and the manner of its election, charging that

> one of [the committeemen], an avowed Republican, had lately met with some disappointments, . . . another had acquired his fortune partly by an illicit trade [in the] last war, . . . another was an illiterate Merchant; another too insignificant to notice, &c. . . . almost all the violent sons of licentiousness are of a particular sect [the Presbyterians?]. . . . I have been assured that there are many on this Committee who could not get credit for twenty shillings, and . . . that not one-sixth of the people ever voted [for the committee] at all—that in the City and Suburbs there were not six hundred votes for the sixty Committee-men, so that you see each one had only to procure ten voters; a mighty easy way this of getting into power.[38]

One can easily dismiss this account as the exaggerated view of an ill-tempered tory, but his colorful observation underlines a central fact about Philadelphia's resistance movement. The rapid growth of committee politics beginning in 1774 had quickly effected a revolution in traditional patterns of leadership.

One should use the word "revolution" with some care in discussing transformations in public leadership. Between 1765 and 1774, Philadelphia's resistance movement experienced a widespread turnover in its leaders, and rapid changes in their attitudes and ideas, but all within a broad business elite. The city's freemen turned from older Quaker and Anglican merchants to younger merchants of several faiths, and to manufacturers and large-scale retailers, to provide guidance in the imperial crisis. This process, Philadelphia's first modest leadership revolution, gradually spread out political power from an extremely narrow upper-class base, distributing it among a broad city elite, defined largely in terms of wealth, family prominence, and education, that was relatively unbounded by age, occupation, or religion. The revolution in leadership that occurred between 1774 and 1776, however, was of another kind. Political power now began to flow downward to men who were less affluent, less well educated, and far more obscure.

Three features of Philadelphia's committeemen convey the magnitude of this change. First, the great majority of these men had never held political office before the resistance movement. Of 150 who served between November 1774 and Independence, 119 (79 percent) had no prior committee experience, and 128 (85

---

38. *N.-Y. Gaz.*, Feb. 23, 1775; also in Force, ed., *American Archives*, 4th Ser., I: 1232.

percent) had not served before May 1774. The growing committee movement had created a very extensive group of new officeholders in just fifteen months. Second, these newcomers were largely men of modest fortune, far better off than the thousands of laborers, domestics, journeymen, and blacks who never sat on Philadelphia's resistance committees, but far less affluent than the city's great merchants. In June 1774, 35 percent of the committee of Forty-Three were assessed less than £45; in 1776, at least 63 percent of the Second One Hundred were in this category. The average assessment of the committeemen fell from £113 to £64 in this period. Finally, the proportion of committee seats held by merchants, manufacturers, and large-scale retailers fell from 81 to 47 percent between June 1774 and February 1776; craftsmen and shopkeepers increased their share of places from 7 to 40 percent in these same months. For the first time in Philadelphia's history, wealthy merchants and elegant lawyers in greatcoats and waistcoats were thrown together with obscure mechanics in shirtsleeves and leather aprons to perform a public service.

Not everything changed, however. It is essential to remember that men of different fortunes and callings, both the prominent and the obscure, shared power and responsibility. Moreover, early trends away from an older, predominantly Quaker leadership, apparent as early as 1769, had almost reached their limit by November 1774. Thereafter, the average age of the committeemen showed little change, and Quakers, Anglicans, and Presbyterians participated in committee politics about equally, as they had in 1769 and early 1774, until pressure from the Society of Friends finally reduced the Quakers' political involvement in 1776.

This continuity in the age and religious identification of Philadelphia's committeemen is too steady, set against changes in committee membership and in the members' wealth and occupations, not to suggest conscious design. Committees that offered scores of new places to eager young patriots and extended to the middle classes an unprecedented invitation to participate in public life had a broad appeal; so did committees that still had room for older men, and for Quakers and Anglicans as well as Presbyterians. This has all the appearance of a design based squarely upon widespread perceptions of what was politically attractive in a large, pluralistic community. By choosing certain Philadelphians as leaders, resistance strategists sought to mobilize other men who identified with the new recruits, either personally or through associations based on common fortune, age, trade, faith, and neighborhood residence.[39] The art of this recruitment lay in selecting committeemen carefully to mobilize the greatest number of Philadelphians.

The history of Philadelphia's Revolutionary committees, then, is one of rapid political mobilization through a sudden expansion in the number and socioeconomic background of its leaders. To understand the importance of this expansion, however, one must answer several larger questions. Was this recruitment

---

39. The evidence for this statement, which is central to the entire argument of this chapter, is of two kinds: Charles Thomson's meeting with six members from each of Philadelphia's several religious denominations, held on May 29, 1774, discussed in chapter 3 above; and the extremely low probability that the steady balance of religious denominations and the steadily growing diversity in wealth and occupation on the committees chosen between 1774 and 1776, summarized in table 12, was accidental.

cosmetic only, or did the new leaders perform vital functions that could not have been done by any other men? Were those who became leaders active agents in their own recruitment? Did socially obscure newcomers obtain real power? And did this expansion in leadership permanently affect the politics of Philadelphia and Pennsylvania?

There are grounds for regarding Philadelphia's new large committees both as pragmatic and as cosmetic aids in achieving the goals of the resistance. The immediate reason for expanding the committees was undoubtedly the pressing need for administrative manpower and occupational expertise to handle the growing volume of technically complex work required in supervising nonimportation and providing for the public defense. And Charles Thomson observed that "the Committee . . . which was elected [in 1775] . . . was, for the purpose of giving them more weight and influence, increased to the number of one hundred."[40] Yet this observation was evidently not intended to suggest that expanded recruitment was simply either a cosmetic maneuver or an attempt to secure bureaucratic depth. Numbers did provide the basic muscle of Revolutionary politics, impress and persuade the public, and offer a broad range of expertise, but they gave the Revolution another dimension as well. A committee of one hundred men, organized into subcommittees based in the several wards in which their members lived and worked, could represent a city of twenty-five thousand in a way that no board of twenty could. The use of larger bodies permitted the constant communication—the passing up from freemen to public officials of attitudes, needs, and desires, and the passing down to the freemen of orders, resolves, and explanations—that Philadelphia needed in the stress of revolutionary times.

Moreover, this intense form of representation did not involve twenty-five thousand undifferentiated constituents. Colonial Pennsylvania was run by Quaker and Anglican merchants and farmers of English and Welsh stock, plus a few Scots and Scotch-Irish Presbyterians. The majority of the artisans and shopkeepers, Germans, and Scotch-Irish were at best on the periphery of the political community. Their talents and drive, fully harnessed in the economy, were lost to the polity. This was perhaps unimportant before 1765, when the city and province were seldom subjected to great political or military pressure from outside forces. To disregard so much manpower in the Revolution, however, when it was so desperately needed to combat and defeat external and internal foes, was unthinkable for the city's radical organizers. The central goal of increasing popular participation in committee politics, then, was to draw a greater proportion of the community into resistance activity. Only by enlisting energetic young leaders and rapidly mobilizing the great majority of the community could Philadelphia defend its autonomy against British imperial power.

The emphasis placed upon a radical design of revolutionary mobilization in this interpretation may give the impression that Philadelphia's new leaders were passive figures chosen by a small elite of committee veterans, but this was clearly not the case. A keen ambition for power or fame undoubtedly motivated many new committeemen, and the fiery patriotic spirit that ran through thousands of Philadelphians in the spring and summer of 1775 certainly impelled others to enter committee service. Far more important, however, was the rise of Phila-

---

40. N.-Y. Hist. Soc., *Colls.,* XI: 283.

delphia's mechanics, who organized independently of the radical merchants between 1770 and 1772, contested county and Assembly elections in 1772 and
1773, and finally forced the merchants to take a few of their leaders into the
Forty-Three in June 1774. When the radical merchants were ready to split from
the moderates in November 1774, the mechanics were ready to ally with them.
The radical strategists who recruited mechanics for the Sixty-Six probably included
both merchant and mechanic spokesmen, but mechanic and manufacturing leaders
dominated the administration of that election, beginning on November 7.[41] The
radical (merchant)-mechanic coalition, which formed at this time, was a true
alliance of factional equals, separated by calling, income, and social status, but
united by their attitude toward the imperial crisis. And so this alliance remained
until Independence.

Yet while radical merchants and radical mechanics were factional equals, they
were not economic or social equals, and the idea of widespread officeholding by
craftsmen and shopkeepers dated only from the formation of the mechanics'
Patriotic Society in 1772. It was probably popular resistance to the novelty of
mechanic equality that most effectively perpetuated the domination of merchants,
manufacturers, and large-scale retailers on Philadelphia's committees until February 1776. Even on the Second One Hundred, moreover, merchants and professionals occupied the highest committee offices. Of the six men who were apparently
continued as chairmen or secretaries of the Second One Hundred, as they had
been on the First One Hundred, three were lawyers and three were merchants.[42]

The monopolizing of high committee office by merchants and professionals can
give a misleading impression of the degree of their power, however, for it was
popularly accepted that the titular heads and corresponding representatives of any
large public body should be well-educated men, who could speak and write most
effectively. Another six members named to assist the Second One Hundred's six
officers, probably in framing policy, included three mechanics.[43] Artisans and
retailers on the November 1774 and August 1775 committees had not been given
such positions of trust, and they are not known to have been prominent in making
committee policy; but in the spring of 1776, such figures as Sharp Delaney, a
druggist, Isaac Howell, a brewer, Christopher Marshall, Sr., a retired druggist, and
Timothy Matlack, who had followed several trades with little success, became
real powers in the formation of committee policy. In June 1776, the Second One
Hundred named seven mechanics and another seven men who had risen from
that class to its twenty-five man delegation to the provincial conference, which in

---

41. On the mechanics' drive for power, see chapters 2–3 and 5 above; and Olton, *Artisans
for Independence.* On the mechanics' prominent role in the November 1774 election, see *Pa.
Gaz.,* Nov. 9, 1774, and Appendix J, where the number of election supervisors of mechanic-
class background is readily apparent.

42. See the "List of the Sub-Committees, appointed by the Committee for the city and
liberties of Philadelphia, . . ." cited in note 8 above. The twelve committeemen who do *not*
appear on this list held some kind of special assignment on the Second One Hundred. Of those
twelve, the six who had been officers of the First One Hundred were Joseph Reed, Thomas
McKean, and Samuel Meredith, chairmen, and John Bayard Smith, Robert Strettel Jones, and
Peter Z. Lloyd, secretaries. Reed, McKean, and Lloyd were lawyers. See Appendix M for
portrait data.

43. These six were John Bayard, James Searles, and Samuel Cadwalader Morris, merchants,
and Sharp Delany, Isaac Howell, and Timothy Matlack, mechanics. See Appendix M for
portrait data.

effect overthrew the old Assembly and ended the colonial era in Pennsylvania. In 1776 merchants were still a powerful force in public life, but in that year, for the first time in Philadelphia's history, they were sharing both committee seats and political power with new public men of the mechanic, or middle classes.

The accelerated recruitment of new leaders in Revolutionary Philadelphia was both necessary for administering the resistance and essential for mobilizing the community. This recruitment resulted from the interplay between resistance strategists seeking certain kinds of leaders and aggressive young men seeking public honor, fame, and power. Many of the new leaders, of all social backgrounds, did rise quickly to positions of real power in the resistance movement. What of our fourth query: did the resistance movement permanently alter Pennsylvania politics?

This vital question invites a resounding affirmative on two grounds. First, the resistance culminated in a total break with Great Britain. What is known of Pennsylvania's old order suggests that the separation of the province from the British Empire probably could not have been achieved peacefully without the new committee politics. To the extent that independence altered the politics of Philadelphia and Pennsylvania, therefore, this alteration must be credited largely to the recruitment of new local leaders.

The lasting effect of Philadelphia's revolutionary politics, however, went deeper than national independence and the many transformations which that new political, economic, and social condition implied. In the early 1770s, Philadelphia entered the age of mass politics; in 1774 this new political behavior spread throughout the province. The Revolution, beginning in the Philadelphia committees, tore Pennsylvania politics wide open. Hundreds of previously obscure young merchants, craftsmen, shopkeepers, Germans, Presbyterians, Anglicans, Baptists, and even Quakers seized this occasion to take part in the public life of their community. While both the concept and the practice of elitist leadership survived in Revolutionary Pennsylvania, they evolved under the impact of the enlarged public role for the ordinary freemen that the committees created.

From this perspective alone can one fully comprehend the origins of the Pennsylvania Constitution of 1776, the most radically democratic organic law in the world at the time of its creation. Only the new revolutionary politics can explain the depth and staying power of Pennsylvania's Constitutionalist-Republican battle, which dominated the life of the new commonwealth from 1776 to 1790. Between 1774 and the Jeffersonian era, Pennsylvania politics would display an ever-changing blend of older elitist and newer mass-oriented elements. This mix and ferment was new in eighteenth-century politics, and produced new political traditions and institutions. Pennsylvania's Constitutional and Republican parties of the late 1770s and 1780s were among the first modern political parties in history.[44] The legacies of Philadelphia's revolutionary leadership recruitment, then, were a successful independence movement and two of the earliest of modern political parties. Major historical processes rarely have one birthdate or one birthplace. Conceding this point, one may say that Philadelphia, between 1774 and 1776, witnessed a birth of modern American politics.

---

44. See Chambers, *Political Parties*, pp. 19–20. I shall have more to say about the contribution of resistance politics to America's political traditions, and particularly to the pattern of urban American politics, in chapter 10 below.

9

"The Revolution is Now Begun"

A change of such importance as that now proposed is not brought about without some contest, ... our opponents will be indefatigable in their endeavors to frustrate . . . every attempt . . . to emancipate the people of this Province from the bondage in which they have been long held.[1]

The Philadelphia Committee of Observation
May 21, 1776

In several respects, Pennsylvania's political condition in May 1776 closely resembled that of May 1774. In both periods the British ministry had just escalated its aggressive actions against America's liberties. In each season, zealous patriots in Philadelphia and in the newer counties, who were most numerous among Presbyterians, young Anglicans, Germans, and the mechanic classes, urged the adoption of stronger countermeasures against England. And in 1776, as in 1774, veteran Quaker party and proprietary faction leaders, under the direction of a widely respected, highly capable leader, blocked the adoption of those countermeasures by Pennsylvania's constituted government.

There were important differences between the two periods, however, which encouraged the radicals to use strategies in 1776 that they had not used in 1774.[2] First, the public was almost evenly divided over the adoption of the last great counter to British policy demanded by the radicals—independence. Popular resistance to this step in 1776 was far greater than popular resistance to a continental congress in 1774. Counterbalancing the hesitancy of the public, however, was the now powerful, ultraradical committee movement, which had been weak and

---

1. Force, ed., *American Archives*, 4th Ser., VI: 520–21.
2. The period May–July 1776 saw the onset of the Revolution proper in Philadelphia—the break with Great Britain, the rejection of the old Assembly leaders, and the drafting of a new constitution. Not surprisingly, these months also saw the redefinition of Philadelphia's "radicals." For this period, I label "radical" all Philadelphians who enthusiastically favored immediate independence, rejected the established Assembly leadership of Pennsylvania, and insisted that Pennsylvanians immediately set up a new government under the firm control of all those who, however rich or poor, were committed to resist British tyranny and, by unmistakable implication, all tyranny against the liberties of America's virtuous freemen. Beginning in July 1776, the ranks of the "moderates" grew, for they included not only all who favored armed resistance to Great Britain while opposing independence, but also all those who, while favoring independence, resolutely opposed any fundamental changes in the framework of Pennsylvania's government, or any social leveling of Pennsylvania's ruling elite.

undeveloped and only partially under radical control in 1774. Their carefully acquired power allowed Pennsylvania's radicals to act more decisively in 1776 than they could have imagined acting two years earlier. Yet as in 1774, they could only advance by the "improvement of occurrences" that the aggressive British ministry obligingly sent their way and by appealing to activist congressmen from other colonies to apply the pressure of exhortation and example to traditionally cautious Pennsylvanians.[3] Both techniques were necessary because, while the radicals were convinced that Pennsylvania's security demanded immediate independence, they could only achieve this goal by sweeping aside constitutional impediments. The public will, expressed on May 1, did present a problem: the radicals had no mandate for the major changes in the polity that they believed were necessary. On this point, however, radical strategists were not troubled for long; within two weeks, public sentiment on independence, under the impact of new measures taken by the British ministry and its military machine, swung their way.

THE DECISION TO OVERTHROW THE ASSEMBLY

As early as January 1776, rumors that Great Britain would send foreign mercenaries to subdue America began circulating in the colonies. Several prominent political figures, including Pennsylvanians noted for their moderation, immediately foresaw a widespread public demand for independence if the British ministry took this step. Most Americans felt that such an act could only mean that Britain was determined to subject them to brutal rapine and pillage by soldiers who would have no respect for the most minimal colonial, and human, rights. Even Dr. William Smith had declared in late March that because Britain had not taken this step, the radicals could not justify independence and a French alliance.[4] Fortune first favored the moderates: news of Britain's decision to send several thousand Hessian mercenaries to America did not reach Philadelphia until six days after the May 1 by-election.[5] Two days later, on May 8, the British warship *Roebuck* sailed up the Delaware and engaged in battle with Pennsylvania's new gunboats, throwing Philadelphians into a brief panic. The skirmish was not serious, and the *Roebuck* was driven off the following day, but war had come to Philadelphia for the first time in its history.[6]

The impending arrival of mercenaries and an attack by a British warship were just what the Independents needed. Confident that many wavering citizens would now support them, they mounted one last drive for independence. This campaign

---

3. The phrase "improvement of occurrences" is Charles Thomson's, in his letter to William Henry Drayton, N.-Y. Hist. Soc. *Colls.,* XI: 281.

4. See Hawke, *Midst of a Revolution,* pp. 92–93; the "Diary of Richard Smith," Jan. 9, 1776, *American Historical Review,* I (1896): 307, and Edward Shippen to Jasper Yates, Jan. 19, 1776, Shippen Papers, vol. VII, HSP, both quoted in Hawke, pp. 92–93; Joseph Shippen to Edward Shippen, May 11, 1776, Shippen Papers, 1727–1783, Library of Congress, quoted in both Selsam, *Pennsylvania Constitution,* p. 105, and Hawke, p. 93; and "Cato," Letter V, *Pa. Ledger,* Mar. 30, and *Pa. Gaz.,* Apr. 3, 1776.

5. *Pa. Packet,* May 6, 1776. The German treaties were signed between January 9 and February 5, presented to Parliament on February 16 and 19, and passed on March 4 and 5, 1776.

6. *Pa. Gaz.,* May 8 and 15; *Pa. Ledger,* May 11, 1776.

was not primarily one of reasoned propaganda; the radicals had already advanced all their arguments for a separation, and after May 4, no anti-Independent essay appeared to counter their earlier claims.[7] Their goal was to bring Pennsylvania to an official declaration of support for independence through direct political action. John Dickinson's coalition of conservative Quaker party members and more moderate proprietary faction delegates, three of whom had been elected on May 1, still held control of the Pennsylvania Assembly, although by a narrow margin.[8] If the radicals were to seek independence at once, rather than wait for the October Assembly elections, they must violate a longstanding Pennsylvania tradition—the acceptance of election results, like those of May 1, as final. They must, in short, destroy the authority of the current Assembly.

The radicals had several powerful motives for attempting this dangerous and unprecedented act. First, they were convinced that only immediate independence would secure vital aid from France and inspire their own citizens to face the imminent onslaught of British forces, which were just then staging for their massive assault against New York. The entire resistance was at stake. Second, many believed that the May 1 by-election had been improperly conducted, and all were confident that events since that day had made enough converts to give independence a majority. Finally, they harbored two keen resentments and one deep fear. They remembered with bitterness the Assembly's refusal to enact a strong militia law in April, which left the province nearly defenseless and exposed poor associators to ridicule by wealthy Quaker and proprietary leaders who scorned military service.[9] And the Assembly's early opposition to independence, in November and again in April, had embarrassed Pennsylvania's radical leaders before Congress and placed the union of the colonies in danger.[10]

The radicals' fear was a simple one. Those who resisted independence, they wrote on the eve of the May 1 by-election, were primarily wealthy proprietary leaders. Many radicals believed that the British ministry had already selected these men for pardons, and some suspected that Andrew Allen and other proprietary figures had secretly been named peace commissioners by the ministry, which could give them even greater power over their neighbors than they had enjoyed under the Penns. Great Britain had a Trojan horse set within Philadelphia's walls even before its army reached America.[11] An Assembly guilty of endangering its people, embarrassing them before their neighbors, and humiliating their most zealous defenders, an Assembly led by avaricious men who were eager to become

---

7. Between May 1 and July 4, seventeen newspaper items and one pamphlet appeared in Philadelphia. The first of these, a standard anti-Independent essay by "A Settled Citizen," appeared on May 4, in the *Ledger*; the remaining seventeen pieces were by Independents, most of whom were quite radical.

8. The proprietary leaders chosen in May were Andrew and James Allen and Alexander Wilcocks.

9. See the Committee of Privates to Congress, May 11, (Force, ed., *American Archives*, 4th Ser., VI: 421), June 3 (*Pa. Gaz.*, June 5, 1776), and June 17, 1776 (Force, VI: 935–37).

10. See the resolves and the "Protest" of Philadelphia's mass meeting of May 20, 1776, in *Pa. Gaz.*, May 22, 1776; the Committee of Observation's circular letter to the county committees, May 21, 1776, Force, ed., *American Archives*, 4th Ser., VI: 520–21; the anonymous "To the Publick. . . ." [May 21?], Force, VI: 521; and the Committee of Observation's May 24 memorial to Congress, in *Pa. Evening Post*, May 25, 1776.

11. See the piece on Andrew Allen, and "To the Tories," by "Old Trusty," both in *Pa. Evening Post*, Apr. 30; "To the Freeholders, . . ." *Pa. Jour.*, May 1; and "A Watchman," Letters I and II, *Pa. Packet*, June 10, 24, 1776.

traitors for gain, did not deserve the respect traditionally accorded to an American legislature.

Such hostile attitudes and beliefs, in greater or lesser degree, were widespread; they commanded a clear majority in every militia unit in the province and in ten out of the eleven county Committees of Observation.[12] Some scholars have argued that independence was achieved in Pennsylvania largely through the efforts of a small core of radical activists who, lacking broad popular support, necessarily worked in the manner of fanatical conspirators.[13] The political passion of Philadelphia's ultraradicals is undeniable, and a small activist core of leaders did indeed form the cutting edge of the radical cause in 1776; even the most zealous radicals, however, operated securely within the established pattern of resistance politics that had developed in Pennsylvania between 1774 and Independence.

The entire thrust of Pennsylvania's committee movement, which from 1774 to 1776 consistently enjoyed broad popular support, had been to offer whatever resistance was necessary to check Great Britain's expansive power and defend the province's autonomy, and to cooperate with the other colonies to insure the unity that would make that resistance effective. From June 1774, the Philadelphia committee always stood ready and willing to persuade, threaten, or ignore the Assembly whenever each strategy was possible and necessary for the cause. From the beginning of 1776, moreover, both county committees and militia units were committed to support the termination of Assembly authority if that should become necessary to defend the province. The Second One Hundred had proven its commitment to this policy in February by calling a provincial convention, and only the Assembly's willingness to offer Pennsylvania's radicals more power through a bill expanding the legislature persuaded the board to rescind that invitation.

It was natural, too, that small bodies of committeemen do the initial work of preparing basic radical strategy, which full committees could then modify, adopt, and implement. Timothy Matlack, who was an officer of Philadelphia's Second One Hundred, and Christopher Marshall, Sr., and Benjamin Rush, who were influential members of that board, were among the most important ultraradical strategists. All three men had fewer commitments to other public bodies than committee chairman and congressman Thomas McKean, for example, and so had the time to plan committee strategy. And the noncommitteeman James Cannon, as secretary of Philadelphia's Committee of Privates, was a logical partner for Marshall, Matlack, and Rush in planning Philadelphia's resistance policy.

The overwhelming majority of the Second One Hundred, however, and several of their official leaders, notably chairman Thomas McKean, secretary John Bayard Smith, and John Bayard, were intimately involved in the overthrow of the Pennsylvania Assembly—indeed, far more intimately than many of them later cared to admit. Given the growing divisive tensions over both policies and personalities within the radical leadership, what is remarkable is how united and aggressive the Second One Hundred was in its campaign to overturn the Assembly. The Philadelphia committee was never a mere "front organization for decisions predetermined in the caucuses of the 'standing committee' " of a handful of ultraradicals

---

12. The Philadelphia County committee was the exception. See *Pa. Gaz.*, May 29, 1776.

13. See Selsam, *Pennsylvania Constitution*; and especially Hawke, *Midst of a Revolution*, whose chapters 4 and 6 give this argument in its strongest form.

but remained a vital agent of revolutionary change right up to Independence.[14] The city committee was, however, a discreet agent of that change. A fundamental alteration in the structure of government was supposed to arise from the people, and the Second One Hundred, the Committee of Privates, and several unofficial radical strategists knew how to work quietly, almost out of sight, to encourage and direct popular sentiment toward the changes in Pennsylvania that most resistance leaders were now convinced were essential.

AN ANNIVERSARY CELEBRATION, MAY 20, 1776

After the May 1 by-election, most Pennsylvania radicals wished to lead the province out of the British Empire immediately, whether by further pressure on the Assembly or through the use of some alternative authority. Philadelphia's radical leadership evidently preferred the second strategy from the moment that the by-election ended, both because they had lost that contest in their city and because, at a time when New Englanders, Virginians, and most congressmen were preparing for the final break, the Pennsylvania Assembly would not even meet for another three weeks.[15] While the timing and substance of the radicals' first strategic decisions in May must remain a matter of some conjecture, they probably decided on May 3 to appeal to Congress for the authority to circumvent the Assembly, and at the same time to declare the May 1 by-election fraudulent, either to damage the legislature's public reputation or to pressure the lawmakers to alter Assembly policy as soon as the House met. On that day, Christopher Marshall, Sr. discussed the election results, which were still coming in from the backcountry, with James Cannon and Samuel Adams' friend, the peripatetic radical Dr. Thomas Young. The three then conferred with Thomas McKean and with Adams himself.[16] Within the next few days, Thomas Paine wrote "The Forester's" fourth letter,[17] which charged that election officials had improperly disqualified many German Independents and closed the polls early on May 1, and the press reported Britain's decision to hire German mercenaries. That news, and the battle with the *Roebuck* on May 8–9, must have figured prominently in a conversation between Marshall and Cannon on May 9, and may have prompted the visits the two men paid to McKean and Samuel Adams on the following day.[18]

Meanwhile, John Adams was busy in Congress devising a formula for dissolving the imperial connection in every colony. The resolution that he framed to this end was directly prompted by Pennsylvania's conservatism, although political conditions in other colonies also motivated his action. Discussed by Congress on May 7–9, and formally introduced and passed on May 10, Adams' resolution recommended to the several provincial assemblies and conventions that "where no government sufficient to the exigencies of their affairs" was established, they "adopt such government as shall, in the opinion of the representatives of the peo-

---

14. Hawke, *Midst of a Revolution*, p. 132.
15. On congressional preparations, see Burnett, *Continental Congress,* chap. 8.
16. Marshall, "Diary" (May 3), Marshall Papers, HSP, quoted in Hawke, *Midst of a Revolution*, p. 131.
17. *Pa. Jour.*, May 8, 1776.
18. Duane, ed., *Passages from Marshall,* p. 79 (May 9); "Diary" (May 10), Marshall Papers, HSP, quoted in Hawke, *Midst of a Revolution*, p. 131.

ple, best conduce to the happiness and safety of their constituents in particular, and America in general."[19] Although Pennsylvania was the resolve's prime target, John Dickinson and his congressional colleagues blithely declared that they had no objection to it, because their Assembly, which could not be prorogued or dissolved by their governor, was "sufficient to the exigencies of their affairs."[20] This forced Adams to write a substantial preamble to his resolution, which Congress narrowly passed on May 15. This weighty introduction specified just how certain provincial governments were unsatisfactory: "And whereas, it appears absolutely irreconcilable to reason and good conscience, for the people of these colonies now to take the oaths and affirmations necessary for the support of any government under the crown of Great Britain, . . . it is necessary that the exercise of every kind of authority under the said crown should be totally suppressed, and all the powers of government [be] exerted, under the authority of the people . . ."[21]

John Adams' exhortation solved the problem of Pennsylvania's radicals neatly. For weeks their propagandists had argued that a government under oath to support George III could not vigorously oppose his tyranny. "The Forester" stressed this inconsistency in his May 8 letter, and Marshall and Cannon probably discussed it in their visits to the Adamses' lodgings on May 3 and 10. The resolve, and its preamble, gave them just the pretext they needed for an appeal to the people to override their legislature's decision to stay in the empire.

Events now moved swiftly. On the evening of May 13, while John Adams was still laboring over his preamble, several zealots, including Paul Fooks, Benjamin Harbeson, Christopher Marshall, Sr., Timothy Matlack, Thomas Paine, and Benjamin Rush, met at James Cannon's home to discuss strategy. They quickly decided to call in more persons to aid them, and on the following evening this larger gathering drew up a "protest" for approval the next day at a still larger meeting.[22] On Wednesday, May 15, at 7 P.M., the radical caucus gathered in the committee room at Philosophical Society Hall, with Thomas McKean, a chairman of the city committee, presiding. This was not an official meeting of the Second One Hundred, because several activists from outside the committee attended. The committee's leaders welcomed these visitors to their informal caucus because they wanted the call to end the current Assembly's authority to appear as if it had arisen from outside the Second One Hundred, spontaneously from the people. The meeting's participants were well prepared, however, for they immediately began debating "the resolve of Congress of the fifteenth instant," that is, of a few hours earlier![23] Adams' preamble was evidently well known to Philadelphia's radicals before it reached the floor of Congress.

Unable to complete their work on the fifteenth, the radicals gathered the following afternoon, a few hours after the Second One Hundred had met in the same room to dispose of routine business. In this most important May 16 session, Philadelphia's radical leaders resolved to call a provincial convention and to protest against the current Assembly's doing any business until that convention

19. *Journals,* IV: 342.
20. Hawke, *Midst of a Revolution,* pp. 119–20.
21. *Journals,* IV: 358. See also Hawke, *Midst of a Revolution,* pp. 120–26.
22. Duane, ed., *Passages from Marshall,* p. 79 (May 13, 14). Little is known about Harbeson, who was a member of the Second One Hundred, or about Fooks, who was not a member.
23. Duane, ed., *Passages from Marshall,* p. 80 (May 15).

determined the sense of the province, and then decided to set plans for the convention in motion by Monday, May 20. Their device would be the traditional mass meeting, and the May 16 caucus must have worked out its agenda, because upon their adjournment the caucus members began distributing handbills throughout the town, which urged the citizens to petition the Second One Hundred to hold an open assembly of citizens on May 20, at which time, the handbills explained, all Philadelphians could discuss both the resolve and the preamble of Congress concerning satisfactory provincial governments. Friday, May 17, was a congressional fast day; the radicals used it to good advantage to circulate their handbills and get up their petition to the city committee to call the mass meeting. On Saturday, the Second One Hundred officially received a request to call such a gathering for 9 A.M., Monday, May 20, and after debating the matter, agreed, with only five dissenting votes.[24] Until this decision, the Second One Hundred, whose members were so intimately involved in the preparations for the May 20 gathering, had kept scrupulously clear of radical politicking as a body, thus projecting the image of a nonpartisan spokesman of the popular will.[25]

Even more thorough preparations than the radicals' handbills and petitions and the city committee's official summons lay behind the May 20 meeting, however, and these preparations directly shaped the deliberations at that meeting. David Hawke has perceptively highlighted the common argument of three powerful exhortations addressed to Philadelphians before that gathering. On May 8, Thomas Paine, as "The Forester," argued that the legislators were not competent to reform Pennsylvania's government and lead their constituents out of bondage to the British Crown, "because *they* cannot sit as *Judges, in a case,* where their *own existence* under their *present form and authority is to be judged of.*" Only a provincial convention could rescue Pennsylvanians from their difficulties.[26] On May 15, Adams' preamble urged "that the exercise of every kind of authority under the . . . crown . . . be totally suppressed, and all the powers of government [be] exerted, under the authority of the people. . . ."[27] And on May 19, the radical broadside "The Alarm," appearing in English and German, reasoned that the Assembly could not suppress all royal authority, as Congress had recommended, because that could only "be done *to them,* but cannot be done *by them.*" Conventions alone were proper bodies to establish government "*on the authority of the people.*"[28]

---

24. Duane, ed., *Passages from Marshall,* pp. 81–82 (May 18).

25. Duane, ed., *Passages from Marshall,* pp. 80–81 (May 16). Hawke contends (*Midst of a Revolution,* p. 133) that the radical caucus clashed with the full Second One Hundred on May 16 over whether to curtail all Assembly power at once or only the legislature's power to establish a new government. This claim is apparently based upon a misreading, and perhaps an overreading, of Christopher Marshall's diary. In summarizing the proceedings on both May 15 and May 16, Marshall does not say that either gathering was an official committee meeting. Hawke apparently thinks that the May 15 session was a committee meeting, but that the May 16 session, in connection with which Marshall first mentions the radicals' plan to end all further Assembly activity, was not. In fact neither was. Moreover, it is not known when the radicals' extreme anti-Assembly plans were modified, or by whom. Nor can one be certain that these plans were so extreme as Marshall tells us they were in his brief phrase (May 16, pp. 80–81). It is quite possible that the radicals never intended to curtail normal legislative activity. If they did have such an intention, it is curious that so little record of it has survived.

26. *Pa. Jour.,* May 8, 1776.

27. *Journals,* IV: 358.

28. Hawke, *Midst of a Revolution,* pp. 134–35; "The Alarm," item 18 (quoted in Hawke), and "Der Alarm," item 59, Broadside Collection (1776), HSP. Hawke speculates quite plausibly (p. 135) that Thomas Paine wrote "The Alarm."

On a rainy Monday morning, two years to the day after that stifling evening when Dickinson, Mifflin, Reed, and Thomson had shrewdly outmaneuvered their conservative opponents at the City Tavern, Major John Bayard, as temporary chairman of the Second One Hundred, called at least four thousand well-drenched Philadelphians to order and blandly informed them "that the meeting was called at the request of a considerable number of respectable citizens."[29] In constructing this elaborate fiction, the committee's leaders achieved two vital objectives that were fully in line with their institutional traditions. They avoided intracommittee conflict by devising a plan of action without long plenary sessions, where probably more than five—but hardly more than a third—of the members might have objected to the proposals that the caucus had approved. More important, they cast the city committee in the role of an impartial agent of the people, above the partisan contention of moderate and radical, eager only to do its community a service. Surviving accounts of the May 20 meeting testify that the Second One Hundred played this role to the final act.

Following Bayard's opening remarks, the Committee of Observation adopted a visible but not overbearing presence. Colonel Daniel Roberdeau, a noncommittee-man popular with the militia, was named moderator of the session. He initiated the day's proceedings by reading first the May 15 preamble and May 10 resolve of Congress, and then the Assembly's November 9 instructions forbidding Pennsylvania's congressmen to vote for independence. Thomas McKean, speaking for the Second One Hundred, then told the crowd that in March the board had petitioned the House to alter its instructions, but that the lawmakers had refused. The crowd then approved several resolves which declared that the Assembly's instructions had "a dangerous tendency to withdraw this province from that *happy union* with the other colonies," that the Assembly was not "competent to the exigencies of [Pennsylvania's] affairs" and had no authority to establish a new government, and that as a result a convention "chosen *by the people*" must form a new government. The last resolve instructed the Second One Hundred to issue a circular letter to the county committees that would call for a conference of committee representatives to arrange for the election of a constitutional convention.[30] Accompanying the passage of the resolves were three major speeches. Colonel Thomas McKean spoke first and may have proposed all of the resolves. Colonel John (?) Cadwalader, a moderate who sat on both the Second One Hundred and the Committee of Safety, tried to have some resolves altered in tone but was insulted by the crowd. Colonel Timothy Matlack spoke last, and probably made a spirited reply to Cadwalader.[31] Although all three men were members of the Second One Hundred, it was their military status that official reports of the proceedings emphasized.

29. On this meeting, see *Pa. Gaz.*, May 22, 1776 (the official account, and Bayard quotation); Duane, ed., *Passages from Marshall*, p. 82 (May 20); William Bradford, Jr., "A Memorandum Book and Register, for the months of May & June 1776," p. 23 (May 20), Col. William Bradford Papers, HSP; John Adams to James Warren, May 20, "Warren-Adams Letters," *Massachusetts Historical Society Collections*, LXXII: 250; "Extracts from the Diary of Dr. James Clitherall," *PMHB*, XXII (1898): 470; and Caesar Rodney to Thomas Rodney, May 22 and 29, 1776, cited in Hawke, *Midst of a Revolution*, pp. 135–38.

30. *Pa. Gaz.*, May 22, 1776.

31. John Adams to James Warren, May 20, cited in note 29 above; and "Diary of Dr. James Clitherall," *PMHB*, XXII: 470. The "Col. Cadwalader" whom Adams mentions could have been either John or his brother Lambert, both militia colonels and both moderates; but John, who was more prominent, is probably meant.

The day's final business was the reading and approval of the "Protest of . . . the inhabitants . . . To the . . . Representatives of the province of Pennsylvania." This memorial, in preparation since May 14, candidly explained why the assembled citizens, and Philadelphia's radicals, wished the House to refrain from having any part in establishing a new government. But the document also declared, "In thus protesting against the authority of this House for framing a new government we mean not to object against its exercising the proper powers it has hitherto been accustomed to use, for the safety and convenience of the province, until . . . a new constitution . . . founded on *the authority of the people,* shall be finally settled by a Provincial Convention to be elected for that purpose. . . ."[32] This may have represented a major concession to moderate Independents by some ultraradicals, but it was a necessary provision for an orderly transition to a new government.[33] The work of Philadelphia's citizens was now done; they thanked the members of the city's Committee of Observation "for their zeal, fidelity and steady attention to the duties of their important station," and all departed.[34] The meeting had lasted three hours, and while both Christopher Marshall, Sr. and John Adams called it orderly, it was zealous enough to intimidate many moderates.[35]

After attending the May 20 gathering, the young militia captain William Bradford, Jr. confided to his diary that "this [meeting] gives the Coup de Grace to the King's authority in this province."[36] Indeed, May 20, 1776, was a watershed in Pennsylvania politics. Before that date, Independents and constitutional reformers had fought an uphill battle and had to act with some restraint, but after the twentieth, they were no longer afraid of alienating moderates and admitting just where they stood. The first product of this new spirit was the circular letter drafted by Philadelphia's Committee of Observation on May 21.

This well-written address wasted little time explaining either the duty given to the committee by the May 20 meeting or the mechanics of electing a constitutional convention, as such a letter would have done in 1774 or 1775.[37] The Second One Hundred evidently felt that the copies of the May 20 resolves and "Protest" that it enclosed explained these questions adequately. The city committee simply asked each county committee to send representatives to Philadelphia on June 18, to prepare for the election of a constitutional convention. Nor did the committeemen bother to review the Assembly's sins, as they had in their March 5 letter. Instead, they launched into a boldly partisan explanation of Pennsylvania's problems, taking the line developed by radical propagandists in late April: the old proprietary elite's lust for power was the root of the province's difficulties.

This interpretation of Pennsylvania's turmoil over independence was neither well balanced nor comprehensive, but it does help to explain the radicals' new candid, unrestrained spirit. In 1774, when Pennsylvania's radicals had more clearly perceived their enemy—the tenacious Quaker party elite in the Assembly—they had kept fairly quiet about it, at least in public. By 1776 many things had changed.

---

32. *Pa. Gaz.,* May 22, 1776.

33. See note 25 above for a summary of and comment on Hawke's argument in *Midst of a Revolution,* p. 133.

34. *Pa. Gaz.,* May 22, 1776.

35. Duane, ed., *Passages from Marshall,* p. 82 (May 20); Adams to James Warren, May 20, cited in note 29 above; and "Diary of Dr. James Clitherall," *PMHB,* XXII: 470.

36. "Memorandum" (May 20), p. 23, Col. William Bradford Papers, HSP.

37. The text of the letter is in Force, ed., *American Archives,* 4th Ser., VI: 520–21.

In the winter of 1775–76, as the power of Quaker party veterans and strict Friends in the Assembly gradually declined, several members of the proprietary elite who had supported the resistance against Great Britain crossed over to the opposition because the resistance movement was rapidly becoming an independence movement. The radicals, who were much stronger in 1776 than in 1774, had nothing but contempt for their old proprietary allies, who had abandoned them when the stakes in opposing British authority increased.

On May 21, Philadelphia's radicals cast aside all restraint and drew the battle lines clearly, both to mobilize the populace and to justify the great reform they were now proposing—a new government and a new constitution for Pennsylvania. The city committee's own words best express its rage at its opponents, and its determination to defeat all those whom it saw as plotting the ruination of the province.

> A change of such importance as that now proposed is not brought about without some contest, arising from the opposition of interests, and the force of prejudice in favor of old and established forms. The Associators [militiamen] will have to contend, in the present instance, against the Proprietaries and all their dependents, influenced by self-interest and holding lucrative offices under them, with all whom they can influence, joined by all the avowed as well as secret enemies of the cause of *American* freedom. . . . [The] party we have already mentioned as our opponents will be indefatigable in their endeavours to frustrate, by falsehood and every other means in their power, every attempt which shall be made to emancipate the people of this Province from the bondage in which they have been long held.[38]

The Second One Hundred would now take on all comers in its drive to reform Pennsylvania's political life.[39]

MODERATE VERSUS RADICAL: AN APPEAL TO THE PEOPLE

Pennsylvania's moderates were fully aware of what the radicals were planning in the spring of 1776; they knew, too, who the leading radicals were and what following they enjoyed. In March and April, Dr. William Smith and James Allen accurately assessed the campaign for independence, discovered its authors, and valiantly attempted to arrest it; but by mid-May, despite their dramatic by-election victory in Philadelphia, moderate leaders no longer believed that they could stem the tide for independence.[40] They ceased publishing newspaper propaganda after May 4, and when William Bradford, Sr. read out Congress's May 10 resolve in Philadelphia's principal gathering place, the London Coffee House, on May 14, the anti-Independent forces felt hopelessly outflanked. James Allen was convinced

---

38. Force, ed., *American Archives,* 4th Ser., VI: 520–21.

39. I do not mean to imply here that there were no moderates who opposed constitutional reform left on the city committee after May 21, but only that they no longer had any influence. It is likely that after mid-May, moderates ceased to attend city committee meetings and turned to more conservative bodies: the Committee of Safety and, especially, the Assembly, to express their political opinions.

40. Poetic introduction to "Cato's" Letter IV, *Pa. Gaz.,* Mar. 27, 1776, quoted in chapter 7 above; "Diary of James Allen, Esq., 1770–1778," *PMHB,* IX (1885): 186.

that if the Assembly refused to alter Pennsylvania's constitution, a convention would supersede the Assembly; and "a convention chosen by the people [would] consist of the most fiery Independents."[41]

Yet Allen and other moderates were still determined to resist the radical tide. Indignant at the "Protest" of May 20, several Philadelphia anti-Independents gathered on the twenty-first and framed a "Remonstrance" to the Assembly in which they refuted the radicals' claims. This memorial pointed out that the resolve of Congress was directed to each assembly, and not to any convention, except where a convention was sitting in place of an assembly that royal officials had dissolved. According to the congressional directive, the *legislators* in each colony were to decide if their present government was "sufficient to the exigencies of their affairs." And why, the "Remonstrance" asked, should Pennsylvania yield up her Assembly, which had strongly supported the American cause and could not be dissolved by Governor Penn, while Connecticut and Rhode Island kept their legislatures intact? The "Remonstrance" closed with the hope that if the lawmakers found it necessary to alter Pennsylvania's constitution, they would do so cautiously, for the purpose of facilitating a reconciliation with Great Britain, which must ever be their goal.[42] Sensing that the fear of constitutional change was more widespread among Pennsylvanians by mid-May than any anxiety over independence, moderate leaders had clearly shifted the focus of their argument. Yet the "Remonstrance" conceded nothing to those who would leave the empire; its authors were unalterably opposed to independence, and most would remain so until July 2, 1776.

In the last two weeks in May, Pennsylvania's Independents and their opponents vigorously contested for support in all parts of the province. The Second One Hundred sent its circular letter, with the "Protest," to every county on May 21; the anti-Independents began distributing copies of their "Remonstrance" on the twenty-second and sought as many signatures for it as possible.[43] By June 1, the moderates claimed 6,000 signatures for the "Remonstrance." Most of the signers must have lived in rural Bucks, Chester, and Philadelphia counties, however, because the radicals claimed that only 461 were city residents, and the moderates were unable even to penetrate most of the eight newer counties.[44] Phineas Bond circulated copies of the "Remonstrance" in Lancaster for Dr. William Smith, and at his request two youths carried the petition to York County on May 25. But the pair arrived in York town just in time to witness the warm farewell accorded to another moderate emissary who had preceded them, and they immediately elected

---

41. "Diary of James Allen," *PMHB*, IX: 187.

42. See the text in *Pa. Gaz.*, May 22, 1776.

43. Duane, ed., *Passages from Marshall*, p. 83 (May 24). The radicals did not really have even one full day's head start on their opponents, for on May 18, the Philadelphia County Committee of Observation, having read Congress's preamble and having learned of the city radicals' plans for their mass meeting in the State House Yard, petitioned the Assembly to resist all attempts to alter Pennsylvania's constitution or to leave the empire (*Pa. Gaz.*, May 29, 1776). Although this committee was the only one under moderate control, the moderates could also count on heavy support among both local officials and the inhabitants of the province's three eastern counties; thus on May 31, the Assembly heard a memorial from the commissioners and grand jurors of Chester County condemning the radicals' "Protest" (*Votes and Proceedings*, VIII: 7532).

44. *Pa. Ledger*, June 8, 1776; and "A Freeman," *Pa. Evening Post*, June 11, 1776. "A Freeman" was skeptical of the moderates' claim to 6,000 signatures for their "Remonstrance."

"to decamp with precipitation."[45] At Reading in Berks County, the "Remonstrance" was burned "in the most ignominious manner, . . . as a seditious and treasonable libel tending to destroy the union of the colonies. . . ."[46] It is unlikely that the memorial ever reached Cumberland, Bedford, Westmoreland, or Northumberland counties.

The failure of Pennsylvania's moderates to build a counterrevolutionary movement in late May owed in part to the backcountry's mounting disillusionment with Great Britain and to the erosion of its confidence in negotiations with British peace commissioners, whom the moderates expected to arrive from London shortly. Nevertheless, a brief but effective campaign by the Second One Hundred and its allies to insure both an enthusiastic response to the "Protest" and a humiliating rejection of the "Remonstrance" was an essential step in terminating British authority in the province. Dr. Thomas Young, with Jacob Barge and other members of the city committee, set off for Lancaster and York, Thomas McKean journeyed to Reading, Robert Strettel Jones and Joseph Watkins, committeemen with a Quaker background, visited heavily Quaker Bucks County, and James Cannon led a delegation to Norristown on May 25, to outflank William Hamilton's conservative Philadelphia County committee.[47] Everywhere success crowned their efforts; militia battalions rushed to approve the principles of the "Protest," and county committees prepared for the selection of delegates to the June 18 provincial conference that the Second One Hundred had recommended. By May 30, militia battalions in Lancaster and Northampton, and county committees in Northampton, York, and Chester had endorsed the resolves of May 20.[48]

The radicals were not content with frustrating the "Remonstrance," however, and on May 24, they framed a memorial to Congress, occasioned by both the "Remonstrance" and the Assembly's decision of the twenty-second to seek an interpretation of John Adams' May 15 preamble and resolve from Congress that would be favorable to continued Assembly rule. Determined to prevent any blunting of the preamble's intended effect, the Second One Hundred informed Congress that it had "with great affliction" watched the Assembly "WITHDRAW from its union with the Congress (in consequence of their instructions to their delegates). . . . [and that] in consequence of the DEFECTION of [Pennsylvania's congressional delegates] from a union with the other colonies, they [the Second One Hundred] apprehended an appeal was made to the people." The committee then asserted that its recent political activities were the immediate result of this appeal, and that it had called the May 20 meeting and written the circular letter to the county committees entirely at the request of the people and in the interest of the public safety. This safety, the memorial continued, was now in jeopardy because most Pennsylvania legislators no longer enjoyed the people's confidence. As for the

45. York Committee of Observation to Philadelphia (city) Committee of Observation, May 28, 1776, in *Pa. Evening Post,* June 4, 1776, and Force, ed., *American Archives,* 4th Ser., VI: 607–8.

46. *Pa. Evening Post,* May 30, 1776.

47. See the vivid narrative in Hawke, *Midst of a Revolution,* pp. 146–47, and citations. Accompanying Cannon to Norristown were Timothy Matlack and Benjamin Harbeson, committeemen, a Lt. Chambers, and one William Miles (Duane, ed., *Passages from Marshall,* p. 83, May 25).

48. *Pa. Gaz.,* June 5 (Lancaster and Northampton references), June 12 (York committee); and *Pa. Packet,* June 17 (Chester committee).

"Remonstrance" of May 21, it was sponsored "by men who hold offices under the crown, or by people connected with them, or by those who have uniformly opposed every measure adopted by the Congress (petitions to the King only excepted) or by those who have published testimonies manifestly injurious to . . . the union of the colonies."[49]

The Second One Hundred concluded its memorial with the assurance that the only changes it sought in Pennsylvania's constitution were a further readjustment in legislative representation and an end to the authority of the governor and the Crown. By this date the moderates, both to prevent these alterations and more extensive changes that they believed the radicals were intending, and to block independence, turned to their last stronghold, the Assembly. They were far from certain that the House could stem the radical tide, but it was their one remaining hope.

THE COLLAPSE OF THE ASSEMBLY

When Pennsylvania's legislature began its spring session on May 22, its members no longer securely occupied the center of their province's political stage. Ultraradicals totally opposed to the exercise of authority by the Assembly dominated Pennsylvania's Independents. These zealots no longer pressed the lawmakers to lead the province but sought only to hamper their work and insure the curtailment of their power. Many opponents of independence, moreover, no longer believed in the Assembly's ability to resist revolution. And for the first time, a provincial conference explicitly designed to supersede the House on the most vital questions facing the province appeared to be a certainty.

In the face of seemingly hopeless odds, however, most Pennsylvania legislators, both Quaker and proprietary anti-Independents led by John Dickinson and the newly elected Allen brothers, and Independents led by Joseph Reed and George Ross, were committed to preserving government by the old Assembly. At the opening of the session they removed one source of both popular and congressional resentment against them by dispensing with oaths of allegiance to the Crown for the new members. Thereupon James Webb, a conservative lawmaker from Lancaster County, walked out of the House. George Ross, the most influential member from Lancaster, declared that he would have left if the oaths *had* been taken.[50] This measure put the Assembly in a position to claim immunity from the May 15 congressional preamble. The necessity of this step was immediately obvious, because the first business of the legislators was to listen to the radicals' May 20 "Protest," a polite death sentence for their body. Their immediate response was to appoint five members "to take into Consideration the Resolve of Congress, and the Preamble thereto; and to draw up a Memorial from this House, setting forth the different Meanings that have been assigned to the said Resolve, and requesting an Explanation in such Terms as will not admit of any Doubt, whether the Assem-

---

49. The text of the Second One Hundred's memorial is in *Pa. Evening Post,* May 25; and *Pa. Gaz.,* May 29, 1776. See also Duane, ed., *Passages from Marshall,* p. 83 (May 24).

50. "Diary of James Allen" (June 16), *PMHB,* IX: 188. Also see James Rankin's letter "To the worthy inhabitants of York County," *Pa. Gaz.,* June 12, 1776.

blies, are or are not the Bodies, to whom the Consideration of continuing the old, or adopting new Governments, is referred."[51] With this decision, anti-Independent and moderate Independent assemblymen began the last defense of Pennsylvania's established government.

But the legislature's resolve to seek a clarification of Congress's May 15 prologue did not signal a durable resistance to the radicals' revolution in government; the Assembly's opposition to the radical assault was effective for just eight days before a sudden, permanent collapse. This failure should not have surprised moderate leaders. They knew that the Assembly majority in favor of remaining in the British Empire was razor-thin, and they sensed that they could not long defend even this margin in the face of growing sentiment for independence. Yet the moderates who controlled the House, led by John Dickinson, continued to link the increasingly unpopular dependency upon Great Britain with the more widely favored retention of Pennsylvania's Constitution of 1701, thereby bringing both to destruction. Their obstinate adherence to this policy quickly made unity within the chamber impossible, even though nearly all members supported the old constitution. For the first time in a decade, the assemblymen divided into two bitterly hostile camps. Both anti-Independents and Independents, whether majority or minority, were strong enough to block legislation by quorum-breaking absences or interminable debates.[52]

From the opening days of the spring session, confusion reigned in the chamber. The decision to dispense with oaths and James Webb's outraged departure went unrecorded in the minutes, and Charles Moore, longtime clerk of the House, submitted his resignation.[53] Yet the moderates pushed on toward their hopeless double goal despite assaults from both the left and the right. The committee appointed on May 22 to draft a memorial to Congress concerning its May 15 preamble had a three-to-two anti-Independent majority, and that same day the House heard the Philadelphia County Committee of Observation's plea that it retain the 1701 constitution.[54] But by May 24, the anti-Independent leadership was already showing signs of strain and growing political insensitivity. A Committee of Safety request for the expansion of its body went unanswered, while the legislators passed a resolve, sure to antagonize the military associators, that provincial troops must pay a monthly charge for arms provided to them by the province. And the draft of the memorial to Congress concerning the May 15 preamble was "referred to further Consideration."[55]

Finally, when the Independents insisted that the dropping of oaths of allegiance by assemblymen made it unnecessary for Germans, great numbers of whom favored independence, to take naturalization oaths to vote, a sharp debate ensued, with the Allen brothers apparently heading the opposition to this innovation. The House

51. *Votes and Proceedings,* VIII: 7516. Of the five, Andrew Allen, Alexander Wilcocks, and Isaac Pearson were then almost certainly anti-Independents; George Clymer and George Ross were Independents.

52. Charles Thomson to John Dickinson, Aug. 16, 1776, Logan Collection, VIII: 78, HSP; "To the People," *Pa. Gaz.,* June 26, 1776; Hawke, *Midst of a Revolution,* pp. 157, 159, 163.

53. *Votes and Proceedings,* VIII: 7514. Moore had been clerk since 1757.

54. *Votes and Proceedings,* VIII: 7517–19. This was the petition drafted on May 18, mentioned in note 43.

55. *Votes and Proceedings,* VIII: 7519–20. The memorial to Congress was evidently approved and sent (see *Votes and Proceedings,* VIII: 7521 on the Second One Hundred's apparent reply to the House memorial, read in Congress on May 25, and Duane, ed., *Passages from Marshall,* p. 83, May 24), but no record of this decision appears in the Assembly's minutes.

finally agreed that if the legislators did not need to take oaths, then neither did any voters, yet the subcommittee named to draft legislation abolishing naturalization oaths contained not only the Independents Reed, Clymer, and Ross, and the anti-Independents Dickinson and Wilcocks, but both Andrew and James Allen.[56] This matter of oaths reached its fitting conclusion on June 5, when the subcommittee's draft was also "referred to further Consideration."[57]

By May 27, these exhausting divisions began to take their toll as the legislators first failed to make a quorum. The next few days were busy, but hardly productive, as the House listened to a Cumberland County petition for independence and made a few routine appointments. The one important matter taken up was a request from the Committee of Safety that the lawmakers conduct an inquiry into the management of the May 8–9 battle between the *Roebuck* and the city's row galleys to determine the board's responsibility for the *Roebuck's* escape. This matter had become a major bone of contention between moderates, who backed the Committee of Safety, and radicals, who supported the galley commanders' claim that the Committee of Safety had not given them adequate ammunition.[58] The Assembly's response to the Committee's request, while predictably conservative, was essentially one of hopeless desperation: it named an investigating subcommittee of twenty-seven members, which was later expanded to thirty-two, at which point it included all but five eligible legislators.[59] The week closed with the reading of the anti-Independent "Remonstrance" of May 21, the resignation of the venerable provincial treasurer Owen Jones, a Quaker, and his replacement by Michael Hillegas, and the appointment of a few routine subcommittees and minor officials.[60]

The legislature's second week of business ended in discouragement and frustration. On Saturday, June 1, when the radicals began a series of crippling absences that prevented a quorum, the lawmakers had yet to do anything of importance. They had not even begun to seek a solution to their militia problems, nor had the military associators asked them to do so; instead the assemblymen only compounded the insensitivity of their military policy, while the militia looked to other men for relief. The legislators' attempt to secure support from Congress for their own legitimacy failed, probably due in part to the Second One Hundred's May 25 countermemorial to Congress and the skillful politicking there of congressmen John and Samuel Adams and Thomas McKean.[61] The whole Congress was hardly

---

56. The principal source here is not the unrevealing *Votes and Proceedings*, VIII: 7520–21, but "To the People," *Pa. Gaz.*, June 26, 1776, wherein the author, evidently a radical Independent, says that opposition to dropping oaths for the Germans was advanced by "one of the proprietary gentlemen, who had taken *his* seat *without* oaths. . . .[He] was seconded by another of the same cast. . . . It is peculiarly remarkable that the persons who objected against admitting the Germans were put on the Committee for taking off their disqualifications. . . ." I have assumed that the two who spoke were Andrew and James Allen, but possibly one of the brothers and Alexander Wilcocks are the persons referred to here (only three "proprietary" figures were elected on May 1).

57. *Votes and Proceedings*, VIII: 7536.

58. *Votes and Proceedings*, VIII: 7521–24. The row galley controversy will be discussed below.

59. *Votes and Proceedings*, VIII: 7523–24, 7538. Of the twenty-six assemblymen not named to the subcommittee, twenty-one were either Committee of Safety members, held other high Assembly offices, or are known to have been absent from this session. The House probably appointed so large a committee simply to avoid charges of political bias and to make the entire Assembly responsible for whatever report the committee made.

60. *Votes and Proceedings*, VIII: 7524–32.

61. Marshall, "Diary" (May 23), Marshall Papers, HSP, cited in Hawke, *Midst of a Revolution*, p. 156.

more sympathetic to the Assembly's plight; too many congressmen, especially from New England, held Pennsylvania responsible for all middle-colony resistance to independence.[62] The Assembly was now stymied: rejected by Congress, spurned by its constituents, and rendered internally helpless by feuding between moderate and radical Independents, led by Joseph Reed, George Clymer, and George Ross, and moderate and conservative anti-Independents under the direction of the Allen brothers. Further confounding this chaos, one radical charged, was John Dickinson, who allied "sometimes . . . with one side, sometimes with the other, sometimes with neither; seeming upon the whole to have no other fixed object in view than HIMSELF."[63]

By June 1, moreover, the Assembly faced not only internal obstruction, but the growing opposition of its constituents. Several conservative lawmakers had sought support outside the Assembly, but to little effect. The Allen brothers probably helped Dr. William Smith and others frame and circulate the "Remonstrance" of May 21, and York County's newly elected James Rankin sent several copies of that document to prominent officials in his constituency. But Rankin's plans badly miscarried; the powerful York Committee of Observation intercepted the petitions, with his covering letter, and publicly denounced his behavior, whereupon his influential correspondents repudiated him. Rankin published a spirited reply in mid-June, in which he defended dependency upon Great Britain and Pennsylvania's established constitution, but his reputation among his constituents was destroyed.[64]

Other events had an even more catastrophic effect upon the position of anti-Independent assemblymen. By May 27, Philadelphia knew that Virginia's provincial convention had instructed its congressmen to introduce a motion that the colonies leave the British Empire.[65] The news flowing in from the countryside was bleak: only in Chester, Philadelphia, and Bucks counties was there significant opposition to independence. By June 1, anti-Independent legislators knew that independence must come to Pennsylvania within a few weeks, once the provincial conference met. To drive this point home, the Second One Hundred, on June 3, requested Philadelphia County's judges to postpone their quarter session to avoid using oaths of allegiance to the British Crown.[66] By this date the Philadelphia press had printed the full texts of the treaties between Great Britain and the German states of Hesse-Cassel and Brunswick, in which George III purchased the services of 20,000 mercenaries, and Congress had scheduled its first debate on independence for June 7.[67] At this critical juncture, Independent assemblymen staged three quorum-breaking boycotts, on June 1, 3, and 4.[68] By June 5, several anti-Independent assemblymen were ready to make some concessions.

62. See Force, ed., *American Archives*, 4th Ser., VI: 517, 1022, 1067 (letters of May 20, May 19–21, June 25, 1776, from congressmen Elbridge Gerry and Josiah Bartlett to friends in New England).

63. "To the People," *Pa. Gaz.*, June 26, 1776.

64. York Committee of Observation to the Philadelphia (city) Committee, May 28, 1776, Force, ed., *American Archives*, 4th Ser., VI: 607–8; York committee resolves, May 30, *Pa. Gaz.*, June 12, 1776; "A Freeman," *Pa. Evening Post,* June 11, 1776; "A Protestor," *Pa. Jour.,* June 12, 1776; "To the worthy inhabitants of York County," by James Rankin, *Pa. Gaz.*, June 12, 1776.

65. Burnett, *Continental Congress*, p. 169. North Carolina also endorsed independence at this time.

66. *Pa. Gaz.*, June 5, 1776.

67. *Pa. Gaz.*, May 24, 1776 (postscript).

68. *Votes and Proceedings*, VIII: 7532–33.

John Dickinson, the anti-Independents' most prominent leader, now realized that the Assembly would have to abandon its prohibition of independence, both to pursue current business and to gain the opportunity to suggest a moderate plan for selecting a constitutional convention for the province. Yet he also knew that New York and Maryland still opposed independence, and that New Jersey, Delaware, and South Carolina were not eager to leave the empire. His aim was to delay independence as long as possible in Congress, arguing that the measure was not yet necessary, nor yet acceptable to the middle colonies.[69] Dickinson could count on most Pennsylvania congressmen to oppose independence without prohibitive instructions, and he hoped that the removal of the instructions might defuse popular resentment against the legislature without actually leading to independence. House Speaker John Morton, whether agreeing with Dickinson or already favoring independence, also saw the necessity for altering the instructions. Thus he skillfully choreographed the legislature's deliberations on the morning of June 5, beginning with a reading of Virginia's May 15 resolve for independence. (Maryland's resolve against independence, also passed on May 15, was not even introduced into the minutes).[70] Then, after reading several anti-Independent petitions "of the same Tenor" as the "Remonstrance" to placate conservative lawmakers, he again took up the recent Cumberland County petition for independence.[71] This moderate piece argued that "to avoid the terrible Consequences of Anarchy, . . . it will soon become, if it has not already become, necessary to . . . form such Establishments, as . . . may be construed to lead to a Separation from *Great Britain*."[72]

No appeal for independence could have been better suited to the moderate temper of the lawmakers. When Morton put the vote for a committee to bring in fresh instructions, the motion carried "by a large Majority," although several members, evidently led by the Allen brothers, objected strenuously.[73] The members appointed to this committee comprised a fair cross section of the legislators now willing to move toward, if not to, independence. Dickinson, congressman Robert Morris, Isaac Pearson, and Alexander Wilcocks were anti-Independents; Dickinson's chief rival, Joseph Reed, along with George Clymer and probably the frontier delegate Thomas Smith, spoke for the Independents.[74]

Whatever the fate of the Assembly's instructions, however, lawmakers who opposed both independence and constitutional change still firmly controlled the House. The presentation of a draft of new instructions the following morning

---

69. Burnett, *Continental Congress,* pp. 169, 174–76.

70. *Votes and Proceedings,* VIII: 7533–34; Burnett, *Continental Congress,* p. 169.

71. *Votes and Proceedings,* VIII: 7535. Hawke's search for these anti-Independent petitions was unsuccessful (*Midst of a Revolution,* p. 160, n. 29), and the *Votes* neither give their texts nor state their origin.

72. *Votes and Proceedings,* VIII: 7522 (submitted May 28).

73. See "To the People," *Pa. Gaz.,* June 26, 1776. This essay's contention that "The rescinding the old instructions was violently opposed by the proprietary party . . ." can only refer to an opposition by conservative Quaker lawmakers from Bucks, Chester, and Philadelphia counties *led* by the proprietary figures Andrew and James Allen (see "Diary of James Allen," *PMHB,* IX: 188). Given the composition of the subcommittee entrusted to draft new instructions, and the low number of votes opposing change in the instructions (see below in this chapter), it seems probable that all others who had ever been connected with the proprietary party, particularly Dickinson, Morris, and Wilcocks, supported altering the directives, although their purposes in doing so were conservative.

74. *Votes and Proceedings,* VIII: 7535. Thomas Smith of Bedford County, although the younger brother of the anti-Independent leader Dr. William Smith, was probably an Independent, because the sentiment for independence was strong in the backcountry.

(June 6) touched off an extended debate, and that afternoon the friends of Pennsylvania's existing constitution initiated one last attempt to arrest the revolution in provincial government.[75] The Assembly's minutes say only that the lawmakers resolved "to take into Consideration the State of this Province" on June 8, but the radical author of an essay, "To the People," a careful analysis of the Assembly's spring session that appeared in the *Gazette* on June 26, asserted that the moderates' intention was to enter "upon the business [of summoning a constitutional convention], by fixing the numbers the Convention should consist of, the proportion to each county, and other matters," thereby circumventing the radicals' provincial conference of June 18.[76] At a time when Pennsylvania's county committees were already nominating delegates to that conference, this belated proposal was sure to confuse the province further, but on the morning of June 7, its backers sought to promote it by reading a Chester County petition against constitutional change.[77]

Moderate anti-Independents and all the Independents, however, insisted that the new instructions had to be approved before the House could transact any other business. On the morning of June 8, the chamber approved instructions that authorized, but did not command, Pennsylvania's congressmen "to concur with the other Delegates in Congress, in forming such further Compacts between the United Colonies, concluding such Treaties with foreign Kingdoms and States, and in adopting such other Measures as, upon a View of all Circumstances, shall be judged necessary for promoting the Liberty, Safety and Interests of America. . . ."[78] The instructions passed by a vote of 31 to 12 (or 13), and the names of its opponents were entered in a ledger at the London Coffee House for all good patriots to see and abhor. With the exception of James Rankin of York and the Allen brothers, these obstructionists were probably all conservative lawmakers of Quaker background from Bucks, Chester, and Philadelphia counties.[79] Upon completing this vote, the legislators, who had deferred considering "the State of this Province" to Tuesday, June 11, also put off debate on a further instruction to its congressmen, and adjourned for the weekend.[80]

The June 8 vote did not end either the matter of independence or that of Assembly power. The House did not officially communicate its new instructions to its congressmen until June 14, and those instructions did not require the approval of, indeed did not mention, independence. Meanwhile, Dickinson and his congressional colleagues, hoping to postpone leaving the British Empire indefinitely,

---

75. *Votes and Proceedings*, VIII: 7537, 7539; *Pa. Gaz.*, June 26, 1776.

76. *Votes and Proceedings*, VIII: 7538; *Pa. Gaz.*, June 26, 1776, also in Force, ed., *American Archives*, 4th Ser., VI: 987. Force dates "To the People" June 20. Its author was either a radical assemblyman or had the confidence of one, because he knew far more than the *Votes* reveal. George Clymer and David Rittenhouse of Philadelphia or Robert Whitehill of Cumberland are likely sources of the information in this piece.

77. *Votes and Proceedings*, VIII: 7538–39.

78. *Votes and Proceedings*, VIII: 7542–43 (full text).

79. Unfortunately, this list has not survived, nor does any roll call appear in the *Votes*, but see Duane, ed., *Passages from Marshall*, p. 86 (which gives the vote as 31 to 12) and "Diary of James Allen," *PMHB*, IX: 188 (31 to 13, including James Allen). Allen says that "We [the anti-Independents] were outdone by false friends in the Assembly, who have since turned out warm independents 'tho they affected to oppose it then." He probably refers to Dickinson, Morris, and Wilcocks, who were certainly not for independence, and to such other likely swing voters as Michael Hillegas, Samuel Howell, Samuel Miles, and Isaac Pearson.

80. *Votes and Proceedings*, VIII: 7539. The content, purpose, and author(s) of this further instruction are not known.

won a delay on June 10, when Congress deferred debate on the matter to July 1.[81] In the Assembly, moderate lawmakers, Independent and anti-Independent alike, turned to a second goal, influencing the choice of delegates to a constitutional convention for the province. But here they faced an immediate problem for which they had no solution. The radicals' incentive for attending Assembly sessions was much weaker after the approval of new instructions, and several delegates probably abandoned the session at this time. Yet some radical lawmakers still had unrealized legislative objectives, in particular the funding of the new active-duty troops requested by Congress on June 3, the settlement of the row galley dispute, which threatened both the integrity of the Committee of Safety and the morale of Philadelphia's defense forces, and the completion of essential militia financing.

The failure of the House to gather a quorum on Monday, June 10, was probably due to normal Monday negligence and to important militia meetings held that day in Philadelphia. Many of Tuesday's and Wednesday's absences were deliberate, however, and the most radical members, who opposed the moderates' attempt to consider "the State of the Province," that is, to initiate the Assembly's own proceedings for a constitutional convention, were the most likely absentees.[82] On Thursday morning, June 13, the Pennsylvania Assembly made its last quorum under the Constitution of 1701. The "Independents" in the House—certainly the more moderate Independents—introduced a motion "to recommend the Choosing a Convention," and the members agreed to consider this proposal, but both that afternoon and on the following day there was no quorum.[83] Again the majority of the absentees were probably radicals who feared that anti-Independents and moderate Independents would combine to interfere with the arrangements to be made by the June 18 provincial conference for the election of delegates to the constitutional convention.[84]

The immediate result of the radicals' absence from the House was the total breakdown of the legislative process on June 14. There was no quorum on that day, and the measures that were taken were not official. The House paid its congressmen and its retiring clerk, and transcribed and signed its new instructions for the congressmen.[85] The legislators then approved a brief report exonerating the Committee of Safety in the controversial row galley affair, although twelve of the

---

81. Congressional debate on independence, set for June 7, was postponed to June 8, then to June 10, and finally to July 1, although the subcommittee named to draft a declaration of independence was filled on June 11 (Burnett, *Continental Congress*, pp. 171–73).

82. *Votes and Proceedings*, VIII: 7540. The quorum was thirty–nine (two-thirds). On Monday, attendance was eighteen (A.M.), and then twenty-seven (P.M.), too low to indicate a boycott by any one faction; but on that day Congress was busy discussing independence, and several militia battalions were meeting (see below in this chapter), which probably caused several absences. Tuesday's attendance, however, was thirty-three, and Wednesday's was thirty-six. Because perhaps only forty-five members had been in attendance as recently as June 8, for the vote on the instructions (31 to 12 or 13), only ten or so men were newly absent, perhaps half of them deliberately, for political reasons.

83. *Votes and Proceedings*, VIII: 7540–41; and Matthias Slough to Jasper Yates, June 13, 1776, Miscellaneous Collection, HSP, quoted in Hawke, *Midst of a Revolution*, p. 162. Hawke's portrait of a three-part division in the Assembly on this date—reactionaries (anti-Independents), moderate Independents, and radical Independents—is persuasive.

84. Attendance fell to thirty-six in the afternoon (*Votes and Proceedings*, VIII: 7541). I am here following Hawke's view (*Midst of a Revolution*, pp. 162–64) that it was the radicals who boycotted the House on June 13 and 14, but see "To the People," *Pa. Gaz.*, June 26, 1776, whose author says that both factions boycotted alternately.

85. *Votes and Proceedings*, VIII: 7541–45.

subcommittee did not sign the document, probably because of absences that were variously motivated and not readily attributable to a particular factional bias.[86]

Despair among the assemblymen was now almost universal. Conservatives as well as radicals had left the chamber, singly, in pairs, or in droves, momentarily or permanently, depending upon each man's reading of the confusing events confronting him. It was not the radicals alone who terminated this last Assembly session so abruptly, although they probably could have done it alone.[87] Nearly all members now realized that it was too late to attend to "the State of the Province"; the radicals in their June 18 conference would have the first opportunity to restructure Pennsylvania's unsettled polity. The Assembly's failure was not simply a matter of time and initiative; the lawmakers' prestige with their constituents had plummeted too far in the spring of 1776 for them to tackle political reform with authority. In a fitting end to a dismal legislative session, hobbled throughout by a failure of vision and courage among Assembly leaders, both the officers and the privates of the Philadelphia militia rudely told the lawmakers that their authority in military affairs had ended. The nomination of brigadier generals for the new continental forces by a House that had been so unattentive to the militia's needs, they declared "will not give Satisfaction to the Associators of the Province, and . . . they will not act under [any such nominees]."[88] With this bold defiance ringing in their ears, the members who formed the rump of the Pennsylvania Assembly dispiritedly adjourned to an August session, not knowing if they would meet again, or what powers they would still enjoy.[89]

The collapse of the Pennsylvania Assembly was not solely the product of moderate and conservative recalcitrance and radical sabotage within the chamber; outside the legislature radical leaders were busy insuring their triumph over the

---

86. *Votes and Proceedings,* VIII: 7544. Hawke, *Midst of a Revolution,* pp. 61–62, uses this list of signers of the report as an indication of political moderation, specifically to show that the moderates did well in the backcountry in the May 1 by-election. Later (p. 163), he regards those that did not sign as radicals. However, although the issue itself seemed to involve a clear moderate-radical conflict, the laconic report may not have had much political significance. Those who did not sign numbered twelve, not seven as Hawke believes (cp. *Votes,* VIII: 7523–24 and 7538, with 7544), and among these twelve were assemblymen Brown, Pyle, Haney, Gibbons, and Jacobs, all moderates or conservatives of Quaker background, and Thomas Smith, whom Hawke himself (p. 60) calls a moderate. Only one non-signer, Robert Whitehill of Cumberland County, was indisputably a radical (Duane, ed., *Passages from Marshall,* p. 85 [June 2]). The report itself was little more than a statement of facts discovered, although it did approve the Committee of Safety's actions. Neither this document nor any other is a certain indication of how many conservatives, moderates, and radicals were elected on May 1, or whether radicals or conservatives were more fully involved in the various deliberate absences that destroyed legislative quorums in mid-June.

87. Although the radicals were probably the more numerous boycotters, as Reed states explicitly (N.-Y. Hist. Soc., *Colls.,* XI: 273), Christopher Marshall says that the House adjourned due to "sundry country members being gone out of town" (Duane, ed., *Passages from Marshall,* p. 88 [June 15]). These two statements may not be incompatible; the signatures on the row galley report indicate that at least half a dozen conservatives and moderates as well as half a dozen radicals had left the session at some time prior to June 14, most of them after June 8. In addition, some assemblymen never attended this session. The repeated failure to reach a quorum was in some measure a factional boycott, but it was not without a large element of bipartisan erosion as well.

88. "The Protest of the Board of Officers of . . . Philadelphia," *Votes and Proceedings,* VIII: 7545. See also "The Protest of the Committee of Privates . . ." (pp. 7546–48).

89. *Votes and Proceedings,* VIII: 7548. Between seventeen and twenty-four legislators gathered again on August 26–28, but lacking a quorum adjourned to September 23, when between twenty-three and twenty-eight legislators, again far short of a quorum, finished routine business (*Votes,* VIII: 7548–87).

House, for which their circular letter of May 21 had prepared the way. In late May the Second One Hundred had outflanked the Assembly's attempted inquiry concerning the May 15 congressional preamble by submitting its own memorial to Congress. A few days later, in petitioning the justices of Philadelphia County to postpone the spring quarter session, the committee stressed the uncertainty of the present state of affairs, and candidly admitted its hope of preventing "a disaffected grand jury or court attempting to censure or condemn the virtuous measures now pursuing for the happiness and safety of the good people of this province," as the Chester County grand jury had just done.[90] The committee's appeal secured its objective: Philadelphia's courts remained aloof from partisan politics. Finally, Christopher Marshall, Sr., James Cannon, and the Committee of Privates kept up a steady pressure against the Committee of Safety for its alleged failure to supply the row galleys with adequate ammunition on May 8 and 9.[91]

More important, however, were the political measures taken by radical military associators in early June. On June 6, the Committee of Privates hit upon a most effective way to discredit and paralyze the Assembly when it voted to poll each militia battalion in Philadelphia to determine the associators' support for Congress's May 15 preamble and Philadelphia's May 20 "Protest." On June 10, all five city battalions assembled. The formal questions put by the officers of the oldest battalions evidently did not raise the issue of independence per se, but focused on the militia's commitment to union with the other colonies and on their resolve to restructure Pennsylvania's government without Assembly interference. In Colonel John Dickinson's First Battalion, only four of the officers and twenty-three privates rejected Congress's preamble and Philadelphia's "Protest." In the Second Battalion, led by the zealous Daniel Roberdeau, only two privates demurred. In the more conservative Third, or "Silk Stocking," Battalion, Colonel John Cadwalader refused to poll his troops, and promptly drew hisses and insults, as he had when he attempted to modify the city's resolves on May 20. The Fourth and Fifth Battalions were newer and more radical, having been formed at a time when Assembly-militia friction was high.[92] Their commanders, Colonels Thomas McKean and Timothy Matlack, evidently used the polling to show support for the Independents in Congress, which was to consider Richard Henry Lee's resolution for independence that same day, because both officers also asked their troops a third question, whether they would join the other colonies in leaving the British Empire.[93] The associators' answer, to this and to the first two questions, was unanimously affirmative.

---

90. "To the Worshipful Justices . . ." *Pa. Gaz.,* June 5, 1776. The board approved this piece on June 3; it may have been suggested by Christopher Marshall, Sr., James Cannon, and their friends, who met informally on May 31 (Duane, ed., *Passages from Marshall,* pp. 84, 85 [May 31, June 1, 3]). Thomas McKean presented it to the justices on June 4.

91. Duane, ed., *Passages from Marshall,* pp. 85, 88 (June 2, 17); and *Pa. Evening Post,* June 4, 1776, wherein the Committee of Privates thanks the row galley crews for their gallant effort of May 8–9, and states that it had only delayed expressing its gratitude "to give the House of Assembly an opportunity of doing it first," a clever attack upon both the Assembly and the Committee of Safety.

92. *Pa. Packet,* June 17; *Pa. Evening Post,* June 11, 1776; Duane, ed., *Passages from Marshall,* p. 87 (June 10); "Diary of Dr. James Clitherall," *PMHB,* XXII: 470.

93. Hawke, *Midst of a Revolution,* p. 171, argues that the Committee of Privates' summons to the June 10 balloting was primarily designed to reinforce the Independents in Congress, but it is not certain that the First and Second Battalions were even asked about independence (*Pa. Evening Post,* June 11, contradicts *Pa. Packet,* June 17, 1776). It appears more likely that the Committee of Privates' principal objective was to force the Assembly to abandon its plans to block constitutional change in Pennsylvania.

The vote in the militia battalions and a host of earlier events argue that Pennsylvania's lawmakers had lost control of their province well before the Assembly's humiliating demise of June 14. Public opinion deserted them after May 9, following news of Britain's intention to use foreign mercenaries, and the warship *Roebuck*'s attack upon the City of Brotherly Love. This loss of popular support was formalized on May 20 in Philadelphia, and within ten days in the backcountry as well. Yet even then, cautious moderates and conservatives securely controlled the House, and the vote of June 8 to change the instructions to Pennsylvania's congressmen was largely a maneuver by John Dickinson and his friends to set up one last defense of dependence.[94] And the new instructions probably did afford Dickinson a few more weeks of safety from the anger of a public that had already deserted him.

It was not until June 10 that the militia, which was alienated from the Assembly far earlier than the civilian population, articulated its rejection of Assembly government. And on or about this day, John Dickinson had not only to face his troops at the militia referendum, but to brave the wrath of his fellow officers as well, when they met to decide whether to warn the House not to appoint Pennsylvania's two new brigadier generals, whom Congress had tacitly allowed the militia to select.[95] Dickinson opposed nomination of the generals by the associators, whereupon a fellow officer retorted by attacking the Assembly's instructions forbidding independence. Dickinson offered a spirited defense of his position. Always a sensitive and ready martyr to his concept of right, regardless of personal cost, this brilliant but stubborn leader freely admitted his authorship of the November 1775 instructions, vindicated the Assembly's resistance policies, and ended on a defiant note: "the loss of life . . . or . . . the Affection of my countrymen shall not deter me from acting as an honest man. . . . I can defy the *world,* Sir, but—I defy not heaven; nor will I ever barter my conscience for the esteem of mankind." Such was the "Farmer's" eloquence and sincerity that even in this dark hour, when he held the most unpopular views and was powerless outside of Congress, he remained an impressive figure. Young William Bradford, Jr., in recording this oration, confessed "he was clearly wrong yet I believed him right."[96] But however persuasive the Assembly's resistance policy might sound coming from Dickinson's lips, it had finally become irrelevant, and on June 14, 1776, it was unceremoniously abandoned. The colonial era had ended; with no nation yet in existence, Pennsylvanians turned to construct a state.

THE REVOLUTION IS NOW BEGUN:
THE PROVINCIAL CONFERENCE OF JUNE 1776

While the Assembly was expiring, the Philadelphia Committee of Observation's summons to the June 18 conference was meeting an enthusiastic reception in most

---

94. I say this because, although most conservative lawmakers evidently opposed new instructions while most radical legislators joined the moderates in supporting them, it was Dickinson and his moderate followers who together engineered this vote.

95. William Bradford, Jr.'s "Memorandum, . . ." p. 41, Col. William Bradford Papers, HSP, is the only source for this meeting, and the entry is undated. The meeting could have occurred at any time between June 7 and 14. On the issue of appointing brigadiers, see *Journals,* IV: 348–414 *passim*; "The Memorial of the Committee of Privates, . . ." *Pa. Gaz.,* June 5, 1776; and *Votes and Proceedings,* VIII: 7545, 7546–48.

96. "Memorandum, . . ." p. 41, June [?], 1776, Col. William Bradford Papers, HSP; "To the People," *Pa. Gaz.,* June 26, 1776.

regions of Pennsylvania. The newer counties were the first to choose conference delegates; Northampton and Berks picked their representatives at once, while Lancaster, Bedford, and other western counties soon followed their lead. Bucks was slower—the decision to scrap the 1701 constitution was certainly not popular in that county—but the county committee finally selected its delegation on June 10. Chester and Philadelphia counties appeared even more reluctant and waited until a few days before the opening of the conference to name their spokesmen.[97] The Second One Hundred also delayed choosing its delegates, perhaps to see what the county boards would do; but on June 13, the city committee named five of its members to compose a delegation for full committee approval the next day.[98]

If cautious sentiments delayed some elections, they had little apparent effect upon the choice of conference delegates. The great majority of the one hundred and eight men chosen were both Independents and radicals. Only three of this body had ever been assemblymen, of whom two were not elected to the House until May 1, 1776. Few June delegates had ever played a major part in establishment politics, and most were eager to see significant alterations in Pennsylvania's political system.[99] The Germans, politically passive under Quaker and proprietary domination, participated in this event in large numbers; Pennsylvania's Provincial Conference of June 1776 saw the first full emergence of Pennsylvania's Germans and of other backcountry peoples into a position of real power and responsibility in Pennsylvania politics.[100] While the June delegates were politically and socially more obscure than those of any earlier province-wide body, however, they were not politically inexperienced nobodies, ignorant of all sound principles of government. Many were prominent county officeholders, and while they technically represented Pennsylvania's committees of observation rather than the people of their counties, those committees rested on the same broad franchise as did the Pennsylvania Assembly.[101]

The several local delegations show this mixture of political radicalism and second-rank political status clearly. The city of Philadelphia's Committee of Observation sent twenty-five members of a distinctly radical stamp. These men varied in occupation and income, but few shared an economic and social background with the old political elite. Few were wealthy and few were Quakers; many were Germans or Presbyterians. The handful of proprietary moderates remaining on the Second One Hundred, like John Allen and John Cadwalader, were not appointed to the conference; instead, the radical strategists Thomas McKean, Christopher Marshall, Sr., Timothy Matlack, and Dr. Benjamin Rush headed the delegation.

97. *Pa. Gaz.*, June 5, 12, 1776; *Pa. Evening Post*, June 11, 15, 1776; the Lancaster Committee Book (MS), entry for June 7–8, 1776, Peter Force Collection, Manuscript Division, Library of Congress; and *Pa. Packet*, June 17, 1776.

98. Duane, ed., *Passages from Marshall*, pp. 87–88 (June 12–14).

99. For a list of the delegates, see *Pa. Archives*, 2d Ser., III: 635ff., and compare *Votes and Proceedings*, VIII: 7513–14.

100. At least 24 of the 108 delegates had German names, while most other backcountry spokesmen were Scotch-Irish. This compares with 17 Germans among the 105 delegates in the January 1775 convention, 12 or 13 out of 75 in the July 1774 provincial congress, and 10 out of 58 in the May 1776 Assembly session, four of whom had entered the House since March 1 (*Pa. Archives*, 2d Ser., III: 545–46, 625–26, 635ff; *Votes and Proceedings*, VIII: 7301–2 and 7513–14).

101. For a view of the conference delegates that emphasizes their inexperience and unrepresentative character, see Selsam, *Pennsylvania Constitution*, pp. 148–51; and Hawke, *Midst of a Revolution*, p. 172. These authors apply this judgment both to the June 18 conference and the July 15 constitutional convention.

Joseph Reed, the committee's nominal first chairman, who had struggled for months to balance Pennsylvania's moderate and radical forces, departed for the army in New York about June 14, the day on which the committee named its delegation. Had Reed stayed in Philadelphia, it is by no means certain that his committee would have sent him to the conference (see table 16).[102]

County delegates were usually more prominent within their localities than the average city delegate: Bucks, Chester, Philadelphia, Berks, and York counties sent veteran lawyers, justices, county officials, and militia commanders of several years' experience. Men like Joseph Hart (Bucks), Elisha Price (Chester), Mark Bird (Berks), and James Smith (York) were the elite of rural Pennsylvania. Yet none had ever sat in the Assembly, and all were evidently critical of the recent policies of that body. All were prepared to accept both independence and some constitutional change. While most delegations were distinctly radical, there were exceptions. Several members from Bucks, Chester, and particularly Philadelphia counties were certainly less zealous than their city and backcountry colleagues.[103] The conference members were essentially a mixture of local establishment officeholders of the second rank—justices, commissioners, and assessors—from several counties, and newly risen, highly skilled radical activists, who were most numerous in the delegations from the city of Philadelphia and Lancaster County. Both groups contributed heavily to the new political elite that was rapidly taking shape in Pennsylvania.

The Provincial Conference of June 18–25, 1776, had two objectives: to organize an election for a constitutional convention as rapidly as possible, and to declare Pennsylvania's support for independence. Most delegates to this conference were radical in the fundamental sense that they sought the creation of a new constitution that would forever reduce the political role of the old Quaker and proprietary elites, whom they held responsible for frustrating the resistance and thereby endangering the liberties of all Pennsylvanians. In response to Congress's May 15 preamble, the delegates unanimously resolved that "the present government of this province is not competent to the exigencies of our affairs," and must be replaced by a new government founded "on the authority of the people only."[104] Any political body that had as its goal withdrawing a province from the British Empire, when that province had a proprietary governor and a legislature that refused to pass an effective militia law, could hardly have done less than this.

Yet the delegates did not go about their business in a rash and partisan spirit. They did not predetermine the kind of government that the constitutional convention would devise, nor did they endorse the most radical of the franchise plans for electing that convention that were suggested to them. Despite the fears of many moderates, the conference did not attempt to legislate any measures that were not immediately necessary in Pennsylvania's perilous situation, and it is evident, both

---

102. For portrait data on these men, see Appendix M. On Joseph Reed's departure for New York, see *Journals,* IV: 419 (his appointment as adjutant to General Washington, June 5, 1776); and Reed to Esther DeBerdt Reed, June [5?], and June 16, 1776, Reed Papers, N.-Y. Hist. Soc.

103. The Philadelphia County Committee sent a conservative memorial to the Assembly on May 18 (see note 43 above), and the board's most prominent members, including chairman William Hamilton and Enoch Edwards, the board's secretary, were delegates to the June 18 conference.

104. *Pa. Archives,* 2d Ser., III: 639.

from the conference minutes and from the correspondence of the radical spokes-man Christopher Marshall, Sr., that the delegates as a whole had no interest in gratuitous expressions of radical fervor.[105] They knew that if Pennsylvania was to become an effective political community, it was imperative that harmony be restored quickly. This did not entail any compromise with the Assembly, for most delegates held the Assembly's obstinacy responsible for the current discord in the province. But the Provincial Conference of June 1776 was looking to the future, not to the past.

The delegates gathered at Carpenters' Hall on June 18, another radical anni-versary: it was two years to the day after John Dickinson, Charles Thomson, and their allies had secured the election of Philadelphia's Committee of Forty-Three. The conference's first business was the election of its officers. Thomas McKean, head of Philadelphia's committee, was named chairman; Joseph Hart, the leading radical in conservative Bucks County, became vice-chairman; and the Philadelphia committee's secretary, John Bayard Smith, and member Samuel Cadwalader Morris were chosen secretaries.[106]

The delegates' major task was to arrange for the election of a constitutional convention. They had no difficulty in setting a date for the poll, July 8, and they quickly decided to allow each county and the City of Philadelphia to elect eight delegates. This last measure, while it ensured constitutional radicals the control of the convention, was more than a partisan proviso. The delegates had agreed to give each county one vote in their own deliberations, as had been the practice in the provincial conventions of July 1774 and January 1775; their decision to appor-tion constitutional convention delegates evenly among Pennsylvania's counties was an extension of this now-established practice.[107] Nonetheless, the apportionment plan was controversial, and both immediate circumstances and the radical temper of the conference delegates played a role in their decision. To have attempted a fair distribution of convention delegates on the basis of either total population or the number of taxpayers, however pleasing this might have been to Pennsylvania moderates, would have been too difficult for the delegates, who had to work in considerable haste. Nor could the conferees have seriously considered apportioning convention delegates as seats were apportioned in the despised Assembly. It was the conference's firm conviction that even after the May 1 by-election, representa-tion in the House was not evenly apportioned throughout the province. Yet the decision to distribute convention seats evenly by county, even if almost unavoid-able, was significant. No fair apportionment plan would have preserved the 1701 constitution intact, for on this point constitutional conservatives simply lacked popular support, but the adoption of a plan that gave the more moderate Bucks, Chester, and Philadelphia counties a greater role in the July convention might have moderated the radical document which that body finally produced.

The conference's second major controversial decision was its definition of the franchise for the July 8 election. At the request of the Committee of Privates and

---

105. *Pa. Archives,* 2d Ser., III: 663–64 ("An Address of the [Conference] . . . To the Associators"); and Marshall to "J. B. at _____ New Jersey," June 30, 1776, Christopher Marshall, Sr. Letter-Book, pp. 191–92, Marshall Papers, HSP. Selsam, *Pennsylvania Constitu-tion*, and Hawke, *Midst of a Revolution*, give a quite different assessment of the June con-ference from that offered here.

106. *Pa. Archives,* 2d Ser., III: 638.

107. *Pa. Archives*, 2d Ser., III: 645–52 (1776), cp. pp. 546 (1774) and 627 (1775).

TABLE 16

The Second One Hundred's Twenty-Five Delegates to the Provincial Conference of June 18–25, 1776

(See Table of Symbols, p. xi)

Members	Age	Occupation	Religion	1774 Tax Assessment	Prior Committee Service
Officers					
Bayard, John	38	merchant	P	£11	43, 66, 100[1]
Delaney, Sharp	ca. 37	druggist	A	8	66, 100[1]
McKean, Thomas, Chairman	41	lawyer	P	20[a]	100[1]
Matlack, Timothy	46	various	Q[disowned]	7	100[1]
Morris, Samuel Cadwalader	33	merchant	Q	173	none
Smith, John Bayard, Secretary	33	merchant	P	12[a]	43, 66, 100[1]
Rank and File					
Barge, Jacob	55	innkeeper	?	94	43, 100[1]
Blewer, Joseph	42	merchant	A	20	100[1]
Bruster, Samuel	?	shipwright	A	27	none
Cox, John, Jr.	ca. 44?	merchant	P	120	1765-Hughes, 1769, 1770, 43, 66, 100[1]
Coates, William[b]	55	merchant	Q[disowned]	340	1765r, 66, 100[1]
Deane, Joseph	38	merchant	P	22	66, 100[1]
Franklin, Benjamin	70	public servant	Deist	330	100[1]
Goodwin, George (Moyamensing)	?	ship chandler	?	41	none

232

Conference of June 18–25, 1776 (continued)

Members	Age	Occupation	Religion	1774 Tax Assessment	Prior Committee Service
Gurney, Francis	38	shopkeeper	A	37	66, 100[1]
Lowman, William (Passyunk)	?	?	?	?	none
Loxley, Benjamin	30	carpenter	B	300	1770, 66, 100[1]
Ludwig, Christopher	56	baker	L	99	43, 66, 100[1]
Marshall, Christopher, Sr.	67	retired druggist	Q[disowned]	70	100[1]
Milligan, James	?	merchant, or tailor	P	4	66, 100[1]
Moulder, Joseph	ca. 40s?	sailmaker	B?	40	19, 43, 100[1]
Robinson, William, Jr.	?	joiner	A?	6	66
Rush, Benjamin	30	doctor	P	per head	none
Schriner, Jacob	?	skinner	?	50	100[1]
Schlosser, George	62	tanner	L	65	1765, 43, 66, 100[1]

Age:
20s —
30s 8
40s 5
50s 3
60s+ 3
? 6

Religion: Q 4 (3 disowned)
A 5
P 7
B 2
L 2
? 4

1774 Tax Assessment:
£200+ 3
100–199 2
45– 99 5
25– 44 4
0– 24 10
? 1

Average: £79.

a. 1775 constables' assessment.
b. Identification uncertain.

233

of several Germans, the conference declared that all militia associators aged twenty-one or over who had been assessed for taxes could vote. In rural areas, this may have increased the suffrage from between 50 and 75 percent to 90 percent or more, except in areas where conscientious objectors—Quakers or German pietists —were numerous. In Philadelphia, this provision may have increased the franchise from 50 percent to 90 percent.[108] Moderate contemporaries and modern scholars alike have regarded this measure as both radical and partisan. It was certainly radical, but there were excellent nonpartisan reasons for it. The militia units were among the resistance committees' strongest supporters; they had demonstrated an ardent desire both for independence and for a new government to defend that independence. Whatever their particular political objectives, all Pennsylvanians were now involved in a war and a revolution, and the militia was vital to both. By June 1776, it was evident to the great majority of Pennsylvanians that resistance to British power must be the principal immediate task of their government, and those who fought surely had a strong claim to vote. If the province were to draft a new constitution, those who would be called upon to defend it could reasonably expect to have some say in its creation. The basic intent and effect of the franchise provision adopted by the conference was to include all adult white males, upon whom any new government would have to depend. The new franchise measure achieved this object admirably. Only those conscientious objectors who were also landless and poor, men who by both choice and circumstance could contribute little to the defense of Pennsylvania's independence, were excluded from the polls.[109]

More objectionable to some Pennsylvanians was the conference's decision empowering the judges and inspectors of the July 8 election to require any voter to take an oath foreswearing allegiance to George III and promising to support "a government in the province on the authority of the people only."[110] Thus the conference, in David Hawke's words, first "widened the voting population to include those who favored independence, then narrowed it to exclude those who opposed it."[111] Again, however, this measure hardly seems unreasonable. On June 8, the Assembly itself had permitted Pennsylvania's congressmen to vote for independence, and all knew that Congress would consider the matter on July 1. If Congress voted for independence, how was the old proprietary government to be retained, and upon what basis could any suitable replacement rest other than "the authority of the people"? The oath devised by the June conference did not commit Pennsylvanians to any specific government (as an oath framed by the July convention would do). Nor were the judges and inspectors of the July 8 election required to administer the new oaths of allegiance; they were only empowered to

---

108. *Pa. Archives,* 2d Ser., III: 639–40. On the franchise, see chapter 1, note 7 above; and Williamson, *American Suffrage,* pp. 33–34, 58, 86–88, 93–97, 111, 120.

109. The conference, it should be noted, ignored the more extreme suggestion that all associators, of whatever age, be enfranchised (see "Elector," *Pa. Packet,* Apr. 29, 1776, cited in Hawke, *Midst of a Revolution,* p. 173).

110. *Pa. Archives,* 2d Ser., III: 641–42. The prospective voter could also be required to pledge not to oppose the formation of a new government by the upcoming convention (p. 640), and all persons who had been branded enemies of their country by local committees and had not been cleared—a few dozen, mostly Quaker, merchants and farmers—were disqualified (p. 641).

111. Hawke, *Midst of a Revolution,* p. 174. Selsam's assessment, *Pennsylvania Constitution,* p. 138, is nearly identical, and both resemble Lincoln, *Revolutionary Movement,* pp. 267–68.

require them whenever they believed them to be necessary. This did enable radical judges and inspectors to bar strict Quaker voters if they chose, and because the local committees themselves named the judges for their respective counties, this power was real.[112] Yet in a community that was becoming increasingly alarmed at the prospect of tories and British-sympathizers in high places, the passage of such a rule reflected something more than mere partisan politics.[113]

The conference could have dissolved at this point if the gathering had limited its goals to settling election procedures for the July convention. But the delegates acknowledged two other obligations that they felt they could not ignore. First, they tackled several pressing provincial matters that required legislation, administration, or arbitration. Critics of their work, observing that they had not convened to exercise any of these powers, termed these actions a "usurpation of governmental functions." The conference's justification for the exercise of these powers, however, went beyond a mere "alleged failure of the Assembly to meet the exigencies of affairs," or "the fact that Congress had advocated the creation of new government."[114] On June 1, Congress had resolved that Pennsylvania should raise 4,500 troops from among its militia, but on June 14, the Assembly, after repeated failures to gather a quorum, professed itself "unable, at this Time, to proceed [to raise fresh troops]," and adjourned to late August.[115] The Assembly *had* failed to meet the exigencies of Pennsylvania's affairs, whatever the cause of its failure, and with Admiral Howe's imminent arrival off New York, the conference passed the necessary resolves to get Pennsylvania's troops into the field.[116]

The conference's recommendation to the upcoming convention that it form a Council of Safety with executive power in military affairs also had its basis in necessity. The delegates had witnessed the inability of the Committee of Safety, which lacked adequate executive powers, to control Pennsylvania's military machine. Once independent, Pennsylvania would have no legal executive at all. In recommending the formation of a council with executive powers in military affairs, the conference did not preclude the creation of the office of governor under the new

---

112. *Pa. Archives,* 2d Ser., III: 648–52. Each county committee was instructed to name three of its members as judges for each election district within its constituency. Inspectors for the July 8 election were to be chosen by the voters, in a poll conducted by these judges, on July 6.

113. The new franchise and oath were, nevertheless, in line with the demands of radical Independents. Compare the June conference's work with "Cassandra," *Pa. Ledger,* Apr. 27; an unsigned piece attacking Andrew Allen, and an item by "Old Trusty," both *Pa. Evening Post,* Apr. 30; an unsigned piece in *Pa. Jour.,* May 1, entitled "To the Freeholders and Electors of . . . Philadelphia"; "The Forester," last paragraph, *Pa. Jour.,* May 8; and "A Watchman," Letters I and II, *Pa. Packet,* June 10, 24, 1776.

114. Selsam, *Pennsylvania Constitution,* p. 142, who concurs with Pennsylvania's moderate political leaders of 1776 in arguing that the conference "usurped" Assembly power.

115. *Journals,* IV: 400, 410, 412–13; *Votes and Proceedings,* VIII: 7545.

116. *Pa. Archives,* 2d Ser., III: 644, 654–55. After the Assembly failed to meet Congress's request for troops, the Committee of Safety's Robert Morris, a congressman, informed Congress on June 20 that Pennsylvania would not be able to raise the troops unless Congress directly empowered the Committee of Safety to do so. Congress, however, declined to do this (*Journals,* IV: 469–70). This information was presented to the conference on June 22, and on the next day the conference issued a resolution for their recruitment. Word of Admiral Howe's arrival, with sixty sail, off Sandy Hook, New Jersey, reached Philadelphia on June 30 (Duane, ed., *Passages from Marshall,* p. 90).

constitution, although this probably was the intention of many of the delegates. Most radical leaders had probably become committed to committee government by 1776 and, never having had a Revolutionary governor, now regarded such a powerful figure as both unnecessary and potentially dangerous. Yet in both of these vital matters—resolving that more Continental troops be recruited and recommending to the constitutional convention the creation of a powerful new Council of Safety—the June conference did not "usurp" the functions of established government. That had already been done informally by radical leaders between May 20 and June 14. Rather, the conference exercised immediate and vital governmental functions which no other public body could or would handle.[117]

Finally, the delegates moved Pennsylvania firmly into the independence camp. The Assembly, on June 8, had removed its instructions prohibiting its congressmen from supporting independence, but it had not encouraged them to support that measure. It was widely suspected that at least half of Pennsylvania's congressmen would reject this final step unless further pressure were applied to them. For this reason, the conference empowered Benjamin Rush, James Smith of York, and its chairman, Thomas McKean, to draft a resolution declaring the sense of the conference with respect to independence. On June 24, the conference approved the committee's draft, which read: "We, the deputies of the people of Pennsylvania, . . . do in this public manner in behalf of ourselves, and with the approbation, consent, and authority of our constituents, unanimously declare our willingness to concur in a vote of the congress, declaring the united colonies free and independent states. . . ."[118] Thus, the June delegates neither declared Pennsylvania's independence nor directed their congressmen to support it; they merely expressed "a willingness to concur in" independence. Their purpose was not to dictate, but to influence Pennsylvania's congressmen gently but firmly, while restoring Pennsylvania's tarnished reputation as a stalwart supporter of colonial unity in the resistance effort.

The essential tasks of the conference were now complete. All that remained was the final approval of two addresses, one to the people of the province explaining their work as a whole, the other to the military associators, explaining the necessity of raising the 4,500 Continental troops that Congress had requested.[119] The address to the people is especially interesting, for it highlights a neglected aspect of the June conference. The delegates informed the province that "we have experienced an unexpected unanimity in our councils, and we have the pleasure of observing a growing unanimity among the people of the province. We beg that this brotherly spirit may be cultivated, and that you would remember that the present unsettled state of the province requires that you should show forbearance, charity and moderation to each other."[120]

The bitter partisan rhetoric of the Second One Hundred's May 21 circular letter

---

117. *Pa. Archives*, 2d Ser., III: 652–53. A recommendation that the July convention select new congressmen, also made at this time, was perhaps more partisan; but several current congressmen were known to oppose independence strongly, and would therefore hardly be suitable if independence carried.

118. *Pa. Archives,* 2d Ser., III: 655, 658 (quotation).

119. *Pa. Archives,* 2d Ser., III: 652, 656, 660, 663.

120. *Pa. Archives,* 2d Ser., III: 656.

to the counties, and of the Philadelphia Committee of Privates' June 14 petition to the Assembly, is totally absent from this appeal.[121] Now that the grand issue had been decided, the rhetoric of the committee movement became just as consensual as it had been in August 1774, when harmony followed the divisive decisions of May–July. Fully as significant, the conference admitted that its harmony was "unexpected," yet the address evidently did not exaggerate the delegates' cooperative spirit.[122] Two delegates argued angrily on the first day of the conference, resulting in the rapid departure of one of them; and when the conference took up the proposal that all July conventioneers take a Trinitarian test oath, Christopher Marshall, Sr. passionately defended the measure against the spirited opposition of his close friend and political ally Benjamin Rush.[123] But these first altercations had little effect upon the smooth cooperation of the conference delegates. In late June 1776, a remarkable harmony prevailed among all the leaders of Pennsylvania's Independents, whether they were constitutional moderates or radicals.

The Provincial Conference of June 18–25, 1776, brought to a close Pennsylvania's long and agonizing search for an effective resistance to British imperial policy. The work of the June conference was worthy of that struggle's original goals and of its entire course. The delegates cooperated warmly in achieving their objectives, for all shared a fine sense of what they should and should not do, a deep feeling of optimism and charity, and a keen awareness that at last, largely against their desires and beyond their dreams, they had become revolutionaries. As the conference neared its end, one local writer sensitively expressed both the achievement of the resistance and the challenge facing Pennsylvanians. "The revolution is now begun," he wrote, "and must be supported."[124]

Twentieth-century students of the Revolution in Pennsylvania have had increasing difficulty accepting this simple truth. Admitting that the June conference "was successful in all that it undertook," one scholar objected that it "had no legal foundation nor any basis at law," an obvious fact that presents no problem to those who accept the revolutionary character of what happened in Pennsylvania in 1776.[125] Again, critics of the June conference view it as both partisan and incompetent.[126] As either an assessment or an explanation of what the conference did, this approach fundamentally misunderstands the nature of the Revolution in Pennsylvania.

The June conference was a revolutionary body. It had to be. Only a revolution could save Pennsylvania from subjection to Britain, war with her neighbors, and internal violence. Partisan ultraradical Pennsylvanians did play a key role in calling the conference, and many of them were delegates. Yet several of the most influential conferees, such as Thomas McKean, Joseph Hart, and John Bayard, were

---

121. For these earlier texts, see Force, ed., *American Archives,* 4th Ser., VI: 520–21; and *Votes and Proceedings,* VIII: 7546–48.
122. See Christopher Marshall, Sr. to "J. B. at _____ New Jersey," June 30, 1776, Christopher Marshall Letter-Book, pp. 191–92, Marshall Papers, HSP.
123. Marshall to "J. B.," Letter-Book, pp. 191–92, HSP.
124. "To the People," *Pa. Gaz.,* June 26, 1776. I have taken the liberty of altering this passage for use in the title of this study, and of this chapter and section.
125. Selsam, *Pennsylvania Constitution,* p. 136.
126. Ibid., pp. 137–39; Hawke, *Midst of a Revolution,* p. 172.

neither the most partisan nor the most radical.[127] The delegates did not try to prepare the way for any one kind of new government, beyond a republican one. Their recommendations to the upcoming constitutional convention did not go beyond the immediate need to provide a strong military machine and appoint congressmen who would support the American cause. They did not try to undermine the authority of the Committee of Safety, the old Assembly's executive arm. And they did not usurp legislative powers for themselves, but simply passed a few vital resolves to insure Pennsylvania's immediate safety.[128]

At the same time, the June delegates knew who and what they were. The Revolution had begun in earnest; there had to be a minimum test of allegiance—independence and republicanism. The conference took the reasonable position that those Pennsylvanians who were unwilling to adopt these measures could not, either as voters or as officeholders, help their community to meet the old challenge that it still faced: stopping Great Britain's threat to America's liberties. Because Pennsylvania was in the midst of a revolution and a war, the conference believed that it could and should demand this minimum allegiance from its active citizens. The conference recognized that its existence, and the existence of Pennsylvania's committees and militia units, was the work of the Revolution, and not of established government.[129] The reputation of this "purely revolutionary" assembly ought not to be "saved from the contumely usually bestowed on such bodies by the high character of some of its members,"[130] but by the fact that its work had a revolutionary necessity and effectiveness, and its members possessed a sound revolutionary self-awareness.

INDEPENDENCE

At about one in the afternoon on Tuesday, June 25, the provincial conference finished its labors, thanked Chairman Thomas McKean for his services, and walked to the Indian Queen tavern for a triumphal banquet.[131] Later that day, McKean read the conference's resolve on independence in Congress. The way was rapidly clearing for an affirmative vote on independence by July 1, the date set for the resumption of congressional debate on the grand question.[132] In Philadelphia, too,

---

127. These three men, plus the more zealous James Smith of York and Dr. Benjamin Rush, were evidently the most influential conference delegates. Timothy Matlack, a notorious ultraradical partisan, was put on the important subcommittee to consider the number and apportionment of July convention delegates, but he had twenty-two colleagues, including several prominent local leaders. Christopher Marshall, Sr. appears to have done nothing except argue for the Trinitarian test oath against Benjamin Rush. Three other well-known ultraradicals, James Cannon, Thomas Paine, and Dr. Thomas Young, were not even conference delegates. Hawke, *Midst of a Revolution*, pp. 102–6, argues that Cannon, Marshall, Matlack, Paine, Rush, and Young were the nucleus of Pennsylvania's ultraradicals in the spring of 1776.

128. In their address "To the Associators of Pennsylvania," the delegates declared, "We presume only to recommend the plan we have formed [to raise troops] to you, trusting that in [a] case of so much consequence your love of virtue and zeal for liberty will supply the want of authority delegated to us expressly for that purpose" (*Pa. Archives,* 2d Ser., III: 663).

129. *Pa. Archives,* 2d Ser., III: 655: "and whereas, the militia of this province at first associated by the advice and under the authority of the committees of inspection and observation of the city and the several counties; . . ."

130. Selsam, *Pennsylvania Constitution,* p. 136.

131. Duane, ed., *Passages from Marshall,* p. 89 (June 25).

132. Burnett, *Continental Congress,* pp. 174–81.

the Revolution's pace quickened, and all opposition momentarily fell silent. On June 27, the Committee of Privates held elections in the militia units for delegates to a provincial assembly of militia associators to be convened at Lancaster on July 4. On the fourth, the militia delegates, in conjunction with their officers' representatives, selected Daniel Roberdeau and James Ewing as the first and second brigadier generals of the Pennsylvania forces, thereby declaring their independence of Assembly control.[133] On Sunday, June 30, word reached Philadelphia that the British fleet had arrived off the coast of New Jersey; on Monday, July 1, a city jury that was condemning two captured British prize ships demanded that the King's arms, mounted in the courtroom, be taken down, and it was done.[134] On Tuesday, July 2, the Second One Hundred appointed seven of their number to be a Committee of Secrecy "to examine all inimical and suspected persons that come to their knowledge."[135]

On the same day, John Dickinson and Robert Morris, bowing to the inevitable but proud to the last, absented themselves from Congress, which then declared the United Colonies independent of the British Empire. Pennsylvania's Benjamin Franklin, James Wilson, and Assembly Speaker John Morton supported the break; Charles Humphreys and Thomas Willing opposed it.[136] Six days later, by order of the Philadelphia Committee of Observation, John Nixon gave the Declaration of Independence its first public reading to the assembled Committees of Safety and Observation and a large crowd at the State House. The King's arms were then ripped from over the State House door and carried to the Revolution's unofficial Philadelphia headquarters, William Bradford's London Coffee House.[137]

Pennsylvania's own revolution in government progressed as rapidly as the drive to independence. On Wednesday, July 3, members of the Committee of Privates and other zealots met to discuss candidates for the City's eight seats in the constitutional convention. James Cannon, Timothy Matlack, and Dr. Young, the principal speakers, urged the nomination of candidates with a broad knowledge, independent fortunes, zeal, and an "uprightness to the determination and result of Congress in their opposition to the tyranny of Great Britain."[138] And on July 6, in a full session of the Second One Hundred, eight men were nominated for the radical slate: congressman Benjamin Franklin, the radical assemblymen David Rittenhouse and George Clymer, radical Committee of Safety member Owen Biddle, German zealots Frederick Kuhl and George Schlosser, and the ultra-radicals Timothy Matlack and James Cannon. Franklin, Kuhl, Matlack, and Schlosser were members of the Second One Hundred; Biddle, Clymer, and Frank-

---

133. *Pa. Archives*, 5th Ser., V: 25.

134. Duane, ed., *Passages from Marshall*, pp. 90–91 (June 30, July 1).

135. Ibid., p. 91 (July 2). Marshall was one of the seven; unfortunately, he does not name his colleagues.

136. Burnett, *Continental Congress*, pp. 181–83. Dickinson had opposed independence the day before in a formally prepared speech (see J. H. Powell, ed., "Speech of John Dickinson Opposing the Declaration of Independence, 1 July 1776," *PMHB*, LXV (1941): 458–81.

137. Duane, ed., *Passages from Marshall*, pp. 93–94 (July 6, 8).

138. Ibid., pp. 91–92 (July 3). Contrast these views with the radical broadside of June 26, 1776, "To the Several Battalions of Military Associators in the Province of Pennsylvania," item 19, HSP, attributed by Hawke, *Midst of a Revolution*, pp. 176–77, to James Cannon. In that broadside, men of great fortune are regarded as improper persons to frame a new constitution, but in the speeches of July 3, according to Marshall, "independent fortune" was stressed, although several of those nominated, including Cannon and Matlack themselves, were not independently wealthy.

lin were Committee of Safety members. On July 8, while John Nixon read the Declaration and the crowd tore down the King's arms, the radical nominees "were elected very quietly" at the State House.[139]

REVOLUTIONARY CONFLICT

In these quiet weeks at the end of June and beginning of July, however, Pennsylvania's new harmony did not penetrate below the surface of political life. Behind the rhetoric of consensus and the ardent desire for unity were strong discordant emotions, centering both on conflicting political policies and on the men who supported them. The new government that was soon to emerge from the constitutional convention would draw this discord into the open. Some of the opposition to Pennsylvania's Revolution would come from outright tories, who by July 1 had organized at least four clubs that met regularly in Philadelphia.[140] Dickinsonian moderates, too, would mount their first effective opposition to radical policies in the fall, after they had finished licking their wounds of May and June. But discontent was not limited to conservatives and anti-Independents; in late June the radical faction itself began to split. On June 21, after arguing with Dr. Benjamin Rush over the need for a religious test oath, Christopher Marshall, Sr. began questioning the orthodoxy of his political allies.[141] By July 1, his doubts turned to disillusionment when his close friend James Cannon told him that his support for the test oath was both ignorant and harmful to the cause.[142]

After July 1, Marshall was an outsider, caustically criticizing the machinations of the very radical leaders whose ally and constant companion he had recently been. Marshall began by condemning the radicals for enlisting "that noisy blunder" Dr. Thomas Young to harangue the Committee of Privates on July 3, thereby stirring up the associators' fears against "certain persons"—perhaps moderate Independents. In this way the ultraradicals secured militia support for a ticket for the constitutional convention that included both Cannon and Matlack. By using the same kind of appeal, Marshall declared, they "unfairly obtained and carried [the slate] in our Committee [of Observation] also, . . . whereby Sundry upright honest men of integrity and probity were shuffeld [*sic*] out: to the great Surprize of Many, who were astonished: and begin now, but too late to see . . . that the Cry of Patriotism was only a blind to Cover their Ambitious intent of Squezing [*sic*] themselves into posts of Profit."[143] Marshall abstained from the Second One Hundred's approval of Cannon and Matlack and objected to holding the election for convention delegates on the day on which the Declaration was to be proclaimed, when he expected Philadelphians to be noisy and tumultuous, but his protests were in vain.[144]

139. Duane, ed., *Passages from Marshall,* pp. 93–94 (July 6, 8).

140. Ibid., p. 91 (July 1).

141. *Pa. Archives,* 2d Ser., III: 642; Duane, ed., *Passages from Marshall,* p. 90 (June 28); Marshall to "J. B. at _____ New Jersey," June 30, 1776, Christopher Marshall, Sr. Letter-Book, p. 192, HSP.

142. Marshall to "J. C." [James Cannon], July 1, 1776, Letter-Book, pp. 193–95, HSP.

143. Marshall to "J. B. at _____ New Jersey," July 27, 1776, Letter-Book, p. 199, HSP. Marshall's remarks are the only extant detailed criticism of the ultraradicals dating from July 1776.

144. Duane, ed., *Passages from Marshall,* p. 90 (July 6).

There were no further defections from the radical core for some weeks, but on July 20, shortly after Pennsylvania's Constitutional Convention of 1776 opened, the radical constitutional reformers began to alienate more of their followers through the appointment of new congressmen. The deletion of the anti-Independents Andrew Allen, John Dickinson, Charles Humphreys, and Thomas Willing, and the addition of the Independent assemblyman George Clymer were probably widely popular, but the inclusion of James Cannon's close ally, Dr. Benjamin Rush, generated opposition even within Independent circles.[145] Then, on July 23, the convention appointed a Council of Safety to replace the Committee of Safety. Reducing this vital executive from thirty-two to twenty-five members, the convention retained only eight veterans from the old Committee, three of whom were assemblymen who rarely attended Committee meetings. Eighteen of the thirty-two old board members had sat in the Assembly after the May 1 by-election, but only five of the twenty-five new councilors were legislators. Thirteen, however, were conventioneers, including five out of the eight delegates from the City of Philadelphia. Several of the old members were evidently deleted because they were committed to active military service outside Pennsylvania, but Andrew Allen, Alexander Wilcocks, John Nixon, John Dickinson, and Robert Morris must all have been removed for their moderation—and Morris had been the moderates' most active committee member. Several moderates were retained, but they had now to cooperate with several new radical members, notably David Rittenhouse, John Bayard Smith, Frederick Kuhl, Timothy Matlack, and James Cannon (see table 17).

Marshall regarded the new Council as the work of Cannon, Matlack, and Rush, whom he accused of conspiring to put themselves on the Council and into Congress. Many Philadelphians, he said, were soon grumbling "of such Autionering [*sic*] and treatment as was transacted in that Election [of the Council of Safety]." The triumvirate, he charged, had first urged their friends to compose lists of candidates for the Council, and then had put aside some of the best nominees and taken their places. These same leaders, Marshall lamented, had earlier condemned the Assembly for the same practice, and their behavior now threw many conventioneers into great confusion.[146] Few Independents broke with the ultraradical leadership in July, however. James Cannon and his allies were still riding high, and at the close of the convention in September, they secured the approval of the ultrademocratic Pennsylvania Constitution of 1776, which was largely Cannon's own work.[147] This document not only provided for a unicameral legislature, which, although traditional in Pennsylvania, was nonetheless controversial, but also advanced quite

---

145. Ibid., p. 96 (July 20). Convention votes for the nine congressmen chosen stood thus: Benjamin Franklin, 78; George Ross, 77; George Clymer, 75; Robert Morris, 74; James Wilson, 74; John Morton, 71; Benjamin Rush, 61; Col. James Smith, 56; and George Taylor, 34. Smith was a radical conventioneer from York County; Taylor an assemblyman from Northampton County. It is not clear why Robert Morris, who with Dickinson abstained from voting on independence, was returned.

146. Ibid., p. 97 (July 23); Marshall to "J. B. at _____ New Jersey," July 27, 1776, Letter-Book, pp. 199–200 (quotation on p. 199). For a comparison of the Committee of Safety and the Council of Safety, see tables 10 and 17.

147. On Cannon's authorship, see Nevins, *American States*, pp. 150–52; Selsam, *Pennsylvania Constitution*, pp. 150, 186; and Hawke, *Midst of a Revolution*, pp. 183, 186, 187–90, and n. 14 on p. 186. Hawke's view that it was Cannon, and not George Bryan, who had the largest share in writing the new constitution is convincing.

TABLE 17

The Council of Safety Appointed by the Constitutional Convention, July 23, 1776

(See Table of Symbols, p. xi)

Members	Residence	Prior Political Service, 1776
Bartholomew, Benjamin[a]	Chester	CS, Assembly (1772–76), 1776 Convention
Blewer, Joseph	Philadelphia Co.	100,[2] Conference, 1776 Convention
Biddle, Owen	City	CS, radical candidate, May 1, 1776, 1776 Convention
Bull, John	Philadelphia Co.	Conference, 1776 Convention
Cannon, James	City	CP, 1776 Convention
Espey, Daniel	Bedford	Conference
Falconer, Nathaniel	City	
Gray, George	Philadelphia Co.	CS, Assembly (1772–76)
Howell, Samuel	City	CS, Assembly (from May 1, 1776)
Hunter, Daniel	Berks	Conference, 1776 Convention
Hubley, John	Lancaster	1776 Convention
Keppele, Henry, Jr.	City	
Kuhl, Frederick	City	radical candidate, May 1, 1776, 1776 Convention
Lyon, William	?	Conference, 1776 Convention
Mifflin, Samuel	City	
Moore, John	Westmoreland	1776 Convention
Morris, Samuel, Sr.	City?	
Morris, Samuel, Jr.	City	CS
Rhoad, Peter	Northampton	1776 Convention
Rittenhouse, David	City	Assembly (from March 2, 1776), 1776 Convention
Smith, John Bayard	City	100[2] (Secretary), Conference
Swoope, Michael	York	Assembly (1768–72, 1774–76), CS
Weitzel, John	Northumberland	1776 Convention
Wharton, Thomas, Jr.	City	CS
Wynkoop, Henry	Bucks	CS, Conference

a. Committee of Safety members are italicized.

novel constitutional ideas like the Council of Censors, and introduced civil test oaths, which at once proved obnoxious to many Pennsylvanians.

The new constitution's many innovations and its patently partisan test oaths, however, turned several staunch radicals against the work of their own faction in the fall. Benjamin Rush himself quickly cut his ties with the zealots, and Thomas McKean attacked the constitution in a mass meeting in Philadelphia on October 21.[148] John Dickinson and his allies now returned to public life and participated in the chaotic elections of October and November for seats in the thoroughly re-

---

148. See Rush to Anthony Wayne, Sept. 24, 1776, May 19, June 5, 18, 1777, in Butterfield, ed., *Letters of Rush,* I, pp. 114–15, 137, 148–51. McKean and Dickinson attacked the Constitution of 1776 at the October 21 meeting, and Cannon, Matlack, and Col. James Smith defended it. Col. John Bayard chaired the session (Duane, ed., *Passages from Marshall,* p. 111).

formed Assembly (each county, and the City of Philadelphia, now had six seats in the chamber). John Bayard, George Clymer, and Samuel Morris, Jr. joined Dickinson and Robert Morris in opposing the new constitution; and in the November elections, which were hotly contested but attracted relatively few voters, the radicals lost both in the City and in Philadelphia County.[149] As 1776 came to a close, Pennsylvania had a government in which many of the leaders, both in the Assembly and on the Council of Safety, were unalterably opposed to the new constitution that gave them their authority. The unstable factional warfare produced by this crisis profoundly unsettled Pennsylvania and posed a severe problem for the Continental Congress and Army for many months. In only slightly milder form, it continued in the commonwealth, with few respites, until the framing of a very different Pennsylvania constitution in 1790.

REVOLUTIONARY ACHIEVEMENT

Yet while the summer of 1776 marked a beginning of the most divisive era in Pennsylvania's history, it also marked an end to the province's resistance movement. With Pennsylvania's and America's decision to declare and fight for independence, Philadelphia's committee movement had finally solved its central problem—to secure political liberty for its citizens on a permanent basis. City, province, and continental union had finally formulated and begun to execute a plan of resistance to counter any threat of suppression by Great Britain. No longer was there the need to make basic decisions about the empire at the local level and convince the public of their merit. What was now required was long, hard fighting. To achieve this, Pennsylvania had formed a militia and was rapidly constructing a government that would be committed to all necessary resistance to British power. After mid-July, the need for local committees quickly diminished; henceforth, the militia, the constitutional convention, the new Council of Safety, and the new Assembly would conduct the Revolution.

The Second One Hundred soon felt the effects of this new political climate. The board kept busy with routine commercial regulation and local political chores through the summer, and in early August its work was still valuable enough for the constitutional convention to extend its term beyond the six months allotted to

---

149. Duane, ed., *Passages from Marshall*, pp. 107, 115–16 (Oct. 4, Nov. 2, 5, 6). Chester, Bucks, and perhaps other counties held their elections early in October, as was traditional, but in the City and County of Philadelphia the poll came on or about November 5 and 6. In the City the results were:

anticonstitutionalists		constitutionalists	
*George Clymer	413	David Rittenhouse	278
*Robert Morris	410	John Bayard Smith	273
*Samuel Morris, Jr.	407	Jacob Schreiner	273
*John Bayard	397	Timothy Matlack	268
*Michael Schubart	393	Thomas Wharton, Jr.	268

both tickets: *Joseph Parker   682

*elected.

In the County, the anticonstitutionalists, including the incumbents George Gray, Thomas Potts, and John Dickinson, also won.

it in February, but on September 3, the Second One Hundred itself considered recommending that any board which should succeed it have only fifty members.[150] In fact, Congress, the constitutional convention, and the militia now ran both the city and the province. On September 17, its work done, Philadelphia's last Committee of Observation, Inspection, and Correspondence extinguished itself, voting "to break up this Committee entirely, except eight members to settle [the] Committee's accounts, and the six members that were appointed to see the salt for each county settled."[151]

JOHN DICKINSON AND CHARLES THOMSON ON PENNSYLVANIA'S TWO REVOLUTIONS

In the hour of the committee movement's triumph, factional strife broke out in Philadelphia and across Pennsylvania. Contemporaries and modern scholars alike have viewed the struggle for independence and the long Constitutionalist-Republican wars following July 4, 1776, as intimately related, but they have sharply disagreed on the nature of that relationship. At issue is the role that certain elements within the resistance movement played in bringing on the commonwealth's decade of party controversy. One approach to this complex problem is to see the Revolution in Pennsylvania as composed of two distinct but closely related and chronologically overlapping developments.

When a radical critic of the Assembly announced that "the revolution is now began" in late June 1776, he meant by "revolution" both a public commitment to full independence from Great Britain and a reshaping of the several colonies into sovereign republics.[152] By July 1776, however, the first Revolution—the development of resistance to British authority and the drive for independence—was completed. This first Revolution somehow generated the second, constitutional Revolution, which began only in the spring of 1776. As Pennsylvanians divided over the Constitution of 1776, so they divided over how their resistance to Great Britain generated the chaos of their political life following Independence. The contrasting views of two major actors in the drama give a good formulation of the argument dividing Pennsylvanians in 1776.

John Dickinson, the leader of Pennsylvania's anti-Independents, was dismissed from Congress by Pennsylvania's constitutional convention on July 20, 1776, and immediately departed for military service in New Jersey. In a speech delivered to his fellow militia officers in Philadelphia in early June, and in his private writings in August, he "held himself completely guiltless of the debacle" in Pennsylvania politics, as Hawke expresses it.[153] Speaking to his militia colleagues, he explained that he had acted according to his principles, and that he sincerely believed that independence was premature in 1776. He offered no apologies. In mid-August he declared to his old friend Charles Thomson his willingness to suffer "all the

---

150. Ibid., pp. 100 (Aug. 17), 103 (Sept. 3).
151. Ibid., p. 105 (Sept. 17).
152. *Pa. Gaz.,* June 26, 1776, "To the People."
153. *Midst of a Revolution,* p. 178. See Dickinson's speech to the officers of the Philadelphia militia, June [8?], 1776, as recorded by William Bradford, Jr., "Memorandum . . ." (June [8?]), pp. 40–41, Col. William Bradford Papers, HSP; and Dickinson to Charles Thomson, Aug. 7, 10, 1776, N.-Y. Hist. Soc., *Colls.,* XI: 29–31.

Indignities that my Countrymen now bearing Rule are inclined if they could so plentifully to shower down upon my innocent head. . . ."[154]

On August 19, Dickinson entertained a friend at his army quarters in New Jersey, and their conversation turned to Pennsylvania politics and Dickinson's fall from power. Whatever was said weighed heavily on Dickinson's mind, for on August 25, in a long and evidently unfinished rough draft to his unnamed visitor, he spilled out his innermost feelings about his political misfortunes. His downfall had occurred, he explained, when Pennsylvania's Presbyterians, who had supported him warmly in political contests for years, gradually turned against him. In part, he wrote, they did so because he married a Quaker heiress in 1770 and became closer to the Friends thereafter, although politically he still opposed the Quaker party. Beginning in 1775, moreover, he increasingly espoused moderate resistance policies that were as favored by Friends as they were deplored by most Presbyterians. But there was more: "The Jealousy of some Gentlemen of Merit . . . desirous of drawing to themselves all the Weight that could be derived from that [religious] Body . . . . [caused them to set out] to destroy that Confidence with which I had been so long, so uncommonly and so affectionately honored by [the Presbyterians]. I mean more especially Col. Read [*sic*] and Dr. Rush. . . ."[155] It was, then, a radical Presbyterian faction, led by the ambitious and unprincipled Joseph Reed and Dr. Benjamin Rush, that had destroyed Assembly power and drawn Pennsylvania precipitously into independence.

Joseph Reed fully reciprocated Dickinson's animosity and regarded all of Pennsylvania's ills in 1776 as the product of Dickinson's vanity and timidity; but a more balanced and sympathetic, and therefore more telling, indictment of Dickinson's conduct came from the pen of "The Farmer's" old ally, Charles Thomson.[156] Thomson defended Dickinson's moderation in 1775, but by the spring of 1776 he had concluded that any opposition to independence was worse than futile.[157] Chiding Dickinson for the angry charges in his August 10 letter, Thomson wrote:

> I cannot help regretting, that by a perseverance which you were fully convinced was fruitless, you have thrown the affairs of this state into the hands of men totally unequal to them. I fondly hope and trust however that divine providence, will . . . restore you . . . to your country, to correct the errors, which I fear those "now bearing rule" will through ignorance—not intention—commit, in settling the form of government. . . .

> Consider, I beseech you and do justice to your "unkind countrymen." They did not desert you. You left them. Possibly they were wrong, in quickening their march and advancing to the goal with such rapid speed. They thought they were right, and the only "fury" they show'd against you was to chuse other leaders to conduct them.[158]

---

154. Dickinson to Thomson, Aug. 10, 1776, N.-Y. Hist. Soc., *Colls.*, XI: 31.

155. Dickinson to ?, Aug. 25, 1776, R. R. Logan Collection, HSP, page 2 (quotation). This nearly illegible four-page draft, which was perhaps never worked into a finished letter, reads like a private confession and apologia.

156. Joseph Reed to [Thomas Bradford?], Aug. 21, 1775, Reed Papers, N.-Y. Hist. Soc.; and "Joseph Reed's Narrative," N.-Y. Hist. Soc., *Colls.*, XI: 269–73 [1777–78?].

157. Charles Thomson to William Henry Drayton [1777–78?], N.-Y. Hist. Soc., *Colls.*, XI: 274–86, a refutation of "Joseph Reed's Narrative," written specifically to defend Dickinson.

158. Thomson to Dickinson, Aug. 16, 1776, "Five Letters from the Logan Papers in the Historical Society of Pennsylvania," *PMHB*, XXXV (1911): 500.

Thomson's judicious remarks to his old friend are an invaluable key to understanding the relationship between Pennsylvania's first and second Revolutions. The committees and their increasingly radical leaders were committed, above all else, to an effective resistance to British imperial authority. This commitment caused no problem so long as the Assembly also accepted the committee's goal. In 1776, however, Pennsylvania's lawmakers opposed independence. Given the dynamics of intercolonial cooperation, the increasingly zealous stance of the New England and southern colonies, and Great Britain's intransigence, Philadelphia's radicals and a growing number of Pennsylvanians had come to regard independence as the only safe policy for America. Still the Assembly chose to defend the status quo. Thus the Pennsylvania legislature's opposition to the Revolutionary tide led to a more total and vindictive destruction of the Constitution of 1701 than either independence or a republican government required.

The American Revolution and the Origin of Modern American Politics

Annuit coeptis novus ordo seclorum.[1]

CHARLES THOMSON
(after Virgil)

The American Revolution was not the first great upheaval of early modern times that historians have seen as revolutionary; the Dutch Revolt, the French Fronde, and particularly the English Civil War (now often called the English Revolution) all exhibited definite revolutionary aspects.[2] America's experience was the first to be labeled a revolution, in part, no doubt, because it was the first to establish political sovereignty formally in the people and to create a new set of integrative symbols and myths for its citizens. These observations are so readily apparent to the modern student of the Revolution that he may easily overlook the impact of the reality behind them upon the actors in that event.

In 1765, there was no revolutionary tradition for Americans to follow. Violent rebellions against oppressive rulers were well understood and heartily approved; so were constitutional coups against tyrannical institutions, such as England's "Glorious Revolution" of 1689. Nearly all colonists agreed with John Locke that men everywhere enjoyed a natural right to resist illegitimate political authority. But Americans did not know, in 1765 or, indeed, in 1775, what a revolution was, as their relative lack of interest in England's "revolution of the saints" in the 1640s demonstrates.[3] No one, before 1774, suggested drastically redesigning the

---

1. This motto was adapted from Virgil's famous fourth *Eclogue*, line 5, by Charles Thomson, secretary to Congress and an avid classical scholar, for the Great Seal of the United States (reproduced on every one-dollar bill). It translates: "In this year [1776] begins a new order of the ages."
2. See Forster and Greene, *Preconditions of Revolution in Early Modern Europe*.
3. The colonists did occasionally refer to Oliver Cromwell, and some ardent revolutionaries developed a good opinion of that regicide and his colleagues as America's quarrel with George III escalated. But whether colonial Americans approved of or despised Cromwell and his followers, they did not see them as revolutionaries, but as rebels. In a February 6, 1775 speech in the House of Commons a revolution was defined as a successful rebellion, and a rebellion as an unsuccessful revolution—by John Wilkes (*The Parliamentary History of England* ["Parliamentary Debates"], XVIII [London, 1813], p. 238). In 1775 this was a most sophisticated definition of revolution, which in itself suggests how little was thought or known about this species of social and political change before 1776.

polity in America; and no one, before 1776, suggested redefining the basis of political sovereignty. While it was well known that these things had been done in the ancient past, all assumed that such measures could not create a sound polity and encourage a harmonious society in their own day.

Thus the creators of the American Revolution transformed the American polity in the absence of a revolutionary tradition, which would begin only in 1776. This reality shaped everything the leaders of the resistance did in the early stages of the Revolution. It was harsh necessity that forced Samuel Adams, Charles Thomson, Christopher Gadsden, and countless more obscure radical leaders to experiment with men and institutions that might check Britain's new imperial policy.[4] In 1765, the American colonies had no extraconstitutional political institutions directed toward mobilizing the populace for political action: no committees, no leagues, no alliances or unions. Nearly every public leader and every public institution—executive, council, assembly, county commission, or town meeting—was a part, however imperfect, of the establishment, pledged to maintain the integrity of the British Empire. Not all established leaders and institutions remained in the establishment; in several provinces, both leaders and institutions defected to the standard of rebellion, and then to the cause of revolution. In many American colonies, however, the established order would not change. Here necessity forced more creative solutions upon the leaders of the resistance; it is in these colonies that one sees the American Revolution at its most revolutionary.

Several British North American colonies were more closely attached to the imperial establishment than Pennsylvania; perhaps no colony, however, was more resistant to change than this Quaker-dominated proprietary province. In the 1760s and early 1770s, Pennsylvania lacked nearly every ingredient for revolution found variously in the New England colonies and in Virginia: a strong dissenting tradition, widely felt economic grievances, or a legislature that was intimately acquainted with royal government.[5] Pennsylvanians felt imperial pressures, but their proprietary executive shielded them from the full force of new British policies for several years and, perhaps more important, led them to believe that problems with their executive were primarily a function of proprietary government and not of empire. Their provincial legislature, while increasingly unhappy with the deepening imperial crisis, ruled out direct confrontation with royal authority for a decade. Confrontation was incompatible with Quaker principles of nonresistance, which powerfully shaped the lawmakers' worldview, directly through the Society of Friends to which so many of them belonged, and indirectly through the tenacious

---

4. I am not trying to suggest here that Americans did not become republicans in 1776 by rational, conscious choice; Pauline Maier has argued the case for this consciousness persuasively in *From Resistance to Revolution,* chap. 9. I do believe, however, that the colonists' range of plausible choices was quite limited in 1776. More to the point here, however, is the fact that in 1776 no one knew what it meant to establish a republic based on the sovereignty of the people, which is simply another way of saying that no one knew what a revolution was. Perhaps significantly, the first occurrence that I have found of the word "revolution" in Philadelphia's political literature, used in a present rather than in a historical sense, is in the essay "To the People," in the June 26, 1776, *Pennsylvania Gazette,* wherein the author declared: "The revolution is now began, and must be supported."

5. Pennsylvania's Quakers were dissenters, but because of their pacifism their dissent could not present so sharp a challenge to the established order of the British Empire as did the dissent of the Calvinist denominations.

and widespread influence of Pennsylvania's Quaker culture. And for the assembly-men, even more than for their constituents, the Penns had become the symbol of threatening outside authority.

In this political culture, it was only natural that most leaders of the early resistance to British policy were not radicals. These men were not dedicated to changing the structure of the imperial bond to restore violated American rights; they were reformers committed to making minor alterations in the imperial system to repair damaged American interests.[6] In 1765 and again in 1769, it was these leaders, Philadelphia's powerful Quaker and proprietary merchants, who possessed the most evident political talents and the greatest capacity for organization. It was to them that the whole community—young merchants, professionals, and mechanics of all nationalities and creeds—looked for guidance in securing reform in imperial taxation and commercial regulation. Those young zealots who felt the need for broader and deeper reforms in the imperial connection were few; in 1768 William Bradford, John Dickinson, and Charles Thomson seemed to be the whole radical faction.

It was the necessity imposed by adversity, the discouragement and defeat of the summer of 1770, which permanently altered the character of Philadelphia politics. In 1770 the major merchants, heretofore well organized behind one common interest, broke into two factions, one attacking and the other defending continued nonimportation to secure the repeal of the tea tax, the last remaining Townshend duty. The conservative boycott-breakers won this struggle, but the conflict destroyed the political reputation of the mercantile class within the community. By late September 1770, most politically active Philadelphians, especially young merchants, mechanics, Anglicans, and Presbyterians, no longer looked to the city's conservative elder merchants for leadership. If they were to resist British authority again, Philadelphians would need new leaders and institutions, and a new set of connections between those new leaders and the community they served.

In Philadelphia, then, and probably elsewhere, the "quiet period" was a time for recovering from the worst defeat suffered by the colonies in the course of resisting British policy.[7] As this period began, the outlook was bleak for those who feared renewed imperial oppression. Conservative merchants were in ill repute, while the radicals had never enjoyed wide political influence. It was from this unpromising beginning that Charles Thomson and his merchant and mechanic friends put together a powerful resistance movement in just four years. They were greatly aided by harsh British measures and by the determination of colonies to the north and south to resist British authority. Fundamentally, however, they had to build up the resistance movement on their own, and here one must consider the central role of local political mobilization in the coming of the American Revolution.

---

6. This is a central theme in Schlesinger, *Colonial Merchants.*

7. I call the collapse of the nonimportation movement the colonies' worst setback because it was the only event between 1765 and Independence that made the colonists confused, divided, and resentful against one another. Further, I am convinced that the picture of a resistance movement growing steadily in power and unity from 1765 to 1776, most recently argued by Pauline Maier, *From Resistance to Revolution,* simply flies in the face of copious testimony, from the radicals themselves as well as from British customs records, that America lost its first round with Lord North (even more clearly in Boston than in Philadelphia), and that American radicals knew that they had lost.

As late as May 1774, every American lived in an intensely localized world. His vision seldom extended beyond his town or county to his province; even more rarely did it reach to other provinces. And while powerful cultural forces had been at work to integrate the continental colonies for a generation,[8] recent resistance efforts had done little to further this process. The immediate result of the collapse of the Townshend Act boycotts in 1770 had been an outburst of recrimination in each major port against the inhabitants of other ports, and many Philadelphians were still wary of intercolonial cooperation in 1774 because of the debacle of 1770. Moreover, as late as the Coercive Acts, there were few symbols or institutions to which all Americans could look with pride. Dr. Franklin and John Dickinson, the celebrated "Pennsylvania Farmer," came closest to filling this role personally, but Franklin had been in England for a decade, and in the early 1770s John Dickinson began to act as if he might drop out of the resistance movement at any moment.

The insularity of colonial America's tiny communities threw a great burden upon a few active resistance leaders in each locality. These men could count on both British policies and radical political pamphlets to generate anger against London and supply good Whiggish reasons for rebellion, but neither distant events nor carefully reasoned essays could generate intense loyalties to any plan of action. Only local men, known and respected at the local level, could do this. Philadelphia's radical organizers quickly realized that recruiting new resistance leaders who were particularly well known in the several neighborhoods and among the several classes or subcommunities that made up their large community would strengthen the entire city's commitment to oppose British authority.

This perception and the particular social structure of Philadelphia together explain why the coming of the Revolution in that city saw a birth of modern American politics. Philadelphia before 1765 was a pluralistic community in which political power was concentrated in a few of its many ethnic, religious, and economic groups. In the next decade, the city was assaulted by an outside power that its political and mercantile elites neither would nor could check. In the course of building a broadly based political movement that could counter British authority in the early 1770s, Philadelphia's radical leaders created the prototype of a modern American urban party.

Philadelphia's resistance movement differed from a modern urban party in several ways. It had no professional politicians, almost no treasury, and only insignificant civil service and public contract resources. It lacked any local opposition that possessed more than a fraction of its own strength. But the fundamentals were there: the resistance committee system was oriented toward mass politics; its representation was by neighborhood or ward, by ethnic-religious group, by occupation, and by relative economic standing. On each index it was radically inclusive by the standards of its day. In just three years, from the tea affair to Independence, Philadelphia's committee movement broadened the leadership base of the city's politics by a factor of several times, thereby generating an intense identification with the cause of the resistance among heretofore ignored nationalities, creeds, and occupational classes. This process produced some of the earliest

---

8. See, for example, Max Savelle, *The Seeds of Liberty: The Genesis of the American Mind* (1948); and Richard Merritt, *Symbols of American Community, 1735–1775* (1966).

pluralistic ticket balancing in urban American politics. In preparing an effective resistance to British power, Philadelphia's revolutionaries first learned that a pluralistic city becomes an effective political community only when its political institutions incorporate its pluralism.

The same fundamental principles underlying the new urban politics in Philadelphia soon extended to a new system of state politics throughout Pennsylvania, but with one important addition. The common denominator among Philadelphia's committeemen, as among the adherents to the new state and then national parties that would follow Independence, was not wealth, occupation, creed, or nationality, but commitment to a central policy or idea. In the resistance movement, through 1775, the unifying idea among politically active Philadelphians of diverse interests and beliefs was a commitment to oppose British authority by the most effective means at hand at any given time, regardless of immediate risks to the fortunes, and ultimately the lives, of the city's many individual leaders.

For several years after the collapse of the Townshend Act boycott, this new radical movement did not face any strong, coherent local opposition. As the resistance moved toward independence and constitutional reform, however, both of these issues, but especially the latter, generated a more cohesive opposition. One student of early American politics has argued that Pennsylvania produced the first two modern parties in the new nation, because all of its citizens divided over the merits of the new ultrademocratic Constitution of 1776.[9] This suggests that the cohesion needed to put together state-wide political parties was initially generated by fundamental divisions over public policy that no concerned citizen could ignore. The development of such a division in Pennsylvania dates from the conversion of the resistance movement to democratic constitutional reform in the spring of 1776, which in turn produced an elitist, antidemocratic (but not antirepublican) party committed to preserving the provincial constitution nearly intact.

Thus Philadelphia's revolutionary committee movement, and the allied militia movement of 1775–76, unwittingly created the foundations of a durable, competitive, two-party system organized around strong commitments to public goals that concerned all active citizens. Both this pluralism and this commitment begin to explain the fundamental difference between Pennsylvania's Quaker party-proprietary faction battles of the 1750s and early 1760s, and the Constitutionalist-Republican campaigns of the 1780s. Before the Revolution, stable but narrow political elites contended over issues that did not vitally affect most Pennsylvanians (the brief royalization contest in the spring and summer of 1764 was something of an exception to this rule). After the Revolution, mass-oriented parties fought not only to hold office and frame public policy, but to secure the power to say what public offices would exist, who would fill them, and who would vote for those who filled them. American politics has adopted two cardinal rules which Philadelphia's resistance leaders discovered in the course of opposing British authority in the 1770s: appeal to every influential subcommunity within the larger community, and find broad, central issues on which diverse citizens will unite.

---

9. Chambers, *Political Parties,* p. 19. Pennsylvania's two parties were probably not the first in America, however. Rhode Island exhibited some signs of a genuine two-party system even before the Revolution, and New York also showed modern party phenomena in the 1780s.

Pluralistic representation and ideological commitment, however, explain only a part of the difference between politics in pre- and post-Revolutionary Pennsylvania. Each of these central features of modern American politics became operative in the 1770s through fundamental changes in the concept of representation which sharply altered the purpose of elections and the nature of the connection between officeholders and the electorate. In British North America's two largest colonies, Massachusetts and Virginia, most adult white males could vote long before the Revolution—and hardly anyone else could vote before the twentieth century. This was undoubtedly true in some other colonies as well; it was certainly true in Pennsylvania, although perhaps not in Philadelphia.[10] At the same time, the concept of political representation before the Revolution was quite different from the modern American idea of representation, both in Pennsylvania and in all other colonies. It was not the purpose of elections in colonial America to select the most popular men for office, or to involve the freemen in the political life of the community, or even to encourage public officials to discuss public policy in an open forum.[11] The fundamental purpose of pre-Revolutionary elections was to allow the freemen to choose, from among two or more contenders who were in effect nominated by their social position, the morally superior candidate. This was essential if the people were to have any protection against possible abuse by their rulers.[12] Voting, then, was a check upon unfit candidates and overbearing magistrates; it was not a means for effecting public policy. For this reason, challengers felt no obligation either to discuss public issues or to explain to the voters their conception of the public good. And incumbents felt no obligation to defend their records in office.

In several of the new states, the Revolution did not immediately transform the old predemocratic politics, but in Pennsylvania that event effected sudden alterations of the greatest importance, both in the mechanics and in the purpose of elections. Pennsylvania was the only new state to extend its already fairly liberal franchise to large numbers of humbler citizens: under the Constitution of 1776, Pennsylvanians enjoyed the broadest franchise of any large polity in the world.[13] Moreover, where Pennsylvania's provincial elections had been only sporadically

---

10. Brown, *Middle-Class Democracy,* and Brown and Brown, *Virginia: Democracy or Aristocracy?* present the definitive argument for a democratic franchise in colonial America. On the percentage of adult white males who could vote in rural Pennsylvania and in Philadelphia, see chapter 1, note 7 above.

11. A partial exception to this may have been town-meeting democracy in New England. The purpose of that system of government, from 1630, certainly was to involve the entire community in the political decisions of the town. Here too, however, the traditions of political and social deference were still strong. Moreover, as Zuckerman has shown (*Peaceable Kingdoms*), as late as 1776 the participants in town meeting democracy were deeply hostile to any decisions made by a simple majority, and the acceptance of this principle is fundamental to modern democratic practice.

12. See Sydnor, *Gentlemen Freeholders*; Bushman, *From Puritan to Yankee, Character and Social Order in Connecticut, 1690–1765* (1967), esp. p. 268; and Buel, "Democracy and the American Revolution," pp. 165–90. The phrase "morally superior candidate" refers, of course, primarily to a candidate's honesty, integrity, and civic morality, which in the eighteenth century was the largest part of the sphere of moral behavor.

13. The Constitution of 1776 declared that all free males of twenty-one years of age who had joined the militia, paid taxes, and lived in Pennsylvania for one year could vote. This could have raised the franchise from some 50–75 percent to 90 percent in rural areas, and from less than 50 to 90 percent in Philadelphia, depending on how many poor young men chose to join the militia. No other new American state in 1776, and no European nation, had provided a way for propertyless, wage-earning men to vote.

contested, its state elections were often fierce battles for power. In 1771, seven out of eight Pennsylvania assemblymen who wished to retire from public life were kept to their tasks by satisfied voters; between 1776 and the mid-1780s, whole county slates of candidates, publicly pledged to defend or to attack the new constitution, moved frequently in and out of the legislature.[14] This remarkable rise in electoral contention is directly related to a fundamental change in the idea of representation in Revolutionary Pennsylvania. It was now accepted, by both parties, that elections were no longer held to weigh the integrity and civic virtue of various candidates, but to elect those candidates who were explicitly committed to certain positions on the major public issues of the day.

Pennsylvania's democratic revolution, which in company with the new politics of other radicalized states would gradually spread over the entire nation in the course of the next two generations, grew directly out of Philadelphia's electoral committee politics. That local revolution had its formal birth on November 12, 1774. In the election held on that day, voters were faced with two slates of candidates of sharply different character. At issue were the public records of many candidates on both slates, and the sentiments of all candidates on the Congress, nonimportation, and other central themes of the resistance. The sole purpose of that election was to effect a particular public policy—a casual or a vigorous enforcement of nonimportation; a cautious or a venturesome defense of America's liberties within the British Empire. The committee tickets of 1774 and 1775, which were the means for conducting vital referenda of this kind, immediately created directly competitive political factions organized around contrasting approaches to the imperial crisis. In 1776 this process accelerated, as first independence and then constitutional reform divided Philadelphians and all Pennsylvanians into two distinct camps. By the fall of that year, two parties had formed, announced their positions on the new constitution, engaged in public debate, and nominated slates of committed candidates. The candidates, of both parties, were nearly all veterans of committee politics and had run in similar competitive elections since 1774.

By the fall of 1776, Pennsylvania's committee movement had completed the fundamental transformation of Pennsylvania politics. In 1765, Philadelphians had asked of their nonimportation committeemen (for whom they had not voted) only that they be honest, energetic, and dedicated to a vaguely defined public interest. In 1776—in the February committee election, the Assembly by-election in May, the July convention election, and the October–November Assembly elections—both Philadelphians and rural Pennsylvanians demanded more of those who would hold public office. Each candidate was asked to support one plan of public action and to associate with other candidates who supported that same plan on one common ticket. By 1776 all politically active Pennsylvanians had accepted, however unwillingly, that political practice which all colonists had been taught to abhor: the direct use of elections to effect positive changes in public policy. Representation in America would never again be the same.

These fundamental alterations in the process, style, and purpose of electoral politics argue that in Pennsylvania the American Revolution was a classic political revolution. Yet these changes were only one part of the transformation the Revo-

---

14. *Pa. Gaz.,* Sept. 26, 1771; *Votes and Proceedings,* VIII, 6724; *Journals of the House of Representatives of the Commonwealth of Pennsylvania* (Philadelphia, 1782).

lution worked in America. One student of comparative revolutionary phenomena has proposed a simple yet comprehensive definition of revolution, against which one may measure the American event. Eugene Kamenka has written: "Revolution is a sharp, sudden change in the social location of political power, expressing itself in the radical transformation of the process of government, of the official foundations of sovereignty or legitimacy and of the conception of the social order."[15]

A comparison of this convenient formula with both the extended argument presented in the foregoing chapters and recent work done on the Revolution by several scholars suggests that the years 1765–76 saw a genuine revolution in Pennsylvania. Taking Mr. Kamenka's points in a somewhat different order, two of the most persuasive studies of the Revolution to appear in the last decade argue that Americans effected a "radical transformation . . . of the official foundations of sovereignty" in their Revolution.[16] Second, it is a major part of the argument in every chapter of this study, and of this concluding essay, that Pennsylvania experienced a "radical transformation of the process of government" in the decade before Independence.

Closely related to changes in both political sovereignty and political process is another fundamental political alteration with which the American Revolution is often not credited, "a sharp, sudden change in the social location of political power." Much recent scholarship, however, has effectively challenged the long-presumed lack of change in the social locus of political power in Revolutionary America.[17] There appears to be no basis for doubting the occurrence of this alteration in Pennsylvania. It has been a major objective of the foregoing analysis, and especially of the quantitative study of committee leadership in both the earlier and later stages of the resistance, to show that the Revolution in Pennsylvania was the creation—and the creator—of new political men. Hundreds of Philadelphians and nearly a thousand rural Pennsylvanians who would not have had the slightest notion—or the slightest opportunity—of serving the public in other times either were pulled in or rushed in to take leading roles in the resistance movement. These men were younger, less affluent, and far less socially prominent than those few figures who had run the small, slow-paced provincial government of colonial Pennsylvania. As soon as one dips below the highly visible level of Pennsylvania's Revolutionary leadership, the Congress and the Assembly, one sees the province's new men—new in origins, in vitality, and in sheer numbers. Pennsylvania's "sudden change in the social location of political power" destroyed forever the old mercantile and Quaker elites of both city and province, and transferred the greater part of both official and effective political power to an aggressive, rising, pluralistic middle class.

Pennsylvania, then, through a radical transformation in its processes of government and in the foundations of its sovereignty, experienced that swift alteration in the social bases of political power that marks a political revolution. Moreover, as the revolutionary transformation became broader and deeper in Pennsylvania, it

---

15. Kamenka, ed., *A World in Revolution?* p. 6.

16. Bailyn, *Ideological Origins,* chap. 5; Wood, *Creation of the American Republic.*

17. See especially Jackson Turner Main, *Political Parties before the Constitution*; and "Government by the People: The American Revolution and the Democratization of the Legislatures," *WMQ,* 3d Ser., XXIII (1966): 391–407.

began to generate spirited opposition. The resulting internal conflict quickly created powerful political passions with strong social overtones. In Pennsylvania, and elsewhere, this led to a widespread demand for a recasting of the relationship between the political and the social order, as many of the new men entering public life began to attack not only arbitrary power but all public recognition of social privilege.[18] And with the arming of the community in 1775, zealous young leaders increasingly took the position that the primary test of a man's worth should not be his birth, his wealth, or his education, but his commitment to the cause of resistance, and then of independence and constitutional reform.

As this sharp challenge to the practice of both social and political deference accelerated in Pennsylvania and in other colonies in 1776, its specific social overtones became unmistakable. At the height of the "wordy war" for independence in Philadelphia, one writer asked: "Do not mechanicks and farmers constitute ninety-nine out of a hundred of the people of America? If these, by their occupations, are to be excluded from having any share in the choice of their rulers, or forms of government, would it not be best to acknowledge the jurisdiction of the British Parliament, which is composed entirely of GENTLEMEN? Is not half the property in the city of Philadelphia owned by men who wear LEATHERN APRONS? Does not the other half belong to men whose fathers or grandfathers wore LEATHERN APRONS?"[19] This revolt against privilege, this demand for a new "conception of the social order," culminated in the radically democratic Pennsylvania Constitution of 1776.

The Revolutionary movement in Pennsylvania probably had the strength and momentum to achieve independence eventually, without either the militia controversy or the conservative opposition to independence that triggered radical outbursts against the traditional social order. British policy alone was probably sufficient to drive Pennsylvania out of the empire. But after 1775, the Revolution in Pennsylvania cannot be understood simply as a resistance movement against British authority that drew many new men into public life. From the summer of that year, the rising demand for a new conception of the social order, soon to be expressed in new democratic processes of government, was an indispensable factor in the pacing, the depth, and the results of Pennsylvania's Revolution.

Two elements were crucial in transforming Pennsylvania's resistance movement of 1774 into an intense and thorough political revolution in 1776. The more visible of these is the keen resentment of two closely allied groups of men who were frustrated by the conservative policies of the established government. The rank-and-file militiamen saw themselves patronized and scorned by an Assembly that intended to rob them of their personal independence and patriotic virtue by making them a mercenary force. The military associators were determined to secure full and honorable support for military service, through the Assembly if possible, around it if necessary. In a similar position of impotent frustration were the committeemen, militia officers, and freelance radical organizers who sought independence from Great Britain. Outraged by the Assembly's refusal to allow Pennsylvania's congressmen to consider leaving the British Empire, a refusal they regarded as pure treason to the safety of the community, the Independents organ-

---

18. For this change generally in the colonies, see Bailyn, *Ideological Origins,* chap. 6; and Wood, *Creation of the American Republic,* pp. 83–90, and chaps. 10, 12.

19. "Queries . . . to . . . Cato," Mar. 14, 1776, *Pa. Evening Post.*

ized radical forces throughout the province to destroy the authority of the legislature and thoroughly reform its organization.

A second characteristic of these revolutionaries is often overlooked, but it was equally critical in creating Pennsylvania's constitutional revolution and in generating the decade of strife that followed. This was the great number of men involved in the resistance. Between 1774 and 1776, over one thousand Pennsylvanians entered public life. They stepped forward because they wanted to serve their community; their ideology had taught them that every good patriot had a keen desire to help lead his country and save it from all harm. And many, no doubt, wanted to stay on even after Independence to enjoy their new-found power and the excitement of public service. Most establishment officeholders, however, had no wish to relinquish their power. These swarms of aggressive men, fighting to gain or struggling to retain the ultimate authority of the state, were the makings of an explosive and continuing revolution.

Viewed from this perspective, the American Revolution was a seminal event in world history, not because it proclaimed the right of revolution, but because it developed the ideological, governmental, and popular means to bring about a revolution. The American Revolution mobilized tens of thousands of ordinary men in hundreds of communities, large and small, to change both the political and the social order and thereby create the local ingredients for a modern political party system. In this way the Revolution quite altered the character of the liberal constitutional state. It also demonstrated that massive political mobilization could readily generate the powerful patriotic emotions that became the foundation of modern nationalism. Such extensive political mobilization and intense identification with a secular cause was new in Western history, and immediately made all existing theories of political science partial or obsolete.[20]

This mobilization, begun in a thousand taverns, streets, squares, and fields throughout the colonies, led directly to the American Revolution's fundamental achievement—the establishment, upon the basis of sovereignty in the people and through the medium of organic law, of the principle of majoritarian democracy. It has been persuasively argued that the great contribution of the American Revolution to the Western political tradition was to establish the people as the "constituent power."[21] This achievement, however, was not possible until America's revolutionaries had first secured participatory, majoritarian democracy as the fundamental principle of American political life. The ideological origins of this concept may be traced back to ancient Athens, but its realization in America is due to a few hundred committeemen, militia leaders, and propagandists in Philadelphia, and thousands of committeemen and local leaders throughout the colonies, who created the American Revolution. In the political world, as the Philadelphia radicals' old master Charles Thomson would soon tell them, 1776 saw "the beginning of a new order of the ages."

20. For a summary of the founding fathers' awareness of how fundamentally they had altered the Western political tradition through their new concept of representation, see Wood, *Creation of the American Republic,* pp. 593–615. In 1816, Thomas Jefferson wrote, "The introduction of this new principle of representative democracy has rendered useless almost everything written before on the structure of government" (quoted in Wood, p. 565).

21. Robert R. Palmer, *The Age of the Democratic Revolution: A Political History of Europe and America, 1760–1800,* Vol. I, *The Challenge* (1959), pp. 213–35.

Appendixes

APPENDIX A

Turnover in Pennsylvania Assembly Membership 1704–80

Year	Members not in Previous Session	Change	Year	Members not in Previous Session	Change
1704	16	62%	1743	4	13%
1705	16	62	1744	2	7
1706	21	81	1745	5	17
1707	5	19	1746	6	20
1708	8	31	1747	4	13
1709	7	27	1748	4	13
1710	26	100	1749[a]	14	44
1711	15	58	1750	8	25
1712	18	69	1751[a]	9	26
1713	17	65	1752[a]	10	29
1714	12	46	1753[a]	6	17
1715	15	58	1754	2	6
1716	18	69	1755	6	17
1717	20	77	1756	15	42
1718	15	58	1757	8	22
1719	14	54	1758	7	19
1720	9	35	1759	4	11
1721	14	54	1760	9	25
1722	8	31	1761	9	25
1723	16	62	1762	7	19
1724	5	19	1763	6	17
1725	8	31	1764	10	28
1726	9	35	1765	9	25
1727	8	31	1766	5	14
1728	5	19	1767	9	25
1729[a]	13	43	1768	5	14
1730	11	37	1769	2	6
1731	10	33	1770	8	22
1732	9	30	1771[a]	5	13
1733	8	27	1772[a]	12	31
1734	9	30	1773[a]	7	18
1735	8	27	1774	8	20
1736	4	13	1775[a]	10	24
1737	7	23	1776[a]	65	90
1738	10	33	1777	36	50
1739	11	37	1778	42	58
1740	4	13	1779	44	61
1741	4	13	1780	43	60
1742	0	0			

a. In these years the House expanded, from 26 to 30 seats in 1729, to 32 seats in 1749, 34 seats in 1751, 35 seats in 1752, 36 seats in 1753, 38 seats in 1771, 39 seats in 1772, 40 seats in 1773, 41 seats in 1775, and 72 seats in 1776. The new occupants of newly created seats are here counted in with new occupants of old seats.

APPENDIX B

Members of the Pennsylvania Assembly, October 1773–September 1774 Session

(See Table of Symbols, p. xi)

	Age in 1774	District and Home Town	Terms Served[a]	Occupation	Religion	Wealth[b] (Tax Assessment or Acreage)
Allen, William	70	Cumberland, Philadelphia	1730–39; 1756–75	merchant, lawyer	P	£780
Bartholomew, Benjamin	22	Chester, East Whiteland	1772–75	farmer	B	150 acres
Biddle, Edward	36	Berks, Reading	1767–75	lawyer	A?	£14
Brown, John	50	Bucks, Falls	1767–75	farmer	(Q)	300 acres
Chapman, Benjamin	?	Bucks, Wrights Town	1758, 1766–75	?	(Q)	3½ acres
Chreist, Henry	?	Berks, Reading	1771–75	?	?	£10.14.4 and 2½ lots
Edmonds, William	?	Northampton, Plainfield	1755, 1770–74	farmer	Moravian?	170 acres
Ellicott, Joseph	ca. 44	Bucks, Solebury	1770–73	miller	Q	?
Ewing, James[c]	38	York, ?	1771–75	farmer	?	162 acres, or 650 acres
Ferree, Joseph	?	Lancaster, Pequea?	1770–74	?	FR	?
Foulke, John	56	Bucks, Richland	1769–75	farmer	Q	140 acres
Franklin, Benjamin[d]	68	City of Philadelphia	1751–63, 1773, 1775	public servant	Deist	£330

a. Given by year of election. Terms ran from October to September. Thus all those listed as serving through 1775 were in the House through September 1776, except Benjamin Franklin, who resigned in February 1776, and Thomas Mifflin, who resigned in November 1775.
b. Acres or town lots owned and/or town and city tax assessments (1774 tax).
c. Identification uncertain.
d. Franklin was living in London for the entire 1773–74 legislative session. All other members attended most debates.

APPENDIX B—Continued

	Age in 1774	District and Home Town	Terms Served[a]	Occupation	Religion	Wealth[b] (Tax Assessment or Acreage)
Galloway, Joseph	44	Bucks, Bensalem	1756–63, 1765–74	lawyer	A?, formerly Q	2,300 acres (Bucks), and £197 (Philadelphia)
Gibbons, James	?	Chester, West Town	1773–75	farmer, miller	(Q)	375 acres
Gray, George	48	Philadelphia Co., Kingsessing	1772–75	ferry-owner	A	£389
Hillegas, Michael	45	Philadelphia Co., Philadelphia	1765–75	merchant	A	£140
Humphreys, Charles	62	Chester, Haverford	1763–75	miller, farmer	(Q)	100 acres
Hunter, Samuel	?	Northumberland, Augusta	1772–75	?	?	?
Jacobs, Israel	ca. 45–50?	Philadelphia Co., Providence	1770–75	farmer?	Q	£13
Jacobs, John	52	Chester, West Whiteland	1762–75	farmer	Q	700 acres
Krewson, Henry	44 or older	Bucks, Southampton	1762–73	farmer	P?	239 acres
Mifflin, Thomas	33	City of Philadelphia	1772–75	merchant	Q	£83
Miles, Samuel	34	Philadelphia Co., Whitemarsh	1773, 1775	merchant	B	£105
Minshall, John	?	Chester, Middletown	1766–73	farmer	(Q)	359 acres

Members of the Pennsylvania Assembly, October 1773–September 1774 Session

(See Table of Symbols, p. xi)

	Age in 1774	District and Home Town	Terms Served[a]	Occupation	Religion	Wealth[b] (Tax Assessment or Acreage)
Montgomery, John	?	Cumberland, Carlisle	1763–75	?	P	?
Morton, John	ca. 50	Chester, Ridley	1756–66, 1769–75	farmer	A	160 acres
Parker, Joseph	?	Philadelphia Co., Philadelphia	1770–1775	tailor?	Q	£35
Pawling, Henry	?	Philadelphia Co., Providence	1751(?), 1764–74	farmer	?	390 acres (?), £72 (?)
Pearson, Isaac	?	Chester, Darby	1761–75	farmer	(Q)	80 acres
Pennock, Joseph	?	Chester, East Marlborough	1773–75	farmer	Q	200 acres
Pope, John	?	York, Tyrone(?)	1772–73	farmer	?	259 acres
Rhoads, Samuel	63	Philadelphia Co., Philadelphia	1761–63, 1770–74	builder	Q	£389
Roberts, Jonathan	?	Philadelphia Co., Upper Merion	1772–75	farmer	Q	300 acres, £25
Rodman, William	?	Bucks, Bensalem	1763–75	farmer	(Q)	280 acres
Ross, George	44	Lancaster, Lancaster	1768–71, 1773–75	lawyer	A	£4.15.0
Shepherd, Peter	?	Bucks, ?	1764–73	?	?	?
Slough, Matthias	?	Lancaster, Lancaster	1773–75	tavern-owner	A	£3.0.0
Thompson, William	?	Westmoreland, Cumberland Valley	1771–75	?	?	300 acres (1779)
Webb, James	?	Lancaster, Lancaster Township	1772–75	innkeeper	(Q)	50 acres
Woods, George	?	Bedford, Bedford	1773	surveyor	P	£0.16.3

APPENDIX C

Members of the 1773–74 Assembly Session: Seniority and Standing Committee Assignments[a]

Assemblymen elected before the royalization campaign, 1756–63

Allen,[b] 1756–, minutes
Galloway,[c] 1756–, speaker, minutes, correspondence
Morton,[d] 1756–, minutes, correspondence
Pearson, 1761–, audit, correspondence
Krewson, 1762–

J. Jacobs, 1762–
Humphreys, 1763–, grievances
Montgomery, 1763–
Rodman, 1763–, correspondence

Assemblymen elected between the royalization campaign and the collapse of the Townshend Act boycott, 1764–69

Pawling,[e] 1764–
Shepherd, 1764–
Hillegas, 1765–, audit
Chapman,[f] 1766–, audit
Minshall, 1766–

Biddle, 1767–, grievances
Brown, 1767–
Ross,[g] 1768–, grievances
Foulke, 1769–, grievances

Assemblymen elected after the collapse of the Townshend Act boycott, 1770–73

Ferree, 1770–
I. Jacobs, 1770–
Parker, 1770–, grievances
Rhoads,[h] 1770–, audit, minutes, correspondence
Chreist, 1771–
Ewing, 1771–
Bartholomew, 1772–, grievances
Edmonds,[i] 1772–, grievances
Ellicott, 1772–
Gray, 1772–
Hunter, 1772–

Mifflin, 1772–, audit, correspondence, grievances
Pope, 1772–
Roberts, 1772–
Thompson, 1772–
Webb, 1772–
Franklin,[j] 1773
Gibbons, 1773
Miles, 1773, audit, correspondence, grievances
Pennock, 1773
Slough, 1773, grievances
Woods, 1773

a. Several members missed some terms between their first election and 1773. Wherever a member missed only one or two terms, I have listed him in the order of his first election. Where he missed three or more terms, the date of his resuming office is used.

Quakers in good standing, men of Quaker background, and men probably of Quaker background are italicized.

b. Allen also served 1730–39.
c. Galloway did not serve 1764–65.
d. Morton did not serve 1767–68 or 1768–69.
e. A Henry Pawling, perhaps the same man, served 1751–52.
f. A Benjamin Chapman also served 1758–59.
g. Ross did not serve 1772–73.
h. Rhoads also served 1761–64.
i. A William Edmonds also served 1755–56.
j. Franklin also served 1751–64.

APPENDIX D

Merchants' Committee Appointed in November, 1765

(See Table of Symbols, p. xi)

Member	Age in 1765	Occupation	Religion	1774 Tax Assessment	1769 Tax Assessment
Chevalier, Peter	34	merchant, distiller	P	£10	£23
Fisher, Joshua	58	merchant	Q	325	143
Fisher, William	52	merchant	Q	160	117
Fuller, Benjamin		merchant	?	57	43
Howell, Samuel		merchant	Q[disowned]	150	197
James, Abel	ca. 45	merchant	Q	240	330
Mifflin, Samuel	41	merchant	Q	229	283
Montgomery, Thomas		merchant, shopkeeper	P		?
Rhea, John	35	merchant	P	?	22
Wharton, Samuel	33	merchant	Q	?	17
Willing, Thomas	34	merchant	A	533	1,032

APPENDIX E

Retailers' Committee Appointed in November, 1765

Member	Age in 1765	Occupation	Religion	1774 Tax Assessment
Bartram, George, Sr.	31	dry goods merchant	A?	£27
Charles, Valentine		?	?	?
Deane, Joseph	27	merchant	P	22
Deshler, David		shopkeeper	Q	79
Doz, Andrew	38	merchant	A	146
Hunter, James[a]		merchant or tallow chandler	P	47 or 19
Ord, John	47	notary public, merchant	A	40
Paschall, Thomas		merchant, hatter	Q	50
Schlosser, George	51	shopkeeper, tanner	L	65
Wade, Francis	ca. 30?	brewer	A	10
West, Thomas		shopkeeper, cordwainer	A?	10

a. There were at least two James Hunters in Philadelphia who could have filled this post.

APPENDIX F

"Joseph Reed's Narrative," Charles Thomson's Letter to William Henry Drayton, and Philadelphia Politics, 1774

For a close understanding of patriot personalities and strategies in the period 1773–76, and especially for May 1774, the two most important narrative sources are "Joseph Reed's Narrative" and Charles Thomson's letter to William Henry Drayton. Reed's account was composed sometime between the fall of 1776 and 1778, and probably toward the end of this period. Thomson's, which shortly followed it, was written in 1777 or 1778. Neither was published for a century thereafter (N.-Y. Hist. Soc., *Colls.* XI [1878]: 269–86).

Although the two narratives disagree on several minor details, they contradict one another sharply only in their respective assessments of the roles that Reed, Thomson, Mifflin, and Dickinson played in the resistance movement. Reed's account is very critical of Dickinson, consistently portraying him as a conservative-to-moderate figure who was constantly hindering the efforts of the radical activists. Reed assigns the role of key radical leader to himself. Mifflin becomes an unsteady supporter who at the last minute declines to speak at the May 20, 1774 meeting. And Thomson is described as merely an important aide to Reed.

Thomson addressed his account of 1773–76 to the South Carolina congressman and Reed opponent William Henry Drayton, with the explicit intention of defending Dickinson, his closest friend, from the charges of Reed's "Narrative," which Drayton had somehow received and showed to Thomson. Thomson's version of the coming of the Revolution in Pennsylvania is the most valuable contemporary account of that event now extant. It is considerably longer and more detailed than Reed's, although it is not without occasional inaccuracies and chronological obscurities. Thomson states that in May 1774 he was the first leader to plan a show of opposition to the Boston Port Act. He further claims that he persuaded Dickinson to write against British policy even before Revere arrived in Philadelphia with the letters of appeal from Boston, and that he asked Reed and Mifflin to join him on May 20 in a visit to Dickinson's home. Moreover, Thomson pictures his own resistance activities as extensive, beginning in the fall of 1773, and says that the outcome of the May 20 meeting was very much as he had planned.

There is no directly corroborating evidence for either of the two pieces, but the present writer has followed Thomson rather than Reed for three reasons. First, Reed's narrative is really little more than a polemic against John Dickinson, with whom Reed was at odds both personally and politically. The two leaders had had a serious falling out in the summer of 1776, which apparently remained a source of bitterness for both men (see Dickinson to ?, Elizabethtown, New Jersey, Aug. 25, 1776 [draft], R. R. Logan Collection, HSP); and in the period 1777–78 Reed was the leader of the radical Constitutionalists, who defended Pennsylvania's Constitution of 1776, while Dickinson had become the leader of the moderate Republicans. It seems likely, therefore, that Reed's "Narrative" is a product of the raging propaganda battle between the two factions. Second, on the basis of both Reed's career and his private letters we know him to have been an occasionally ambivalent patriot. A man who could, in fairly rapid succession, take on conservative and then radical roles, Reed was even more tortured and indecisive in his private expressions than in his public acts and statements. Thomson's career, in contrast, manifests a remarkable consistency from late 1765 until his retirement from public life in 1789, a consistency strongly echoed in his private and even in his secret writings. Finally, all of the evidence from this period points to Thomson, not Reed, as the foremost organizer of Philadelphia's resistance efforts at every stage until

September 1774, when he was drawn away from local politics by his appointment as Secretary to the Continental Congress.

Thomson's letter to Drayton does, however, present two important analytical problems. The first is his very favorable treatment of Dickinson. Here Thomson smoothly glosses over his good friend's strong reservations about involving himself in the resistance in 1774. John Adams records a brief anecdote which presents a very different image of Dickinson, and which Thomson himself related to Adams. This incident may well have occurred around May 20, 1774, although it could have happened as late as June 1775. Adams wrote in his *Autobiography* that

> Mr. Charles Thompson [sic], . . . told me, that the Quakers had intimidated Mr. Dickinson's Mother, and his Wife, who were continually distressing him with their remonstrances. His mother said to him: "Johnny you will be hanged, your Estate will be forfeited and confiscated, you will leave your Excellent Wife a Widow and your charming Children Orphans, Beggars and infamous." (*John Adams' Diary, 1771–1781,* Lyman H. Butterfield, ed. [1961], III: 316).

This story fits nicely with a remark in Reed's narrative, where he says:

> But by this time Mr. Dickinson began to repent of his engagement to attend the meeting [of May 20, 1774]. . . . On the other side the other gentlemen [Mifflin, Reed, and Thomson] kept him to it, & resolved that he should not be left alone in the interval least his wife or mother would speak with [him] & overthrow at once all that had been done. They were in an adjoining room, appeared very uneasy, & only waited for such an opportunity. . . . (N.-Y. Hist. Soc., *Colls.,* XI: 271).

The other problem in Thomson's analysis lies not in its assessment of the attitudes of individuals, including that of Thomson himself, but in the very extent of his claims concerning the broad conceptual scope and the great success of his, or any resistance leader's, various stratagems for mobilizing the populace. The fundamental goal of the present study has been to investigate these stratagems, to measure the degree of their success, and to explain that success.

APPENDIX G

Committee Appointed by the Mechanics on June 9, 1774

(See Table of Symbols, p. xi)

	Age	Occupation	Religion	1774 Tax Assessment
Barge, Jacob[a]	53	innkeeper, sugar-baker	?	£94
Duffield, Edward	54	clockmaker	A	192
Fleeson, Plunket	62	upholsterer	A	44
Howell, Isaac	ca. 35–40?	brewer	Q	25
Masters, William	39	distiller	Q or A?	107
Morris, Anthony, Jr.[a,b]	36	brewer, merchant	Q	55
Pryor, Thomas	38	baker, flour merchant	Q	342
Rittenhouse, David	42	clock and instrument maker	P	12
Ross, John	59	lawyer	A	208
Rush, William[a]	56	blacksmith	P	92
Smith, Robert[a,c]	ca. 40+	builder	P	110

a. Served on the Forty-Three.

b. Morris's father, A. M., Sr., was also a brewer and merchant, and one of the ten wealthiest men in Philadelphia, if the 1774 assessment is any guide.

c. There were several Robert Smiths; this one seems the most probable. The others were also of the artisan class, and evidently much less affluent than the one listed here.

APPENDIX H

Spokesmen Whom the Mechanics and Germans Sought to Add to the Forty-Three (Chosen June 17, 1774)

(See Table of Symbols, p. xi)

	Age in 1774	Occupation	Religion	1774 Tax Assessment	Prior Activity
Mechanics' spokesmen					
Ball, William	45	silver and gold smith	A?	£304	
Craige, William	?	merchant?	?	91[b]	
Fleeson, Plunket	62	upholsterer	A	44	11
Loxley, Benjamin, Jr.	28	builder	B	300	1770, 1773
Pryor, Thomas	38	baker, flour merchant	Q	342	11
Ross, John	59	lawyer	A	208	11
Worrell, James	?	carpenter	A	97	
Germans					
Farmer, Lewis	?	innkeeper	?	10[b]	
Hillegas, Michael[a]	45	merchant	A	140	
Hubley, Adam[a]	30	merchant	A	6	
Ludwig, Christopher[a]	54	baker	L	99	
Melchior, Isaac	?	innkeeper	J	per head	
Schlosser, George[a]	60	shopkeeper, tanner	L	65	1765r

a. These men were elected to the Forty-Three.
b. 1772 tax assessment.

APPENDIX I

Committee Appointed by a Meeting of Tradesmen, July 8, 1774

(See Table of Symbols, p. xi)

Member	Age in 1774	Occupation	Religion	1774 Tax Assessment
Affleck, Thomas	ca. 30–35?	joiner, cabinetmaker	Q	£10
Bedford, Gunning	37	carpenter	?	58[a]
Fleeson, Plunket	62	upholsterer	A	44
Morgan, Jacob	32	distiller, merchant	A	20
Rush, Jacob	27	lawyer	P	per head
Wade, Francis	ca. 40?	brewer	A	10
Wetherill, Joseph	34	carpenter	Q	16

a. 1772 tax assessment.

APPENDIX J

Supervisors of the November 10 Election and Judges of the November 12 Election, 1774

(See Table of Symbols, p. xi)

	Ward	Age	Occupation	Religion	1774 Tax Assessment
Supervisors for the November 10 (preliminary) Election (2 for each ward)					
Bayard, John	High Street	36	merchant	P	£11
Bradford, William	Chestnut	55	printer	P	10
*Bright, Jacob	Upper Delaware	45	biscuit maker		35
Claypoole, George	South		joiner		6[a]
Deane, Joseph	Chestnut	36	merchant	P	22
Delany, Sharp	South	ca. 35	druggist	A	8
*Donaldson, Arthur	Southwark		merchant		8[a]
Donnell, Captain	Dock				
Duffield, John	Lower Delaware		merchant		47[a]
*Hollingshead, William	High Street		goldsmith	P	2
Howard, John	Middle		joiner		45[a]
*Howell, Isaac	North	ca. 35–40?	brewer	Q	25
*Hubley, Adam	Walnut	30	merchant	A	6
*Humphreys, Richard	North		tailor	Q	40[a]
Jackson, William	Dock		merchant	P	55
Knowles, John	Lower Delaware		merchant		84[a]
*Masters, William	Northern Liberties	39	distiller	Q or A?	107
Melchior, Isaac	Mulberry		innkeeper	J	per head
Moore, Philip	Upper Delaware		merchant		6[a]
*Penrose, Thomas	Southwark	40	ship builder	A	196
*Simpson, Samuel	Middle	54	cordwainer		90
Taylor, John	Walnut				
Thatcher, Joseph	Northern Liberties				
Winey, Jacob	Mulberry		merchant		35
Judges for the November 12 Election					
Bayard, John		36	merchant	P	11
*Howell, Isaac		ca. 40?	brewer	Q	25
Jones, Blaithwaite		48	ship captain	A	96

All persons italicized were elected to the Sixty-Six on November 12, 1774. All persons who are asterisked served on some city committee, or sought committee office unsuccessfully, or served in the militia or other local military forces.

a. 1772 tax assessment.

APPENDIX K

Tickets Run on November 12, 1774

---

1. The Radical-Mechanic Ticket (in the order printed)

1. *J. Dickinson*	31. J. Shee
2. *T. Mifflin*	32. *O. Biddle*
3. C. Thomson	33. W. Heysham
4. J. Cadwalader	34. *J. Milligan*
5. *R. Morris*	35. J. Wilcox [Wilcocks]
6. *S. Howell*	36. *S. Delaney*
7. G. Clymer	37. *F. Gurney*
8. J. Reed	38. J. Purviance
9. *S. Meredith*	39. R. Knox
10. J. Allen	40. F. Hassenclever
11. *W. Rush*	41. T. Cuthbert, Sr.
12. J. Mease	42. *W. Jackson*
13. J. Nixon	43. I. Mechior
14. J. Cox	44. S. Penrose
15. J. Bayard	45. *I. Coates*
16. C. Ludwig	46. *W. Coates*
17. T. Barclay	47. B. Jones
18. G. Schlosser	48. T. Pryor
19. J. B. Smith	49. S. Massey
20. F. Wade	50. *R. Towers*
21. B. Marshall	51. H. Jones
22. L. Cadwalader	52. J. Wetherill
23. *R. Keen*	53. *J. Copperthwaite*
24. *R. Bache*	54. J. Deane
25. *J. Benezet*	55. B. Harbeson
26. *H. Kepple, Jr.* [Keppele]	56. J. Ash
27. J. Winey	57. B. Loxley
28. J. Rush	58. W. Robinson
29. *J. Falconer*	59. R. Albertson
30. W. Bradford	60. *J. Irvine*

APPENDIX K—Continued

2. The Moderate Ticket (in the order printed)

1. *T. Mifflin*	31. A. Brickley [Bickley]
2. *R. Morris*	32. A. Usher
3. *S. Howell*	33. W. West
4. *S. Meredith*	34. A. Hubley
5. *W. Rush*	35. P. Benezet
6. *R. Keen*	36. J. Steinmetz
7. *R. Bache*	37. R. Wells
8. *J. Benezet*	38. J. Potts
9. *J. Falconer*	39. T. Affleck
10. *R. Towers*	40. J. Palmer
11. *O. Biddle*	41. J. Evans
12. *J. Milligan*	42. T. Willing
13. *S. Delany*	43. P. Reeve
14. *F. Gurney*	44. J. Morton
15. *I. Coats* [Coates]	45. J. Brown
16. *W. Coats* [Coates]	46. A. Brunner
17. *J. Copperthwaite*	47. W. Wishart
18. T. Penrose	48. R. S. Jones
19. *J. Irwin* [Irvine]	49. J. Pemberton
20. J. Paschall	50. R. Hare
21. J. Craig	51. E. Lewis
22. W. Morrel	52. D. Robinson
23. E. Duffield	53. E. Pennington [Penington]
24. L. Hollingsworth	54. *J. Dickinson*
25. J. Browne	55. *W. Jackson*
26. E. Middleton	56. T. Fisher
27. B. Paschall	57. J. Reynell
28. T. Shields	58. S. Shoemaker
29. A. Liddon	59. R. Meredith
30. *H. Keppele, Jr.*	60. J. Barge

Note: All those italicized appeared on both tickets; all names are spelled here as they appeared, with the author's spelling of variant names given in brackets.

APPENDIX L

Tickets Run on August 16, 1775

"The Mechanics' Ticket"[a]

1. Benjamin Franklin
2. Thomas Miflin [Mifflin]
3. John Cadwalader
4. George Clymer
5. Robert Morris
6. Joseph Read [Reed]
7. Samuel Meredith
8. John Allen
9. William Rush
10. James Mease
11. John Cox
12. John Bayard
13. Christopher Ludwig
14. Thomas Barclay
15. George Schlosser
16. Jonathan B. Smith
17. Francis Wade
18. Benjamin Marshall
19. Lambert Cadwallader [Cadwalader]
20. Richard Bache
21. John Benezet
22. William Bradford
23. John Shee
24. Owen Biddle
25. William Heysham
26. James Millegan
27. John Willcox [Wilcocks]
28. Sharpe Delaney
29. Francis Gurney
30. John Purviance
31. William Jackson
32. Thomas Pryor
33. Samuel Massey
34. Joseph Wetheril [Wetherill]
35. Benjamin Harbison
36. James Ash
37. Benjamin Loxley
38. James Irvine
39. Thomas Cuthbert, Sen.
40. Christopher Marshall, Sen.
41. Isaac Howell
42. Joseph Parker
43. William Ball
44. John Linington
45. Robert Strettle Jones
46. Joseph Moulder
47. Daniel Joy
48. Samuel Mifflin
49. Charles Massey
50. Fredrick Kule [Kuhl]
51. Paul Ingle [Engle]
52. Timothy Matlock [Matlack]
53. Richard Willing
54. Thomas Wharton, Jun.
55. Nathaniel Brown
56. Thomas McKean
57. Moore Furman
58. David Potts
59. James Cresson
60. Joseph Watkins, Jun.
61. Andrew Caldwell
62. Thomas Lawrence
63. James Read
64. Peter Lloyd
65. Christopher Pechin
66. William Wister
67. John Wood, Watchmaker[b]
68. Thomas Affleck
69. John Patton
70. Thomas Leech
71. Samuel Morris, Jun.
72. Nicholas Hicks
73. Philip Boehm
74. Jacob Shriner
75. Jacob Morgan
76. Jacob Barge

Northern Liberties

77. John Dickinson
78. William Masters
79. Isaac Coates
80. Thomas Britton
81. Charles Thompson [Thomson]
82. William Coats [Coates]
83. Joseph Cowperthwaite
    [Copperthwaite]
84. John Brown
85. Thomas Hopkins
86. John Britton
87. Jacob Miller[b]
88. Benjamin Eyre[b]

a. The names on this and the following tickets are given exactly as they were printed, with the author's spelling of variant names given in brackets.

b. Wood, Miller, and Eyre were not elected. Apparently voters scratched out their names in favor of Joseph Deane, John Williams, and George Leib, who appear in Appendix M.

APPENDIX L—Continued

"The Moderate Ticket"

1. Doctor Franklin
2. Thomas Mifflin
3. John Cadwallader [Cadwalader]
4. Robert Morris
5. George Clymer
6. Joseph Read
7. Samuel Meredith
8. John Allen
9. William Rush
10. James Mease
11. John Nixon
12. John Cox
13. John Bayard
14. Christopher Ludwig
15. Thomas Barclay
16. George Schlosser
17. Jonathan B. Smith
18. Benjamin Marshall
19. Lambert Cadwallader [Cadwalader]
20. Reynold Keen
21. Richard Bache
22. John Benezet
23. Jacob Rush
24. William Bradford
25. John Shee
26. Owen Biddle
27. William Heysham
28. James Millegan
29. John Wilcox [Wilcocks]
30. Sharp Delany
31. Francis Gurney
32. John Purviance
33. Francis Hassenclever
34. Thomas Cuthbert, Senr.
35. William Jackson
36. Blaithwaite Jones
37. Thomas Pryor
38. Samuel Massey
39. Robert Towers
40. Henry Jones
41. Joseph Wetheril [Wetherill]
42. Joseph Copperthwaite
43. Joseph Dean [Deane]
44. Benjamin Harbeson
45. Benjamin Loxley
46. James Irvin [Irvine]
47. Andrew Allen
48. Thomas Wharton, Junr.
49. John Maxwell Nesbit
50. Robert Erwin
51. Alexander Wilcocks
52. John Chevalier
53. Richard Peters
54. Robert Ritchie
55. James Allen
56. John Gibson
57. Tench Tilghman
58. Thomas Fitzsimmons [Fitzsimons]
59. William Richards
60. Joseph Stiles
61. Richard Tilghman
62. Samuel Mifflin
63. Samuel Caldwell
64. Doctor Rush
65. Thomas Lawrence
66. Phineas Bond
67. Thomas McKean
68. David Rittenhouse
69. Jacob Morgan
70. Samuel Morris
71. Moore Furman
72. Thomas Afflick [Affleck]
73. Jacob Barge
74. Richard Willing
75. James Wharton
76. Jacob Bright

Northern Liberties

77. John Dickenson [Dickinson]
78. Charles Thompson [Thomson]
79. Trench Francis
80. Isaac Coates
81. William Coates
82. Emanuel Eyres [Eyre]
83. Peter Knight
84. John Salter
85. John Rice
86. Captain Leib
87. John Williams
88. William Masters

Southwark

89. John Wharton
90. Joseph Marsh
91. Robert Smith
92. Robert Knox
93. Samuel Penrose
94. Carpenter Wharton
95. William Robinson
96. Ricloff Albertson [Alberson]
97. Joseph Blewer
98. Elias Boyce [Boys]
99. Abraham Jones
100. Thomas Robinson

APPENDIX L—Continued

"The Conservative Ticket"

1. Doctor Franklin
2. Thomas Mifflin
3. Thomas Willing
4. John Cadwalladar [Cadwalader]
5. Dr. Clarkson
6. George Clymer
7. Joseph Read [Reed]
8. Samuel Meredith
9. Samuel Fisher
10. William Rush
11. Christopher Marshall, Senr.
12. Doctor Morgan
13. John Cox
14. John Bayard
15. Christopher Ludwig
16. Thomas Barclay
17. George Schlosser
18. Jonathan B. Smith
19. Benjamin Marshall
20. Lambert Cadwallader [Cadwalader]
21. Isaac Howell
22. Richard Bache
23. John Benezet
24. William Bradford
25. John Shee
26. Owen Biddle
27. Peter De Haven
28. Captain Cox
29. John Wilcox [Wilcocks]
30. Sharp Delany
31. Francis Gurney
32. Edward Milner
33. Francis Hassenclever
34. Thomas Cuthbert, Sr.
35. William Jackson
36. Blaithwaite Jones
37. Thomas Pryor
38. Samuel Massey
39. William Wishart
40. Charles Massey
41. Joseph Wetheril [Wetherill]
42. Joseph Copperthwaite
43. Joseph Dean [Deane]
44. Joseph Paschall
45. Robert Stevenson
46. Jacob Duche
47. James Irvine
48. Andrew Caldwell
49. Thomas Wharton, Junr.
50. John Maxwell Nesbit
51. Robert Erwin
52. Alexander Wilcocks
53. John Chevalier
54. Richard Peters
55. Robert Ritchie
56. James Allen
57. John Gibson
58. Tench Tilghman
59. Thomas Fitzsimmons [Fitzsimons]
60. Stephen Collins
61. Joseph Stiles
62. James Cresson
63. Samuel Mifflin
64. Samuel Caldwell
65. Doctor Rush
66. Thomas Lawrence
67. Phineas Bond
68. Thomas McKean
69. David Rittenhouse
70. Jacob Morgan
71. Samuel Morris
72. Moore Furman
73. John Mifflin
74. Richard Willing
75. James Wharton
76. Jacob Bright

Northern Liberties

77. John Dickinson
78. Charles Thomson
79. Tench Francis
80. Isaac Coats [Coates]
81. William Coats [Coates]
82. Emanuel Eyres
83. Peter Knight
84. John Salter
85. Thomas Hopkins
86. Captain Leib
87. John Williams
88. William Masters

Committeemen Who Served Between May 1774 and February 1776

(See Table of Symbols, p. xi)

Committeeman	Age in 1774	Occupation	Religion	1774 Tax Assessment	Committee Service
Affleck, Thomas		cabinetmaker	Q	£ 4	100[1]
Alberson [Albertson], Ricloff		ship captain		56	66
Alexander, Charles		ship captain		5	100[1]
Allen, John	32	merchant	P	34	1773, 43, 66, 100,[1] 100[2]
Allison, Robert		carpenter	P	9	100[2]
Annis, John William		sailmaker	A	9	100[1]
Ash, James	24	hatter	A	5	66, 100,[1] 100[2]
Bache, Richard	37	merchant, postmaster	A	5	66, 100,[1] 100[2]
Ball, William	45	silver and gold smith	A?	304	100,[1] 100[2]
Barclay, Thomas	46	merchant	P	74	1773, 19, 43, 66, 100,[1] 100[2]
Barge, Jacob	53	innkeeper, sugar-baker		94	43, 100,[1] 100[2]
Barnes, James		painter	A?	3	100[2]
Bayard, John	36	merchant	P	11	43, 66, 100,[1] 100[2]
Benezet, John		merchant?	A?	?	66, 100[1]
Biddle, Owen	37	watchmaker	Q	8	66, 100[1]
Blewer, Joseph	40	ship captain	A	20	100,[1] 100[2]
Boehm, Philip		shopkeeper		40	100,[1] 100[2]
Boys [Boyce], Elias	27	merchant	P	6	66, 100[2]
Bradford, William	53	printer	P	10	66, 100,[1] 100[2]
Britton, John		merchant, distiller	Q[disowned]	118	100[1]
Britton, Thomas		lumber merchant	Q?	46	100[1]
Brown, John[a]		distiller	Q[disowned?]	178	100,[1] 100[2]

a. Identification uncertain.

Committeemen Who Served Between May 1774 and February 1776

(See Table of Symbols, p. xi)

Committeeman	Age in 1774	Occupation	Religion	1774 Tax Assessment	Committee Service
Brown, Nathaniel	ca. 40+?	blacksmith	Q?	115	100,[1] 100[2]
Bruster [Brewster], Samuel		shipwright	A	27	100[2]
Cadwalader, John	32	merchant	A?	143	1770, 66, 100,[1] 100[2]
Cadwalader, Lambert	31	merchant	Q?	2	1773, 66, 100[1]
Caldwell, Andrew		wine merchant	P	12	100[1]
Casdrop [Casdorp], Thomas		shipwright	A	10	100[1]
Chevalier, Peter	43	merchant, distiller	P	10	1765m, 1770, 43
Clymer, George	35	merchant	A	230	1770, 1773, 19, 43, 66, 100[1]
Coates [Coats], Isaac		brickmaker	Q	122	66, 100,[1] 100[2]
Coates [Coats], William[a]	53	merchant?	Q[disowned]	340	66, 100,[1] 100[2]
Colladay [Colladа], William, Jr.	ca. 35?	house carpenter		18 (1775c)	100[2]
Copperthwaite, Joseph		chairmaker	Q	5	66, 100,[1] 100[2]
Cox, John, Jr.[a]	42?	merchant	P	120	1769, 1770, 19, 43, 66, 100,[1] 100[2]
Cresson, James	34	lumber merchant, carpenter	Q	81	100,[1] 100[2]
Cuthbert, Thomas, Sr.	61	mastman	A	198	66, 100,[1] 100[2]
Davis, William[a]	21?	ship captain	Q or A?	17?	100[2]
Deane, Joseph	36	merchant, retailer	P	22	1765r, 66, 100,[1] 100[2]
Delaney, Sharp	ca. 35	druggist	A	8	66, 100,[1] 100[2]
Dennis, Richard		shipwright	A	60	100[1]
Dickinson, John	42	lawyer	Q[lapsed]	710	19, 43, 66, 100,[1] 100[2]
Donnell, Nathaniel		shopkeeper		?	100[2]
Drewry, William		ship chandler		93	100[1]
Duche, John		boat builder	A	13	100,[1] 100[2]
Engle [Ingle], Paul		shopkeeper		36	43, 100[1]
Engles [Engle], Silas		carpenter		5	100[1]
Erwin, Samuel		?		28	43
Eyre, Emanuel	38	shipwright	A	24	66
Falcone-, Joseph		shopkeeper	A	15	66, 100[2]

APPENDIX M–Continued

Committeeman	Age in 1774	Occupation	Religion	1774 Tax Assessment	Committee Service
Fitzsimons, Thomas	33	merchant	RC	8	43
Fox, Joseph	65	merchant, builder	Q[disowned]	609	19
Franklin, Benjamin	68	public servant	Deist	330	100,[1] 100[2]
Furman, Moore		merchant	A	10	100,[1] 100[2]
Gibson, John	45	merchant	A	163	1769, 1770, 19
Gray, George	49	ferry owner	A	389	43
Gurney, Francis	36	shopkeeper	A	37	66, 100,[1] 100[2]
Haines, Reuben	47	brewer	Q	238	43
Harbeson, Benjamin	45	coppersmith	P	65	66, 100,[1] 100[2]
Hare, Robert	22	brewer	A	28 (1775)	100[2]
Hassenclever, Francis Casper		bookseller		8	66
Heysham, William	54	merchant	A	34	1773, 66, 100,[1] 100[2]
Hicks, Nicholas		bricklayer	A	19	100,[1] 100[2]
Hillegas, Michael	45	merchant, iron manufacturer	A	140	43
Hollingshead, William		goldsmith	P	2	100[2]
Hopkins, Thomas	ca. 40?	baker	A	41	100,[1] 100[2]
Howell, Isaac	ca. 35–40?	brewer	Q	25	43, 100,[1] 100[2]
Howell, Samuel	ca. 40–50?	merchant	Q[disowned]	150	1765m, 1769, 1770, 19, 43, 66
Hubley, Adam	30	merchant	A	6	43
Huddle, Joseph		cooper	A	48	100[1]
Irish, Nathaniel	39?	carpenter	A	44	100[2]
Irvine [Irwin], James[a]	39	hatter?	A or P?	per head	66, 100[1]

Committeemen Who Served Between May 1774 and February 1776

(See Table of Symbols, p. xi)

Committeeman	Age in 1774	Occupation	Religion	1774 Tax Assessment	Committee Service
Jackson, William[a]	ca. 30?	merchant	P	55	66, 100,[1] 100[2]
Jones, Abraham		carpenter	Q?	158	66
Jones, Benjamin		hatter?		per head	100[1]
Jones, Blaithwaite	48	ship captain	A	96	66
Jones, Henry		ship captain	Q[disowned]	5	66
Jones, Robert Strettel	29	gentleman	B	104	100,[1] 100[2]
Joy, Daniel[b]		?	A?	8	100,[1] 100[2]
Keen, Reynold	36	distiller	SL	330	66
Keppele, Henry, Jr.[a]	29	merchant	L	108	66
Knox, Robert		lumber merchant	P	90	66, 100[2]
Kuhl, Frederick	46	gentleman?		204	100,[1] 100[2]
Lawrence, Thomas	30	cooper	Q or A?	2	100,[1] 100[2]
Leech, Thomas		ship captain	Q?	115	100[1]
Leib, George		tanner		20	100,[1] 100[2]
Linington, John		joiner, board merchant	Q[disowned]	45	100,[1] 100[2]
Lloyd, Peter Z.		lawyer	A?	per head	100,[1] 100[2]
Loughead, James		vendor, merchant		2	100[2]
Loxley, Benjamin	28	carpenter, builder	B	300	1770, 1773, 66, 100,[1] 100[2]
Ludwig [Ludwick], Christopher	54	baker	L	99	43, 66, 100,[1] 100[2]
McKean, Thomas	39	lawyer	P	20 (1775)	100,[1] 100[2]
McMullen, William		joiner		3	100[2]
Marsh, Joseph		shipwright		23	100[1]
Marshall, Benjamin	37	merchant-manufacturer	Q	178	1773, 19, 43, 66, 100[1]
Marshall, Christopher, Sr.	65	retired druggist	Q[disowned]	70	100,[1] 100[2]
Massey, Charles		baker	Q	10	100,[1] 100[2]
Massey, Samuel	39	merchant	Q[disowned]	112	66, 100,[1] 100[2]
Masters, William	39	distiller	Q or A?	107	1770, 100,[1] 100[2]
Matlack, Timothy	44	various trades	Q[disowned]	7	100,[1] 100[2]
Meade, George	32	merchant	RC?	36	100[2]
Mease, James	30–35?	merchant	P	52	1769, 1770, 1773, 43, 66, 100[1]

b. Possibly Dominick Joyce, assessed £128 in 1774.

APPENDIX M—Continued

Committeeman	Age in 1774	Occupation	Religion	1774 Tax Assessment	Committee Service
Mease, John	28	merchant	P	13	100[2]
Melchior [Melcher], Isaac		innkeeper	J	per head	66
Meredith, Samuel	33	merchant	Q[disowned]	11	66, 100,[1] 100[2]
Mifflin, Jonathan	21	merchant	Q	per head (1775)	100[2]
Mifflin, Samuel	49	merchant	Q[disowned]	229	1765m, 100[1]
Mifflin, Thomas	30	merchant	Q	83	1769, 1770, 1773, 19, 43, 66, 100[1]
Miles, Samuel	34	merchant	B	105	43
Miller, Jacob		shipwright	Q?	11	66
Milligan [Mulligan], James[a]		merchant or tailor	P	4	66, 100,[1] 100[2]
Moore, Samuel		brewer		10	100,[1] 100[2]
Morgan, Jacob	32	distiller	A	20	100[1]
Morgan, George		merchant	A	4	100[2]
Morris, Anthony, Jr.	36	merchant, brewer	Q	55	43
Morris, Robert	40	merchant	A	116	1769, 43, 66, 100[1]
Morris, Samuel, Jr.	40	merchant	Q	152	100,[1] 100[2]
Morris, Samuel Cadwalader	31	merchant	Q	173	100[2]
Moulder, Joseph	ca. 40–50?	sailmaker	B?	40	19, 43, 100,[1] 100[2]
Moulder, William	50	grocer	B	4	1773, 43
Nesbit, John Maxwell	46	merchant	P	11	1769, 1770, 19, 43
Nixon, John	41	merchant	A	108	1773, 19, 43, 66
Parker, Joseph		tailor	Q	35	100,[1] 100[2]
Paschall, Benjamin		cordwainer	Q	10	100[2]
Patton, John[a]	30	merchant?	A or P?	?	100,[1] 100[2]
Pechin, Christopher	ca. 30 + ?	merchant		7	100,[1] 100[2]

Committeemen Who Served Between May 1774 and February 1776

(See Table of Symbols, p. xi)

Committeeman	Age in 1774	Occupation	Religion	1774 Tax Assessment	Committee Service
Penington, Edward	48	sugar-baker	Q	100	19, 43
Penrose, Samuel	32	merchant	A	31	66
Penrose, Thomas	40	shipwright	A	196	1773, 19, 43
Potts, David	33	merchant	Q or A?	18 (1775c)	100[1]
Pryor, Thomas	38	baker, flour merchant	Q	342	66, 100,[1] 100[2]
Purviance, John	32	merchant	P?	7	66, 100,[1] 100[2]
Reed, James	ca. 30?	merchant	A	4	100,[1] 100[2]
Reed, Joseph	33	lawyer	P	10	1773, 19, 43, 66, 100,[1] 100[2]
Roberts, George	37	merchant	Q	148	1769, 1770, 43
Roberts, John	53	miller	Q	143	43
Robinson, Daniel[a]		merchant or mariner	A or P?	6?	100[2]
Robinson, Thomas	23	?	Q[disowned]	25	66
Robinson, William, Jr.[a]		joiner?	A or Q?	22?	66, 100[2]
Rush, Benjamin	28	doctor	P	per head	100[2]
Rush, Jacob	27	lawyer	P	per head	66
Rush, William	56	blacksmith	P	92	43, 66, 100,[1] 100[2]
Schlosser [Slosser], George	60	shopkeeper, tanner	L	65	1765r, 43, 66, 100,[1] 100[2]
Schriner, Jacob		skinner		50	100,[1] 100[2]
Schubert [Schubart], Michael		distiller		20	100[2]
Searles, James	44	merchant	A	?	100[2]
Shee, John	ca. 35?	merchant	A?	12	1770, 1773, 66, 100[1]
Simpson, Samuel	54	cordwainer	A	90	100[2]
Skinner, James		clerk		3	100[2]
Smith, John Bayard	31	merchant	P	12 (1775c)	43, 66, 100,[1] 100[2]
Smith, Robert	ca. 40	builder	P	110	43
Smith, Robert[a]		hatter	P	44	100[2]
Smith, William	47	minister, teacher	A	47	19, 43
Thomson, Charles	45	merchant	P	12	1769, 1770, 1773, 19, 43, 66, 100[1]
Towers, Robert		skinner	A or Q?	48	66
Turner, Joseph[a]	34	merchant	A?	150	66

APPENDIX M—Continued

Committeeman	Age in 1774	Occupation	Religion	1774 Tax Assessment	Committee Service
Tybout, Andrew	38	hatter	P	16	100[2]
Wade, Francis		brewer	A	10	1765r, 66, 100,[1] 100[2]
Warder, Jeremiah, Jr.	30	merchant	Q	10	1769, 1773, 19, 43
Watkins, Joseph, Jr.		joiner		58	100,[1] 100[2]
Wetherill, Joseph	34	carpenter	Q	16	66, 100,[1] 100[2]
Wharton, Thomas, Sr.	43	merchant	Q	166	43
Wharton, Thomas, Jr.	39	merchant	Q[disowned]	86	19, 43, 100[1]
Wilcocks, John[a]	ca. 30?	merchant	A	72	1773, 66, 100,[1] 100[2]
Will, William		pewterer		14	100[2]
Williams, John	30	carpenter	Q or P?	23	100[1]
Willing, Richard	29	merchant	A	17	100,[1] 100[2]
Willing, Thomas	43	merchant	A	533	1765m, 43
Winey, Jacob		merchant		35	66
Wister, William	28	merchant	Q	?	100,[1] 100[2]
Worrell, James		carpenter	A	97	100[2]

For Moyamensing, 1776

Goodwin, George
Tittermary, John
Whitman, Jacob

For Passyunk, 1776

Deshong, Frederick
Lowman, William
Mesmer, John

APPENDIX N

Men Nominated to Committee Tickets in 1774–75, But Never Elected to Committee Office After May 1774

(See Table of Symbols, p. xi)

	Age in 1774	Occupation	Religion	1774 Tax Assessment	Prior Political Activity
Allen, Andrew	34	lawyer, attorney general	P	£290	1770, 1773
Allen, James	32	lawyer	P	250 (1775c)	
Benezet, Philip	52	merchant	A	65	1770 boycott-breaker
Bickley [Blockley], Abraham	ca. 35+	merchant	B	260	1773
Bond, Phineas	25	lawyer	A	per head	
Bright, Jacob	45	merchant, biscuit maker		35	
Browne, Jonathan[a]		merchant		10	
Brunner [Bunner], Andrew	34	merchant	A	6	
Caldwell, Samuel	36	merchant	P	10	
Chevalier, John	30s or 40s?	merchant	P	117	
Clarkson, Dr. Gerardus	37	doctor	A	18	
Collins, Stephen		merchant	Q	58	
Cox, Captain John		ship captain	P?	4	
Craig, James	57	merchant, ropemaker	A?	116	
DeHaven, Peter	55	gentleman	A	85	
Duché, Jacob[a]	37	minister	A	171	
Duffield, Edward	54	clockmaker	A	192	June 1774 mechanics' comm.
Erwin, Robert		gentleman		220	
Evans, Jonathan	late 50s	merchant, cooper	Q	147	
Eyre, Benjamin	27	shipwright	A	14	
Fisher, Thomas	33	merchant	Q	12	1769, 1770 boycott-breaker
Fisher, Samuel[a]	29	merchant	Q	per head	
Francis, Tench	44	merchant	A	196	1769
Hollingsworth, Levi	35	merchant	A	8	
Knight, Peter	51	merchant	A?	95	1773
Lewis, Ellis	40	merchant	Q	64 (1775c)	
Liddon, Abraham		shopkeeper		58	

a. Identification uncertain.

APPENDIX N—Continued

**Men Nominated to Committee Tickets in 1774–75, But Never Elected
to Committee Office After May 1774**

(See Table of Symbols, p. xi)

	Age in 1774	Occupation	Religion	1774 Tax Assessment	Prior Political Activity
Meredith, Reese	66	merchant	Q	558	
Middleton, Edward	40s?	baker		16	
Mifflin, John	54	merchant	Q	196	
Milner [Milne], Edward	51	merchant	B	43	Phila. Co. comm. (rural)
Morgan, Dr. John	39	doctor		60	
Morrel, William		merchant	A	68	
Morton, John	ca.30	merchant	Q?	10	
Palmer, John	57	mason	A	76	
Paschall, Joseph	34	merchant	Q	43	
Pemberton, James	51	merchant	Q	358	
Peters, Richard, Jr.	30	lawyer	A	20	
Potts, John	36	lawyer	A or Q?	67	
Reeve, Peter	ca. 54	merchant, mariner		104	
Reynell, John	66	merchant	Q	140	1769
Rice, John		shipwright?		10	
Richards, William		druggist	A	16 (1775c)	1765 Hughes
Ritchie, Robert	ca. 29?	merchant	P	8	
Rittenhouse, David	42	clock and instrument maker	P	12	
Salter, John		baker?		43	
Shields, Thomas	30s?	gold and silver smith	B	46	
Shoemaker, Samuel	49	merchant	Q	135	
Steinmetz, John	52 +	merchant, shopkeeper		80	
Stevenson, Robert		merchant	A	14	
Stiles, Joseph		schoolmaster	Q	5	
Tilghman, Richard	28	lawyer	A	16 (1775c)	
Tilghman, Tench	30	merchant	A	per head	
Usher, Abraham	late 30s?	merchant	A	10	
Wells, Richard	40	merchant	Q	50?	
West, William	50	merchant	A?	143	1769, 1773
Wharton, Carpenter	27	hatter	Q?	6[b]	
Wharton, James	42	merchant	Q	30	
Wharton, John	37	shipbuilder, merchant	Q	150	
Wilcocks, Alexander	32	lawyer	A	20	
Wishart, William		merchant	Q	76	
Wood, John	38	watchmaker	A	104	

b. 1772 assessment.

A Note on Sources
For Studying the
Committee Movement

Basic accounts of the activities of Philadelphia's committees have generally survived only in print, primarily in the city's newspapers. The *Pennsylvania Gazette, Journal,* and *Packet* are the most useful sources here. For the years 1768–70, the *Chronicle* is also helpful, as is the *Mercury* for 1775, and the *Ledger* and the *Evening Post* for 1775–76. The reader is particularly referred to the *Gazette,* May 10, 24, June 7, Sept. 20, 27, Oct. 1, 1770; Dec. 29, 1773; May 25, June 8, 15, 22, July 6, 20, 27, Nov. 2, 9, Dec. 22, 1774; Feb. 1, Aug. 9, 16, 23, 1775; and Feb. 14, 21, Mar. 6, 27, May 8, 22, 29, June 12, 19, 26, and July 3, 10, 1776, for details of the most important meetings, lists of committee members, circular letters, transactions of provincial conventions, extracts from votes of the Assembly, and results of elections. Some interesting variants and important addenda to this information appear in the corresponding issues of the *Journal, Packet,* and *Evening Post.* Most political essays that relate to the committee's work first appeared in these same papers. See also the broadside entitled *At a Meeting at the Philosophical Society's Hall, on Friday, June 10th,* . . . Philadelphia, 1774 (Evans No. 13534), copies in the Historical Society of Pennsylvania (HSP), American Philosophical Society (APS), and Library Company of Philadelphia; and broadside committee election tickets for November 1774 (2), August 1775 (3), and February 1776 (1), all Library Company. Several important additional printed sources for the period 1774–76 may be found in Peter Force, ed., *American Archives,* 4th Series (Washington, 1837–46).

The proceedings of a few public assemblies and committee meetings have survived in manuscript, notably in "Joseph Reed's Narrative" [n.d.], and Charles Thomson's letter to William Henry Drayton [n.d.], both in *Collections of the New-York Historical Society,* XI (1878): 269–86, and both commenting extensively on the May 20, 1774, meeting; "Notes on a meeting of a number of Gentlemen convened on 10 June 1774," in Charles Thomson's "Memorandum Book, 1754–1774," Gratz Collection, HSP; a manuscript list of forty candidates for the committee of Forty-Three, nominated on June 10, 1774, probably in John Dickinson's hand, and a transcript of a mechanics' meeting held on June 17, 1774, both in the John Dickinson material, R. R. Logan Collection, HSP; an anonymous and fragmentary account of the June 18, 1774, meeting in "Tea Papers," Am 30796, HSP; the minutes of the Forty-Three, June 18–July 11, 1774, Yi 965 F, Du Simitière Papers, HSP; and transactions of several district sub-committees of the Sixty-Six, December 1774–August 1775, in "Manuscripts Relating to Non-Importation Agreements, 1766–1775," APS; and Am 817 and 3079, HSP.

Bibliography

PRIMARY SOURCES

Manuscripts

The Samuel Adams Papers. The New York Public Library. Manuscript Department.

An untitled manuscript transcript of the proceedings of the Committee of Forty-Three, June 20–July 11, 1774 (Minutes), vol. Yi 965 F. Du Simitière Collection. HSP.

Colonel William Bradford Papers. "A Memorandum Book and Register, for the months of May and June 1776," HSP.

Committee of Observation district subcommittee books, 1774–1775. Catalogued Am 807, No. 1–4, and Am 3079. HSP.

Coates and Reynell Papers. John Reynell-Samuel Coates Letter-Book, 1769–1784. HSP.

The John Dickinson Material. The R. R. Logan Collection. HSP.

The Henry Drinker Papers. Letter-Book, domestic, 1772–1786. Letter-Book, foreign, 1772–1785. Loose Correspondence. HSP.

Joshua Francis Fisher Papers. HSP.

The Benjamin Franklin Papers, vol. LXIX. APS.

The Du Simitière Collection. HSP.

The Gratz Collection. HSP.

James and Drinker Correspondence. HSP.

The Logan Collection. HSP.

"Manuscripts Relating to Non-Importation Agreements, 1766–1775." APS.

Christopher Marshall, Sr. Papers. Letter-Book. Diary. HSP.

Material on Committee of Observation district 3 sub-committee, 1775–1776. Catalogued Am 973.2 M 31, vol. 2. APS.

"Minutes of the Lancaster County Committee of Safety." The Peter Force Collection. The Library of Congress, Manuscript Division.

"Minutes of the Monthly Meeting of the Northern District of Philadelphia, 1771–1781" (microfilm). The Friends Historical Library, Swarthmore College. Swarthmore, Pennsylvania.

"Minutes of the Philadelphia Monthly Meeting, 1765–1771" (microfilm). The Friends Historical Library, Swarthmore College. Swarthmore, Pennsylvania.

"Minutes of the Philadelphia Monthly Meeting, 1771–1777" (microfilm). The Friends Historical Library, Swarthmore College. Swarthmore, Pennsylvania.

"Minutes of the Southern District Meeting, 1772–1778" (microfilm). The Friends Historical Library, Swarthmore College. Swarthmore, Pennsylvania.

"Papers Relating to the Shipment of Tea, . . ." HSP.

The Peters Papers. HSP.

The Proud Collection. HSP.

The Joseph Reed Papers. N.-Y. Hist. Soc.

"Report of the Committee appointed to Wait on the Tea Commissioners, 17 [18] October, 1773." "Non-Importation MSS." APS.

Dr. William Smith Manuscripts. "Notes & Papers on the Commencement of the American Revolution" (1869 MS transcription). HSP.

The Society Collection. HSP.

The Charles Thomson Papers. "Memorandum Book, 1754–1774." Gratz Collection. HSP.

The Charles Thomson Papers. The Library of Congress, Manuscript Division.

"A Transcription of the Assessment of the Seventeenth 18d. Provincial Tax laid the 8th day of April 1774 on the Inhabitants of the City and County of Philadelphia" (MS and microfilm). The Pennsylvania Historical and Museum Commission. Harrisburg, Pennsylvania.

Thomas Wharton, Sr. Collection. Letter-Book, 1773–1784. Letters. HSP.

Newspapers

The New-York Gazette. New York, 1775.
The New-York Journal. New York, 1775.
The Pennsylvania Chronicle. Philadelphia, 1767–73.
The Pennsylvania Evening Post. Philadelphia, 1775–76.
The Pennsylvania Gazette. Philadelphia, 1765–76.
The Pennsylvania Journal. Philadelphia, 1765–76.
The Pennsylvania Ledger. Philadelphia, 1775–76.
The Pennsylvania Mercury. Philadelphia, 1775.
The Pennsylvania Packet. Philadelphia, 1774–76.
Rivington's New-York Gazetter. New York, 1773–75.

Broadsides and Pamphlets

An Account of the Baptisms and Burials in all the Churches and Meetings in Philadelphia, From Dec. 25, 1774 to Dec. 25, 1775. Philadelphia, 1775.

An Account of the Births and Burials in the United Churches of Christ-Church and St. Peter's . . . From December 25, 1774 to December 25, 1775. Philadelphia, 1775.

The Alarm. Philadelphia, 1776. Broadside Collection, item 18. The Historical Society of Pennsylvania.

At a Meeting at the Philosophical Society Hall, Friday, June 10th. . . . Philadelphia, [June 13?] 1774.

Committee . . . 1. John Dickinson . . . [59 other names follow]. Philadelphia, 1774. Broadside Collection, 960.F.52. The Philadelphia Library Company.

Committee . . . 1. Thomas Mifflin . . . [59 other names follow]. Philadelphia, 1774. Broadside Collection, 960.F.53. The Philadelphia Library Company.

Committee, For the City of Philadelphia, District of Southwark and Northern Liberties. Philadelphia, 1775. Broadside Collection, 960.F.71. The Philadelphia Library Company.

Committee / For the City of Philadelphia and Northern Liberties, to be and continue until the 16th / day of February A.D. 1776 and no longer. Philadelphia, 1775. Broadside Collection, 960.F.70. The Philadelphia Library Company.

Committee / For the City of Philadelphia and Northern Liberties to continue for Six Months. Philadelphia, 1775. Broadside Collection, 960.F.73. The Philadelphia Library Company.

Dickinson, John. *An Essay on the Constitutional Power of Great Britain over the Colonies in America.* Philadelphia, 1774.

An Earnest Address to the People called Quakers. Philadelphia, 1775.

Fellow Citizens and Countrymen. Philadelphia, 1772.

Galloway, Joseph. *A Candid Examination of the Mutual Claims of Great Britain and the Colonies with a Plan of Accommodation on Constitutional Principles.* New York, 1775.

List of the Sub-Committees, appointed by the committee for the city and liberties of Philadelphia. . . . Philadelphia, 1776.

Paine, Thomas. *Common Sense Addressed to the Inhabitants of America on the Following Interesting Subjects. . . .* Philadelphia, 1776.

The Testimony of the People Called Quakers, Given Forth . . . at Philadelphia the Twenty-fourth Day of the First Month, 1775. Philadelphia, 1775.

This is True Liberty. . . . by "A Tradesman." Philadelphia, 1774. Broadside Collection, Ab (1774) 9. The Historical Society of Pennsylvania.

To the Free and Patriotic Inhabitants of the City of Philadelphia and Province of Pennsylvania. Philadelphia, 1770.

To the Manufacturers and Mechanics of Philadelphia, the Northern Liberties, and District of Southwark. Philadelphia, 1774. Broadside Collection, 992.F.77. The Philadelphia Library Company.

To the Several Battalions of Military Associators in the Province of Pennsylvania. Philadelphia, 1776. Broadside Collection, item 19. The Historical Society of Pennsylvania.

Other Printed Materials

Adams, Thomas R., *American Independence, The Growth of an Idea.* Providence, R.I., 1965.

Barratt, Norris Stanley. *Outline of the History of Old St. Paul's Church, Philadelphia, Pennsylvania.* Philadelphia, 1917.

Bronson, Rev. William White. *The Inscriptions in St. Peter's Church Yard, Philadelphia.* Camden, New Jersey, 1879.

Butterfield, Lyman, ed. *Adams Family Correspondence.* Cambridge, Mass., 1963.

Butterfield, Lyman, ed. *John Adams Diary, 1771–1781.* Cambridge, Mass., 1961.

Butterfield, Lyman, ed. *The Letters of Benjamin Rush,* Vol. I. Princeton, 1951.

Conway, Daniel Moncure, ed. *The Writings of Thomas Paine.* New York, 1894–96; reprinted 1967.

Duane, William, Jr. *Passages from the Remembrancer of Christopher Marshall.* Philadelphia, 1839.

Force, Peter, ed. *American Archives,* 4th Series. Washington, 1837–46.

Ford, P. L., ed. *The Writings of John Dickinson, 1764–1774,* Vol. I. Philadelphia, 1895.

Ford, W. C. et al., eds. *Journals of the Continental Congress.* Washington, 1904–37.

Galloway, Joseph. *Historical and Political Reflections on the Rise and Progress of the American Rebellion*. London, 1780.

Graydon, Alexander. *Memoirs of His Own Times with Reminiscences of the Men and Events*. Philadelphia, 1846.

Hinshaw, William Wade, ed. *The Encyclopedia of Quaker Genealogy*. Ann Arbor, Michigan, 1938.

Johnson, Allen, and Dumas Malone, eds. *The Dictionary of American Biography*. New York, 1928–44.

Jordan, John W. *Colonial and Revolutionary Families of Pennsylvania*, 3 vols. New York, 1911. Continued by Wilfred Jordan, Vols. 4–15 (1932–55), and by Thomas H. Bateman, Vols. 16–17 (1960–65).

Jordan, John W. *Colonial Families of Philadelphia*. New York, 1911.

Journals of the House of Lords, Vol. XXXIV. London, n. d.

Journals of the House of Representatives of the Commonwealth of Pennsylvania. Philadelphia, 1782.

Keith, Charles P. *The Provincial Councillors of Pennsylvania, 1733–1776*. Philadelphia, 1883.

Labaree, Leonard W. et al., eds. *The Papers of Benjamin Franklin*. New Haven, 1959–.

Martin, John Hill. *Martin's Bench and Bar of Philadelphia*. Philadelphia, 1883.

Minutes of the Provincial Council of Pennsylvania. In *Colonial Records*, Vol. X. Harrisburg, 1852.

Montgomery, William. "Pew Renters of Christ Church, St. Peter's, and St. James from 1776 to 1815, Compiled from Existing Records." August 1948, typescript. American Philosophical Society Library.

Munford, Robert. "The Patriots." *The William and Mary Quarterly*, 3d Series, VI (1949).

New Jersey Archives, 1st Series, X. Newark, N.J. 1886.

The Parliamentary History of England. Vol. 18. London, 1813.

Pennsylvania Archives, 2d Series, Harrisburg, 1874–80; 3d Series, 1894–97; 5th Series, 1906; 8th Series, 1931–35.

A Record of the Inscriptions on the Tablets and Grave-Stones in the Burial-Grounds of Christ Church, Philadelphia. Philadelphia, 1864.

Reed, William B. *The Life and Correspondence of Joseph Reed*. Philadelphia, 1847.

Sharpless, Isaac. *A History of Quaker Government in Pennsylvania*. Vol. II: *The Quakers in the Revolution*. Philadelphia, 1900.

Thomson, Charles. "The Charles Thomson Papers." *Collections of the New-York Historical Society*, XI. New York, 1878.

Votes and Proceedings of the House of Representatives of the Province of Pennsylvania, 1682–1776, ed. Gertrude MacKinney. In *Pennsylvania Archives*, 8th Series. Harrisburg, Pennsylvania, 1931–35.

"Warren-Adams Letters," Vol. I. *Massachusetts Historical Society Collections*, LXXII. Boston, 1917.

Wells, William V. *The Life and Public Services of Samuel Adams*. Boston, 1865.

SECONDARY WORKS

Books and Dissertations

Ammerman, David. *In the Common Cause: American Response to the Coercive Acts of 1774*. Charlottesville, Va., 1974.

Bagnall, William R. *The Textile Industries of the United States*. Cambridge, Mass., 1893.

Bailyn, Bernard. *The Ideological Origins of the American Revolution.* Cambridge, Mass., 1967.

Bailyn, Bernard. *The Origins of American Politics.* New York, 1968.

Bauman, Richard. *For the Reputation of Truth: Politics, Religion, and Conflict among the Pennsylvania Quakers, 1750–1800.* Baltimore, 1971.

Beard, Charles A. *An Economic Interpretation of the Constitution of the United States.* New York, 1913.

Becker, Carl Lotus. *The History of Political Parties in the Province of New York, 1760–1776.* Madison, Wisconsin, 1909.

Benson, Lee. *The Concept of Jacksonian Democracy: New York as a Test Case.* Princeton, 1961.

Boyd, Julian P. *Anglo-American Union: Joseph Galloway's Plans to Preserve the British Empire.* Philadelphia, 1941.

Bridenbaugh, Carl. *Mitre and Sceptre: Transatlantic Faiths, Ideas, Personalities, and Politics, 1689–1776.* New York, 1962.

Brown, Richard D. *Revolutionary Politics in Massachusetts, The Boston Committee of Correspondence and the Towns, 1772–1774.* Cambridge, Mass., 1970.

Brown, Robert E. *Middle-Class Democracy and the Revolution in Massachusetts, 1691–1780.* Ithaca, N.Y., 1955.

Brown, Robert E. and B. Katherine Brown, *Virginia, 1705–1786: Democracy or Aristocracy?* East Lansing, Michigan, 1964.

Brunhouse, Robert L. *The Counter-Revolution in Pennsylvania, 1776–1790.* Harrisburg, Pa., 1942.

Burnett, Edmund Cody. *The Continental Congress.* New York, 1941.

Bushman, Richard L. *From Puritan to Yankee: Character and the Social Order in Connecticut, 1690–1765.* Cambridge, Mass., 1967.

Chambers, William Nisbet. *Political Parties in a New Nation: The American Experience, 1776–1809.* New York, 1963.

Diamondstone, Judith M. "The Philadelphia Corporation, 1701–1776." Ph.D. dissertation, The University of Pennsylvania, 1969.

Douglass, Elisha P. *Rebels and Democrats: The Struggle for Equal Political Rights and Majority Rule During the American Revolution.* Chapel Hill, 1955.

Etzioni, Amitai. *The Active Society: A Theory of Societal and Political Processes.* New York, 1968.

Foner, Eric. *Tom Paine and Revolutionary America.* New York, 1976.

Forster, Robert, and Jack P. Greene, eds. *Preconditions of Revolution in Early Modern Europe.* Baltimore, 1970.

Friedrich, Carl J., ed. *Nomos VIII—Revolution.* New York, 1966.

Goodman, Nathan G. *Benjamin Rush: Physician and Citizen, 1746–1813.* Philadelphia, 1934.

Greene, Jack P. *The Quest for Power: The Lower Houses of Assembly in the Southern Royal Colonies, 1689–1776.* Chapel Hill, 1963.

Gurr, Ted Robert. *Why Men Rebel.* Princeton, 1970.

Hanna, William S. *Benjamin Franklin and Pennsylvania Politics.* Stanford, California, 1964.

Hawke, David. *In the Midst of a Revolution.* Philadelphia, 1961.

Hawke, David Freeman. *Benjamin Rush, Revolutionary Gadfly.* New York, 1971.

Henderson, H. James. *Party Politics in the Continental Congress.* New York, 1974.

Hunt, N. C. *Two Early Political Associations.* Oxford, 1961.

Huntington, Samuel P. *Political Order in Changing Societies.* New Haven, 1968.

Hutson, James H. *Pennsylvania Politics, 1746–1770, The Movement for Royal Government and Its Consequences.* Princeton, 1972.

Jensen, Merrill, *The Founding of a Nation: A History of the American Revolution 1763–1776.* New York, 1968.

Jenson, Arthur L. *The Maritime Commerce of Colonial Philadelphia.* Madison, Wisconsin, 1963.

Kamenka, Eugene, ed. *A World in Revolution? The University Lectures 1970.* Canberra, 1970.

Labaree, Benjamin Woods. *The Boston Tea Party.* New York, 1964.

Labaree, Leonard W. *Royal Government in America, A Study of the British Colonial System before 1783.* New Haven, 1930.

Lee, Robert, and Martin Marty. *Religion and Social Conflict.* New York, 1964.

Lemon, James T. *The Best Poor Man's Country: A Geographical Study of Early Southeastern Pennsylvania.* Baltimore, 1972.

Lincoln, Charles H. *The Revolutionary Movement in Pennsylvania 1760–1776.* Philadelphia, 1901.

Lynd, Staughton, *Class Conflict, Slavery, and the United States Constitution.* New York, 1967.

McDonald, Forrest. *We the People: The Economic Origins of the Constitution.* Chicago, 1958.

McKinley, Albert Edward. *The Suffrage Franchise in the Thirteen English Colonies in America.* Philadelphia, 1905.

Maier, Pauline. *From Resistance to Revolution: Colonial Radicals and the Development of American Opposition to Britain, 1765–1776.* New York, 1972.

Main, Jackson Turner. *Political Parties before the Constitution.* Chapel Hill, N.C. 1973.

Main, Jackson Turner. *The Sovereign States, 1775–1783.* New York, 1973.

Merritt, Richard L. *Symbols of American Community 1735–1775.* New Haven, 1966.

Morgan, Edmund S. and Helen M. Morgan. *The Stamp Act Crisis.* Chapel Hill, N.C. 1953; New York, 1963.

Morris, Richard B. *Government and Labor in Early America.* New York, 1946.

Namier, Louis. *England in the Age of the American Revolution.* London, 1930.

Namier, Louis. *The Structure of Politics at the Accession of George III.* London, 1929.

Nash, Gary B. *Quakers and Politics, 1682–1726.* Princeton, 1968.

Nelson, William H. *The American Tory.* Boston, 1961.

Nettl, J. P. *Political Mobilization: A Sociological Analysis of Methods and Concepts.* New York, 1967.

Nevins, Allan. *The American States during and after the Revolution.* New York, 1924.

Newcomb, Benjamin H. *Franklin and Galloway, A Political Partnership.* New Haven, 1972.

Olton, Charles S. *Artisans for Independence: Philadelphia Mechanics and the American Revolution.* Syracuse, N.Y., 1975.

Palmer, Robert R. *The Age of the Democratic Revolution: A Political History of Europe and America, 1760–1800,* Vol. I. Princeton, 1959.

Savelle, Max. *The Seeds of Liberty: The Genesis of the American Mind.* Seattle, Wash., 1948.

Schlesinger, Arthur M. *The Colonial Merchants and the American Revolution 1763–1776.* New York, 1918.

Selsam, J. Paul. *The Pennsylvania Constitution of 1776, A Study in Revolutionary Democracy.* Philadelphia, 1936.

Shepherd, William R. *History of Proprietary Government in Pennsylvania.* New York, 1896.

Sydnor, Charles. *Gentlemen Freeholders: Political Practices in Washington's Virginia.* Chapel Hill, N.C., 1952.

Thayer, Theodore. *Pennsylvania Politics and the Growth of Democracy, 1740–1776.* Harrisburg, 1953.

Tolles, Frederick B. *Meeting House and Counting House: The Quaker Merchants of Colonial Philadelphia.* Chapel Hill, N.C., 1948.

Warner, Sam Bass. *The Private City: Philadelphia in Three Periods of Its Growth.* Philadelphia, 1968.

Wellenreuther, Hermann. *Glaube und Politick in Pennsylvania 1681–1776: Die Wandlungen der Obrigkeitsdoktrin und des* Peace Testimony *der Quaker.* Cologne, 1972.

Williamson, Chilton. *American Suffrage from Property to Democracy, 1760–1860.* Princeton, 1960.

Wood, Gordon S. *The Creation of the American Republic, 1776–1787.* Chapel Hill, N.C. 1969.

Young, Alfred F. *The Democratic Republicans of New York: The Origins, 1763–1789.* Chapel Hill, N.C. 1967.

Zemsky, Robert M. *Merchants, Farmers, and River Gods, An Essay in Eighteenth-Century Politics.* Boston, 1971.

Zuckerman, Michael. *Peaceable Kingdoms: New England Towns in the Eighteenth Century.* New York, 1970.

Articles and Essays

Bockelman, Wayne L., and Owen S. Ireland. "The Internal Revolution in Pennsylvania: An Ethnic-Religious Interpretation." *Pennsylvania History,* XLI (1974): 125–59.

Buel, Richard, Jr. "Democracy and the American Revolution: A Frame of Reference." *The William and Mary Quarterly,* 3d Series, XXI (1964): 165–90.

Diamondstone, Judith M. "Philadelphia's Municipal Corporation, 1701–1776." *The Pennsylvania Magazine of History and Biography,* XC (1966): 183–201.

Greene, Jack P. "Changing Interpretations of Early American Politics." In Ray A. Billington, ed., *The Reinterpretation of Early American History.* San Marino, California, 1966. Pp. 151–84.

Greene, Jack P. "Foundations of Political Power in the Virginia House of Burgesses, 1720–1776." *The William and Mary Quarterly,* 3d Series, XVI (1959): 486–506.

Greene, Jack P. "The Growth of Political Stability: An Interpretation of Political Development in the Anglo-American Colonies, 1660–1760." In John Parker and Carol Urness, eds., *The American Revolution: A Heritage of Change.* Minneapolis, Minn., 1973. Pp. 26–52.

Hutson, James H. "Benjamin Franklin and Pennsylvania Politics, 1751–1755: A Reappraisal." *The Pennsylvania Magazine of History and Biography,* XCIII (1969): 307–71.

Hutson, James H. "An Investigation of the Inarticulate: Philadelphia's White Oaks." *The William and Mary Quarterly,* 3d Series, XXVIII (1971): 3–25.

Ireland, Owen S. "The Ethnic-Religious Dimension of Pennsylvania Politics, 1778–1779." *The William and Mary Quarterly,* 3d Series, XXX (1973): 423–48.

Jacobson, David L. "The Puzzle of 'Pacificus.'" *Pennsylvania History,* XXXI (1964): 406–18.

Kenyon, Cecilia. "Republicanism and Radicalism in the American Revolution: An Old-Fashioned Interpretation." *The William and Mary Quarterly,* 3d Series, XIX (1962): 153–82.

Klein, Philip Shriver. "Memories of a Senator from Pennsylvania, Jonathan Roberts." *The Pennsylvania Magazine of History and Biography,* LXI (1937): 469–70.

Leonard, Sister Joan de Lourdes. "Elections in Colonial Pennsylvania." *The William and Mary Quarterly,* 3d Series, XI (1954): 385–401.

Leonard, Sister Joan de Lourdes. "The Organization and Procedure of the Pennsylvania Assembly 1682–1776." *The Pennsylvania Magazine of History and Biography,* LXXII (1948): 215–39, 376–412.

Main, Jackson Turner. "Government by the People: The American Revolution and the Democratization of the Legislatures." *The William and Mary Quarterly,* 3d Series, XXIII (1966): 391–407.

Nash, Gary B. "Social Change and the Growth of Prerevolutionary Urban Radicalism." In Alfred F. Young, ed., *The American Revolution: Explorations in the History of American Radicalism.* De Kalb, Ill., 1976.

Nash, Gary B. "The Transformation of Urban Politics 1700–1765." *The Journal of American History,* LX (1973–74): 605–32.

Nash, Gary B. "Urban Wealth and Poverty in Prerevolutionary America" *The Journal of Interdisciplinary History,* VI (1976): 545–84.

Newcomb, Benjamin H. "Effects of the Stamp Act on Colonial Pennsylvania Politics." *The William and Mary Quarterly,* 3d Series, XXIII (1966): 257–72.

Oaks, Robert F. "Philadelphia's Merchants and the First Continental Congress." *Pennsylvania History,* XL (1973): 149–66.

Olton, Charles S. "Philadelphia's Mechanics in the First Decade of Revolution 1765–1775." *The Journal of American History,* LIX (1972–73): 311–26.

Thayer, Theodore. "The Quaker Party of Pennsylvania, 1755–1765." *The Pennsylvania Magazine of History and Biography,* LXXI (1947): 19–43.

Warden, G. B. "The Proprietory Group in Pennsylvania, 1754–1764." *The William and Mary Quarterly,* 3d Series, XXI (1964): 367–89.

Young, Henry J. "Treason and Its Punishment in Revolutionary Pennsylvania." *The Pennsylvania Magazine of History and Biography,* XC (1966): 292–93.

Index